The Lost Pubs of Bath

The Lost Pubs of Bath

by

Andrew Swift & Kirsten Elliott

AKEMAN PRESS

Published by AKEMAN PRESS
www.akemanpress.com

ISBN 0 9546138-4-8

Designed by Niall Allsop in Bath
Printed by SRP in Exeter

Set in Frutiger, Sabon and Broadsheet

ACKNOWLEDGEMENTS

As always, special thanks to Colin Johnston and Lucy Powell of Bath Record Office, Stuart Burroughs of the Museum of Bath at Work, and Stephanie Round of Bath Central Library for their help and advice, and permission to reproduce material from their archives.

Thanks also to:

Ruth Moppett of the Victoria Art Gallery for help with tracking down pictures of lost pubs and permission to reproduce the two paintings on the cover.

The staff of Bath Central Library, Bristol Reference Library, the National Newspaper Library, and the Somerset, Wiltshire and Buckinghamshire Record Offices.

Trevor Becker, Mike Bone, Isobel Brewer, Neil Coombs, Maurice Cottle, Paul De'Ath, Michael Lee, Marek Lewcun, Richard Lovett, Simon Newton, Julian Peters, Val and Reg Russell, and Matthew Zuckerman.

Julian Peters for permission to reproduce material from the Ivo Peters Collection.

Jean Fry who advised on the trilogy at an early stage, but sadly did not live to see its completion.

The hundreds of people we have taken round Bath on the Great Bath Pub Crawl and whose questions and comments led us to ask questions we might not otherwise have done.

Those people not mentioned by name because of disorganisation and amnesia (ours, that is).

PICTURE CREDITS

Bath Record Office: 23, 39 (all), 46 (both), 48 (bottom left), 49 (all), 50 (both), 56 (bottom), 57 (bottom), 66, 68, 69, 70 (top), 72 (left), 78, 93, 99 (top & middle), 102, 107, 108 (bottom), 109 (both), 110 (both), 112, 114 (all), 116 (middle), 117, 121 (top right), 122 (bottom), 138, 140, 142 (bottom), 143 (bottom), 152, 154 (bottom), 157 (top left & bottom), 159, 160 (top), 161, 168 (top), 169 (top), 181, 182 (centre left & bottom), 183 (bottom), 192 (centre & bottom), 193, 194, 200 (top), 208, 213, 215, 216, 222 (bottom), 225, 232, 237, 241 (bottom left), 246 (top), 256 (bottom), 258 (top), 261 (bottom), 270 (bottom), 274 (bottom), 281 (top), 298, 299, 303 (bottom), 305 (top), 306 (both), 308 (both), 311, 312, 315 (top centre & top right), 316 (bottom), 317, 320, 324, 326, 327 (right), 328 (bottom), 331 (top left), 337, 354 (bottom), 375 (both); Bath Central Library: 12 (middle & bottom), 20 (top right & bottom left), 22, 27, 44 (bottom), 111 (top left), 118 (bottom), 132 (bottom), 142 (top), 157 (top right), 164 (top), 165 (top), 169 (middle), 173, 178 (top), 179 (top), 222 (top), 246 (bottom), 247 (top), 267, 272, 297 (right), 310 (top), 316 (top), 318 (top), 321 (top); Museum of Bath at Work: 75, 77, 123, 202 (bottom), 204, 218, 219, 228, 245, 250 (both), 253 (right), 287, 288, 290, 305 (bottom), 309 (top), 315 (top left), 331 (bottom right); Isobel Brewer: 205; Neil Coombs: 296; Maurice Cottle: 201 (top & centre); Paul De'Ath, 101 (centre right), 330 (top); Richard Lovett: 100, 101 (centre left); Simon Newton: 184; Julian Peters, 126 (top) (© Ivo Peters Collection); Val & Reg Russell: 201 (bottom); Tim Wheeldon: 365 (bottom).

All other photographs and illustrations are from the Akeman Press Archive.

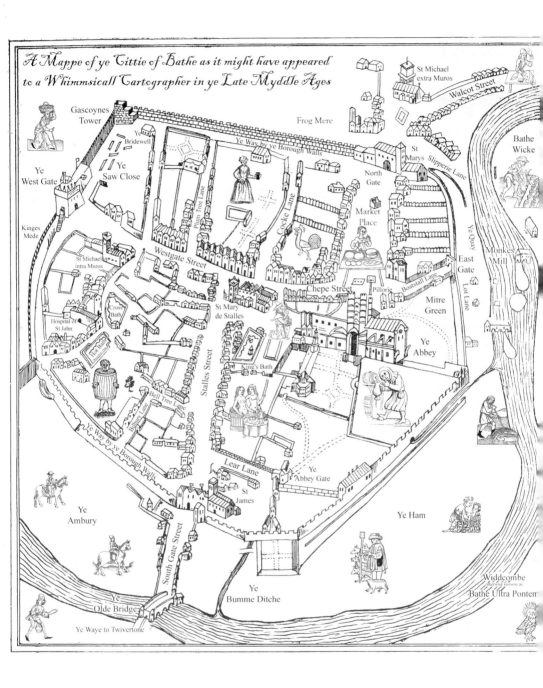

A Mappe of ye Cittie of Bathe as it might have appeared to a Whimmsicall Cartographer in ye Late Myddle Ages

Gascoynes Tower

Ye Bridewell

Ye Saw Close

Ye West Gate

Kinges Mede

Frog Mere

St Michael extra Muros

Walcot Street

Bathe Wicke

St Marys

Slipperie Lane

North Gate

Plum Tree Lane

Cocke Lane

Market Place

Westgate Street

St Michael intra Muros

Cross Bath

Hospital of St John

Hot Bath

Bell Tree Lane

Bilbury Lane

Ye Way by ye Borough Walls

Stalles Street

St Mary de Stalles

King's Bath

Chepe Street

Pillorie

Boatstall Lane

East Gate

Mitre Green

Ye Abbey

Ye Quay

Lot Lane

Monkes Mill

Ye Way by ye Borough Walls

Lear Lane

St James

Ye Abbey Gate

Ye Ambury

South Gate Street

Ye Olde Bridge

Ye Waye to Twivertone

Ye Bumme Ditche

Ye Ham

Widdcombe otherwise knowne as Bathe Ultra Pontem

CONTENTS

The authors wish it to be known that the following excursions (with the honourable exception of the first), although occasionally elliptical, are non-orbicular, or, in the common argot of the day, non-circular. The second, third, fifth and sixth excursions, in particular, leave the reader at a considerable distance from the point of departure. Being apprised of the possible inconvenience that may be attendant on such a circumstance, they have made enquiries and been advised that fast and expeditious omnibus services (which the enterprising traveller may wish to avail him or herself of) operate at regular intervals from the outlying parts of the city to the centre of the same, on payment being tendered in coin of the realm.

The authors further wish it to be known that they accept no responsibility for disfigurement or injury caused by inappropriate use of this book, whether due to dehydration, rehydration, overindulgence, underindulgence, ignorance, confusion, information overload, lack of public conveniences, seagulls, ice, rain, internal combustion engines, external combustion engines, hail, sun, landslides, the wrong sort of leaves, the right sort of leaves, the other sort of leaves, any leaves not covered by the above, lack of leaves, falling trees, bollards, drunkenness (whether intentional or not), indifference, insouciance, ennui, act of dog, or reading while under the influence.

PROLEGOMENON

In which the authors endeavour to attract the reader's attention to the bit that most people skip when it's called the introduction.

This is the final part of a trilogy, which also includes *Bath Pubs* (2003), the history of the city's existing pubs, and *Awash With Ale* (2004), the history of drinking in Bath. *The Lost Pubs of Bath* tells the story not only of pubs that closed within living memory, but of many that called last orders centuries ago.

The first problem we faced when writing it was determining what was a pub. Today the term refers to a wide range of licensed premises, but 200 years ago there were inns, taverns and alehouses. The differences between them were not always clear; at different times the same establishment could be known by all three terms. The only term that was specific was beerhouse, which came into existence with the Beerhouse Act of 1830. In the end, we decided to trace the lot, from the grandest inn to the lowliest alehouse, with all the taverns and beerhouses in between.

One problem was that, in many cases, not only were the pubs lost – the buildings have gone as well. The Georgians virtually rebuilt the city. Many of the bits they spared were pulled down by the Victorians. In turn, large swathes of eighteenth- and nineteenth-century Bath disappeared in the twentieth century, some as a result of Hitler's bombs, but most at the decree of developers. The Sack of Bath continues today, albeit in a more insidious form. And with it go more pubs. They may be gutted and turned into style bars. They may become offices or homes. They may, like the Windsor Castle on the Upper Bristol Road, retain only a façade behind which "exciting new developments" spring up. They may simply be demolished.

It has been suggested that this book, tracing, as it does, a path through pubs that are no longer there, and attempting to recreate the past through a psychogeographical odyssey defining the parameters of a lost city, can be viewed as a poststructuralist model of intertextuality. That's as maybe.

It comprises a series of excursions, and can be used as a virtual guide, enabling readers to make a series of journeys into the past from the privy of their own home. It can be taken in hand and used to explore what's left of Bath's lost pubs on foot. It can be placed in a convenient room and dipped into at random to while away what is sometimes referred to as "down time." Alternatively, it can be used to support a table with one extremely short leg.

In the excursions which follow, we have set ourselves the task of recording all of Bath's pubs since 1776 (in the city centre at least), as well as including any we can trace back any further. 1776 was the year full licensing records – or alehouse recognizances – began to be kept for the city of Bath. At that time, Combe Down, Twerton, Weston, Widcombe, and part of Walcot lay outside the city. Records for these areas were kept separately and, until the early nineteenth century, only included the name of the licensee, not the name of the pub. As a result, a number of late eighteenth-century and early nineteenth-century pubs in these outlying parishes may have slipped through our net.

Despite all our efforts, we discovered two more pubs as we prepared the book for the printer. We would be very interested to hear of any we may have missed, in the hope that they can be included in a revised edition of this book. Information on the pubs we have included would also be welcome. As we also run the "Great Bath Pub Crawl" throughout the summer and give regular talks on old pubs, the information will certainly not be filed away and forgotten about, even if it does not immediately find its way into print.

Perhaps attempting to list every pub in Bath in this way seems a bit obsessive. But the quest for inclusivity appeals to the inner anorak in all of us. And just remember, every pub was once someone's local. It may not have been your idea of a place for a good night out, it may have been as rough as hell, but somebody loved it and mourned its demise. One thing we have avoided, however, is giving lists of landlords. While these may be of interest to family historians or the current licensee of a particular pub, en masse they are about as interesting as a telephone directory, and a good deal less useful. Wherever possible, we have tried to tell a story and give some sense of what each pub was like. That does not mean all landlords are excluded, for many feature in the story – indeed some were such colourful characters they are the story.

Several people have wandered around Bath's pubs before and written down their findings. In 1903, E Newton Fuller prepared a report for the Licensing Justices. He visited every pub in the city and, while he did not mention what the beer or the clientele were like, he faithfully recorded the layout and general state of repair. One thing that particularly interested him was the condition of the toilets. A hundred years on, his descriptions of the facilities on offer make fascinating (if occasionally gut-churning) reading. Pubs with facilities for ladies could be counted on the fingers of one fish (leading one to wonder how those ladies of the night who spent much of their time in pubs coped); facilities for men were often so dire that, for many, they must have been a convenience of last resort. You will find many of Mr Newton Fuller's observations, both lavatorial and non-lavatorial, on the pages that follow.

Then, early in 1976, Fred Pearce visited every pub in the city to produce his highly entertaining *Critical Guide to Bath Pubs*. The Campaign for Real Ale was just getting under way and beer was less than 25p a pint. *Mamma Mia* had just toppled *Bohemian Rhapsody* from the Number One slot. Demis Roussos and the Brotherhood of Man were the current pop idols. The sizzling summer of '76, with the Wurzels belting out *I've Got a Brand New Combine Harvester*, was still months away.

THE LOST PUBS OF BATH

THE CRITICAL GUIDE TO BATH PUBS
by Fred Pearce

Eighteeen pubs have closed since Fred Pearce produced his guide in 1976

Smith's seen here in the 1950s, is now DYMK

The Garrick's Head called last orders a few months short of its bicentenary

Over the course of a few weeks, Fred set himself the task of visiting every pub in Bath, mostly at lunchtimes, and writing mini-reviews of what he found. Even though he stuck to beer, there is more than a whiff of *Last of the Summer Wine* about the booklet he produced. Eighteen of the pubs Fred visited have since closed; sixteen have undergone a change of name; many more have changed beyond recognition, while seven new ones have opened.* Some he condemned now make a regular appearance in the *Good Beer Guide* while some of his favourites have been given a total makeover. His pithy comments give an invaluable insight into how much Bath's pubs have changed in the last quarter of a century and we draw on them frequently.

It doesn't take a quarter-century to register a significant impact on the Bath pub scene, however, and just now the pace of change seems to be hotting up. There have been many changes since we published *Bath Pubs* in 2003.

In February 2004, Smith Bros in Westgate Buildings, one of Bath's top lad-and-lager pubs, was revamped by Eldridge Pope as a gay venue called DYMK (Does Your Mother Know?).

The Garrick's Head in St John's Place closed early in 2005, a few months short of its bicentenary. Despite having been taken over by the landlord of a former Gloucestershire CAMRA Pub of the Year, the management decided it would be more successful as a wine bar. That is what it will become when it reopens in 2006.

---

*Those that have closed include the Beaufort, the Beehive (Belvedere), the Beehive (Southdown), the Bladud's Arms, Broadley's, the Empire Bars, Fortt's, Fuller's (Broad Street), the Full Moon (latterly Sam Weller's), the Golden Fleece (Widcombe), the Garrick's Head, the Hat & Feather, the Heath Robinson, the Mason's Arms (Combe Down), the Railway, the Seven Stars, the Viaduct (Monkton Combe), and the Windsor Castle. Those whose names have changed include the Argyle Wine Vaults (now the Boater), the Barley Mow (now the Barley), the Britannia (now the Piccadilly), the Burnt House (now the New Burnt House), the County Wine Vaults (now Flan O'Briens), the Devonshire Arms (now the Bath Tap), the First In Last Out (now abbreviated to Filos), the Grove (now the Rummer), Hatchett's (now the Raven), the Lansdown (now Mandalyns), the Regency (now the Delfter Krug), the Royal Oak, Larkhall (now the Brains Surgery), the Spirit Vaults (now DYMK), the Talbot (now the Hobgoblin), the York Street Wine Vaults (now the Alehouse), and the White Horse (now the Dark Horse). Pubs opened since Fred's guide was published include the Ha Ha! Bar, Lambrettas, the Litten Tree, O'Neills', the Pig & Fiddle, and the Slug & Lettuce. Two pubs not surveyed in the 1976 *Guide* – the Angel in Westgate Street and the Christopher in the High Street – are now the Rat & Parrot and All Bar One.

The Full Moon a century ago ... and in spring 2005.

Inside the Full Moon 50 years ago: wood panelling, screens, drop-down seats, gilt, glass, mahogany and silvered backs.

Spring 2005 also saw the closure of Sam Weller's on Upper Borough Walls, with metal shutters going up a few days later. Strangely enough, the passing of a pub which had been there since at least 1739 was marked by not a word of protest or lamentation. It did not even make it to the pages of the *Bath Chronicle*. The closure may only be temporary; it may be by the time you read this that it is open for business again. The chances of it becoming a wine bar or a shop, however, given what has happened elsewhere, are alarmingly high. The sad thing about Sam Weller's is that its character had been so comprehensively ripped out of it in a series of revamps, there is little left to mourn. Pictures of Sam Weller's – then known as the Full Moon – from the 1960s show that it had a traditional wood-panelled interior, like thousands of other pubs. Like them, it was gutted and revamped in the name of progress. If it had remained unchanged – as the Star and the Old Green Tree have done – its closure would have sparked protests not just in Bath but across the region.

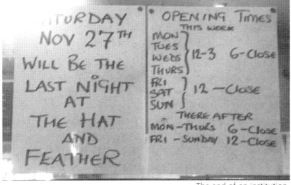

The end of an institution.

One closure that did spark vigorous debate was that of the Hat & Feather in London Street. Almost certainly dating from the 1660s, and taking its name from the distinctive headgear of Royalists during the Civil War, it was rebuilt around 1900. The Hat was a Bath institution, famed not for the quality of its beer, but as "Bath's original underground hangout – not a style bar, more a way of life – the kind of pub legends are made of – or at least tall stories." That's a quote from its website, which, like the pub, is no longer on line. Following a dramatic rent hike by the pubco, the leaseholder, Ian Wood, decided to cut his losses and concentrate on his other pub, the Bell. The Hat went out on a high, with a spectacular firework display. A few weeks later, the pubco put in a temporary manager and the Hat reopened; then, on a miserable night at the end of November 2004, it closed for good. The lease was taken by Richard Fenton, who already owned the Grappa Bar (formerly the Beehive pub) on Belvedere. After an extensive revamp it opened in April 2005 as the Hudson Bar and Grill, "located in a restored former Victorian pub at the top of Walcot Street in Bath's artisan quarter." The move sparked a heated, and at times vituperative, exchange of views in the letters page of the *Bath Chronicle*, much of it condemning the loss of a name that had lasted almost 350 years.

A little further out of town, a pub which closed shortly before *Bath Pubs* was published, the King William on Thomas Street, has not only reopened, but is one of the success stories of the decade. The prognostications for the King William were not good. With no car park and limited on-street parking, it was too far out of town, too small, too run down, and had a somewhat unenviable reputation. But, against all the odds, Charlie and Amanda Digney took the lease and spent months revamping the place, before reopening it – without a change of name – early in 2004. Real ale, fine wines, an adventurous and upmarket food policy, and an object lesson in how an unloved street-corner boozer can be brought bang up to date without compromising its essential character, has ensured that the King William has been popular right from the start. It isn't only beer buffs who've been singing its praises either: in September 2005, the King William received a glowing full-page review in the *Guardian* weekend supplement.

Another pub in line for a listing in the *Good Beer Guide* is the Raven on Queen Street, formerly Hatchett's. The formula here was much the same as for the King William. Jill Forsey and Tim Perry took over the pub, scrubbed it down, smartened it up, and introduced a range of local real ales, plus a choice of ten wines. A year later, it's not only one of the city's top real-ale venues, and a genuine free house, it is increasingly popular as a lunch or dinner venue. The upstairs room, so long under-used, is now a stylish no-smoking bar with some of the best views in the city.

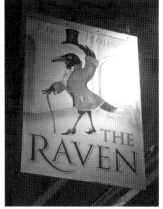

And then there's the Royal Oak on Lower Bristol Road. Closed in 1999, and earmarked for demolition in 2002, few people thought that it would ever bounce back. But bounce back it has, with a vengeance. After lengthy, and extremely sympathetic, restoration, it opened on 5 August 2005 with no less than 10 hand

pumps on a bar running virtually the width of the building. John and Becky Whinnerah have big plans for the Royal Oak – restaurant, beer garden, beer festivals, and an ever-changing selection of real ales. Already the work of local artists is appearing on the walls; there are weekly Irish music sessions, a reading group, and one-off events, such as an evening of Breton music. Initial reports from the city's beer drinkers indicate that, even though it's half an hour's walk from the city centre, this is set to be one of Bath's top pubs – and not just because of the beer.

No survey of changes to Bath's pub scene would be complete without mentioning the Brave New World of Wetherspoons. Bath was probably the last city in the country to fall to the Wetherspoon's juggernaut, which rolled into the new Kingsmead Leisure Complex in 2004, under the banner of the King of Wessex.

As we went to press, more changes were reported. The Rummer on Grand Parade opened after a total refit; the Chequers on Rivers Street temporarily closed. The past two years have seen some positive developments on the Bath pub scene; the range of beer, too, has improved, with new microbreweries opening at Keynsham and Timsbury. The new licensing laws to be introduced in November 2005 bring with them challenges as well as opportunities. Some seem to imply they spell the end of civilisation as we know it – but they implied that when all-day drinking was introduced in 1988; today, nobody seems eager to return to the bad old days of afternoon closing. But even if it is just a storm in a beer mug, generated by newspaper columnists to buoy up sales, the next few years are likely to see many more changes to the Bath pub scene. We can only hope that they are, on balance, as positive as those of the last two.

Before launching into the first of our excursions, a word about sources. Some information came from talking to people who remember Bath's lost pubs, or whose families ran them, but most came from record offices. The Wiltshire Record Office has the Usher's archive, with records and inventories of pubs once owned by the brewery. The Somerset Record Office has a wide range of archives relating to inns and pubs in Bath and the surrounding area.

Most of our information, however, came from the Bath Record Office. Bath is uniquely privileged in the range and extent of its archives. Most of the old city was owned either by the council or by charitable foundations it administered. As a result the history of most sites within the city can be traced back several centuries – some as far back as the twelfth or thirteenth. The extent of the material held is astonishing: for the White Hart Inn in Stall Street, for example, there are over 200 separate documents. Until recently, the sheer bulk of the material was liable to defeat the most indefatigable researcher.

Not until 1967 was a full-time archivist, Robert Bryant, appointed to bring some order to the mass of ancient deeds and documents in the basement of the Guildhall. In the words of the *Bath Chronicle*, "for years, Bath's archives, which occupy four basement rooms, corridors and strong rooms at the Guildhall, had been something of a mystery, even to those most closely connected with them." Mr Bryant transformed it into a properly functioning public record office, and, in 1984, was succeeded by Colin Johnston, who, along with Lucy Powell, still runs it today. It is a measure of how far things have come since 1967 that anyone with access to the internet can now log on to the Bath Record Office website (www.batharchives.co.uk), enter the name of a street or building and come up with a list of leases, deeds, and other documents, giving an outline of its history. Armed with this information, they can then visit the Record Office to take their enquiries a step further. It is no exaggeration to say that without such access to Bath's archives, this book would have been far too slim to support that table.

Documents examined included leases, deeds, conveyances, council minutes, committee reports, alehouse recognizances, coroners' reports, and a host of miscellaneous items. Also invaluable were Postal Directories; a near complete run from the early nineteenth century is held in both the record office and Bath Central Library. Newspapers, especially the *Bath Journal* (founded in 1744) and the *Bath Chronicle* (founded in 1760) also provided much information. Photographic archives held by the record office and the library were also of immense value in bringing the past to life. Full acknowledgement for permission to reproduce these, as well as pictures from other sources, appears on page 5.

That, dear reader, explains the wherefores and the whys, not to mention the hows, behind *The Lost Pubs of Bath*. Now read on....

EXCURSION THE FIRST

WITHIN THE WALLS

This excursion starts just inside the old North Gate, in the High Street, or, as it was known for centuries, the Market Place. People have lived within the city walls since Roman times, but very few pre-eighteenth-century buildings have survived in anything like their original state. Just about all that survives from Tudor Bath are the Abbey and Abbey Church House. There is another pre-eighteenth-century survival in the Market Place, however, that predates the Abbey by at least a hundred years. The beams in the archway leading to Northumberland Passage form part of the oldest building above ground in Bath, hidden inside an eighteenth-century shell. Although a remarkable survival, it would not excite much interest in a city such as York or Canterbury, where so much medieval building has survived. Because Bath has been so comprehensively redeveloped, however, it is something to cherish. It also indicates the scale of the problem that faces us when we try to delve into the history of pre-eighteenth-century Bath.

Of the Market Place onto which this building looked when it was new, nothing is left. We do not even know what the Norman abbey – pulled down to build the present one in the late fifteenth century – looked like.

The Market Place that early eighteenth century visitors to Bath would have seen as they passed through the North Gate has also disappeared. We can, however, piece together what it looked like from old documents and prints. The old Town Hall and Market House stood in the middle of the street. In front of it stood a fountain "in the Dorick Order, covered with a Cimasium Roof." According to John Wood, when Charles II was crowned in 1661, the fountain flowed with claret, in a ceremony involving 400 virgins.

Right up against the walls of the Abbey was a cluster of buildings, some dating from the time of the Abbey's dereliction in the sixteenth century, others added later. One was built by Thomas Atwood (who also built the Paragon) as late as 1718. It blocked up two of the Abbey's northern windows and drew vigorous protests from clergy and parishioners, but to no avail.

Just inside the North Gate, on the left, was the old church of St Mary by the Northgate, abandoned at the Reformation, its nave converted to a school, its tower to a prison. And then there were the coaching inns, vying with each other for the

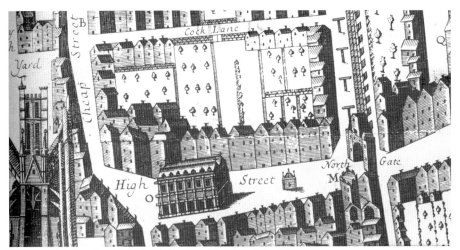
The Market Place in 1694, with the Guildhall and conduit in the middle of the street.

custom of newly-arrived visitors. Everything except the Abbey has long disappeared.

We do not have to go back to the early eighteenth century, however, to find a Market Place which bears no resemblance to the one we know today. Here is a description of what it was like on a typical Saturday night in the mid 1800s:

> Up to the passing of the City of Bath Act in 1851, the Market Place assumed on a Saturday night quite a different appearance to what it does now. Itinerant vendors of almost every class of article for household purposes took their stand on each side of the street. Some – especially the retailers of Staffordshire ware, such as pans and pitchers – laid out their stock on the ground, as also did the vendors of vegetables and greens ... If an execution had recently taken place, a well-recognised old character, known by the sobriquet of "Yam Yam," would be bawling out "the last dying speech and confession" of the culprit. "All the newest and latest songs of the day" were in abundance – "Child of earth with golden hair," "Has your mother sold her mangle?," "All round my hat," "She wore a wreath of roses," etc. Sweets in profusion. Stay and boot laces. Pens and Bath Post letter paper. Pills whose curative properties superseded, so the quack said, either Morrison or Holloway, were to be obtained at the low price of one penny per box. Baked potatoes, pies, all hot! Toss or buy; mutton, beef, or pork. Mussels, hot cockles, etc. ... More than once I have seen a fire kindled in the Market Place, and fish sufficient to fill a cart, which had been pronounced unfit for human consumption, heaped on the fire and burnt ... From the Upper Borough Walls to Cheap Street was one continuous line of vendors. When evening arrived some of these were lit up with naptha, some with oil and many with candles, for neither paraffin nor petroleum had come into use. Most of these conveyed their goods on lightly built barrows drawn by a couple of lurcher dogs, harnessed as a pair of ponies would be; these travelled at a remarkable pace, and wherever the stand was pitched, they were also good caretakers of their owner's property.

THE LOST PUBS OF BATH

And so, with the voice of Yam Yam in our ears, the smell of hot cockles in our nostrils, torchlight flickering on the faces of the passers-by, and ghostly shadows dancing on soot-blackened walls, let us weave our way past the lurchers to revisit the Market Place's ancient inns.

Two doors down from the corner of Upper Borough Walls was the **Greyhound**, with the large figure of a seated greyhound above its entrance. It may have opened in 1585, when "Robert Chilton assignee of William Sherston, Alderman," took a 100 year lease on a "messuage or tenement with a garden and a backside thereto belonging" in the Market Place. When the lease was renewed by John Sherston a century later, in 1685, the messuage was identified as the Greyhound. At the time it had gardens front and back. By 1724, however, the gardens had gone: stables had been built on those at the back; those at the front had fallen victim to road widening. In 1744, the Greyhound was advertised for sale as "a very good and well-accustom'd inn with very good stables."

The entrance to the Greyhound yard was about 35 yards along Upper Borough Walls. Although the Greyhound was not the largest of Bath's coaching inns, it had daily coaches to London. An accident report from February 1752 shows that, even a century and a half before the advent of the motor car, drunken driving could have fatal consequences:

> Last Saturday, in the afternoon, one John Dursley, a coachman, was killed as he was driving the London coach into the Greyhound Inn in the Market Place. Dursley being at present out of place, went about a mile out of Bath to meet the caravan; and upon meeting it, desired to ascend the box; this the driver readily consented to, as he wanted to get down on a particular occasion; so Dursley drove it home: But unhappily for him; for the driver's seat being much higher in the caravan than in any coach, and he not stooping low enough when he enter'd the inn, was crushed against one of the beams over the entrance, and died immediately. 'Tis believed the deceased had been drinking before this happen'd, otherwise he night have taken a more proper care.

In December 1766, William Tucker, from the Shakespeare in Westgate Street, moved to the Greyhound and renamed it the Greyhound & Shakespeare. It kept this name, through several changes of licensee, until it was acquired by the Northgate Brewery in 1793. Thereafter, it had a variety of names – the Greyhound Inn & Tavern (1805), the Greyhound Family & Commercial Inn (1826) and the Greyhound Commercial Hotel (1841). In the early nineteenth century, the Greyhound was the home of the Royal Sussex Masonic Lodge.

Like other coaching inns, the coming of the railway dealt a serious blow to the Greyhound's trade. The landlord of the Greyhound, William Clarke, tried to attract travellers who had switched to the railway by running "an elegant and commodious omnibus to and from the railway station." Despite his best efforts, however, the Greyhound closed in the early 1860s. By 1866 the building housed the London & South Western Bank, as well as Wilkinson's Engravers and James Dutilk's Wine

Four stages in the transformation of the Greyhound: as an inn, c1850; as a bank and printing office, c1900; as Cater, Stofell & Fortt's, c1950; as an outdoor clothing store, c2000.

THE LOST PUBS OF BATH

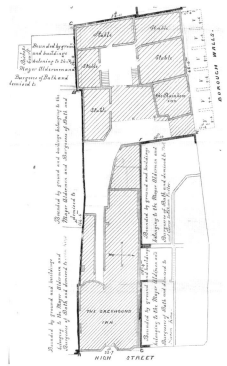

A plan of the Greyhound in 1861, with the High Street at the bottom and Upper Borough Walls on the right. The Rainbow Inn can be seen just above the entrance to the coachyard on Upper Borough Walls.

Merchant's. James Dutilk also ran a public bar called the Greyhound Vaults around the corner in Upper Borough Walls. This relic of the old inn survived the takeover of the premises by Cater. Stofell & Fortt, and remained open until 1964, when the whole block was demolished. Despite the redevelopment of the site, a faint echo of the old Greyhound still lingers in Upper Borough Walls, where the entrance to a service yard stands on the site of the entrance to the coachyard.

The Greyhound's most famous visitor was Samuel Taylor Coleridge. By his early forties, he was hopelessly addicted to opium. He had left his wife and spent much of his time as the guest of various friends who could tolerate his addiction. One set of benefactors were the Morgans. In late 1813, he moved into a cottage at Ashley, near Box, with Mary Morgan and her sister Charlotte. He was not the easiest of house guests, and on the evening of 5 December, things came to head. Although the details of what happened are unclear, he swallowed a massive dose of laudanum and stormed out of the house, taking only a small satchel of books with him.

He set off for Bath, trudging along the muddy, unlit road into the driving rain, as the effects of the drug began to take hold. He dragged himself through Batheaston, along the London Road, down Walcot Street – stopping perhaps for a drink at an alehouse en route – until he reached Northgate Street and the Greyhound Inn. He probably remembered it from 17 years earlier, when he had taken lunch there after delivering a sermon at the Unitarian Chapel in Frog Lane.

He somehow managed in his delirious and dishevelled state to convince the innkeeper to take him in. He was, despite all appearances to the contrary, a national celebrity. His play, *Remorse*, had been performed at the Theatre Royal nine months earlier. Even so, he was consigned to a small garret room, where he collapsed into a nightmare of hallucinations, sweating, agonising muscular pains, and a burning fever that left him unable to sleep, eat or talk coherently. The landlord, William May, thought he was dying and called a doctor. By a stroke of luck, it was Dr Caleb Parry, the father of an old friend of Coleridge's, who turned up.

On 19 December, Coleridge wrote to Mary Morgan:

Yesterday was the first day, Mary! that I could leave my bed, except in a blanket to have it made – even from the day I quitted you – the terrors of the Almighty

The Katherine Wheel after conversion to Oliver's shoe shop. The entrance to Bishop's Court can be seen on the left.

have been around and against me – and tho' driven up and down for seven dreadful days by restless pain, like a leopard in a den, yet the anguish and remorse of mind was worse than the pain of the whole body ... Dr Parry, who was called in by accident (for I was too wild with suffering to direct anything myself) attended me day after day, and often twice a day, with parental kindness. Mrs May says, he did what she never knew him do – stay with me two and three hours at a time – and to him under God's mercy I owe that I am at present alive.

Later that day he took a postchaise to Bristol to stay with Josiah Wade in Queen's Square where he continued his convalescence.

Next door to the Greyhound was the **Katherine Wheel**.* Although it can only be traced back to 1585, its name suggests it may have dated from before the reformation. Because the wheel on which St Katherine had been martyred looked like a spinning wheel, she had been adopted as the patron saint of weavers. In Bath, whose prosperity was based on weaving, St Katherine was one of the saints whose name was most frequently invoked, with altars dedicated to her in several churches.

There were Katherine or Catherine Wheels in many other towns and cities, but, when hagiolatry was outlawed after the reformation, many of them changed their names – often to the innocuous (but meaningless) Cat in the Wheel. We have political correctness; the sixteenth century had religious correctness. But it was something the landlords of Bath's Katherine Wheel do not seem to have subscribed to, and the inn survived – with its name unchanged – for another couple of hundred years.

In 1650, Mrs Power, who had taken the lease, was let off paying rent for five years, because of the damage done to the inn by Puritan soldiers billeted there six years earlier. It was last recorded as an inn in 1747, and closed sometime before

*Bath's Katherine Wheel Inn was unusual, although not unique, in that the saint's name was spelt Katherine rather than Catherine.

THE LOST PUBS OF BATH

The end of the Katherine Wheel. The buildings on the right were soon to follow.

1782. The building was restored in 1800, although some early or mid-eighteenth century features were retained. It has been suggested that, because of similarities to buildings in Kingsmead Square and elsewhere, the frontage may have been redesigned in the early eighteenth century by the Bristol architect, John Strahan.

The back part of the Katherine Wheel – possibly its tap – survived to become the **Crown**, which by 1833 had been leased to the Anchor Brewery. The Crown was set well back from the Market Place at the end of a yard called Bishop's Court (the old yard of the Katherine Wheel, perhaps?). Whatever the old Katherine Wheel was like, by the mid-nineteenth century the Crown had more to do with sinners than saints, as this newspaper report from November 1837 indicates:

> Jane Sherston, 28, who could read and write imperfectly, was charged with robbing John Cross of 4/-. The prosecutor deposed that on the 11th of September he met the prisoner in the High Street, who asked him to treat her to a glass of beer. He went with her to the Crown public house in the same street, and gave her some. When they were on their return, she drew the money from his pocket in the Crown Passage.

Asking to be treated to a glass of beer was a common way for prostitutes to approach potential customers. If they agreed to a drink, the next step was to coax them upstairs to one of the pub's bedrooms. In this case, Mr Cross thought things had gone far enough, with the result that Miss Sherston took matters into her own hands. She ended up with four month's hard labour.

The Crown (which was known as the Crown & Thistle for a brief period) closed in 1876. When the old Katherine Wheel became Oliver's shoe shop, the Crown became the warehouse. Despite the ground floor of the Katherine Wheel being extensively remodelled, with a new shop front added in the early twentieth century, the upper floors and the buildings at the rear were largely untouched. On the fourth floor there was a curious top-lit room with stone panelling. Photographs in the archive of the Building of Bath Museum, taken in 1964, just prior to demolition, also contain particularly poignant reminders of the dim, distant past – diamond-scratched signatures on old window panes – a common practice in the eighteenth century. Who knows what other irreplaceable relics were reduced to rubble in the destruction of one of Bath's last links with the coaching era?

There was also an inn called the **Hare & Hounds** on the west side of the Market Place, although information about it is very sketchy. In 1721, when Philip Bennet leased it off the Corporation, it was described as having a tenement occupied by Samuel Howse on the north, a tenement occupied by John Axford on the south, other buildings to the west, and the street on the east. In 1722, Philip Bennet paid for a feather of water to be laid "to his house called the Hare & Hounds in the Market Place." And that is the last we hear of it.

Across the street from the Greyhound and the Katherine Wheel, on the site now occupied by the northern extension of the Guildhall and the Art Gallery, was the **White Lion**. This was one of Bath's top coaching inns, but it has a somewhat convoluted history. Its principal claim to fame was that the first stagecoach from Bath to London set out from the White Lion in 1667. However, this White Lion was next door, and was pulled down when the Guildhall was built in the 1770s.

The White Lion on the corner of Bridge Street. The entrance to its coachyard can be seen on the left.

THE LOST PUBS OF BATH

To the north of the original White Lion was an inn called the **Unicorn**, into which the White Lion moved in 1780. The Unicorn dated from the mid-seventeenth century, when the lease was held by John Biggs, a member of the Corporation. In 1699, the lease passed to Messrs Stibbs, Bushell and Webb. Mr Stibbs was the Mayor; his two associates were also councillors. In 1720, the Unicorn "with orchard, garden and two tenements adjoining" was leased to Ambrose Bishop; in 1742 it passed to Benjamin Collibee.

The Unicorn was bounded on the east by the city wall and on the north by the old church of St Mary by the Northgate, which had been deconsecrated at the Reformation. By the 1760s, when William Pulteney applied to pull it down to build Bridge Street, its tower was in use as the city gaol. The Council agreed that "the ground on which the prison stands … be granted to Mr Pulteney on condition that he procures for the city a piece of ground 80 feet by 60 feet by the river and within 300 yards from the east end of the intended bridge, for the purpose of building a new prison." So it was that Bridge Street came into being, with the Unicorn on the corner.

When the White Lion, on the other side of the Unicorn, was demolished in 1780, its licence – and its name – was transferred to the Unicorn. In a move reminiscent of musical chairs, the Unicorn's licence and name was transferred to the Boat in Northgate Street (of which more in the third excursion).

The new White Lion had one of the most enviable positions in the city, wrapped round the first street corner visitors to the city saw as they entered the Market Place. Yet its location was not without its drawbacks. The main problem was the proximity of the market. In July 1819, Julia Arnold, the landlady, wrote to the council "complaining of the nuisance occasioned by the exposure of fish, fruits, etc., on sale on the pavement adjoining the White Lion Inn." Despite the Mayor's promise that the nuisance would be removed, nothing seems to have been done until, five years later, the councillors themselves complained

THE BATH, BRISTOL, and LONDON POST-COACH, carrying four Infide Paffengers, and MACHINES fix Infides, belonging to the Original Proprietors, fet out at the Times and from the refpective Inns, as under:

AFTERNOON FLYING POST-COACHES, every Day, (Saturday excepted) from
The White-Lion, Briftol, at 2, to the Swan, Holborne-bridge; Bufh Tavern, at 3, to Three-Cups, Bread-ftreet; White-Lion, Bath, at 2, to Golden-crofs, Charing-crofs Three Tuns, and Chriftopher, Bath } at 4, to Belle-favage, Ludgate-hill.

MORNING POST-COACH, at 4 o'Clock every Day, From the White-lion, Bath, to the Bolt and Tun, Fleet-ftreet.

POST-COACHES in TWO DAYS, every Monday, Wednefday, and Friday morning, at eight o'clock, From the White-Hart, Bath, to the Rofe, Holborne-bridge; And every Tuefday, Thurfday and Saturday morning, From the White-Lion, Bath, to the Golden-Crofs, Charing-Crofs.

MACHINE in ONE DAY, every Night (except Saturday) from White-hart, Briftol, at 8 } to Three-Cups, Bread-ftreet, and Greyhound, Bath, at 10 } & Saracen's-head, Friday-ftreet

Prices in the above Poft-Coaches and Machines as follow:

		l.	*s.*	*d.*
Each infide paffenger to or from Briftol, by Poft-Coach	-	1	8	0
Each infide to or from Bath, by Poft-Coach	—	1	6	0
Each infide to or from Bath, by two-day Poft-coach	1	8	0
Children in lap, and Outfides, half-price.				
Each infide to or from Briftol, by Machine	—	1	3	0
Each infide to or from Bath, by ditto	—	1	1	0
Children in lap, half-price.				
Outfides to or from Briftol, by Machine	—	0	12	6
Outfides to or from Bath, by ditto	-	0	11	6

Half the money to be paid on taking the places, the other half on entering the Machines, or Poft-coaches.

Infide paffengers in the above Carriages allowed 14lb. children in lap and outfides 7lb. of luggage; all above to pay in the Poft-coaches 1d¾. and in the Machines 1d. per lb.

The Proprietors will not be accountable for any jewels, plate, money, writings, &c. (if loft) unlefs entered and paid for as fuch.

They call at the Old and New White-horfe Cellars, the Black and White-Bear Inns, Piccadilly, London, both going in and coming out of Town.

Performed (if GOD permit) by
JOHN GLAZIER, ROBERT MOODY, } Bath.
JAMES WHITE, Caftle-Inn, THOMAS HANCOCK, } Marlborough
ANN BANNISTER, Reading.
THOMAS HALLIWELL, WILLIAM CLARK, JOHN HARRIS, GEORGE SIMCOCK, } Speenhamland
JOHN RIMELL, Maidenhead.
JOHN WHALLEY, { Three-Cups, Bread-ftreet, London.

Details of the Bath, Bristol & London Post Coach – the forerunner of the Mail Coach – in 1780.

of the "offensive smell [of fish] in the Mayor's Room and the Town Clerk's and Chamberlain's Offices." This time they wasted no time in instructing the City Architect, George Manners, to draw up plans "for removing the fish stalls."

In 1830, the Corporation announced plans to enlarge the markets, which entailed taking over part of the White Lion. Six years later, the council took possession "of those parts of the White Lion which [had] by a recent contract been surrendered" and set about determining "the use they [could] best be put to."

The White Lion was the meeting place for numerous societies, such as the Bath Catch Club. In January 1792, the following notice appeared in the *Bath Chronicle*:

BATH CATCH CLUB, WHITE LION

The Master of Ceremonies' Ball being on Friday next,

the Club will be held on the preceding evening

- Mr Pigott in the chair -

Catches and Glees to begin precisely at seven o'clock

W. Wordsworth, Secretary.

The name at the end may give us pause. Could it possibly be *the* W Wordsworth? Sadly, not. He was in France around this time, revelling in the revolution and having an affair with Marie-Anne Vallon, who bore him a daughter on 15 December 1792. This W Wordsworth was an actor who regularly appeared at the Theatre Royal in Orchard Street in the 1780s and 1790s.

One famous figure who did stay at the White Lion was Isambard Kingdom Brunel. He was there on the night of the census on 7 June 1841. Just over three weeks later, the final section of his Great Western Railway opened, linking Bath with London and sealing the fate of the coaching business which had been the lifeblood of Bath's inns. Not that innkeeping was an automatic road to riches before the railway arrived. In October 1830, for example, when few people took the threat of the railways seriously, the leaseholders of the White Lion, George Arnold and Charles Smith, had gone bankrupt.

Unlike many Bath inns, the White Lion survived the coming of the railway by almost half a century. In 1872, a report "on the advantages offered by the site of the White Lion Hotel for a new Post Office" was prepared, but never acted on. Two years later, the diarist Francis Kilvert visited Bath and found an unusual variety of street entertainment outside the White Lion:

At the door of the White Lion Hotel in Bath we found a large crowd gathered round the donkey and cart of the nobleman organ grinder. The disguised nobleman and his organ were putting up at the Hotel and the people were waiting for him to finish breakfast and come out. No one knows who he is. There are many reports. Some say he is an Irish baronet, some say that he is a Lord. It is believed that he has made a wager for £30,000 that he will go about for three years with the same donkey, and live by his earnings. People give him gold in the street and some days it is said he makes as much as £15. Perhaps he has run through one fortune and taken this means of getting another. Or perhaps a fortune of £30,000 was left him to be inherited on this condition.

Three years after this bizarre character passed through, in September 1877, part of the back of the old inn, facing onto Bridge Street, was demolished. This included the White Lion Tap, a pub for the servants and tradesmen who would not have been allowed into the main part of the inn. To cater for them, a new pub – the Bridge Street Brewery, later renamed the Bridge Street Vaults – was opened. It only lasted a few years, for in 1891 the whole of the site was cleared to make way for the

The White Lion shortly before demolition.

Technical College (now part of the Guildhall) and Art Gallery, and all trace of one of Bath's most familiar landmarks for over 350 years disappeared.

On the east side of the Market Place – probably somewhere near where the main entrance to the Guildhall is today – was an inn called the **King's Arms**. In 1722, Ann Bushell paid £20 a year to have a feather of water supplied to the "King's Arms in the Market Place." In 1732, the property was described as having a tenement occupied by Thomas Short to the north, one occupied by James Parker to the south, the city walls to the east and the street to the west. In 1744, the lease was taken by Edward Marchant, a distiller. It was demolished soon afterwards to make way for an extension to the market.

The **Turk's Head**, Bath's first coffee house, also on the east side of the Market Place, was opened by Robert Sheyler around 1679. Around 15 years later, he moved to a new coffee house on the corner of Cheap Street. However, the building in the Market Place continued to be known as the Turk's Head and may have continued as a coffee house under new ownership. The building was demolished in 1745, when the Corporation instructed the Chamberlain

> to contract with the persons interested in the house called the Turk's Head near the Shambles in the possession of John Rees, for the purpose of enlarging the market.

There was also an inn called the **Noble Science** in the Market Place. This opened sometime before 1694, and was last recorded in 1715 when "a feather of water [was] taken into the house called the Noble Science in the Market Place. However, it may have been renamed the **Fencer's Arms**, recorded as an inn in the Market Place in the 1740s. Fencing was regarded as a "noble science" in the eighteenth century and was a popular spectator sport. Large wagers were placed on the outcomes of contests, and skilful swordsmen achieved celebrity status. The most famous swordsman to visit Bath, in the 1790s, was a notorious French transvestite, the Chevalier d'Eon. During his visit, wagers were even placed as to whether the Chevalier was a man or a woman pretending to be a man dressed as a woman! Earlier in the century, marathon fencing matches lasting a couple of days and attracting huge crowds, were held in the Market Place. Much of this activity probably centred on the Fencer's Arms.

It was also the venue for other diversions. In January 1748, for example, the *Bath Journal* announced that "a famous strong woman is to be seen at the Fencer's Arms, who among other curiosities lifts six hundredweight by the hair of her head." A year later, "a curious collection of wild beasts" was displayed there. The last large-scale fencing matches took place in the 1760s – possibly as a result of a crackdown by the Corporation – and the Fencer's Arms closed around the same time.

On the east side of the Market Place, just up from the corner of Orange Grove, was a "tenement in the tenure of Henry Chapman," which in 1662 was described as a "new tavern" called the **Sun**. Henry Chapman was a prominent Royalist and, during the Civil War, the Sun was a meeting place for Royalist soldiers. In 1661, after the Restoration of Charles II, it was the scene of curious post-election celebrations. The Corporation, overwhelmingly Parliamentarian in its sympathies, had elected two anti-Royalist Members of Parliament. Incensed by this, Henry Chapman organised a rival election to return two alternative Members of Parliament. The election was conducted in "a most tumultuous manner," and was followed by a party at the Sun, where Chapman's cronies "caroused so long that many of them were scarce able to return home." When parliament assembled, all four Members turned up, the two with Royalist sympathies being ejected.

From 1662 to 1672 and again from 1681 to 1690, the Sun also housed Bath's Post Office. On the north side of the tavern, an alleyway, lined with butchers' shops, led through to the old council house (part of which was also a tavern). The Sun lasted only about 40 years. An entry in the Council Minutes for 6 October 1701 reads:

Mr Fran. Pearce pays 20/- for lease of 42 years of a messuage called the Sun … provided he produces his old lease.

However, the entry is crossed out, suggesting that he failed to produce the lease and the deal fell through. By 1709, the Sun was a private house in the possession of Francis Bave; the tavern's name may have been transferred to a new tavern called the Sun on the site now occupied by the Empire Hotel.

Next to the Sun, on the corner of what later became the Orange Grove, was the **Horse's Head** or Corner House. In an indenture of 1617 we read that

Frauncis Blisse and Mary his wife doe hold … all that messuage or tenement commonly called the Horsehead or Corner House and a backside thereunto adjoining between a tenement then in the tenure of Henry Chapman on the north side and a lane that leadeth to the East Gate on the south side and abutteth backward upon the Guildhall east and openeth against the said market house west.

The inn's name probably indicated that horses could be hired there. In 1626, the lease of the Horse's Head was taken by John Atwood. He still held it in 1662, but by then had renamed it the Nag's Head. It closed shortly afterwards.

After a lapse of almost 300 years, another inn opened on the same site. The **Abbey Hotel**, with a bar, tap room, and seven bedrooms, opened in the 1860s and closed in 1891 to make way for the southern extension of the Guildhall.

The corner of High Street and Cheap Street, with Eureka Trading and the Jamuna Restaurant at Nos 9-10, was redeveloped in the 1880s. Formerly, the buildings extended further south. On the corner, at 1 High Street, was a beerhouse called the **Guildhall Tavern**, opened by James Downton around 1860. It closed about five years later and became a tobacconist's.

§

The north side of Cheap Street in the mid nineteenth century, showing the sites of four lost inns.

Six hundred years ago, Cheap Street, leading off the Market Place, was known as Soutor Street. A soutor was a shoemaker, but of the alehouses which slaked the thirst of the workers in this notoriously thirsty profession, we have no record. In 1399, the council decided that the name of the street should be "changed into the more fair and honourable name of Cheap Street." A cheap was a market, and the renaming indicates that the stalls that once filled the Market Place continued along here as well.

It would have been very crowded, for Cheap Street was notoriously narrow. "The streets are most of the narrowest size," wrote Henry Chapman in 1673, "especially that nearest the centre, called the Cheap Street, the greatest eye-sore to its beauty." In 1749, John Wood called it a "narrow, inconvenient way, being only 13 feet broad." It was also a black spot for pedestrian casualties. Probably its highest-profile victim was the Bishop of Worcester, who was knocked down and killed there in 1780. It was rebuilt, and the buildings set back, under the auspices of the Bath Improvement Act of 1789. By then, however, all of Cheap Street's inns had closed.

All the inns stood on the north side of the street. Two doors up from the Market Place, at Nos 7-8, was the **King's Head**. In 1717, it was leased from St John's Hospital by William Horton, a maltster. In 1747, it passed to the Rev Duel Taylor, Rector of Bath Abbey, who promptly closed it down. The building later passed to the Shum family and was rebuilt around 1790. It became a pork butcher's, and today houses the Early Learning Centre. The words DILL'S FAMOUS BATH POLONIES can still be seen above the first-floor windows, while the name of Shum survives in the name of Shum's Court, which can be reached through a door at the side of the shop.

A couple of doors along, at No 4 Cheap Street, where Burger King now stands, was the **Bird Cage**. It opened sometime before 1752 and had closed by 1780. It has bequeathed nothing to us nothing except a cautionary tale of short measures from 1769:

> This day fortnight William Badham, who keeps the Bird Cage alehouse in Cheap Street, was convicted before the Mayor and Justices of the City for drawing drink in a pewter pot that held barely three half pints; he paid the penalty of six shillings and eight pence. One half went to the informer, the other half to the poor of the parish. If some of the injured public in such like cases will only give themselves the trouble to make information, it would be serving the poor, and prevent the great abuse of short measures in general.

THE LOST PUBS OF BATH

Next door but one to the Bird Cage, at 2 Cheap Street, on the eastern corner of Cock Lane (now Union Passage), was the **Queen's Head**. In 1603, when Mabel Mountayne took the lease, it was described as "all those roomes of houseinge lyeinge in Cheape Street viz. a shopp, a little chamber adjoyninge, a butterie, an entrie, a hall with a little butterie therein, a parlour, a stable, and three upper roomes or chambers over the said parlour of the said hall." In 1714 John Saunders took the lease, and in 1727 Bath's first Masonic lodge held its inaugural meeting there. Richard "Beau" Nash, the Duke of St Albans, Viscount Cobham, the Duke of Bedford, and the Earl of Lichfield were among those present. A year later, John Saunders was granted "liberty to make a common shore [sewer] from the upper end of the Queen's Head under Cox Lane into the main shore, under Cheap Street, paying rent for the same."

In January 1747, the inn was advertised to let, complete with stables. It was taken by Henry Trinder, who promptly changed its name and placed an advertisement to that effect in the *Bath Journal*:

> The Lebeck's Head in the Market Place is now removed to the house in Cheap Street, formerly the Queen's Head, where may be had good eating and good wines of all sorts, in the best manner, and at the most reasonable rates.
>
> NB Good lodgings at the Lebecks Head, and an ordinary every day in the season at three o'clock.

The Lebeck's Head in the Market Place was, in fact, the Christopher (now All Bar One), which Henry Trinder had also renamed during his tenure. There were four Lebeck's Heads in London in the mid-eighteenth century and one on Broad Street in Bristol. Mr Lebeck was a celebrity chef whose portrait was used as an inn sign. Whether Henry Trinder was operating a franchise or serving food in the style of Mr Lebeck, however, is unclear.

In 1769, it was taken over by Mr Strange, who announced his arrival in the *Bath Chronicle*:

> The Old Queen's Head Tavern & Eating House in Cheap Street ... is taken by N Strange, Cook, who has fitted up the same in a Neat Manner, for the reception of Ladies, Gentlemen, and others. Where may be had all sorts of Soops, in as small a quantity as agreeable; with Chops, Steaks, and Made Dishes of every kind; likewise Hams, Tongue, Brawn, Sausages, etc. ... NB A genteel ordinary every day at two o'clock.

Food was not the only attraction at the Queen's Head. In October 1772, over 2,000 people visited the inn to see the "Chronoscope" on display there. "Never," rhapsodised the *Bath Chronicle*, "was anything so admired, or ever met with greater applause." Life at the old Queen's Head was not without its problems, however, as this report from April 1774 indicates:

> Joseph Thwaites at the Queen's Head returns his sincere thanks for the many favours he daily receives; and is extremely sorry that many of his customers should be offended and leave his house, owing to a want of measures to serve them: The real cause of which proceeds from the great number sent out of doors,

and the difficulty to get them returned. He therefore hopes that those who have any of his measures will be kind enough to return them or let him know where he may send for them, as he doubts not but there are many in the houses of those who are not his constant customers, he having lost six dozen within the last six months … Joseph Thwaites having been informed that several of his measures have been wilfully melted, and otherwise destroyed, and sold for old metal, or concealed for that purpose, offers a reward of one guinea to anyone who will give information of the persons guilty of the said offence, so that they may be brought to justice.

Joseph Thwaites was the tenant of Richard Hay and Mr Strange. By 1778, he had been replaced by Peter Appleby, but by 1786 the Queen's Head had closed. However, it kept its name. In 1800, for example, when Daniel Godwin, a shoemaker, took the lease, it was still referred to as "a messuage called the Queen's Head." The plan accompanying the lease shows that, although it only had a frontage of 22 feet, it broadened out further back, and extended 91 feet along Union Passage, with an entrance to a courtyard beyond that.

On the western corner of Cock Lane, at 1 Cheap Street (now part of Dixon's), was the **Raven**. The earliest recorded leaseholder was Paul Hopkins, who was there in 1585. By 1654, it had been taken over by George Bennett, who renamed it the Three Goats. George Bennett was succeeded by George Collibee in 1679; he was succeeded by John Masters in 1688. When Richard Masters (presumably John Masters' son) took over the lease in 1697, he renamed it the Three Crowns & Sceptre. In 1744, however, when John Henshaw, a Doctor of Physick, took the lease, it was described as a "former inn," with its brewhouses having been taken over by the Bear.

The **Bear** was not only the biggest inn in Cheap Street, but, in its early years, the biggest building in Bath after the Abbey. It covered the whole of what is now Union Street. It was first recorded in 1585, but was almost certainly older. One of its early landlords was Peter Chapman (1506-1602), the son of Thomas Chapman, who kept the White Hart at the top of Stall Street. Other early leaseholders included George Chapman (1673), John Masters (1691), John Martin (1698), Henry Townsend (1701), and Thursby Robinson (1733). Until the York House opened in 1769 the Bear was, with the possible exception of the White Hart, Bath's top inn.

In 1608, Lionel Cranfield, First Earl of Middlesex, stayed four nights at the Bear and left a record of what it cost. He paid two pounds and a shilling for bed and board, one pound and eleven shillings for stabling his horses, one shilling and sixpence for "the boy who brought the beer and washed the linen," and twopence each for the maids and the chamberlain (the man who looked after the chambers).[*]

Not everyone found the Bear to their liking. A lady called Elizabeth Noel, for example, wrote to her sister after arriving in Bath in January 1774, that "the Bear was

*To get an idea what these figures represent in today's terms, they need to be multiplied by 120.

An artist's impression of the Bear.

so very noisy & dismal & so very indifferent that I could not forbear crying." Another visitor whose sojourn at the Bear proved less than felicitous was Sir William Smith, who arrived in March 1752:

> On Thursday evening, Sir William Smith, Alderman of Aldgate Ward, London, arriv'd here for the recovery of his health; but he came too late, for Friday morning, he died at the Bear Inn, having deferr'd coming to this place too long; a case which very often happens.

A less partisan observer may have wondered whether it was the journey from London that killed him. The *Bath Journal*, however, was keen to avoid saying anything that might deter potential visitors. The Bear was fully equipped to cope with moribund clients: the yard accommodated "that valuable concern called the black work" (a funeral director's) consisting of three hearses, four coaches, a chariot, and 20 horses.

In 1733, a masonic lodge was established at the Bear. Originally known as the Bear Lodge, it was absorbed into the Royal Cumberland Lodge in 1785, although meetings continued to be held at the Bear. On 27 December 1784, Thomas Dunckerley, Provincial Grand Master of Somerset, together with 120 freemasons, attended a service in the Abbey before walking in procession to the Bear, where they spent the rest of the day in "festivity, harmony and fraternal affection." Three years later, Thomas Dunckerley became Grand Master of the Knights Templar in England and established a Templar Lodge at the Bear.

Throughout the latter part of the eighteenth century, there were plenty of indications that the Bear had failed to keep up with the times. Despite Bath's growing sophistication, it never aspired to be anything more than the chief inn of a prosperous market town. Take this advertisement from the *Bath Journal* in March 1747, for example:

> This is to give notice to all gentlemen and others, that there will be kept at the Bear Inn in Bath all this season, a beautiful well-bred strong stallion for covering. He was bred by Edward Jones, Esq. of Langford, and was got by Mr Robinson's horse Spare, who was bred by Lord Godolphin ... He is now come but four years old, 15 hands and an inch high ... The price of covering is one guinea the stint, to be paid at the stable door, and any gentleman may have his mare try'd as often as is needful all the season, gratis.

In January 1795, "the original Bath Repository" was moved "from the Pelican Inn, Walcot Street, to that most commodious situation the Bear Inn yard, for the sale of horses by auction every Saturday as usual at one o'clock. The entrance is by the large gates on the Borough Walls."

It was not just the character of the inn that was a problem. As soon as John Wood started to build north of the old city walls, it became clear that the Bear was a serious impediment to visitors travelling from their lodgings to the baths and Pump Room. When Matthew Bramble, in Smollett's *Humphrey Clinker* (1771), visited Bath, he

> was impatient to see the boasted improvements in architecture, for which the upper parts of the town have been so much celebrated; and t'other day I made a circuit of all the new buildings. [Queen] Square, though irregular, is, on the whole, pretty well laid out, spacious, open, and airy; and, in my opinion, by far the most wholesome and agreeable situation in Bath, especially the upper side of it; but the avenues to it are mean, dirty, dangerous, and indirect. Its communication with the baths is through the yard of an inn, where the poor trembling valetudinarian is carried in a chair betwixt the heels of a double row of horses, wincing over the curry-combs of grooms and postillions, over and above the hazard of being obstructed, or overturned, by the carriages which are continually making their exit or their entrance. I suppose, after some chairman shall have been maimed, and a few lives lost by these accidents, the Corporation will think in earnest about providing a more safe and commodious passage.

When the Rev. John Penrose visited Bath in 1766 he wrote that "there is an Act of Parliament passed this Session, to enable the Corporation of Bath to make great alterations for the beauty and convenience of this city: particularly all the houses are to be pulled down, that are between Staul and Milsom Streets, and a grand street to be built from the higher end of the former to the lower end of the latter. So many alterations are to be made, that beautiful as Bath now is, it will be much more so in very few years."

Penrose was over-optimistic. Coming from Cornwall, he did not know how long things could take in Bath. John Wood and the developers who followed him could throw up magnificent squares, crescents and terraces in a few years. When the Corporation got involved, however, it was a different story. Although they had parliamentary approval to demolish the Bear and build Union Street, negotiations with the landlord, Henry Phillot, and later with his executors, rumbled on for years.

It is hard to know what to make of Mr Phillot. He moved to the Bear from the Three Tuns in Stall Street in 1767, when plans for Union Street had already been approved by Parliament. Was he hoping for a handsome pay-off when the Bear was pulled down or did he take it on the promise of some deal by the Corporation? It is impossible to say. What we do know is that, as a result of the Bath Improvement Act in 1789, he was offered £13,500 (over £900,000 in modern terms) to build a new inn on the west side of "the street to be called Union Street." The deal was that the Bear would stay open until the new inn was built and then be demolished to make way for Union Street. It never happened, but whether that was due to Mr Phillot's intransigence, a change of heart by the Corporation, or the financial crisis of 1793, is unknown.

By 1801, 35 years after Penrose confidently predicted that a "grand street" would soon run between "Staul and Milsom Streets," still nothing had been done. Then the King announced he was coming to Bath. A Bath chronicler of the time, with the resounding name of Captain Mainwaring, takes up the story:

> At this period the communication between the upper and lower parts of the town was generally through that lane now called Union Passage, the street bearing the name of Union Street not being in existence. This confined thoroughfare was then considered a grievous nuisance, and a suggestion was thrown out, whether a commodious passage might not be made through the Bear yard so as to afford the Royal visitors a safe and uncontaminated walk from the Pump Rooms to their intended residence [in the Royal Crescent]. However, their Majesties' visit having been relinquished, this plan likewise was given up.

Nevertheless, things finally started to happen. In the following year "the different tenants, contiguous to the Bear, received notices to quit their several premises." It was not until 1806, however, 40 years after Penrose's visit, that things really got under way:

> In the early part of this year a notice was issued, inviting such persons as were desirous of contracting for the purchase of certain plots of ground, to build a new street, intended to be called Union Street, leading from the north side of Cheap Street, to other streets and places in the upper town.

The Bear, which had long presented a seemingly immovable obstacle to progress – a relic of Elizabethan Bath staring the Georgian city full in the face, like an embarrassing old regular with snuff stains down his shirt and a dubious line in personal hygiene hogging the seat by the bar in the old Dog & Duck long after its transformation into a trendy wine bar – was reduced to a pile of rubble. Captain Mainwaring described its passing:

> Towards the conclusion of [1806], we find these improvements rapidly progressing; and, as if by magic, convenient openings, spacious streets, and elegant edifices presented themselves in every direction: Union Street nearly finished, and New Bond Street opening a short and easy access from Milsom Street to the Market Place.

§

Stall Street, facing the Bear Inn, took its name from the church of St Mary de Stalls which once stood on the spot now occupied by the Roundhouse – the only pub left in the street. Stall Street was always very busy, leading as it did to the South Gate. In 1749, John Wood wrote that it contained "82 houses, some of which have the aspect of as much magnificence as one would expect to meet with in a King's Palace" In 1776, the first year for which accurate figures are available, it also had twelve inns or pubs.

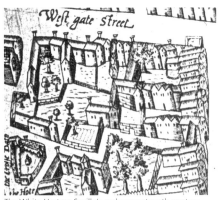

The White Hart on Saville's early-seventeenth-century map, showing White Hart Lane snaking its way through to the Cross Bath on the south of the inn.

Facing the Bear at the top of Stall Street, where the mock Georgian shopping complex now stands, was its great rival, the **White Hart Inn**. It was Bath's most famous inn, immortalised by Jane Austen and Charles Dickens, and ultimately the biggest. However, a much-reproduced picture by an artist called John Maggs has muddied the waters somewhat as far as its appearance is concerned. For much of its history, its Stall Street frontage was a mere 36 feet. To the rear, however, it extended back almost the length of what is now Bath Street, in a jumble of stables, yards, coach houses and offices. Its curtilage also included dilapidated cottages which provided accommodation for the staff, but also had a more dubious function, as we shall see.

The White Hart was Bath's oldest recorded inn, dating back to at least 1503. The earliest White Harts appeared in the reign of Richard II (1377-99). His heraldic device was a white hart; calling an inn the White Hart was tantamount to hanging up a sign saying "By Royal Appointment." Inns continued to be named the White Hart after Richard's death, so we cannot be sure whether Bath's was established in the fourteenth century or not.

The earliest recorded landlords included Thomas Chapman, a clothier, who died in 1524, his grandson John Chapman (twice Mayor of Bath), who died in 1603, and Walter Chapman (three times Mayor of Bath), who died in 1624. Later came Henry Chapman (Mayor of Bath in 1627 and 1637) and Richard Chapman.

The White Hart on Gilmore's map of 1694, showing a short colonnade in front of the Stall Street entrance.

Like Bath's other major inns, the White Hart's primary business from the late seventeenth century onwards was coaching. Few visitors stayed there for more than one or two nights before taking rooms in a lodging house. In Ned Ward's *A Step to the Bath* (1700), he arrives at the White Hart after a three-day trip from London in the company of two women. They were unknown to him when he set off, but, as he records, three days gave him plenty of time to put that right:

Being come to the White Hart, our long-wish'd for port, we refreshed ourselves with much joy, for our tedious, mortifying journey... Then, enquiring for a lodging, we were recommended to a tonser's [barbers], whose wife kept a milliner's shop in the same house, where was good accommodation for us all, tho' he had several other lodgers in the house of good quality. That night my widow and I had an opportunity to enjoy ourselves to our mutual satisfaction, without any suspicion ... In the morning we were saluted by the whole fraternity of cat-gut scrapers, and could not get rid of them without the assistance of an angel [a gold coin]. My mistress and her sister would not appear in public, till all their baggage arriv'd from London, which they did not expect in three or four days time, so I had the liberty to stroll alone.

It may seem strange that, despite the "tedious, mortifying journey" and despite the refreshment offered by the White Hart, Ned Ward and his two companions wasted no time in finding lodgings elsewhere. In contrast to spa towns in the north of England, where visitors stayed at inns for weeks or months at a time, visitors to Bath almost invariably preferred to stay in lodging houses. Some inns, including the White

Hart, had their own lodging houses. The Hart Lodgings, on the east side of Stall Street, next to the King's Bath, appears on Gilmore's Map of 1694 as a tall gabled building with a colonnaded front. In the early eighteenth century, the Masters family ran both the inn and the lodging house. As the century wore on, and the standard of new lodging houses improved, the Hart Lodgings fell out of favour, and in 1757 was described as "formerly the Hart Lodging."

If the Hart Lodgings did not prosper in the new climate, the inn certainly did. In 1722, coaches calling at the inn were causing such congestion that local residents petitioned the Corporation to put up bollards. The Corporation

> agreed that the inhabitants about the Cross Bath [had] liberty to put up posts
> from the White Hart back gate to the house in possession of Mr William Waters
> to prevent coaches standing in the lane leading from Stalls Street to the Cross
> Bath that passengers and chairs may pass without difficulty.

By 1745, a regular coach service was running from the White Hart to the White Lion in Bristol. The fare was five shillings.

In 1747, Thomas Mullins advertised the White Hart Inn & Tavern to let. A wine merchant called Richmond Day took the lease and contracted Joseph Haycock, an innkeeper from Market Harborough in Leicestershire, to run it. Haycock placed a notice in the *Bath Journal* informing the public that "the best wines, rum, brandy, arrack" were available at the White Hart. Mullins added a testimonial:

> As I have declin'd keeping the White Hart Inn & Tap, I recommend Mr J Haycock,
> and hope my friends and acquaintances will frequent it as before.

In 1771, Samuel Woodhouse, the innkeeper of the White Hart, was granted "liberty to make a carriageway into the yard behind the White Hart from Westgate Street." By this time, the lease of the inn had passed to the Bradbourne family, who split it into two business units. The Bradbournes – and later their relatives the Webbs – ran the coaching business, while the inn was sublet.

In 1778, Samuel Woodhouse left to open a new hotel – the Alfred – on Lower Borough Walls, and the White Hart was taken by Charles Taylor from the Rummer in Bristol. The White Hart was closed for several weeks while "great improvements" were made. These included "a new kitchen, quite detached from the house" – possibly in the carriageway leading from Westgate Street. Two years later the White Hart was again advertised to let. The new tenant was the most celebrated of Bath's landlords, Eleazar Pickwick, who had previously kept the Angel in Westgate Street and the Packhorse in Northgate Street.

As one of Bath's top inns, it was a natural choice for masonic meetings. On 19 August 1784, the first Provincial Grand Lodge in Somerset was held at the White Hart. The *Bristol Journal* reported that the attendance was "very numerous and respectable and the entertainment plentiful and elegant … The day was spent with that social harmony which has ever characterised the brotherhood and was indeed 'the feast of reason and the flow of soul.'" The White Hart was also the meeting-place of the Bath Harmonic Society, a glee-club in which gentlemen met to sing songs often specially written for the occasion, with a drink between each song.

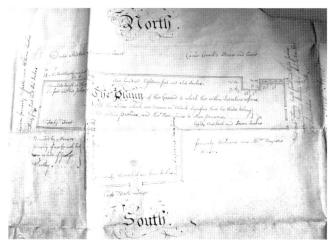

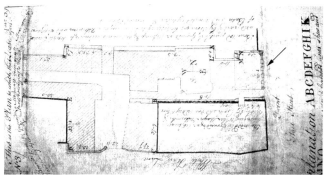

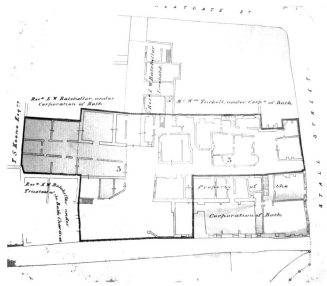

The White Hart in 1748, 1772 and 1863. The arrow on the 1772 plan indicates what appears to be the colonnade shown on Gilmore's map

THE REVEREND WOODFORDE COMES TO BATH

Friday 28 June 1793

We got up about four o'clock this morning and at five got into the Bath coach from the Angel and set off for Bath. The coach carried only four inside passengers. We had a fat woman with a dog and many band boxes, which much incommoded us, and also a poor sickly good kind of man that went with us. We breakfasted at Maidenhead on coffee and tea. For strawberries at Maidenhead paid one shilling. For our breakfast paid two shillings. We were very near meeting with an accident in Reading, passing a wagon, but thank God we got by safe and well. It was owing to the coachman. As we went out of Reading we met a regiment of soldiers, some militia going into Reading. At Reading there were two young gentlemen by name Joliffe that got up on top of the coach, being going home from school for the vacation. I remembered their father at Winchester School. We dined at the Pelican Inn, Speenhamland. The young gentlemen dined with us. Their father lives about ten miles beyond Bath. For our dinners, coachmen, etc., paid about fourteen shillings. Paid at Speenhamland for extra luggage about four shillings.

About ten o'clock this evening, thank God, we got safe and well to Bath, to the White Hart Inn, where we supped and slept – a very noble inn. As soon as the young Joliffes got to Bath, they hired a chaise immediately and set off for home. The fat lady that came with us, supped with us.

Saturday 29 June 1793

We breakfasted at the Hart and after breakfast paid for the inn for our suppers last night, etc., nine shillings and sixpence; to servants at the inn, barber included, five shillings ...

Although this sounds a splendid idea, what the singing would have sounded like by the end of the evening is best left to the imagination.

In 1791, the Corporation carried out road improvements, for the purposes of which "a piece of ground at the upper part of Stall Street, measuring 569 superficial feet, was bought by the Corporation from Messrs Webb and Pickwick at the rate of £3.5.11½d per foot; and besides this a sum of £2,000 was paid to Mr Pickwick for new-fronting his house, the White Hart, and the inconvenience he suffered in his business."

The White Hart, which had remained unchanged for centuries, was now made to fit into a planned streetscape, which included the newly-built Bath Street. The whole area was redeveloped, but, as far as the White Hart was concerned, the changes were only superficial. Behind the new façade lurked the old inn.

Unchanged too was the maze of stables and old buildings along White Hart Lane. The lane remained as well, its entrance hidden behind a door. This area, approached through the White Hart yard, was a well-known pick-up place for prostitutes. Jane Austen seems to have alluded to this in *Persuasion*. Mary Musgrove, who is staying at the inn, looks out of the window and sees Mrs Clay and William Elliott having an assignation. William Elliott is trying to persuade Mrs Clay to abandon her designs on Sir Walter Elliott and elope with him, which she later does. Those among Jane Austen's readers who knew Bath and were aware of the White Hart's reputation would almost certainly have seen the parallel between the assignation in the book and the assignations that took place in the stable yard. To underline the link with the women who plied their trade at the White Hart, Jane Austen tells us that Mrs Clay uses Gowland's Lotion to clear away freckles. At the time, freckles were seen as a sign of sexual disease; Gowland's Lotion, which contained mercury, was used, among other things, for treating syphilis.

Despite the dubious reputation of the White Hart's postern regions, the Rev James Woodforde stayed at the inn on several occasions in the 1790s and regarded it as "a very noble inn"; in 1794, a lady visitor found it "an excellent inn, the business very great but everything managed with regularity and comfort."

In April 1795, tragedy struck the Pickwick family:

Thursday died in his nineteenth year after a lingering illness, Mr William Pickwick, son of Mr Pickwick of the White Hart Inn. He had been entered at Oxford but a short period when the rupture of a blood vessel impaired a constitution naturally good, and which has deprived society of a valuable young man, and his distressed parents of an only child.

So it was that Moses Pickwick, Eleazar's nephew, was appointed his heir, and carried on the business Eleazar had so successfully established. Moses seems to have been as astute a businessman as his uncle, yet it was common knowledge that "the books of the hotel were never properly balanced. In fact, errors in adding were the rule rather than the exception … The accounts were never audited and no indication is given as to the exact income."

Despite this slapdash accounting, in the first 20 years of the nineteenth century, the White Hart went from strength to strength, no doubt helped by the demolition of its great rival, the Bear, in 1806. In 1803, the White Hart took over the stables, coach houses and yard of the old Bell Inn in Bell Tree Lane, which had previously been leased to the Three Tuns. In 1806, an adjoining house known as the Lanthorn House, dating back to at least 1292, was incorporated into the White Hart. It was described as ruinous, and was promptly pulled down and replaced by stables. The following year, the Corporation appointed a committee "to inquire into the value of the ground late Scrope's by the Cross Bath, which is desired … for improving the White Hart Inn."

In January 1810, an American called Louis Simond paid a flying visit to Bath and recorded his impressions of the White Hart:

We arrived at Bath last night. The chaise drew up in style at the White Hart. Two well-dressed footmen were ready to help us to alight, presenting an arm on each side. Then a loud bell on the stairs, and lights carried before us to an elegantly furnished sitting-room, where the fire was already blazing. In a few minutes, a neat-looking chambermaid, with an ample white apron, pinned behind, came to offer her services to the ladies, and shew the bedrooms. In less than half an hour, five powdered *gentlemen* burst into the room with three dishes, etc. and two remained to wait. I give this as a sample of the best, or rather of the finest inns. Our bill was two pounds eleven shillings sterling, dinner for three, tea, beds, and breakfast. The servants have no wages – but, depending on the generosity of travellers, they find it in their interest to please them. They (the servants) cost us about five shillings a day.

Not only was the White Hart one of the top coaching inns in the West Country; Moses Pickwick became the most famous innkeeper of all time when he was immortalised by Charles Dickens in *The Pickwick Papers*. Here is the famous scene where the fictional Mr Pickwick, about to board the coach from London to Bath, first becomes aware of his real-life counterpart:

Mr Tupman and Mr Snodgrass had seated themselves at the back part of the coach; Mr Winkle had got inside; and Mr Pickwick was preparing to follow him, when Sam Weller came up to his master, and whispering in his ear, begged to speak to him, and with an air of the deepest mystery.

"Well, Sam," said Mr Pickwick, "what's the matter now?"

"Here's rather a rum go, sir," replied Sam.

"What?" inquired Mr Pickwick.

"This here, sir," rejoined Sam. "I'm wery much afeerd, sir, that the proprieator of this here coach is a playin' some imperance with us."

"How is that, Sam?" said Mr Pickwick; "aren't the names down on the way-bill?"

"The names is not only down on the vay-bill, sir," replied Sam, " but they've painted vun on 'em up, on the door o' the coach." As Sam spoke, he pointed to that part of the coach door on which the proprietor's name usually appears; and there, sure enough, in gilt letters of a goodly size, was the magic name of Pickwick."

"Dear me," exclaimed Mr Pickwick, quite staggered by the coincidence; "what a very extraordinary thing!"

"Yes, but that ain't all," said Sam, again directing his master's attention to the coach door; "not content vith writing up Pickwick, they puts 'Moses' afore it, vich I call addin' insult to injury, as the parrot said ven they not only took him from his native land, but made him talk the English langwidge arterwards."

The Pickwick Papers was an instant success. No sooner had the last instalment appeared than an adaptation, Sam Weller and the Pickwickians, was staged at the Theatre Royal. Moses must have been the toast of the town. Dickens' observation that the White Hart's "waiters, from their costume, might be mistaken for Westminster boys, only they destroy the illusion by behaving themselves much better," would have done the inn's business no harm either.

Despite the White Hart's continuing success, there were problems. In the early nineteenth century, Eleazar Pickwick sublet the White Hart to Richard Woodhouse, leaving himself free to concentrate on the lucrative coaching business. The company's office, known as the Universal Coaching Office, was in the inn. It faced onto Stall Street; the coffee room was to the south, the main entrance to the north; the staircase behind it led to the rooms from which Mary Musgrove saw Mrs Clay.

In 1817, Richard Woodhouse entered into partnership with Messrs Bishop and Cooper. When Woodhouse left the partnership in 1826, and a new lease needed to be drawn up, the Corporation announced that they did not own the freehold. This caused considerable consternation. The immediate reaction was recorded in the Council Minutes:

No lease of the premises of the White Hart, etc., on the west side of Stall Street, to be granted until the expiration of the existing one, the greater part of the property belonging to the Black Arms and Free Grammar School Charities, as lately ascertained by the commissioners.

While this legal tangle dragged on, Eleazar Pickwick decided to retire from the coaching business, leaving his nephew Moses in charge. He chose a good time to leave; rocky times were ahead for the White Hart Inn.

In 1831, the company became embroiled in another legal battle with the Corporation, as a result of an attack on the inn during the Reform Act riots.

Until October 1831, there had been no unrest in Bath. But then the disaffected and unenfranchised of Bristol rose, burning great swathes of the city and getting hopelessly drunk on wine looted from dockside warehouses. Neighbouring cities were called upon to send troops to re-establish order. In charge of the Bath Yeomanry was Captain Wilkins – a shrewd choice, for as a friend of reform, he was well placed to defuse volatile situations. But the mob that assembled outside his lodgings in the White Hart was in no mood to listen to anyone.

The Bath Reform Riot of 1831 was one of the earliest in which the red flag was raised as a symbol of rebellion. It had been flown at the Spithead Mutiny in 1797, but its first recorded use on land was in Wales in June 1831. The rioters were defeated, not by force of arms, but by red hot pokers, suggested by one of the volunteers who happened to be a chef at the inn.* The White Hart was seriously damaged, however, and, after the rioters were dispersed, they moved on to sack two other inns run by Bishop and Cooper, including the Red Lion at Odd Down.

The claim for compensation against the Corporation foundered on a technicality. The summons was taken out against the inhabitants of the City of Bath, when it should have been taken out against Bath Forum, the group of parishes which constituted the city. Heated correspondence was exchanged between the innkeepers' lawyer and the city solicitor, during which the latter said he had no idea, until he took legal advice, that this invalidated the claim. Records show, however, that this was a lie: he had raised the same point himself, before seeking advice.

The entrance to the White Hart yard in Westgate Street.

Bishop and Cooper's next move, in 1833, was to petition the Corporation for a reduction in rent; the Corporation responded by pursuing a "claim for dilapidations of the White Hart" caused by the rioters two years earlier. Bishop decided enough was enough, and sold his share of the business to Cooper for £30,000 – well over £1M in today's terms.

A year later, the city architect, George Manners, reported that repairs were "absolutely necessary … for the safe occupation of the building." When these were carried out, Thomas Cooper took the opportunity to remodel the ground floor, creating two new servants' rooms and converting the waiters' room into a bedroom. Two years later, the gateway from the White Hart yard into Westgate

* An account of the riot can be found in *Awash with Ale*, p84.

A vision of grandeur: Charles Maggs' famous painting of the White Hart ...

... and the reality: a photograph of the White Hart taken shortly before demolition in 1867.

THE LOST PUBS OF BATH

Street was widened, and Cooper took over the stables formerly in the hands of the Webb family. During all this time, the issue of the lease remained unresolved.

It was about this time that John Maggs produced his famous painting of the White Hart. Some details – the coaching company office and the figure of the white hart above the entrance, for example – were accurate. However, he extended the building on the northern side by over ten feet, and made the coaches and people in the foreground less than life-size, thus making the inn appear far larger than it actually was. Fortunately, a photograph, taken just before the inn was demolished, survives to give an accurate impression of its size.

Despite all the problems of the early 1830s, the White Hart's future looked bright. Control of the inn and the coaching business was back in the hands of one man, and improvements were underway to provide increased accommodation. The Corporation finally drew up a lease, despite admitting that it did not own the freehold. There was one problem the White Hart could not possibly hope to overcome, however. Its success, like that of other inns, depended on the coaching trade. If that went, everything went. The twentieth century saw several instances of one mode of transport superseding another – cars and lorries taking traffic from the railways, planes taking over from liners. But those changes took place over decades. When the railway took over from stagecoaches, it happened overnight. There was no time for those dependent on the coaching trade to adjust or make contingency plans. Bath's coaching industry remained busy right up to the night before the railway arrived. There was no scaling down, just a sudden collapse.

In 1846, five years after the railway opened from London to Bath, Thomas Cooper Jr., who had succeeded his father, wrote to the Corporation asking for an abatement of rent due to loss of trade caused by the opening of the railway. We do not know whether his appeal was successful, but he eventually passed the lease on to a Mr Sabin from Coventry. He was the last landlord of the White Hart. When he left in 1861, the shutters went up, and the inn which had been at the centre of Bath life for centuries fell silent, its corridors deserted, its gilded chambers unheated and unlit. For six years it stood, its stonework crumbling, the paint flaking from its window frames, a gaunt reminder of a vanished age, mocking those who were trying to pull Bath into the nineteenth century.

In June 1869, the *Bath Chronicle* reported that

> the desolate and tenantless condition of the old White Hart, having long been an eyesore and the subject of complaint, the attention of the Town Council was called to the building. Advertisements for tenders were issued in, we believe, the early part of 1862, but only one offer to take the building was received, viz from Mr Henry Eve, who proposed to rent the building ... to spend £500 on it and to utilise it for chambers and for professional men, sale and store rooms. The Council rejected this offer, and when the subject came before them, several members suggested that the site was an admirable one for a first class hotel.

The White Hart was demolished in 1867. On 26 October 1867, James Irvine, who was involved in the subsequent excavation of the site, wrote to the Rev HM

Scarth, of the Bath Royal Literary & Scientific Institute, informing him that the remains of a Roman temple had been discovered a foot below the cellars of the inn.* The following extract from the *Bath Chronicle* gives further details of the discovery:

At a meeting last week of the Bath Natural History and Antiquarian Field Club some interesting particulars were brought forward by the Rev Earle and others with reference to excavations now being made on the site of the old White Hart Hotel. These excavations which have been carried down to a great depth, have passed through 18 inches of red clay, largely impregnated with iron, which is supposed to be the sediment of the Bath waters. Immediately above this deposit several traces of the Roman period in Bath have been found. The most important is the discovery of a large building, and the continuation of the friezes of the great Roman temple dedicated to Minerva, a portion of which is preserved in the museum of the Bath Literary and Scientific Institution. In Collinson's

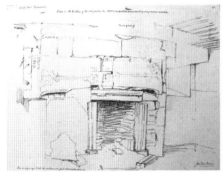

Two of Irvine's drawings of the White Hart during demolition showing ancient stone coffin lids used as lintels above a fireplace in the White Hart Tap, and a window found in the foundations.

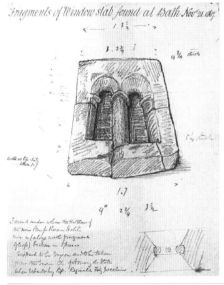

Antiquities of Somerset, 1791, it is stated that the "site of this stupendous edifice had been plainly indicated by the late discoveries made in laying the foundations of the new buildings at the top of Stall Street, near the White Hart Hotel. The temple stood on the east side of the great Fosse Road, running through the city from north to south, and nearly midway between the Porta Decuma or north gate and the Porta Flumenana or south gate, leading to the river. Its front was towards the west, and consisted of a portico supported by very large fluted columns of the Corinthian order, crowned with rich sculptured capitals. The architraves were charged with inscriptions to the Deae Campestres, and to the other local deities, and the frieze was enriched with gigantic images, figures of animals and groups of foliage. The internal recesses contained the votive altars, inscribed with the names of

* This forms part of a much larger correspondence concerning the discoveries in the BRLSI Archive.

THE LOST PUBS OF BATH

relations either oppressed with lingering disease, or engaged in military perils." Behind the temple, towards the east, stood the splendid Roman Baths, the foundations of which were discovered in 1755, at the depth of 20 feet beneath the surface of the ground. The recent excavations have laid bare a kind of concrete pavement, leading to the inference that there had been a large area of parade ground adjoining the temple. Other discoveries show that the Roman Forum extended considerably beyond the east end of the present Abbey Church Yard. Various relics of the Roman period have been found, the most notable being richly sculptured stones, and a coin of Marcus Agrippa, bearing a date of 30 years before the Christian era; hitherto the earliest known coin found in or near Bath had been of the time of Augustus. A terracotta head, with a strong Egyptian expression has also been discovered. We may add that the present discoveries of Roman remains confirm the theory already advanced that all the walls built by that people in Bath ran like those in Roman Silchester, north and south, and east and west. Careful drawings of all the antiquities found have been made by Mr Irvine, who is engaged under Mr Scott in superintending the restoration of the Abbey.

The only relic of the old inn to survive was the figure of the white hart over the entrance, which was moved to the White Hart in Widcombe. In 1999, it was stolen, and, although its body was later found in a ditch, its head was never recovered. A replacement head was made and stuck onto the body, along with a set of antlers from a venison farm. The new white hart was ceremoniously unveiled at the White Hart in Widcombe by Lady Margaret Oswick in March 2003.

The **Grand Pump Room Hotel**, built on the site of the old White Hart in French Chateau Style, opened in 1869. It had a public bar, known as the Grand Pump Room Hotel Vaults, in Stall Street. The hotel was a temple to conspicuous consumption, to a style of living that died, like so much else, in the First World War. Although it stayed open after the war, it grew increasingly shabby, increasingly difficult to maintain, and increasingly out of touch with the demands of the new age. In the 1930s, there were plans to revamp it in art-deco style, but then came another war and its requisition by the government. After the war, it enjoyed a brief spell in the unlikely stewardship of British Railways, before demolition in the late 1950s.

The old White Hart was unique among Bath's inns for having two taps – one for domestic servants and one for those whose business lay in the stables and coach houses. To the south was the **Jolly Footman**, which catered for indoor servants. It first appears in an advertisement from 1748:

> To be lett, a house in Stall Street, next door to the White Hart, known by the sign
> of the Jolly Footman, with cellars and brewhouses convenient.

It was still there in 1776 but was absorbed into the White Hart soon afterwards as a coffee room.

The entrance to the Grand Pump Room Hotel.

The corner of Stall and Westgate Streets. Apart from the roof, the building is very similar to the former Lloyd's Bank (now the Litten Tree pub) at the top of Milsom Street.

The servants at the Grand Pump Room Hotel were no less superior than those encountered by Charles Dickens at the White Hart Inn.

THE LOST PUBS OF BATH

To the north of the White Hart, on the corner of Stall Street and Westgate Street, was the **Saddler's Arms**. As its name suggests, it catered for liverymen, grooms, and ostlers. The first record of the Saddler's Arms comes in 1737, when George Rogers leased it from the Corporation. An advertisement in the *Bath Journal* in 1748 informed readers that

> Flying Stage Coaches ... will begin to set out from Bath to London on Monday the fourth of April and will carry passengers at 25/- each ... Places taken at the Saddler's Arms, Bath.

In 1792 an advertisement appeared in the *Bath Chronicle*:

> George Bishop (late waiter at the White Hart Inn) begs leave to inform his friends and the publick that he has taken and entered upon ... the Saddler's Arms at the

Six views of the Grand Pump Room Hotel shortly before demolition: the Lounge and main staircase; the Smoke Room; the Inner Lounge; the Billiard Room; the Dining Room looking towards Cheap Street; and the Dining Room looking towards Westgate Street.

On **TUESDAY**, the 23rd of **October**, at One for Two o'Clock precisely,
THE FOLLOWING

VALUABLE PROPERTY:

LOT 1.—The Desirable and most Centrically-situated PREMISES, known as

THE SADDLERS' ARMS

STALL STREET,

*Close to the "White Hart" Hotel, and in the very centre of the City, in which a most lucrative trade has been carried on
for many years; now let to Mr. JOHN HAYMAN, at the low Rent of £45 per Annum.
There is a convenient Bar and large Bar-Parlour, a Tap-Room at the back, 2 large Drawing-Rooms, and 8 good Bedchambers, with Kitchen and Scullery, and a great extent of Cellarage running under this and the adjoining House, affording
ample room for a small Brewery to be erected, and offering a tempting opportunity to a Purchaser of converting these Premises into a **HOME-BREWED HOUSE**, the undeniable situation being a sufficient guarantee of a most profitable return.
The Property is held under the Corporation of Bath for Three Lives, (which are renewable,) aged respectively about 59, 56, and 53 Years, subject to
an Annual Quit Rent of £1 16s. per Annum.*

The lease of the Sadler's Arms offered at auction in 1848.

top of Stall Street, where he has laid in an excellent stock of beer and porter, with genuine good spirits.

In 1848, when the Saddler's Arms was put up for auction, it was described as:

close to the White Hart Hotel and in the very centre of the city, in which a most lucrative trade has been carried on for many years; now let to Mr John Hayman, at the low rent of £45 per annum. There is a convenient bar and large bar parlour, a tap room at the back, two large drawing rooms and eight good bedchambers, with kitchen and scullery, and a great extent of cellarage running under this and the adjoining house, affording ample room for a small brewery to be erected, and offering a tempting opportunity to a purchaser of converting these premises into a home-brewed house, the undeniable situation being a sufficient guarantee of a most profitable return.

The lease was acquired by Williams' Brewery on the Quay, who re-engaged Hayman. While other inns, including the White Hart, were struggling, he continued to improve the Saddler's Arms, expanding it into two rundown properties at the back, which he knocked into one. His writing-paper, with a splendid coat of arms, was designed to show what a superior establishment the Saddler's Arms was. It survived the closure of the White Hart, with Hayman at the helm, until compulsory purchase and demolition in 1867. It ended up under the coffee room of the new Grand Pump Room Hotel.

There was – briefly – another tap at the White Hart. The **White Hart Tap** was in the passageway leading from Westgate Street to the stable yard.* Here among assorted stables, bakehouses, and ruinous buildings was a little lane called York Buildings. In the early nineteenth century, the old buildings were demolished and a cottage, stable

*There is still a modern archway leading to a service yard on this site.

THE LOST PUBS OF BATH

and coach-house built in their place. By 1858, Henry Ryman had opened this range of buildings as the White Hart Tap. A couple of years later, it was taken over by William Feaver, a servant from 2 Camden Cottages. It is unclear why it opened. Perhaps some of the horsy fraternity were no longer welcome at the Saddlers Arms as it went upmarket; perhaps it was just more convenient. We may never know. It survived until demolition in 1867.

There was also an alehouse called the **Queen Charlotte** on White Hart Lane, which closed around 1786.

A century earlier, there was an inn called the **Cross Daggers** on the north side of "the street leading to the Cross Bath."* In 1678, Mary Berriman and Mary Stevens, her daughter, leased it from the Corporation. In 1690, Robert Chivers took over the lease, which passed to Thomas and Mary Jefferis six years later. It was last recorded in 1698.

Only a couple of small shops divided the White Hart from the **Crossbow**, which stood roughly where Bath Street is today. In 1605, it was described as "a common inn on the west side of Stall Street," in the possession of Barnabie Harrold. It was still known as the Crossbow when Hamon Lewkenor took the lease in 1682. By 1688, when John Pocock took over, however, it had been renamed the New Inn. By 1703, the lease was held by George Trim, who later built Trim Street. We last hear of it in 1715, when the lease was taken by William Collibee, an apothecary.

Just south of the Crossbow, where the south side of Bath Street stands today, was the **Nag's Head**. It was first recorded in 1711, but by then it had already closed. In a lease dated 2 October 1711, it was described as "a messuage and garden formerly called the Nag's Head in Stauls Street."
　　In 1791, Bath Street was built to the north of the old Nag's Head, replacing a narrow alley called Union Passage (not to be confused with the present Union Passage). In 1813, Thomas Parfet refronted and set back the building, which was described as "fronting east to Stall Street, with a garden and some buildings adjoining with vaults under part of the north-east part of Bath Street." As late as 1835, over a century after it closed, it was still known as the "former Nag's Head."

At 4 Bath Street, on the corner of Bilbury Lane, now occupied by the Portman Building Society, was a beerhouse called the **Eagle**. This doubled as the showroom of the noted sculptor, Stefano Pieroni, who built the fountain that once stood at the end of Bath Street, but has now been moved to Bog Island. Mr Pieroni opened his showroom around 1852 and starting selling beer around a decade later. Its name

*It has been suggested that the Cross Daggers was in Bell Tree Lane (now Beau Street), but the description of it as being in the street leading to the Cross Bath indicates it was in White Hart Lane.

Bath Street only ever had one pub – the Eagle. When it was turned into a film set in the 1950s, they added a few more, including the Duke of Normandy, the Golden Fleece and the Cross Keys.

was probably a reference to St John, to whom the nearby hospital was dedicated, and whose emblem was an eagle. By 1876, Mr Pieroni and his sculptures had gone and George Ley had taken over the beerhouse. In 1882, when Walter William took over, the Eagle had a bar (with a circular gas stove, oak casks, spirit tap and five-motion beer engine), a coffee room, a bar parlour and a billiard room.

A year later, the Eagle closed and its contents were sold to a consortium which included JB Bowler. It became a Forester's Hall and from the 1890s also housed a Friendly Society Medical Institute. It later became a homeopathic dispensary and an Exclusive Brethren Society Meeting House.

York Street, the entrance to which faces the old Nag's Head, dates from around

The former Union Tavern in York Street.

1796, and was named in honour of the Duchess of York, the first person to drive along it in a carriage. At 10 York Street (on the west corner of Swallow Street) was the **Union Tavern** beerhouse, opened around 1840 and closed about 20 years later. It later became the office of Stuckey's Livery Stables.

A mystery pub from the 1770s, before York Street was built, was the **Bath Side House**. It was renamed the Blue Tub in 1777, and closed shortly afterwards. Its address was "Near the King's Bath." The lack of any reference to it in contemporary accounts suggests that it was not patronised by the type of visitors who wrote accounts.

THE LOST PUBS OF BATH

On the east side of Stall Street, facing down Beau Street, (where Whittard's and Thornton's are today) was the **Three Tuns**, a seventeenth-century inn whose history is recounted in *Bath Pubs*, on account of its lodging house in Abbey Green having survived as the Crystal Palace.

At 32 Stall Street was the **Bell**, which started off on the north side of Beau Street (then known as Bell Tree Lane), before expanding into an adjoining property on Stall Street. In the late eighteenth century, the original property in Bell Tree Lane was given up, leaving just the Stall Street property. This closed in 1850, when the landlord moved to the Crispin Tavern on Lower Borough Walls, which he renamed the Bell.

Bell Tree Lane took its name from the tree from which a mote bell was rung in Saxon times to summon people to motes or meetings. Bell Tree House, on the south side of the lane, was, until the Reformation, the Parsonage House for St James's Church, which belonged to the Abbey. After St James's came under the control of the Corporation, the Parsonage House was deemed surplus to requirements and leased to a Mr Hussey of Marnhull in Dorset, who turned it into a meeting place for the city's Catholics. In the run-up to the foiled terrorist attack on Parliament in 1605, several of the Gunpowder Plot conspirators met at Bell Tree House to draw up their plans to return England to the true faith.

Bell Tree House survived as a centre for Catholic recusants until the late eighteenth century, when, in a climate of increasing tolerance, a new chapel was built near St James's Parade. It is ironic that, while the old Catholic meeting

At one time, Stall Street was lined with a succession of coaching inns. Today, when the shops close, it is generally deserted.

house managed to survive for almost 250 years in the face of official hostility and persecution, the paint was hardly dry on the new one before it was burnt down by the Gordon Rioters.* Bell Tree House was eventually pulled down in 1824 to widen Beau Street.

On the north side of Bell Tree Lane was another building which once belonged to the Abbey. Its post-Reformation history may come as a surprise to anyone familiar with the fate of Richard Whiting, the last Abbot of Glastonbury. Whiting was one of the last religious leaders to stand out against Henry VIII's policy of suppression and sequestration, and paid for it with his life. On 15 November 1539, after a show trial, he was dragged – although "a very weak man and sickly" – through the streets of Glastonbury and up the slopes of the Tor on a hurdle. There, along with two monks who had stood by him, he was hanged till he was near death. He was then cut down, disembowelled, beheaded, and hacked into quarters. His head was stuck on a spike above the Abbey gateway, and his body's quarters, boiled in pitch, displayed at Wells, Ilchester, Bridgwater and Bath.

The part of Abbot Whiting's body displayed at Bath would have been seen by William Gibbs, the last Prior of Bath Abbey, who no doubt shuddered at the thought of what might have happened to him if he had stuck more firmly to his principles. He had resisted, it is true, the commissioners on their early visits. As custodian of the most modern abbey in the country, a showpiece of architectural design and decorative art, he hardly relished the prospect of being booted out and seeing it ransacked. But when he found out that Dr Layton, who had visited the Abbey to report on the state of play, reported that the monks were "worse than any I have fouwnde yet, both in bugerie and adulterie," he must have realised it was a foregone conclusion. The end came on 27 January 1539, when he signed the deed of surrender. Even at this stage, the Abbey might have been saved, for Henry VIII offered it to the Corporation for £330 (between £100,000 and £150,000 in modern terms). They turned the offer down and soon the lead had been stripped from the roof "for the King's profit," and the stained glass windows and ironwork sold for £30.

The Prior – now plain William Gibbs – was not thrown onto the street. Henry rewarded co-operation as lavishly as he punished opposition. He was granted a pension of £80 a year and the use of the former abbey building on the north side of Bell Tree Lane, "with rights to profit from the hot baths." He embraced this new challenge enthusiastically, installing a network of pipes in the building, through which he diverted water from the hot springs, making it almost certainly the first centrally-heated house in Bath since Roman times. His interests did not stop at civil engineering, however. He was also an alchemist.

Elias Ashmole, whose collection formed the nucleus of the Ashmolean Museum in Oxford, has bequeathed us the following story:

> Shortly after the Dissolucon of Bath Abbey, upon the pulling down of some of the Walls, there was a Glasse fond in a Wall full of Red Tincture, which being flung away to a dunghill, forthwith it coloured it, exceeding red. This dunghill

*See *Awash With Ale*, pp 69-80.

(or Rubish) was after fetched away by Boate by Bathwicke men, and layd in Bathwicke field, and in the places where it was spread, for a long tyme after, the Corne grew wonderfully ranke, thick and high: insomuch as it was there look'd upon as a wonder.

Ashmole, however, was not told the story until 1651 – over a century after the event – and contemporary reports suggest that the tincture was discovered, not shortly after the dissolution of the Abbey but years later. Ashmole was, however, another alchemist, and, even if he got the timing wrong, he would have understood the nature of the tincture. It was, in fact, the Philosopher's Stone, capable of working miracles, such as producing superabundant corn. Whether this was due to radioactive properties, as some have suggested, is unknown. A century before Ashmole penned his account, however, another alchemist called Thomas Charnock recorded not only that Gibbs had left the tincture in the wall, but that, when he discovered his loss, "he did go blind and mad in his selfe, and for the rest of his days did wander divers ways about the country, led by a boy."

After Gibbs' death, in 1552, the house "late in the tenure of the late Prior" (the freehold of which had been granted to King Edward's School) was leased, along with the hot baths, to Humphrey Cotton. At what date the building became the Bell Inn is not known. The first definite reference to it as an inn comes in a deed of 1631, which describes it as "a tenement called the Bell and a garden thereunto belonging … between a tenement of William Bennett being hospital land on the eastside, a garden of Thomas Ireland on the west, a garden of Anthony Harding on the north, and [the] street south." By 1659, its lease was held by a Walter Gibbs. It remained in the Gibbs family until at least 1754, when Alderman Thomas Gibbs held the lease. It may be coincidence – Gibbs was not an uncommon name in Bath – but it is just possible that Prior Gibbs' descendants were still running the inn over 200 years after the dissolution of the Abbey.

It is possible that the ex-Prior himself opened the house as an inn. He was granted "rights to profit from the hot baths," and as the building was right next to them, an obvious way to make money was by accommodating visitors. In this he may even have perpetuated a tradition of hospitality established by the Abbey, as, for example, at the George & Pilgrims Inn in Glastonbury. In this scenario, the Bell would have been of monastic foundation, dating from the fifteenth century or even earlier. But, in the absence of any supporting evidence, this too must remain conjecture.

When Rosewell Gibbs took the lease of the Bell in 1718, part of it consisted of "certain rooms heretofore used for malting now converted to stables" – a clear indication of the growing importance of the coaching trade to the city's economy. At some stage, the inn was expanded to take over the adjoining property in Stall Street.

In 1792, Williams' Brewery took over the Bell, and, sometime in the late eighteenth or early nineteenth century, the original property in Bell Tree Lane was given up. This may have been as late as the 1820s, when the Corporation, which had taken over administration of most of the property granted to King Edward's

St Katherine's Hospital, built on the site of the original Bell Inn.

School, did a deal with the Trustees of St John's Hospital, exchanging the land on which the old Bell had stood for land elsewhere. Around 1830, after they had acquired the land, the Trustees of St John demolished the old Bell and built St Katherine's Hospital on the site.

The Stall Street property was two doors up from the corner of Bell Tree Lane and backed onto the inn yard. As it was much smaller than the part of the inn that had been given up – little more than an alehouse, in fact – it did not need such a large yard. While redevelopment of the old site was still under discussion, the yard was leased (much as an overflow car park would be today) to the Three Tuns, and, when that closed, to the White Hart.

In 1801, the frontage of the Stall Street property was set back about six feet to widen the road. An auction notice from 1849, just before the Bell made its final move, described it as having "a bar, tap-room, large bar-parlour, and another room designated 'The Soldiers' Room,' this house always being the headquarters of the different recruiting parties; two large dining rooms, and six good bedchambers, with kitchen and washhouse, yard and ample cellarage."

In 1850, the Bell closed and its last landlord, David Garrett, moved to the Crispin on Lower Borough Walls, which he renamed the Bell. The final chapter in the history of the Bell must wait, therefore, until we get to Lower Borough Walls.

LOT 2.—The Well-accustomed HOUSE, called the
BELL INN, STALL STREET,

In which a thriving trade has been successfully carried on by the present Tenant, Mr. DAVID GARRETT, who has been in possession as Yearly Tenant, at the low Rent of £29 per Annum, for nearly 20 years.

The Premises are in very excellent repair, and consist of a Bar, Tap-Room, large Bar-Parlour, and another Room, designated "The Soldier's Room," this House always being the head-quarters of the different Recruiting Parties; two large Dining-Rooms, and 6 good Bedchambers, with Kitchen and Washhouse, Yard, and ample Cellarage.

It is held under the Corporation of Bath for Three Lives, (which are renewable,) aged respectively 66, 61, and 23 Years, at an Annual Quit Rent of £1 4s.

Despite the thriving trade promised in this sale notice of 1849, the Bell Inn on Stall Street closed the following year.

The **Horse & Jockey**, on the north side of Beau Street, one door down from the corner of Stall Street, was quite a survivor. Judging from its name and location, it may have started life as the tap for the Bell, or for the Three Tuns on the other side of Stall Street. It opened, as the Horse & Groom, sometime before 1776. In August 1784, Charles Griffin renamed it the New Mail Coach to celebrate the introduction of mailcoach services, which called at the Three Tuns. After a while, the New was dropped from its name and it was known simply as the Mail Coach.

One night in 1822, a serious fight, involving at least seven men, spilled out of the pub into the street. After the landlord, who also happened to be a constable, came out with a staff to break it up, they adjourned to a piece of waste ground on the

THE LOST PUBS OF BATH

Beau Street today, looking towards the old Three Tuns on the far side of Stall Street with the old Horse & Jockey on the left.

A vertiginous view of the Horse & Jockey in the 1960s.

Lower Bristol Road called Collier's Field and continued fighting. Subsequently, one of the combatants died and another was charged with manslaughter.

After the novelty of the mailcoach had worn off, the pub was renamed the Horse & Jockey. It survived the revamping of Bell Tree Lane, and by 1851 was one of seven pubs in Bath which the police wanted shut because "keepers of these houses, after repeated cautions, had some of them kept open their houses on Sunday mornings, and others allowed prostitutes and other bad characters to resort to them." It managed to survive, finally closing in the 1970s.

There was at least one other alehouse in Bell Tree Lane. The **Coach & Horses** was first recorded in 1773 when John Dover moved from there to the Lamb in Stall Street. By 1776 Ann Witney was the licensee. Joseph Wilmot took the licence the following year, but by 1778 he was recorded as the landlord of the New Coach & Horses, with Robert Spencer holding the licence of the Old Coach & Horses. By 1786 both the old and new Coach & Horses had closed. There is no indication where either of them were.

Just south of the Hot Bath, there was once an inn called the **George**, built in the late sixteenth or early seventeenth century on land owned by St John's Hospital. When leased to Edith Smith in 1633, it was described as "lying within the tything of Bimbery between a tenement of Tobias Fenne, Doctor of Physick, south-east, the Hot and Lazers' Bath north, the way leading by the Burrow Walls west." In 1665, it was leased by Tobias Rustatt. The lease later passed to Councillor Samuel Wintle, who also held the lease of 14 acres of land in Widcombe, where he kept geese, horses and cattle. In 1717, when William Skinner took over, the George was described as having "a room for entertaining poor people that use the Lepers' Bath" on the north.

In 1777, the George featured in a particularly nasty murder case. Elizabeth Gingell, servant to the master of the George, Daniel Charmbury, was standing at the door of the George around eight o'clock one June evening, when a friend of hers called Ann Emery came by. She asked her to go to the Three Tuns yard with her to look for her brother.* There they met Robert Briggs, an under-ostler, who picked Elizabeth Gingell up in his arms and carried her into one of the stables "where they continued together about two minutes." They then came out and the two women walked to the Cross Bath, where they parted, Elizabeth telling Ann that "she believed she would never go back to her master's house."

The following day, two men were walking by the river when a lad came up to them shouting that he had seen a body in the river. They managed to drag it ashore and found it was a young woman who had been strangled with a linen handkerchief, still tied around her throat, and thrown into the river. She was later identified as Elizabeth Gingell. At the inquest, the coroner drew particular attention to the fact that the handkerchief was "of the value of four pence." He obviously thought this a vital clue to the identity of the murderer, probably because it indicated he was a gentleman of means.

In May 1781 the George was advertised for sale as an "old accustom'd inn," its cellars "well stock'd with fine old beer, ale and other liquors, warranted prime; stabling for eighteen horses, coach houses and granary." Daniel Charmbury renewed the lease and advertised the fact in the *Bath Journal*:

> D Charmbury most respectfully informs the public that the well-known eating house the George Inn near St James' Parade is now revived and will be constantly supplied with the best beef, mutton and pork for stakes, veal for cutlets and meat cut out ... with the best home-brewed ale, beer, Bath and London porters, wine and the best of spiritous liquors.

The George had a reputation for entertainment. Here are a few samples of what was on offer in the mid-eighteenth century:

From the *Bath Journal*, 4 April 1748:

> This evening the Fair Penitent with Miss in her Teens will be acted at the George for the benefit of Mr & Mrs Kennedy, being the last time of performing here

From the *Bath Journal*, 7 May 1753:

> This is to acquaint the curious that there is come to the George Inn at the Cross Bath and will begin his performance on Wednesday next, Mr Powell, the celebrated fire eater from London. Tickets 2/6 each ... He licks with his naked tongue red-hot tobacco pipes flaming with brimstone; he fills his mouth with red-

---

*Although the Three Tuns was on the east side of Stall Street, in 1777 it used the old yard of the Bell in Beau Street, which was only a few yards from the George.

THE LOST PUBS OF BATH

hot charcoal and broils a slice of beef or mutton upon his tongue; and any person may blow the fire with a pair of bellows at the same time; he discharges as much gunpowder out of his mouth as will load a small fowling piece

From the *Bath Chronicle*, 13 August 1761:
The sagacious and beautiful little animal, the learned canary bird, exhibited a short time since in London and lately at Bristol (at both which places it has gain'd universal applause from the nobility and gentry, all declaring that it surpassed the imagination) is now exhibited at the George Inn near the Cross Bath … for four days, but positively no longer. The ingenious little creature does by the means of typographical cards read, write and cast accounts, spells persons' names with several other extraordinary performances

From the *Bath Chronicle*, 31 December 1761:
This is to acquaint the curious that there is come to this city at the George Inn near the Cross Bath a Wonderful Man – a Wonderful Man indeed! that is born with a Double Voice; as soon as one voice speaks, the other answers in the same breath. He pleases the curious and astonishes the wise. His Performances are next to Impossibilities and the Satisfactions they give Universal:

> All that in Miracles rejoice,
> Come and hear this change of voice,
> And to this little fairy haste
> Who will not fail to please your taste.

Hot Bath Street, built on the site of the George Inn in the early nineteenth century.

WITHIN THE WALLS

All the fun and frivolity came to an end when the George was pulled down to make way for Hot Bath Street. In January 1796, the council appointed a committee "to treat with Mrs Betty Charmbury or others for the purchase of certain premises near the Cross Bath called the George Inn." In January 1798, the Council instructed Mr W Clark and John Palmer, the architect, to attend the public auction of the George and bid up to £600. In July the following year, they appointed a committee "to meet Dr John Chapman, Master of St John's, regarding purchasing their interest in Bellott's Hospital, the George Inn, and that part of the City Dispensary Estate owned by St John's." Finally, in May 1802, they ordered that the George, now derelict, "be taken down for the safety of the public." Four years later, John Allen leased part of the site to build "a messuage on a plot of ground (parcel of the late George Inn and stables)." This became 5 Hot Bath Street, and now forms part of the Hetling Building.

There was also an inn called the **Red Lion** near the Hot Bath. In 1649, it was leased to Robert Latter. In 1657, it was described as "ye tenement called ye Red Lyon in the possession of Henry Chapman." In 1680, the lease was transferred to William Burford. It does not appear on Gilmore's Map of 1694 and the lack of any subsequent reference suggests that it closed between 1680 and 1694. Although no trace of it survives, one thing has come down to us from over three centuries ago – an inventory of its contents, drawn up in 1680, and preserved in Somerset Record Office, which gives a fascinating glimpse of how an inn was furnished in the late seventeenth century. Its rooms had wonderfully evocative names – the Swan Parlour, the Green Chamber, the White Chamber, the Red Coloured Hanging Room, the Purple Hanged Room, the Little Middle Room, the Castle Room, the White Upper Room – as well as the more prosaic hall, kitchen and cellar.

In the Swan Parlour was a bedstead mattress, three curtain rods, an old sheet for a tester, a calico head, a trundle bedstead and cord, a flowered calico quilt lined with green, a pair of blankets, a set of large green curtains and valance with a green silk fringe, a set of white calico curtains and valance, three high turkey-work chairs, two low turkey-work chairs, a little table board, a joint stool, a looking glass, and a set of green printed hangings.

The White Chamber had a bedstead mattress and cords, two curtain rods, an old sheet for a tester, three white striped fustian curtains and valance, a white rug, a pair of blankets, four turkey-work chairs, a Spanish table, and an old carpet. The furnishing of the other rooms followed the same pattern, with one or two individual touches – a calico flowered quilt in the Red Coloured Hanging Room, a purple bath gown and three close stool boxes in the Castle Room, brass andirons, three pewter chamber pots, a brass pot weighing 16 pounds, two pairs of old Bath stools, and so on.

In the kitchen were an iron dripping pan, two "whole spitts," a pair of iron andirons, a pair of bellows, a skimmer, a matted chair, a table board, and a flour trough. In the cellar were a butt, two hogsheads, a tunn and two wooden horses.

There was also an inn or lodging house called the **Crown** near the Hot Bath, where John Wood stayed in the 1720s, while working on Chandos Buildings. It was demolished in 1804.

To the north of the Cross Bath is St Michael's Place. Although publess today, it has a rich history of alcoholic consumption. It takes its name from the chapel of St Michael Intra Muros (St Michael Within the Walls), which fell into disuse after the Reformation. By 1610 it was a "ruinous church called little St Michaels"; by 1699 it housed "a little shop," measuring five and a half feet by five feet. In 1734, John Chapman was charged with "permitting alcohol to be sold and billiards played" there (although how anyone could have played billiards in a room less than six feet square with people standing around drinking is unclear). The building was demolished in the late eighteenth century.

In April 1729, "Mr Billing, now Mayor," took a 42-year lease of "the **Fleece Tavern** in the lane leading from Westgate Street to the Cross Bath." It closed sometime before 1748, for on 18 July 1748, "part of the old Fleece, fit for a wine cellar, leading to the Cross Bath," was advertised to let.

Around 1780 a pub called the **Chequers** opened, its address being variously recorded as 4 St Michael's Place, 4 Chandos Buildings, 4 New Chandos Buildings, or Cross Bath Lane. It was, in fact, on the corner of St Michael's Place and Chandos Buildings, the site now occupied by the Little Theatre. One night in June 1840,

> some mischievous person put a quantity of gunpowder in a blacking bottle, and by means of a train, set fire to it in the street near the Chequers Inn at the bottom of Bath Street. The explosion shook the houses near, and, the bottle bursting, the pieces flew and broke a pane of glass in the shop of Mr Burridge, grocer, of St Michael's Place.

Eight years later, in May 1848, another night-time disturbance was reported:

> A young man named James Eglon was charged with being drunk and disorderly. A policeman stated that he found him at four o'clock on Sunday morning knocking violently at the door of the Chequers public-house, St Michael's Place, and on his refusing to go on, he took him into custody. The prisoner said he had been out late, and knowing the landlord, he was trying to get admission for the purpose of taking rest for an hour till daylight.

On Christmas Eve 1857, several children were found lying drunk near Chandos Place. One girl was so drunk that, had she not received urgent medical attention, she would have died. It later transpired that they had been drinking gin obtained from the Chequers. Given its reputation, it is unlikely that its neighbours shed too many tears when it was demolished in 1883.

By this time, however, there was another pub in St Michael's Place, on the site of the old chapel. In 1812, Thomas Snell, a tailor, leased a plot of waste ground at the

back of the Grapes to build a house. The terms of the agreement included a clause prohibiting use of the premises as an alehouse. Fifty-six years later, however, James Appleby opened a beerhouse there called the **Queen**. It closed in 1912, but the building is still there, looking much as it did when last orders were called, but now housing St Michael's Day Centre.

The Grapes, on the corner of St Michael's Place and Westgate Street, has only been a pub since around 1794, although the building is much older. Over the road, on the western corner of Parsonage Lane, is the site of Bath's oldest recorded pub, **John Wissy's Tavern**. John Wissy was one of the most prominent citizens of Bath and Bristol in the late thirteenth century, and served as Mayor of Bristol in 1272. Among the buildings he owned was this tavern on the corner of Parsonage Lane.

The former Queen in St Michael's Place, now St Michael's Day Centre.

Parsonage Lane, formerly known as Plumtreotwichene or Plum Tree Lane, takes its name from a parsonage that stood at the top of the lane, on the site now occupied by the nineteenth-century extension to the Mineral Water Hospital. There were three pubs on Parsonage Lane in the eighteenth century. The Rat & Parrot, formerly the Angel Inn, dating from the seventeenth-century, opens backward onto Parsonage Lane, and it is probable that the **Coach & Horses** was its tap. In 1744, Thomas Brown leased "that tenement being two rooms of a floor and a brewhouse thereto adjoining called … the Coach & Horses" in Parsonage Lane. That is the last we hear of it, and it is likely that it was absorbed into the Angel.

The other two pubs on Parsonage Lane closed around 1780 as part of the Corporation's clampdown on licensed premises. These were the **Catherine Wheel** and the **King Bladud**. The King Bladud was there by 1730, when John Crouch leased it from the Corporation. In March 1758, it was advertised as "a house in Parsonage Lane known by the sign of the King Bladud [with] a very good conveniency for brewing." Its last landlord was John Peterswald, who in 1780 placed an advertisement in the *Bath Journal* announcing his move "from Parsonage Lane to the Star & Garter near the North Parade."

Near the bottom of Parsonage Lane, where John Wissy's Tavern once stood, is a series of elaborate Jacobean-style carvings whose provenance is a total mystery. Estimates as to their age range from the seventeenth to the early twentieth century. It is possible, however, that they date from around 1810, when a brewery opened here. The building, which housed the *Bath Chronicle* for much of the twentieth century, is still there, and is still recognisable as a typical tower brewery. The carvings may have been added, as decorative touches, to the principal offices of the brewery, although, in the absence of documentary evidence, it is impossible to prove this.

The Westgate Brewery building in Parsonage Lane.

On the south side of Westgate Street, almost opposite Parsonage Lane, was the **Rose**. In 1619, when it was leased from the Corporation by George Stoughton, it was described as a "tenement, stable and backside lyeinge in Westgate Street commonly called the Rose." In 1645, it was divided into three parts, but the lease remained with the Stoughton family. They still held it in 1661, but by then the Rose had been renamed the Rose and Crown – probably in celebration of the restoration of the monarchy. In 1696, John Stibbs, a baker who later became Mayor, took the lease, which he renewed in 1707. However, by 1745, when George Stibbs and John Hicks took the lease, the property was described as the former Rose and Crown. Its stable almost certainly became part of the ever-expanding empire of the coachmasters at the White Hart Inn.

On the north side of Westgate Street, between the Rat & Parrot and Union Street, was the **White Swan**, originally known as the Lower Swan, which dated from the late sixteenth century.* In August 1604, during a plague epidemic, Captain John Wintle of Dyrham wrote to Robert Cecil, James I's Secretary of State, informing him that 50 people had died in Bath, but the disease was now confined to four houses,

*Confusingly, the inn next door was originally the Three Swans before it became the Angel. Today it is the Rat & Parrot.

one of which was the White Swan. Six people had already died at the inn; two more died before the epidemic ran its course a month or so later.

In 1645, the White Swan was leased by Carew Davis. Giles Davis took over in 1691, and stayed till at least 1710, when his tenant was Widow Boyce. The tenancy later passed to her son, who stayed there until his death in 1743. The following May, a notice appeared in the *Bath Journal*:

> The White Swan in Westgate Street, late in the possession of William Boyce, deceas'd, is now occupied by John Eccles, who formerly kept the King's Arms in the Market Place; and the stables of the said inn are taken by George Palmer, who lived with Mr Thursby Robinson at the Three Tuns in Stall Street, and the Bear in Cheap Street, upwards of 20 years, the greatest part of which time in the station of an ostler; where all gentlemen and ladies may be assur'd of the civillest treatment and the best accommodation, by the humble servants, John Eccles, George Palmer.

The White Swan was a popular venue for auctions and sales. A horse auction was held there in October 1747; in February 1752, it was the venue for a sale of "Silesian Lawns, Muslins, Hollands, and other Linnens … considerably cheaper than was first design'd." Five years later, following John Eccles' death, it was the inn itself – "with or without the tap" – which was on the market, and by 1769 it had become a private house.

Opposite the White Swan was the Three Jacks, renamed the **Shakespeare** (or the Shakespeare's Head) in 1741. In December 1766, William Tucker moved from the Shakespeare to the Greyhound in the Market Place and renamed it the Greyhound & Shakespeare.

Like the White Swan, the Shakespeare was used for auctions. Appropriately, given its name, a book auction was held there in December 1773; in January 1792, there was an "auction … of linen drapery, hosiery and jewellery goods, being the stock of a bankrupt." The Shakespeare closed in the 1780s and by 1787 was described as a private house. It was later converted to a shop

On the far side of Union Street is Union Passage, formerly known as Cock Lane, and rebuilt by Thomas Baldwin in the late eighteenth century. In the nineteenth century, it was home to four beerhouses.

On the east side at No 27 was the **Military Arms**. This started out as an eating house, before getting a beer licence around 1868. It closed around 1906. The building later housed the Bath Gas Company and now forms part of Oasis.

A little further along on the east side, at No 24, was the **Albert Tavern**, a single-roomed beerhouse opened by Albert Stiles around 1868. It closed in 1935 and now forms part of Melson Wingate Opticians.

Finally, north of Northumberland Place, on the west side, was the **Rising Sun** at No 12. This was another eating house which got a beer licence around 1864, took a few years out as a furniture store, reopened as a beerhouse around 1870 and closed in 1905. It consisted of a bar with seats around it and another small room. Today it is the back entrance to Thornton's Chocolate Shop.

A right turn at the top of Union Passage takes us back to our starting point, the old North Gate. It is also the starting point for the second part of this excursion – a

The former Rising Sun beerhouse in Union Passage.

circuit of the old city. The inns and pubs we have visited so far have all been within the city walls. Many of those we will visit next were built upon them.

§

Our route takes us westward along Upper Borough Walls. The first steps towards making this a street were taken in September 1674, when the council "agreed that the burrow walls shall be railed for the convenience of walking thereon." Half a century later, in June 1715, they "agreed that the footway leading by the city wall shall be new pitched and posts fixed there, from Gascoine's Tower [in the Sawclose] to Richard Horler's house, near the Northgate of the city."

Most of the buildings on the north of the street date from the mid-eighteenth century. However, the block next to the North Gate is much older. It can be seen, for example, on Speed's map of 1610. The block included the old **Seven Stars**, which opened sometime before 1687, when "William Harford paid £5 for the lease of two messuages called the Seven Stars." The inn consisted of two buildings, which were in different parishes – St Michael's and St Peter & St Paul's. The boundary mark can still be seen on the wall dividing the two properties.

When William Harford's widow, Anne, took over the lease after his death in 1695, the address of the inn was Northgate Street. When Samuel Jones took the lease in March 1727, it was described as being "within the North Gate," with a house on the east, "the way leading by the city wall on the south and west, and the said wall north." By 1762, when Catherine Howe took the lease, its address was "on Borough Walls." Five years later, on 20 August 1767, the Bath Chronicle announced that "Monday was married Mr Fuller of Batheaston to the Widow Cottle at the Seven Stars on the Borough Walls."

In August 1756, an advertisement appeared in the *Bath Journal*:

BUGS, be they ever so intolerable, are effectually destroyed (no cure no pay) by Benjamin Bridges, the first inventor of that art, at the Seven Stars in Brook Street, near the Market Place, Bath; where hospitals, workhouses, infirmaries, gentlemen's houses, rooms, walls, wainscots, floorings, bedsteads, and bedding furniture, are warranted to be cleansed from bugs for any number of years at reasonable prices – and as he has practised for these eight years, and cured upwards of 10,000 beds, for people of the best rank and property, in and about London, the bugs not returning: To avoid disputes, he chuses his character might be first enquired after, before he is employ'd. Those who please to favour him with their commands, shall be waited on, and shall have twelve months time for trial, provided the sum be large. NB What he does makes no smell, neither does it hurt the furniture; and if any complaint should happen, he visits again gratis.

As far as we know, this is the only reference to a street called Brook Street in Bath. It is possible that Upper Borough Walls was known as Brook Street for a short time; it is more likely, however, that Mr Bridges got the name wrong. At the time, there was a brushmaker's shop on the corner of the High Street and Upper Borough Walls, owned by William Brook. Perhaps Mr Bridges – in all probability a stranger to the city, lodging at a convenient inn – saw the name Brook on the corner and took it to be the name of the street.

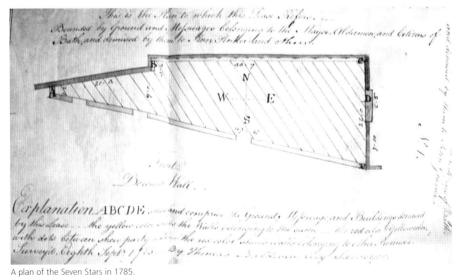

A plan of the Seven Stars in 1785.

THE LOST PUBS OF BATH

In 1785, William and Catherine Purlewent and Charles Gunning took the lease of the Seven Stars. A plan drawn up at the time shows that the building was shaped like a wedge of cheese – 67 feet long at the front, with an east wall measuring 22 feet, and a west wall measuring two feet two inches.

A sad incident from 1827 is worth recounting because it indicates that, back then, twenty-four-hour drinking was a reality. Joseph Smith had gone to the Wheatsheaf in Broad Street at 5.15am and downed three pints before going on to the tap room of the Seven Stars at six o'clock and ordering another. He then ate the fat off a beefsteak and fell asleep with his head on the table. When they came to move him, they found he was dead.

At one time, there was a family connection between the Seven Stars and the Greyhound Inn, the entrance to whose yard was over the road. In 1837, John Brinkworth held the lease of the Seven Stars while George Brinkworth held that of the Greyhound. Three years later, George Brinkworth took over the Seven Stars. In the early nineteenth century the Seven Stars was the meeting place of a benefit society called the Friends of Humanity. One early Victorian who tried to benefit himself, but ended up getting six months' hard labour, appeared in the *Bath Chronicle* in April 1840:

> William Cook, aged 18, was indicted … for stealing a silver spoon, the property of George Brinkworth of the Seven Stars public house. The prisoner called for a glass of gin and water, which being brought him, he took out of it the silver spoon and put in its place one of inferior metal.

Eight years later, a serious accident highlighted the shortcomings of the Seven Stars' health and safety policy. In June 1729, Samuel Jones had been granted "a piece of ground five feet by three feet under the parlour of his house called the Seven Stars to let down casks into his cellar, his paying 1/- per annum rent for the same." One day in August 1848, as John Parker, of Prospect Buildings on Wells Road, was passing the Seven Stars, he fell through the open trapdoor. The *Bath Chronicle* later reported that "the sufferer is in a doubtful state."

By the mid-nineteenth century, the Seven Stars consisted of a bar, a bar parlour, a tap room, two dining rooms, ten bedrooms and a brewery. There were three entrances from Upper Borough Walls, two to the bars and one to the hotel. An exit from the back led into Barton Passage (a relic of Barton Lane) which contained a public urinal. In 1857, following complaints from nearby residents, the Corporation received an engineer's report on this urinal, "the effluvium from which is exceedingly bad."

In 1970, with the threat of demolition hanging over it, Roy Packer, who had taken the Seven Stars on a short lease from Courage's, transformed what had become "a nondescript back street bar into a trendy and cosy Victorian pub with art nouveau wallpapers and lampshades, and pictures of the Duke of Wellington and Captain Cook on the walls." He also painted "the fluted and carved woodwork on the exterior … in imperial red, gold and black." This brought him into conflict with council officials, who told him that he had to restore it to its original colour

The Seven Stars in the 1950s.

THE LOST PUBS OF BATH

(dirty brown) because the pub was in a conservation area – even though it was scheduled for demolition! Once the absurdity of the situation had been pointed out, they reluctantly agreed that the colour scheme could stay. The Seven Stars closed in 1974, with the threat of demolition still hanging over it. Today, with nothing left of the old pub but its frontage, the building has been converted into shops.

A few doors along, at No 7, was – very briefly – the **George Tavern**. In 1860 a hatter occupied the premises; in 1870 they were occupied by a tailor. In between, from around 1863 to around 1868, they were a beerhouse. The site has since been redeveloped.

On the south side of Upper Borough Walls, one door up from the High Street, was the **Squirrel**, which opened some time before 1739. When Elizabeth Marchant, a distiller, took the lease of the Squirrel in 1767, it was described as being situated on and fronting the Borough Walls on the north, with stables to the south and west, and a passageway on the east. This passageway was, in fact, the entrance to the Greyhound yard. In June 1808, the lease was taken by William May, who "agreed to take down and set back the premises" to widen the road. Later renamed the Greyhound Vaults, it survived the closure of the inn from which it took its name, finally closing in 1964 when the whole block was redeveloped.

When the Northgate Brewery leased the Greyhound in the Market Place in 1794, they also acquired "a certain other messuage, tenement or dwelling house erected and built on part of the said premises … at the north east end or side thereof fronting the street called the Borough Walls." This was the Greyhound Tap, on the right-hand side of the entrance to the Greyhound yard. In 1800 it was renamed the Jolly Coachman; eight years later it was the Coach & Horses. Finally, in 1826, it became the **Rainbow**.

Cater's Wine Vaults, formerly the Greyhound Vaults, as rebuilt in 1808. Before that it was the Squirrel.

Although connected with the Greyhound, the Rainbow was licensed separately and had its own coachyard and brewery. In March 1849, it was advertised for sale as an "old established home-brewed public house" comprising "bar, tap room, large smoking room and four bedchambers." By 1860 the licensee was William Weeks, who ran a coaching business from the yard. His son, Sambourne Weeks, who later took over the pub and coaching business, went bankrupt in 1893. Among the items seized by the bailiffs were seven horses, two landaus, one cab and a dogcart. The Rainbow was taken over by Thomas May, who let Sambourne Weeks stay on, living in a cottage in the yard and running a scaled-down coaching business. By all accounts, the Rainbow was a fairly rough establishment, with frequent convictions for drunkenness. It closed in 1922.

West's Grill on the corner of Union Passage.

Today, Dollond & Aitchison's opticians covers the site of both the Rainbow and the building next to it, on the corner of Union Passage. This was the **London Dining Rooms**, which opened around 1870 and formed part of West's Commercial Hotel. Athough not primarily a pub, it had a drinking bar at the back of the dining room. It was renamed West's Grill in 1956 and closed in 1963.

Across the road, at No 10 Upper Borough Walls, was the Royal Oak, later the Owl's Nest and now the Central Wine Bar, whose history is covered in *Bath Pubs*, as is Sam Weller's, formerly the Full Moon.

At 17 Upper Borough Walls, on the corner of Old Bond Street, was the **White Hart Vaults**. It opened around 1886 and closed in 1919. The bar, which was divided into several compartments, was used for light meals as well as drinking. Today, Caffè Nero occupies the building.

The City Dining Rooms, later Fuller's Wine Vaults.

Next door, at No 18 Upper Borough Walls (now 10 Trim Street), was the **City Dining Rooms**, later known as Fuller's Wine Vaults, which opened around 1858. The 1903 report makes somewhat queasy reading for those of a delicate disposition: "Premises consist of bar with three compartments. Luncheons supplied. Urinal in corner of bar." It closed around 1912 and became a Nurses' Home for the Mineral Water Hospital.

BATH CITY DINING ROOMS,
UPPER BOROUGH WALLS.
A Respectable and Good DINNER Every Day,
from Twelve to Four, Cheap.

An advertisement for the City Dining Rooms in 1858.

THE LOST PUBS OF BATH

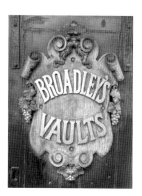

BROADLEY & ANSWORTH

BEG to call attention to their STOCK of CHOICE

OLD WINES AND SPIRITS,

Which they offer at the Lowest Remunerative Prices.

CONSIGNEES FOR GUINNESS & CO.'S EXTRA STOUT.

AGENTS FOR ALLSOPP'S, BASS' & YOUNGER'S ALES.

Gascoyn Place (opposite the Blue Coat School.)

At the end of Upper Borough Walls, in Gascoyne Place, stands one of Bath's most recently lost pubs, and one which may yet reopen – **Broadley's Wine Vaults**. It takes its name from John Broadley, who, with Charles Answorth, opened a wine merchant's here in the nineteenth century. Later, it became a pub; in the 1970s it was one of the top real ale pubs in Bath. It had three bars, known as the Corner Bar, the Middle Bar, and the Dugout Bar. In 1976, Fred Pearce described the Dugout Bar as "dominated by aging customers," with "one long bar the length of the room … divided with wood partitions." In 1980, the pub was taken over by ex-jockey Mick Leak, who renamed two of the bars the Saddle and the Paddock. Broadley's was the last pub in Bath to have a men-only bar.

By the time it closed in 2001, it had survived for some time on short-term contracts and was pulling in a young, rather indiscriminate crowd. The *Itchy Bath Guide* for 2001 regarded its impending closure as inevitable, but added that its loss would not be too keenly felt. It is to be hoped that its future will be brighter than its recent past.

We now retrace our steps to Bridewell Lane, between the old Bluecoat School and the Mineral Water Hospital. A Bridewell, or House of Correction, was established here in the 1630s, when "a barne stable and backside" were converted "for the setting of poore people on worke." The name came from a former royal lodging at St Bride's Well in London, which Edward VI endowed as a hospital, but which later became the model for houses of correction throughout the country. Bridewells differed from gaols in that you did not have to commit a crime to end up in one: you simply had to be destitute. The Bridewell in Bath was for paupers from outside the city, as an incentive for them to leave. It was demolished around 1715 when the Blue Coat School was built.

There were three pubs in Bridewell Lane in the eighteenth century:

The **Crown & Cushion**, whose exact location is unknown, closed around 1776.

At 15-16 Bridewell Lane, about halfway along on the east side, was a pub which had a variety of names – the Chairmen (1776), the Chairman (1783), the Glass

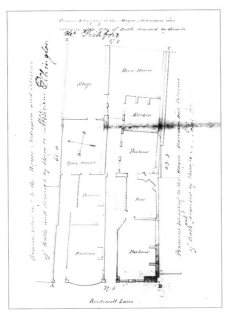

Above A nineteenth-century plan of the Sedan Chair in Bridewell Lane – four parlours, bar, kitchen, shop, and brewery – and that's just the ground floor.

Top right The Sedan Chair Brewery advertising its wares in 1866.

Bottom right The Sedan Chair today.

Chair (1789), the Bath Chair (1795), the Chair (1800) – before finally becoming the **Sedan Chair** in 1809. It was first recorded in 1720, when Christopher Palmer, a victualler from Marshfield, leased it from St John's Hospital. An inventory carried out in 1877 draws a picture of a spacious establishment, with four bedrooms, sitting room, smoking room, bar, bar parlour, tap room, brewery, hop room (with Kent and Farnham hops), and spirit cellar. It closed in 1892, but the building, although extensively remodelled, survives.

On the west side of the lane, at No 12, was the **Prince of Wales**, first recorded in 1792. In the early nineteenth century it was the meeting place for a benefit society called the New Bath British Society. It was leased by the Northgate Brewery and renamed the Victoria Tavern around 1844. It was closed and demolished around 1859, when the Blue Coat School was rebuilt and extended.

We now head down Bridewell Lane, turn right and walk along Westgate Street to find the **Boar's Head Tavern**. This stood roughly where the corner of Westgate Street and Westgate Buildings is today, although it projected much further into the road. It opened sometime before 1719, when Mary Edney took the lease. By 1728, it had been taken over by a vintner called John Billing. Although it was on the south side of the street, its yard and stables were tucked away behind the buildings on the north side, with an entrance in the Sawclose. The Boar's Head closed around 1776,

THE LOST PUBS OF BATH

but the building survived until 1805, when William Elkington took the lease of a "messuage formerly the Boar's Head" and pulled it down to erect a new building set further back.

Beyond the south-western corner of Westgate Street, right up against the old Borough Walls, stood another building which may have been a tavern. In 1625, John Hayward leased a "tenement lyeing in Westgate Street [with] a newe erected shop of the said John Hayward's sometymes parcell of a tenement called the Westgate House on the west side and openeth into the said street on the north side." In 1694, the property was described as a "tenement, malt house, stable, backside, coach house and garden thereunto adjoining, on part of which a messuage or tenement is lately erected." It extended "as far as the ancient porch of another messuage of the same Robert Hayward on the east," abutted a garden of Walter Gibbs on the south and the Borough Walls on the west, and contained "in length about 18 yards fronting Westgate Street."

The Haywards were maltsters who had an interest in several licensed premises; various details in the leases – the shop, the malt house, the coach house, and the size of the property – suggest that this was an inn or tavern. It was probably the **Golden Ball**, listed on Gilmore's map of 1694 as one of three inns in Westgate Street, but mentioned in no other documents. Whatever it was, it would have been demolished no later than the 1770s, when a new street was built south from Queen Square past the old West Gate to the top of Southgate Street. With it probably went the most intriguing item of all – the "ancient porch" on the building next door. In an age which regarded the medieval as barbarous, it is extremely unlikely that, if the porch had dated from that period, anyone would have considered it worth mentioning. It is more likely that it was a Roman relic, removed from wherever it was found to adorn the house in Westgate Street.

We are now at the West Gate of the city. In 1572, in preparation for a state visit by Queen Elizabeth, the old West Gate was rebuilt in grand style, with lavish apartments to the north to accommodate the Queen and her entourage. In 1591, Thomas Parker leased "all that tenement and buildings erected and made upon the west gate of the said cittie called **Westgate House**, one barn or stable lying on the north side thereof upon the walls of the said cittie, one barton adjoininge on the west side thereof as the same barton is now inclosed and bounded together with one garden lyeinge within the walls … next adjoyninge unto the south side."

Westgate House, which subsequently opened as an inn, suffered extensive damage when Bath was used as a garrison by Parliamentary troops in the Civil War. In March 1652, the landlord, Mr Ernley, was "abated 40/- of the rent being £6 formerly due for the Westgate House in lieu of his wife's loss and damage suffered by reason of the Court of Guards being kept there in the time of this city being a garrison." By 1678, when William Duckett was the landlord, a malthouse had been built.

East and west views of Westgate House.

The apartments over the gate continued to be used for royal visitors. In May 1728, for example, Princess Amelia watched from the windows as celebrations in her honour – including an ox roast, "maurice dancers" and fireworks – were held on Kingsmead Fields.

In 1754, the Corporation ordered the demolition of the town gates. The West Gate was still there in 1767, however, when an unfortunate incident highlighted its inconvenience and danger. The Rev John Penrose, who was directly involved, takes up the story:

> As we went through the postern at West Gate, which as you know is a narrow pass not capable of two abreast, without some inconvenience, I was at the head of our little company, when I heard some noisy fellows behind cry out, "stand away," and one of them rushing along pushed the ladies in upon me. I put back my hand to screen them from violence, when a fellow with too much liquor in his pate pushed me with his backside against the wall. I then took him by the shoulder, and pushed him in my turn, and with my stick gave him a little

rap on the head. The fellow turned about, lifted up his club, and attempted to strike me. I warded the blow with my stick, and hit him again on the head, no mortal blow ... Indeed, I was most easily disarmed; the fellow got my stick into his possession. My stick however was soon restored by the undaunted courage of Mr Scoble, who was in a furious passion with the fellow for attempting to strike a clergyman, and laid on manfully. The Doctor from behind stretched out a Herculean club, very knotty and broke the fellow's head, which streamed with blood.

When the party finally got out "into the open street in Kingsmead Square," their adversaries "rallied and made a fresh attack." They finally managed to make their way to safety, suffering no serious injuries, but the affair so shocked Bath society that it was soon "in everybody's mouth." News of it even reached Bristol.

Penrose's tale of woe gives us a vivid insight into a side of Bath we rarely hear about. Not only was there an ever-present threat of violence, generally fuelled by drink; Bath was also a very difficult place to get around. Before the walls came down, the only way into or out of the city was through one of four narrow gates. If you walked through the main gate, you risked being mown down by a coach or cart; if you walked through the postern gate at the side, you had to squeeze past people coming the other way.

New Westgate House, later known as the Westgate Tavern, stood in the middle of the road leading from Westgate Street to the Sawclose.

Westgate House survived the demolition of the West Gate, which was pulled down a few months after the attack on the Rev Penrose's party. However, it probably suffered serious structural damage in the process, for nine years later it was described as "greatly decayed and ruinous" and not worth "the expense of repairing." Westgate House was compulsorily purchased by the Corporation in 1775, along with "eight little tenements adjoining," so that "Mr Palmer's plan ... to make a road from Queen Square, along the Borough Walls to Horse Street [could] go ahead."

However, no sooner had it been demolished than a new row of buildings was erected on part of the site. New Westgate Buildings was a free-standing block completely surrounded by public thoroughfares (similar to – but narrower than – the Bond Street/Burton Street block at the bottom of Milsom Street).

The southernmost building was an inn, which opened in September 1779 as the **New Westgate House**. James Pinnock, its first landlord, described its facilities in glowing terms:

> The house and yard are pleasantly situated, the stables furnished with the best hay and corn, and careful attendants. The house is neatly finished, and as neatly furnished with good beds, etc., and the best provisions, which he hopes, with his steady attention to his customers' commands, will merit their favour.

Originally, the block consisted of the inn and two fairly upmarket shops at the northern end. In 1791, the shops were occupied by Mr Rogers, a jeweller, and Mr Molineux, a hairdresser. By the mid-nineteenth century, however, any pretence at gentility had gone, and part of the inn was converted into shops. The New Westgate House, now known simply as the Westgate House, got so rough that the magistrates took away its licence, forcing the landlord to turn it into a beerhouse. A new landlord took over and tried to get the licence reinstated, but, as the report of the licensing session for 14 September 1851 indicates, he was unsuccessful:

> A beerhouse keeper, named Parker, who had applied for a spirit licence on the first day, now appeared to renew his application and was attended by Mr Higgins, attorney. The applicant said he had taken the house known by the sign of the Westgate House and had laid out a considerable sum to fit it up, in the expectation that he should have a renewal of the spirit licence, which had been suspended.
>
> Mr Oakley said this was one of the houses from which the magistrates withheld licences last year on account of their disorderly character, and as there were two licensed houses in close proximity to it, there was no reasonable ground for entertaining the application; and besides this, according to a resolution passed by the bench at the last meeting, that no beerhouse should have a spirit licence granted, the request of the applicant should not be complied with. As it respected

The Westgate Tavern from Kingsmead Square, with the County Wine Vaults (now Flan O'Brien's) in the background.

> the inconvenience and expense to which he said he had subjected himself, he was informed when he first entered the house, that there was no probability that he would have the licence renewed.
>
> Mr Higgins said that the house was one of the oldest licensed houses in the city; and it was hard that the applicant should have the misconduct of his predecessor visited upon him by the refusal of the licence.
>
> The Mayor said that, as the applicant took the house with a knowledge that the house had been discontinued on account of its bad character, his plea was inadmissible; and, as a resolution had been passed by the bench to the effect that no houses should be newly licensed, the application must be refused.

If there were any subsequent attempts to overturn the magistrates' ruling, they were unsuccessful. The

THE LOST PUBS OF BATH

Westgate House, which was renamed the Westgate Hotel, and later the Westgate Tavern, was still a beerhouse in 1903. As the inspector's report from that year indicates, hygiene was not high on the landlord's agenda:

> WC in basement; apparently whole of basement used as urinal, there being a sink
>
> in the floor for the water to run away. Very unsatisfactory.

It closed in 1938.*

A little way along Westgate Buildings is Chandos House, now part of St John's Hospital. John Wood built it for James Brydges, Duke of Chandos, in the late 1720s. By 1848, part of it had become a pub called the **Chandos Arms**, with John Gill as the landlord. In 1877, John Gill's widow died and left the Chandos Arms to Enoch Tutton, who already had an interest in other Bath pubs and may have been related to the Gills by marriage. Mr Tutton leased it to William Hinton, a fly proprietor. The inventory drawn up at the time records that it had four bedrooms, a small dining room, a tap room and a bar.

---

*The old New Westgate Buildings, the freehold of which was held by King Edward's School, disappeared when the street was widened. The current New Westgate Buildings stand to the west of the old ones, on the site of what was once known as John's Lane. Another inn – the Seven Dials – stood on the corner of John's Lane and Monmouth Street. Its history is covered on pages 138-40 of *Bath Pubs*.

Chandos House is now part of St John's Hospital; a century ago it was the Chandos Arms.

In 1898, Thomas Pearce acquired the property and "spent £700 on transforming an old-fashioned sort of place into a modern public-house." He extended the pub "into a large room which was part of the house next door, and [pulled] down an old wall to give access to it." He also blocked up "an old doorway at the back of this room which communicated with the other part of Chandos House. He [built] a doorway into this room from the front path … to use it for an order office." Despite this refurbishment, the Chandos Arms only lasted another 16 years, closing in 1914.

Continuing into Lower Borough Walls, we come to Bilbury Lane. Its name may lead the unwary to assume that bilberry fields once covered this area. In fact, Bilbury is a corruption of the Anglo Saxon Binnebury, meaning "within the borough walls."

On the western corner of Bilbury Lane was an inn called the **Blue Anchor**. In 1672, Benjamin Lewis leased "three tenements called or known by the name of the Blue Anchor being heretofore a barne, situate and being in the tything of Binbury … directly against the Burrow Walls." In 1719, the lease passed to Dr Charles Bave. In 1753, when Edward Harington took the lease, the property was referred to as "three messuages formerly the Blue Anchor."

By this time, Dr Bave had built a magnificent four-storey house nearby. It had eight bays, the central ones being enclosed under a broken pediment held up by two giant order Corinthian columns stretching over the first and second floors. On the third floor, reaching through the broken pediment was another window with a small triangular pediment above. On the first floor, between the columns, was a Venetian window. After Dr Bave's

Dr Bave's House on Lower Borough Walls – later the Alfred Hotel, later the City Infirmary, later demolished.

death in 1774, it was advertised as "a large and substantial well-built messuage facing St James's Parade, built by the late Dr Bave, deceased, for his own residence and fit for a large family. Consisting of a large good kitchen, two servants' halls, a large hall, a handsome staircase, three large and lofty parlours, and a lodging room on the ground floor, a large, elegant and lofty dining room, three good large lodging rooms on the first floor, five good lodging rooms in the attic storey, and seven good garrets, a wash house, brew house and laundry adjoining to and in front of the house, and two lodging rooms for servants over the same, a good seven-stall stable, and a coach house for two carriages. There is plenty of both sorts of water and a good carriageway to the premises."

Four years later, in October 1778, Samuel Woodhouse from the White Hart opened it as the **Alfred Hotel**. The announcement of its opening included the information that Mr Woodhouse "keeps a man cook. His liquor and provisions of every sort shall be the best that can be purchased. A good yard for carriages; stabling for any number of horses." It also informed prospective patrons that it was "opposite the new Catholic Chapel.* The Royal Cumberland Masonic Lodge were so impressed by the Alfred that they adopted it as their meeting place, before moving to the Greyhound in the Market Place in 1780.

The choice of name may have been influenced by the celebrated historian, Catherine Macaulay, who lived at Alfred House in Alfred Street. The bust of King Alfred above her front door was a mark of her veneration of him as "a prince of the most exalted merit that ever graced the English throne." The Alfred Hotel closed in 1792, after a career of only 14 years, and became the Bath City Infirmary. Judging by a newspaper report from November 1792, however, this change of use did not meet with the approval of some of the local youth:

> On Sunday night a party of young bloods came to the door of the Bath City Infirmary, and made a great noise to obtain entrance; insisting, contrary to the asserverations of the matron, that the house (formerly the Alfred Hotel) was still destined to its former purpose. The next time they go on a similar errand, it is hoped the matron will give each of them a fever patient for a bedfellow.

It was pulled down in the 1860s when the Royal United Hospital was extended. Extensive Roman remains, including a tessellated pavement, were found under the building.

Across the road from the Lamb & Lion, at 6 Lower Borough Walls, was the **Crispin Tavern**, opened around 1826. It was named after the patron saint of shoemakers, which suggests that the licensee, Thomas Pranket, like many others at the time, made or mended shoes.

The Crispin stood next to St James's Burial Ground, at the entrance to St James's Court. By the mid-nineteenth century, this was one of the most notorious spots in Bath, with up to 60 prostitutes crammed into its 20 small hovels. When David Garret closed the Bell in Stall Street in 1850 and moved to the Crispin, he brought the name with him. Renaming it did nothing, however, to improve its character.

When a new vicar, the Rev WJ Bolton, came to St James's Church, at the bottom of Stall Street, in 1881, he wasted no time in spearheading a campaign to have the Bell closed and the court at the back of it pulled down. "By day," he wrote, "even on Sundays, and within a stone's throw of St James's Church, dissolute women, half dressed, would stand in groups, soliciting passers-by. At night, riots, fighting and piano playing disturbed the whole neighbourhood. Respectable people were ashamed to live in or pass through such a district." After a two-year struggle, the vicar and his parishioners were successful. The licence of the Bell was revoked in August 1883, on the grounds that it harboured prostitutes, and the court was demolished. St James's Memorial Hall was built on the site of the court, and George Troutt, the last landlord of the Bell, opened up an auction house in the pub.

The old Bell is still there, with its nineteenth-century sign bracket intact, although now it is dedicated to nymphs of a more rarified kind, as Bath's Faerie Shop. But there are a couple more twists to this tale.

*This was burnt down in the Gordon Riots less than two years later.

The Crispin Tavern, later the Bell, was notorious as the haunt of piano-playing prostitutes. Today it is the Faerie Shop.

St James's Church, from where the Rev Bolton launched his crusade against the cesspit of iniquity and piano playing that was the Bell, was badly damaged in the Second World War. Its gaunt remains survived until April 1957, when the site was redeveloped. They could – indeed should – have been preserved as a lasting reminder of what Bath suffered during its two terrible nights of bombing. Go to Bristol, to Exeter, to Coventry, to Portsmouth, or to many other cities devastated during the Second World War, and you will find similar sites preserved to remind future generations of the inhumanity and imbecility of war. But Bath has nothing,

The vicar of St James's Church spearheaded the campaign to close the Bell.

nothing, that is, except the pockmarked walls of the old Labour Exchange opposite the Trinity in James Street West. What should have been Bath's blitz memorial was sacrificed on the altar of commercial greed. What would the pious parishioners who prayed to have the Bell closed down think if they could return and see the greetings-card superstore that now stands on the site of their church?

THE LOST PUBS OF BATH

If they survived the initial shock, an even ruder one would be waiting for them round the corner, where St James's Memorial Hall has become Inventions Studios, an arts centre with fully licensed bar and cutting-edge music, comedy, and much else besides. Somehow you feel that the Rev Bolton would not be too impressed by the Cosmic Sausages or Bedlam Cabaret – and after listening to the warblings of bands with names such as Punk You Too Mate he would probably wish he had never got rid of the piano players.

A few doors down from the Bell, at 3 Lower Borough Walls, was the **White Swan**, which opened in the 1850s. Around 1868 it became the Queen's Head before changing to the Foresters' Arms in 1869. The last licensee was Robert Hoskins, who, in July 1869, was "summoned for selling beer at an illegal hour on Sunday the 11th." When the policeman who caught him "said he should report the house, the defendant asked him not to as he was a young beginner." A couple of years later the pub closed and become a grocer's shop. The building no longer exists.

The **French Horn**, at No 11, stood much further out into the road than the current building, with its front wall built on top of the old city wall. It was opened in 1779 by William Cottell who had previously kept the Ring of Bells in Stall Street and the Seven Stars in Upper Borough Walls.

In the eighteenth century, French horns were primarily open-air instruments. They were valveless and more akin to hunting horns than modern French horns. Open-air performances were held at spots where echo effects could be obtained. Bath, surrounded by hills, was ideal for showing them off to their best advantage. An advertisement in the *Bath Journal* in May 1751 gave notice

> that Messrs Charles, the French Horn Masters, with a Band of Musick, are to perform a concert at breakfast, upon a variety of instruments, at Lyncomb-Spaw House near Bath on Tuesday … for the benefit of John Taber, who keeps the said house. If the ladies should be desirous, after the concert, of dancing country dances, proper hands will be ready to attend.

A poem on the delights of Bath written in 1775 indicates that French horns accompanied boat trips along the river, in the same way that saxophones do today:

> Sailing, the voice of musick soothes our cares,
> Whose magic sounds enchant th'enraptured ears:
> Hark! – the French horns the vocal woods awake,
> And teach the pendant rocks and hills to speak,
> While doubly – trebly – all our barge around,
> The mimick echo mocks the dying sound.

The entertainment at the French Horn in Lower Borough Walls was somewhat less refined. Even though it was the meeting place of the St James's Benefit Society, it was probably a good place to avoid unless you were looking for a fight. In 1817, for example, John Brown, a chairman who had upset some of his colleagues by working for lower rates than those generally agreed, was invited outside. As so often happened, the bout which followed was not some rough and ready free for all, but a proper bare-knuckle contest, with a series of rounds. To accommodate spectators, it was held on Kingsmead Fields. Unfortunately, during the fight, the two men fell into a pit of stones and broken bottles, and, although the fight ended with a handshake and a drink, Brown later complained of being short of breath and subsequently died. At the inquest, his death was put down to the fall. A few months later, another chairman, Samuel White, died after being challenged to a fight at the French Horn. This time the contest took place several days later in the pouring rain at Lansdown Fair. Although White won the fight, he died later of his injuries.

The French Horn closed in the 1850s, became a grocer's and was later demolished when the street was widened.

§

We have now arrived at the old South Gate of the city. On the corner of Stall Street and Lower Borough Walls, where Evans' store is now, was the **Royal Oak**, which Thomas Atwood leased in 1728. In 1768, the lease was taken by George Compton, a schoolmaster. Three years later, it was transferred to his widow, Susannah Compton. It closed around 1780. The Royal Oak is one of the most common pub names in the country, and recalls the incident after the Battle of Worcester when the future King Charles II hid in an oak tree at Boscobel in Shropshire. On his restoration to the throne, his birthday, 29 May, was declared a holiday called Royal Oak Day, and pubs throughout the land were renamed in an outbreak of patriotism.

Next to the Royal Oak was the **Chequers**, opened sometime before 1776 and converted to a temperance hotel around 1811.

The South Gate in 1694.

Across the road, where Marks & Spencer's stands today, was the **Golden Lyon**. In 1656, it was leased from the Corporation by Thomas Biggs. In 1721, its layout was altered, part of the old inn was redeveloped, and Richard Cornish paid £24 for a "messuage in Lear Lane, with the newly built tenement adjoining, formerly part of the inn called the Golden Lyon." Four years later, Henry Woolmer leased "an inn called the Golden Lyon, with appurtenances, in Stall Street, between Mr Morley's house on the north, the way to St James's Church on the south [and] Henry Woolmer's malt house on the east." And that is the last record we have of it.

On the other side of the street, a little further along, were the Lamb & Lark (which now lies under Burton's) and the Lamb Inn (now the Halifax Building Society), both of which are featured in *Bath Pubs* in the section on the Lamb & Lion. There were eight other inns and pubs in Stall Street whose precise location is unknown. These included:

the **Admiral Rodney**, which closed around 1786;

a cider house called the **Apple Tree**, which featured in a crime report in December 1764:

> Saturday last a young woman was robbed on Claverton Down of eight shillings by a footpad; and on Monday evening one William Bryan, an Irishman, was apprehended at the Apple Tree in Stall Street, on suspicion of committing the said robbery. A loaded pistol was found in his pocket, which he pretended to pick up on the London Road; but the woman swearing positively to his person, he was committed to Shepton Mallet Gaol.

the **Bath Coffee House**, which held a licence to serve alcohol. It was renamed the Coffee Pot in 1779 and disappeared by 1786. It was on the east side of the street;

the **Crown**, which closed in the early 1780s;

the **White Horse** or White Horse Cellar, opened by the Anchor Brewery around 1820 and closed around 1830;

the **Ring of Bells**, opened sometime before 1760 and closed around 1780;

the **Shoulder of Mutton**, first recorded in 1782 and closed around four years later;

the **Wheatsheaf**, possibly dating from 1620, when an inn of that name was licensed in Bath by Sir Giles Mompesson. The first definite reference to it comes in February 1752, when an early picture restorer placed an advertisement in the *Bath Journal*:

> This is to give notice that James Calder, who has had the honour of cleaning the paintings of the Town Hall, Bath, cleans, mends and lines. He is to be spoken with at ... the sign of the Wheatsheaf in Stall Street, Bath.

In August 1755, "a grand collection of living wild beasts and birds [were] to be seen at the sign of the Wheatsheaf in Stall Street, Bath, including porcupines, vultures, hyaenas." A few years later, in 1766, a fire eater performed there. The Wheatsheaf closed around 1780.

We now head down Abbeygate Street, originally known as Lear Lane. Around 1777, it was renamed Abbey Lane, and received its present name in the nineteenth century. Lear was an Old English word meaning empty or barren, which suggests that the land was unproductive. The side entrance to Marks & Spencer's stands where St James's Street South once branched off Abbeygate Street. St James's Street South ran through to New Orchard Street and Philip Street, and consisted of 26 large houses, mostly built in the 1740s.

The Talbot, later renamed the Painter's Arms, stood on the corner of Abbeygate Street and St James's Street South.

On the western corner of Abbeygate Street and St James's Street South stood the **Talbot**, which may have dated from 1620, when Sir Giles Mompesson issued a licence for an inn of that name. It was a timber-framed building which Major Davis believed was built by the Abbey around 1500.

In 1762, James Atwood, a brassmaker, whose workshop was next door, leased the Talbot from the Corporation. In 1763 he advertised for a tenant:

> To be lett, a very good-accustom'd house known by the sign of the Talbot in St James' Street, Bath, with the stock of beer, consisting of between 30 and 40 hogsheads, all entire sound and good, together with the horses, vessels and brewing utensils; also the boxes and tables, copper sign and sign iron; with some other fixtures.

In 1796, it was advertised for sale as "that desirable public house, the Talbot, comprising two commodious dwelling houses in St James's Street and Abbey Lane, now in full business and in the occupation of William Tucker."

The Talbot seems to have had close links with the Raven a few yards away in Abbey Green. In 1806, for example, Arthur Cook, the landlord of the Talbot, moved to the Raven. Twenty-six years earlier, in 1780, Thomas Bell had also moved from the Talbot to the Raven, but he caused what must have been no end of confusion by renaming it – temporarily – the Talbot & Raven.

The Talbot was renamed the Painter's Arms in the early 1840s. It survived until 1851, when William Titley took the lease, together with that of "the house in the rear," a "salt house at 8 Abbeygate Street," and an adjoining salt refinery, "on the understanding that the old buildings are to be forthwith taken down and rebuilt."

On the north side of Abbeygate Street was a "messuage or tenement called or known by the name of the **Nag's Head**," which closed around 1780.

There was also a **Chequers** in Abbeygate Street, which closed around 1782.

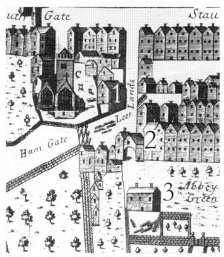

Abbeygate Street in 1694, showing: 1) the Talbot; 2) the Abbey gateway; 3) the Raven.

Before the redevelopment of the area in the 1740s, the Abbey gateway straddled Lear Lane just beyond its junction with St James's Street South. After the dissolution of the Abbey, John Hall of Bradford-on-Avon acquired part of the land inside the gate. In 1620, he granted a building lease to Edward Byam. In 1631 or 1632, Byam increased the size of his plot, and built Nos 5 & 6 Abbey Green (now 5 Abbey Green and 7-8 Abbeygate Street, the former NSJ Levi Store and Evans' Fish Restaurant). The south wall of the building incorporated an old boundary wall which can still be seen in the alley beside Marks & Spencer's.

This was the **Raven**, which may have been a pub from the start, although the first reference to it comes no earlier than 1759. In July 1778, it was advertised for sale as an "inn or public house called the Raven … with convenient stables [and] a remarkably healthy cellar room, sufficient to contain one hundred butts of beer." The Raven also claimed to have the best private clubroom in Bath; among the clubs that met there were a friendly society and a catch club.

The Raven, later the Freemason's Tavern, was built in the 1630s.

Although a raven appears in several coats of arms, it is believed that the sign of a raven in the eighteenth century indicated Jacobite sympathies. In the late eighteenth century, the Raven had a variety of names, including the Druids' Head and the Bladud's Head. In 1812, the Sussex Masonic Lodge started holding their meetings at what was then known as the Bladud's Head, prompting the landlord, John Purnell, to change its name once again, to the Freemasons' Arms.

In 1832, Charles Gear took over the Freemasons' Arms and embarked on a full-scale refurbishment, including the installation of the large round-headed windows on the first floor. He renamed it the Freemasons' Tavern and announced its relaunch in the *Bath Chronicle* on 15 March 1832:

Charles Gear respectfully informs his friends and the public that he has, at considerable expense, fitted up the above house with a view to the comfort and accommodation of those who favour him with their company, and he intends to supply a good article on reasonable terms. Steaks, chops, etc. at the shortest notice ... Old wines and spirits, London and Bath papers daily.

Five months later, however, another advertisement appeared in the *Chronicle*, announcing an auction of the tavern's contents. The following March, Mr Gear received a letter:

Take notice that I have this day, by virtue of the warrant from Mr Orchard yr. landlord taken and distrained the several goods and chattels mentioned in the inventory hereunder written and impounded them in the premises for the sum of £30 arrears of rent of the house you rent of him situate in the Abbey Green in the City of Bath and known by the name of the Freemasons' Tavern:

Kitchen: fender & irons, 4 saucepans, pot, kettle, plate rack, frying pan, gridiron, 3 chairs, candlesticks, warming pan, 2 dish covers, lot of ware;

Garret No 1: Bedstead, bed & bedding;

Garret No 2: 2 bedsteads, 1 bed & bolster, 2 blankets & quilts;

Attic no 1: Field bedstead, bed & bolster, bedding, basin, stand & ewer;

Attic No 2: 4 best bedsteads of furniture, feather bed & bolster, lot of bedding, basin & stand, basin & ewer table, chest of drawers, 6 carpets;

Drawing Room: Bagatelle board & balls, 6 tables, 6 chairs, 7 stools, lamp, 3 blinds, sundries;

Parlour: 4 tables, 2 blinds;

Bar: 6 spirit cocks, beer engine, 35 beer measures, 2 sets spirit ditto, 40 various glasses, 6 bottles, teaware, 6 stools, counter, 2 tables, glass, fender, irons, 9 beer cans, sundry fixtures;

Tap Room: 4 tables, 2 stools, fender;

Cellar & stable: 7 casks, beer pulley, pony & harness.

After Mr Gear left, the Freemasons' Tavern went downhill fast. By 1851 it was one of seven pubs in Bath which the police wanted closed, on the grounds that the "keepers of these houses, after repeated cautions, had some of them kept open their houses on Sunday mornings, and others allowed prostitutes and other bad characters to resort to them." Despite this, it soldiered on till 1911. The 1903 report on its facilities, however, suggests that they left a lot to be desired. There was a urinal in the corner of the yard, without a flush, which was described, with a degree of understatement, as "unsatisfactory."

The large room on the first floor, looking down Abbeygate Street, was remodelled in 1832 when the Raven became the Freemason's Tavern. It is seen here in the 1950s when the building was taken over by Evans' Fish Restaurant.

In 1912 the Freemasons' Tavern was advertised for sale as "a public house, now unlicensed, at 6 Abbey Green, a

THE LOST PUBS OF BATH

The north side of the Raven looked onto Abbey Green. The gateway dates from 1973.

messuage, tenement and stable used as a brewery, and a yard." It was bought by Arthur Evans and turned into a hostel for girls of slender means and a temperance restaurant called the Abbeygate Tavern. The part of the building fronting Abbeygate Street later became Evans' Fish Restaurant; in July 2005, Black's camping and outdoor store moved into the building. The archway leading into Abbey Green from Abbeygate Street, incidentally, which reinforces the impression that the former Freemasons' Tavern is two separate buildings, only dates from 1973.

In 1789, Thomas Farmer opened the **London Inn & Tavern** on Abbey Green. Three years later, in November 1792, it was taken over by John Thomas, before disappearing from the records. There is no clue as to its exact location, although it may have reopened around 1851 as the Crystal Palace.

Lilliput Alley, leading off Abbey Green, was originally known as Segar's Alley, then as Evelyn Street, and there was once an attempt to call it Abbey Green Street. Today it is officially called North Parade Passage, although, not surprisingly, most people prefer to call it Lilliput Alley. The history of the range of buildings on its northern side is no less complicated. For a start, the level of the pavement is much higher than it was originally – so much so, in fact, that what is now the ground floor of the houses on the north side was once the first floor. What is more, they were once the other way round – or,

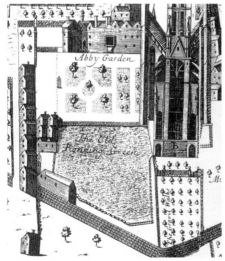

The houses in Lilliput Alley (on the extreme left) were built around 1622. They looked over a bowling green bounded by the city wall.

to be more precise, their back entrances were once their front entrances. It is hard to imagine, picking our way down the grubby alley at the side of the Huntsman, that this was once the front way into Sally Lunn's and the buildings either side, but one look at the architectural embellishments and ashlar blocks on this side (in contrast to the rubble stone on the other) should convince us. And, if more evidence is needed, it is provided by early maps, which show these buildings looking out across a bowling green to the Orange Grove.

Sally Lunn's has never been, as far as we know, a pub, but it once had pubs on either side of it. Before looking at them, however, a word of caution to those who may be tempted to go to the pub after visiting Sally Lunn's. The following report comes from the *Gentleman's Magazine* in 1752:

> William Chiseldon, Esq., an eminent anatomist, lithotomist, and surgeon to the Royal Hospital at Chelsea; [died on April 11] at Bath. He had drunk ale after eating hot buns, upon which being very uneasy, he sent for a physician, who advised vomiting immediately, which advice, had it been taken, might, it is thought, have saved his life.*

The King's Arms in Lilliput Alley, after closure but before the present ground-floor windows were added.

These hot buns were not known as Sally Lunn's until the 1770s, when a pastrycook called Sally Lunn came down from Yorkshire and took over the franchise for what, until then, had been known as Spring Garden Rolls.† Spring Gardens, on the far side of the river, was owned by the same consortium that owned the Parade Coffee House (now the Huntsman pub); the bakery behind the coffee house where the buns were made is now Sally Lunn's restaurant.

To the left of Sally Lunns', was the **King's Head** at 3 Lilliput Alley. Built around 1622, and known as Blanchard's Tenement, it was first recorded as a pub in 1779, when it was known as the Crown. It became the King's Head in 1786 and was acquired by the Northgate Brewery in the 1790s. Sometime during the eighteenth century – possibly when

---

*Lest this be thought a singular occurrence or occasioned by a surfeit of ale, the reader is referred to an obituary in the *Gentleman's Magazine* for October 1742, in which the sudden death of Ralph Thicknesse was attributed to "eating a hearty breakfast of spongy rolls" after imbibing liberally of the Bath waters. His memorial can be seen in the Abbey. Years later, in 1780, his brother, Philip Thicknesse, published a *Valetudinarian's Bath Guide*, in which he warned his readers against the habit of invalids who "first drink three pints or a quart of Bath Waters, and then sit down to a meal of Sally Lunns, or hot spongy rolls, rendered high by burnt butter. I have known and seen it produce almost instantaneous death to valetudinarians." This is one of the earliest instances of the rolls being described as Sally Lunns.

†The confusion over Sally Lunn's nationality seems to have come about because a nineteenth century writer, denying the existence of Sally Lunn, came up with the bizarre theory that the buns were originally called *Soleil-lunes* (Sun-moons), in the same way that croissants got their name because they were crescent shaped. Quite apart from the fact that Sally Lunn was a real person, this theory falls down because of the lack of any similarity between the buns and either of the celestial orbs alluded to. A further point is that the surname Lunn is of Scandinavian origin; there are thousands of Lunns in Yorkshire and those parts of England settled by Scandinavians in the centuries before the Norman Conquest, but remarkably few in France.

THE LOST PUBS OF BATH

Left Gallaway's Buildings, built around 1749.
Above The blocked-up archway leading through to the Pineapple on Old Orchard Street.

it became a pub – it was refronted in a curious mixture of ashlar and rubble stone. It closed in 1906, and today the building is occupied by Tilley's Bistro and a tailor's. The shop windows on the ground floor were added after it closed as a pub.

On the other side of Sally Lunn's was the Star & Garter, which now forms part of the Huntsman, and features in *Bath Pubs*.

Gallaway's Buildings (or North Parade Buildings), which lead off Lilliput Alley, were built, probably by Thomas Jelly, for an apothecary called William Gallaway around 1749. Orchard Street (or Old Orchard Street as it is now known) was built at the same time. A blocked-up archway at the end of Gallaway's Buildings once led through to a pub called the Pineapple, which we will visit in the eighth excursion.

In 1785 John Wicksteed, from the Bagatelle Pleasure Gardens at Lyncombe, opened a shop in Gallaway's Buildings selling engraved seals. Around the same time, the ultra-fashionable Mrs Delaney took lodgings here. But, perhaps because of its proximity to some rather dubious streets, by the early nineteenth century Gallaway's Buildings had been abandoned by fashionable society. A report from 1845 concluded that they were "occupied almost entirely by poor. The dwellings are very crowded with inmates." At No 3, for example, lived a "vendor of watercress," whom we know about only because he fell down the stairs when drunk and made it to the pages of the *Bath Chronicle*. In 1852, a 16 year-old boy from Gallaway's Buildings called Charles Lane was sentenced to seven years transportation for stealing a purse from a lady in a railway carriage. Respectable it wasn't. Which is why, for a brief period in the mid-nineteenth century, there were three beerhouses there.

In the late 1840s, Richard Avery opened the **Waterloo** beerhouse at 2 Gallaway's Buildings. In May 1847, he was fined for serving after hours and "allowing a riotous disturbance to take place in his house." It closed shortly afterwards.

At around the same time, James Parfitt opened a beerhouse called the **Woodman** at 9 Gallaway's Buildings. This too lasted for no more than a couple of years.

The lost pubs of Gallaway's Buildings: the Waterloo at No 2; the Woodman at No 9; the Queen's Arms at No 4.

The third beerhouse in Gallaway's Buildings was more of a survivor, although it was open for less than 30 years. The **Queen's Arms** at No 4 was opened around 1833 by Hezekiah Hawkins, and renamed the Sterling Tavern around 1848. In July 1851, the licensee, Richard Melhuish, was charged with serving after 11pm. He excused himself by pointing out that it was the day after the election. The excuse was, needless to say, not accepted. The Sterling Tavern closed in the 1860s.

The North Parade Tavern.

Gallaway's Buildings remained publess for a few years until, in the early 1870s, the **North Parade Tavern** opened at No 10. Its name reflected Gallaway's Buildings' change of name to North Parade Buildings – an attempt, perhaps, to get rid of the insalubrious connotations of the old name.

The bar of the North Parade Tavern was divided into three rooms – bar, bar parlour and tap – with a brewery at the back. There were two front entrances and a back exit through the brewery into Lilliput Alley. By 1903, its name had changed to the North Parade Brewery and it supplied beer to the Chandos Arms in Westgate Buildings and the Three Crowns in London Street. In 1912, William Shackell, the landlord of the North Parade Brewery, took over the Barley Mow in Bathwick Street. The North Parade Brewery closed in 1923 and became a Salvation Army Hostel. Today it is an apartment block known as Hamilton House. The round-arched windows to the right of the front door – out of keeping with the rest of the building – are almost certainly a legacy of its conversion to a pub in the 1870s.

We now head east along Lilliput Alley, turn left past the Huntsman – originally the Parade Coffee House and later a wine merchant's – to the Orange Grove. Today, dominated by the Empire Hotel, Orange Grove seems unsure whether it wants to be a traffic island or a coach park. It was not always so. Originally the litten or graveyard of the Abbey, it appears on Gilmore's map of 1694 as Miter [Mitre] Green, with a single building nestling against the city walls. This was erected by Walter Werratt around 1648 and may have been a tavern. Although its name is not recorded, a

THE LOST PUBS OF BATH

The Huntsman, built as a coffee house in the 1740s, later became the Institution Wine Vaults.

likely candidate would be the Mitre, a popular name for taverns connected with cathedrals in other cities. The building disappeared when Orange Court was built around 1740.

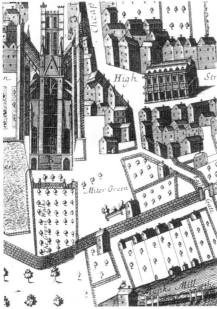

Miter – or Mitre – Green later became the Orange Grove. The building in one corner, hard against the city walls, may have been a tavern.

In the early eighteenth century the Grove was laid out with gravelled walks and planted with sycamore trees. By 1730 these had grown so big that "many people were obliged to dine by candlelight at four o'clock in the afternoon in the month of May." Another problem was rooks, which found the sycamores ideal for nesting in, and created the same sort of aerial inconvenience that seagulls do today. So the sycamores went – to be replaced, not with orange trees, but with elms. The Grove was renamed the Orange Grove in 1734 to commemorate the visit of the Prince of Orange to Bath. Beau Nash commissioned John Wood to erect an obelisk to record the visit and ensure that nobody started making up fanciful stories about orange trees.

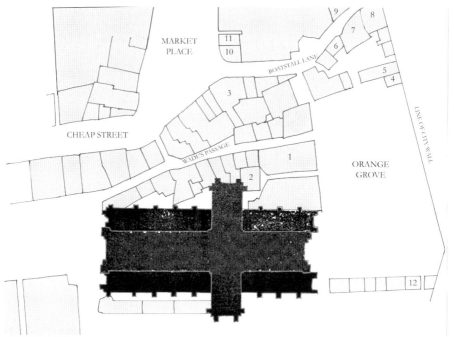

Inns and taverns north of the Abbey in the seventeenth and eighteenth centuries included: 1) Morgan's Coffee House; 2) Sot's Hole or the Ring of Bells; 3) the Cross Keys; 4) the Mitre (?); 5) the Sun (18th century); 6) Old Tumble Down Dick; 7) the Butcher's Arms; 8) the Grove Tavern; 9) the Beefsteak Tavern; 10) the Horse's Head; 11) the Sun (17th century);12) the King's Arms.

The Orange Grove gradually acquired a coffee house, elegant lodgings and upmarket shops. Not that it was without its problems. John Wood later recalled that "the ground on the east side of the Grove ... then lay in two levels, with steps to rise from one to the other ... It was, in effect, the common jakes for the rabble of the whole city; the better sort retiring, at the same time, to one publick lay-stall on the north side of the Grove, and to another on the west side of the same area. Of such little value was the land in this part of Bath in those days." John Wood set to work improving the area, and by the 1740s the Orange Grove was one of the most fashionable places in the city. The development of the Circus, however, was instrumental in shifting the fashionable centre of Bath north-westward, and by the early nineteenth century, the Orange Grove had definitely seen better days. In 1819, Pierce Egan declared that the houses in Orange Grove "are irregularly built, but notwithstanding this defect, it is a pleasant, though not an elegant, residence."

As well as shops and lodging houses, the Orange Grove had a numbers of inns and taverns, ranging from the upmarket to the down at heel. Today, all that is left of eighteenth-century Orange Grove is the row of shops on the south side, built around 1724 and savagely refronted in the late nineteenth century. So our stroll around this area must perforce be an imaginary one. But, as you lean against the wall above Parade Gardens, trying to summon up the glory that was the Orange Grove, just remember, before clipping on your rose-tinted pince-nez, that the manicured lawns and dazzling flower beds below you were once a vast open-air karsey.

For a brief period in the mid-eighteenth century, the building that now houses Aqua Glass, on the corner of Orange Grove and Terrace Walk, was an inn called the **King's Arms**. At the time there was another building to the east, built up against the city walls, with an alleyway between it and the King's Arms.

Our next pub requires more than a little imagination. Remember the cluster of buildings up against the walls of the Abbey? You've guessed it – one of them was a pub. It was the tap for a coffee house, built by a member of the Sheyler family in 1718 and enlarged three or four years later. In 1724, when Robert Whatley visited the coffee house, he found "a fine spacious room for the gentlemen to meet in, to converse together, and to read the advices of the *Times*, which was provided there for their entertainment." In 1731, it was taken over by Charles Morgan, who was related to the Sheylers, and was thereafter known as **Morgan's Coffee House**. Its social exclusivity was ensured by a subscription system. By the 1740s it had up to 400 subscribers a season. Viscount Percival, who used it during a visit to Bath in 1730, noted that the other subscribers included the Speaker of the House of Commons, a High Court judge, and the Dean of Exeter. Around 1793, it was renamed the Grove Coffee House. It closed around 1818 and was converted into three shops.

Its location can be seen on the map opposite. A narrow alleyway separated it from another building to the south, which abutted the Abbey. This was built by William Collibee as a private house around 1718, and later became the home of Lord Hawley. Later still it was converted into two shops. At the end of the alleyway between the two houses was the tap for the coffee house, known as Sot's Hole or the **Ring of Bells**.

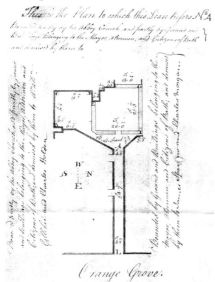

A plan drawn by Thomas Baldwin, the City Architect, showing the Ring of Bells built against the walls of the Abbey, with the alleyway leading from the Orange Grove, and Morgan's Coffee House on the right.

If you had walked the 50 feet or so down the alley, you would have ended up in a small courtyard, hemmed in by high walls, facing the Ring of Bells, twenty-six feet square and nestling against the buttresses of the Abbey. The first record we have of it comes from 1747, but it probably opened at the same time as the coffee house. In 1780, John Whittaker, a victualler, leased it from the Corporation, together with a plot of "void ground." In 1796, a perfumier called John Carsley took the lease. After his death in 1815, his widow, Hannah, continued to run it as a pub until 1822, when the Corporation paid her £500 for the lease. The following year, they awarded the tender for "the removal of … the Ring of Bells" and the adjacent building to Abraham Fisher.

Looking down the Market Place towards the Abbey in the late eighteenth century. The original Cross Keys, with bay windows on the first and second floors, is on the far left.

No sooner had the pub disappeared than the churchwardens from the Abbey approached the council, "requesting to know the terms upon which [they] would dispose of a plot of ground in Orange Grove whereon on the Ring of Bells and Mr Webster's house lately stood, to be used as a place of internment." Fortunately, the council declared that they had no intention of letting the ground be used for such a purpose.

Although the Ring of Bells disappeared almost two centuries ago, it has left one ghostly reminder of its existence behind – a diagonal roofmark high on one of the buttresses of the Abbey.

Our next pub stood just south of where the southern extension of the Guildhall stands today. The **Cross Keys**, its name a reference to the emblem of St Peter, probably opened around 1724, when it was leased to two maltsters called John and William Hayward. They installed David Lewis as their tenant. By 1754, the leaseholder was a victualler called Thomas Bishop. Around 1792, the Cross Keys was taken over by Sainsbury's Brewery.

In 1780, crowds flocked to the Cross Keys to see a monkey that could sit in a chair and drink out of a bottle. As performing animals go, it was hardly even in the PG Tips league. Still, if you had not seen a monkey before, it might have had some novelty value.

In the early nineteenth century, the Cross Keys was "the recognised house of the guardians of the peace, for here they sat and talked over the matters of the day, under the refreshing influence of a long churchwarden and a glass of grog." One of the Cross Keys' regulars in the closing years of the coaching era has left us this reminiscence of what it was like:

THE LOST PUBS OF BATH

When Mrs Brittan went to the Cross Keys ... she gave up the large room on the first floor to a number of tradesmen who met there every night to smoke their pipes and drink their – well, it was chiefly beer in metal cups – I think many were silver. She would get for those who wished it a nice little supper – a chop, a welsh rabbit, or a bit of pickled salmon. In 1837 I joined that party – the youngest therein. I forget the names of most of them, but I remember Mumford and Baily, Salmoni, Simms, Harman. Harman was usually the chairman. The *Times* then came in at eight o'clock in the evening; it was handed to him and he read out any important news for the benefit of the company. Harman was a saddler, his house was immediately in front of St James's Church facing the Borough Walls, and by the side of the house was the stocks.

The Cross Keys had a downstairs bar as well, where the customers were somewhat less upstanding. So far from the straight and narrow were they, in fact, that, in 1828, Robert Peel, the Home Secretary, wrote to the Mayor of Bath asking him to investigate complaints he had received about the goings on there. As the lease of the inn was held by the Sainsburys (who had friends in high places), the Mayor fended off the enquiry and the Cross Keys stayed open.

As early as 1819, the council had resolved that the houses between the Abbey and the Market Place should come down, and notice was given "to the several lessees" that the houses were to be removed. Fourteen years later, however, the Cross Keys was still there. Although its days were clearly numbered, the Sainsburys were not going to let it go without a fight. A report in June 1833 declared that

> the Cross Keys Public House with an adjoining shop occupied by P Ferbrache, hairdresser, and a tenement behind occupied by Mr Scovell belonging to Mrs Sainsbury [has been] lately issued to Messrs Sainsbury, Brewers, for a term of 21 years at £200 per annum. They require for the leasehold interest of all parties the sum of £3,000, and will accept a lease of the Beefsteak House adjoining the market for a term of 21 years at £70 per annum.

In November, there was a further report:

> The Committee appointed ... for the purpose of treating and concluding with the owners and occupiers of houses at the bottom of the Market Place for the purchase of the same with a view to their removal, report that they have encountered great difficulties in effecting arrangements with Mrs Sainsbury, the lessee, under this Corporation, of the Cross Keys Public House, and an adjoining tenement in the occupation of P Ferbrache; also with Messrs JPG and C Sainsbury, her sub-lessees, principally on account of their inability to procure an eligible situation for the continuance of the business. The committee have however lately received a proposal from them for the payment to Mrs Sainsbury of the sum of £4,000 for the Cross Keys and the adjoining tenement ... on condition that the tenants may be allowed to remove the whole of the materials of the buildings; and that the Corporation will grant to Messrs JPG and C Sainsbury ... a lease of the buildings immediately behind and adjoining the house occupied by Mr Munday at the corner of the Orange Grove, including the eating house in the occupation

of Mr Prangley which they purpose removing and erecting a public house on the site thereof ... with liberty also to make the necessary cellarage in Boatstall Lane and in the Grove.

A month later the council offered Sainsbury's a "plot of ground on the north side of the Orange Grove ... to erect a substantial stone and timber messuage to be called the Cross Keys." The new inn opened the following year.

In 1866, the "guardians of the peace" got their own brand-new purpose-built police station next door to the new Cross Keys. In the 1870s, a new fire station was built behind the police station, and, as access to it was needed from the Orange Grove, the new Cross Keys followed its predecessor into oblivion, after less than 50

The Orange Grove in the 1860s, with the second Cross Keys and the Abbey Hotel on the right.

THE LOST PUBS OF BATH

Pubs around Orange Court in the late nineteenth century included: 1) the Beefsteak Tavern; 2) the new Cross Keys; 3) the Grove Tavern; 4) the Newmarket Tavern; 5) the Rummer; 6) the Sun.

The Sun stood beside the archway leading to Orange Court. The sign of the Cross Keys was moved to the Sun when it was demolished in the 1870s.

years. The sign of the Cross Keys, which had moved with the inn, was moved one last time, to the Sun in Orange Court, where it stayed until that too was demolished. The archway on the site of the Cross Keys, that led to the fire station, is still there, although the fire station moved out to Bathwick years ago. The police station, which closed in 1966, is now Brown's Restaurant.

Wade's Passage was a narrow alleyway, named after Field-Marshal Wade, MP for Bath, that led from the Abbey Church Yard to the Orange Grove. In May 1754, "a house in Wade's Passage, now in the possession of William Cabbell, and known by the Sign of the **Chair**," was advertised to let. It was suitable, the advertisement continued, "either for a Publick House, a Shop or a Private house, as it may suit." Although there is no further record of it, it is possible, especially given its name, that it was a pub catering for sedan chairmen prior to 1754.

The Empire Hotel, built around 1900, ceased being a hotel when the Admiralty requisitioned it in the Second World War. Today it is divided into retirement flats and the closest it has to a bar is Garfunkel's (named, so it is said, after the nearby bridge over troubled water). Many people will remember when what is now Caffé Uno housed the **Empire Bars**. In 1976 Fred Pearce found them "very spacious and well carpeted [with] rich wood panelling (note especially the Gents loo door). The long green bench sofa at the far end is especially fine … Mirrors, small chandeliers and big rather bad paintings help make it rather like a superior station bar."

The Empire stands on the site of four lost pubs – the Sun, the Old Tumble Down Dick, the Butcher's Arms, and the Grove. The **Sun** was first recorded in 1776, but may have opened at the beginning of the eighteenth century when the Sun in the Market Place became a private house. In 1815, when it was acquired by Oakhill Brewery, it was described as "a messuage, etc., on the east side of Orange Court, next to Lot Lane, with the arched way over Lot Lane leading to Orange Court." It closed in 1900, when it was pulled down to make way for the Empire.

At the back of the Sun, in Orange Court, was the **Old Tumble Down Dick**. It was named after Oliver Cromwell's son, Richard, who became Lord Protector after his father's death, but resigned in 1659. Old Tumble Down Dick was one of the kinder epithets applied to him. It is said that the use of dick as a term of abuse dates from this time. There are still pubs called the Tumble Down Dick in Camberley and Farnborough. It is possible that Bath's Tumble Down Dick was so called because Richard Cromwell stayed there when it was a lodging house run by Henry Chapman, the landlord of the Sun in the Market Place. According to Mr S Sydenham, "it is evident … that in 1658 the Lord Protector Richard Cromwell spent some considerable time in Bath and was in favour with its citizens. It is not improbable that he lodged at one of Chapman's houses, perhaps at his tavern the "Sunne" and that, as many another Royalist of the time, Chapman was attracted to and supported the authority of Richard Cromwell." The Old Tumble Down Dick closed around 1786.

Although there is no trace of the Old Tumble Down Dick, the remains of the pub that stood next to it can be seen just above the old East Gate. The East Gate was a lot or postern gate, and stayed open at night, except in times of war, to allow benighted travellers to enter the city. Boatstall Lane, the silent, padlocked alleyway that leads through it, was once a hive of activity. Until Pulteney Bridge was built in the early 1770s, Boatstall Lane turned left where it met the river and ran along a narrow quay until it met Slippery Lane, that dingy remnant of old Bath that dives down off Northgate Street and now leads only to a locked door.

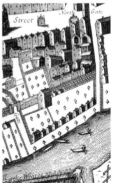

The East Gate as it looked in the late nineteenth century …

… and as it looks today. The Butcher's Arms was on the extreme right.

Boatstall and Slippery Lanes in 1694.

THE LOST PUBS OF BATH

LOT 3.—The Well-situated HOUSE, known as
THE BUTCHERS' ARMS,

Formerly called the "RED COW," advantageously placed close at the back of the Market, at the top of Boat Stall Lane, now let to Mr. BRACHER, as Yearly Tenant, at the low Rent of £20 per Annum; consisting of a Bar, with a glazed Shop Front, Parlour, and Tap-Room, front Sitting-Room, and four Bedrooms, with Kitchen, Scullery, and Cellarage.
Held under the Corporation of Bath for Two Lives, (which are renewable,) aged 62 and 24 Years, and subject to a Quit Rent of £1 14s.

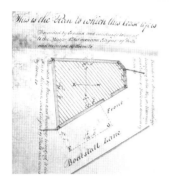

Above An auction notice from 1849.
Left A plan of the Butcher's Arms in 1827.

The **Butcher's Arms**, whose blocked-up doorway can be seen in the wall just inside the East Gate on the right-hand side, was one of the oldest pubs in the area. Around 1822, it was taken over by Williams' Brewery who changed its name to the Red Cow. The change did not last long, for in 1849 it was advertised for sale as "that well-situated House, known as the Butcher's Arms, formerly called the Red Cow, advantageously placed close at the back of the Market, at the top of Boatstall Lane, now let to Mr Bracher, as Yearly Tenant, at the low rent of £20 per annum, for nearly 20 years; consisting of a bar, with a glazed shop front, parlour and tap-room, front sitting-room, and four bedrooms, with kitchen, scullery and cellarage." It closed a few years later.

A newspaper report from September 1824 indicates that there was a pub beyond the east gate:

> At the east gate of this city, the only one now standing, leading to Monk's Mill, stood a priory with its gate, which a few years ago was occupied as a public-house. It was lately purchased by John Tiler, of the Beefsteak Tavern, and taken down, and on its site were found some human bones, together with a glass vessel beautifully ornamented and many hundreds of Roman coins.

The Grove Tavern from Orange Court – demolished, like the Sun, to make way for the Empire.

Above Boatstall Lane, to the south, was the **Grove Tavern**. Built in the 1730s as a house for Mary Chandler, a prosperous milliner, it became a tavern after her death. Its full story can be found on pages 158-59 of *Bath Pubs*. On the north side of Boatstall Lane is Newmarket Row, formed when the new market was built on a terrace high above the river in the 1770s. There were three pubs in Newmarket Row: one still open, one a restaurant, the third demolished.

At the top of Newmarket Row was the **Beefsteak Tavern**. Although the

Richard Miles Lovett, landlord of the Beefsteak Tavern, holding the pub cat; with him is his son, William Miles Lovett, landlord of the Turk's Head on Broad Street.

THE LOST PUBS OF BATH

The Beefsteak Tavern during celebrations to mark the laying of the foundation stone of the Guildhall extension.

Far left A loving cup, bearing the name of Richard Miles Lovett, from Curtis's china merchant's at 30 Westgate Street.
Left A china tankard from the Beefsteak Tavern.

The demolition of the Beefsteak Tavern in November 1947.

building has gone, its beefsteak-shaped outline, like the ghostly echo of long-lost voices, can still be seen. It consisted of a brewery, tap room (with a settle and fixed seating), bar (with pewter-topped serving counter and glazed, sliding sashes above), bar parlour (with three spittoons, two bell pulls and an oil painting) and smoking room (with fixed seating, two screen boards, painted oak-back casing and prints and engravings on the walls). In the early nineteenth century, a benefit society called the New Bath British Society met there. In the mid-nineteenth century, it was famous for its "annual cucumber and mushroom show"; Meehan, in his survey of Bath's famous inns, noted cryptically that it was also noted for "sporting incidents."

In 1908, the trustees of the Holburne Museum, then in Charlotte Street, were looking for larger premises. They considered "purchasing the buildings occupied by the Beefsteak Tavern and the Rummer" to house the collection. Eventually, however, they moved into the old Sydney Hotel. The Beefsteak closed in 1923, and stood empty until November 1947, when the following report appeared in the *Bath Chronicle*:

> The Beefsteak Tavern, the derelict inn behind the Guildhall, which is to be demolished to provide car parking space, seems to have had a history like its position – obscure. Books and old magazines studied by a member of Bath Library's staff yielded this information – Nothing definite has been found as to the exact date of construction, but Allen started building in the Orange Grove in 1727 and, as Orange Grove Court is mentioned in connection with Orange Grove building, it may be assumed that the tavern dates from the mid-eighteenth century. The inn certainly has the appearance of Georgian architecture.

For much of the twentieth century, the Rummer was known as the Grove, having taken the name of the old Grove when it was demolished in 1900. The Clifton cycle shop, next door (now Marmaris restaurant), was formerly the Newmarket Tavern.

THE LOST PUBS OF BATH

Unfortunately, Orange Court was south of the East Gate. The area north of the gate was not developed until the 1770s, so, although the Beefsteak was Georgian, it was considerably later than suggested by the *Chronicle*.

At the eastern end of Newmarket Row is the Rummer, which has been a pub since it was built. Between the Rummer and the entrance to the market was another pub – the **Newmarket Tavern**, opened around 1792. It was destroyed by fire in 1848 and rebuilt a year later. Only the left-hand side of the new building reopened as a pub; the right-hand side became a fishmonger's. The last landlord of the Newmarket Tavern was Thomas Clack, who also ran the fishmonger's next door. He closed it in 1881 and made the whole building a fishmonger's. It later became a cycle shop. Today, it is Marmaris Restaurant.

The redevelopment of the Guildhall and market area in the 1770s saw the disappearance of several pubs whose locations we can only guess at. Other buildings disappeared as well, including the medieval Guildhall, which was in a lane leading from the Market Place to the East Gate. In the early seventeenth century, a new Guildhall had been built, reputedly to a design by Inigo Jones, in the middle of the Market Place. The main body of the old Guildhall was converted into a meat market or shambles; the old council chamber became a pub called the **Jolly Butchers**. Despite its name, this was a fairly upmarket establishment. In December 1751, for example, the *Bath Journal* informed its readers that "Mr Parrot's Rock Shell Work and Fountains that are to be seen at the Jolly Butchers in the Shambles is, by desire of certain persons of quality, to continue here this week and no longer; after which it will be shown in Bristol."

A story from the *Bath Journal* of 26 September 1757, with a decidedly modern ring to it, suggests that, even then, you couldn't believe everything you read in the papers:

> In the account of the drawing of the lottery in last week's paper we made the following mistake, viz "Thursday No. 62172 was drawn a prize of £50" which should have been 62272. The number we inserted being the property of a young man of this city, he immediately went to the Jolly Butchers in the Shambles (where the correct list of prizes, publish'd by the managers, is taken in every day) in order to see if it was true, but on enquiry, had the mortification to find it a mistake.

Christmas celebrations at the Jolly Butchers were spectacular. In 1759, for example,

> the large Christmas loaf which Mr Brookman at the Jolly Butchers entertained his customers with according to annual custom, weighed above 400 pounds; was above twelve feet long, five feet and a half in circumference, two feet broad and nine inches thick.

The Felliniesque picture this conjures up, of eighteenth-century butchers sitting in a medieval hall, with candlelight flickering on the wainscoting, tucking into a twelve-foot loaf, is like a surrealist vision of Merrie England. The Jolly Butchers was pulled down in the mid-1770s.

Newmarket Row from the river before the construction of the Empire Hotel. Four pubs can be seen in this picture – the Rummer, the Newmarket Tavern, the Grove Tavern, and the Pulteney Stores on Pulteney Bridge, featured in chapter nine.

There was another pub called the **Noah's Ark** in the market area. The only clue to its location comes from John Wood, who tells us that it was off the Market Place and had a court at the back of it. In 1761, the Council ordered that "the house called the Noah's Ark ... be pulled down and the garden market placed there." It was still open in 1776, but closed and was demolished soon afterwards.

Even after the market area had been redeveloped, there were still plenty of reminders of the bad old days. In May 1781, for example, the council ordered "the use of the slaughterhouses opposite Newmarket Row to be discontinued on account of the complaints received of nuisance caused from the owners of houses in Bridge Street, Newmarket Row, Orange Court, and Orange Grove." They had strong constitutions in the eighteenth-century. For them to complain about slaughterhouses, they must have been pretty bad. Even well into the nineteenth century, the area had more than a hint of the farmyard about it. And things occasionally got out of hand. In 1824, for example, a herd of bullocks being driven to a butcher's in Boatstall Lane stampeded and charged through the Market Place before they could be rounded up.

Two hundred and fifty years ago, we could have walked down Boatstall Lane to the "boat stall," starting point for the Bathwick ferry, and wandered along the quay, past tenements of tanners and weavers, past the ancient cross where fish were sold, past the ducking stool "for the punishment of disorderly women," to find our last alehouse, the **Crown & Thistle** (closed around 1783), before turning up Slippery Lane, below the walls of the city, and come at last – by a commodious vicus of recirculation – to the North Gate and environs.

THE LOST PUBS OF BATH

EXCURSION THE SECOND

STEPPING WESTWARD

Our second excursion starts on the site of the South Gate. Rebuilt in 1326, with statues of Edward III, Bishop Ralph and Prior John in niches over the arch, it was the principal entry to the city for travellers from the south and the south west. It was also the first of Bath's city gates to be pulled down, in 1755.

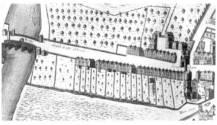

Southgate Street in 1694.

In the early eighteenth century, Southgate Street was renamed Horse Street. The name may have been chosen because, in the seventeenth century, there had been a horse bath nearby, fed by water from the hot springs. When the lower part of the street was redeveloped in the 1820s, the old name was readopted.*

In 1726, Southgate Street was devastated by a fire which destroyed most of its thatched buildings. It was rebuilt with 48 new houses. Fifty years later, in 1776, fourteen of them – almost a third – were inns or pubs. The biggest were the Golden Lion and the Exeter Inn, "at each of which," wrote Pierce Egan in 1819, "stages to London and Bristol are continually calling for passengers, and where good ordinaries are also held daily." At the beginning of the twentieth century, there were still eight pubs in Southgate Street. All have gone, along with all trace of the old Southgate Street.

Tracing the history of the pubs in Southgate Street – partly because of their number, partly because the street was renumbered at least once, and partly because no trace of the old street survives – is a complex and frustrating business. Even the large-scale 1880 Ordnance Survey map, which marks public houses, got it wrong, showing both the Golden Lion and the Exeter Inn one door further up the street than they actually were. What follows is an attempt to recreate a pub crawl down a street whose licensed history is as rich and fascinating as any in Bath, but for which we have had to rely entirely on documentary evidence and reminiscence.†

*To avoid confusion, we refer to it as Southgate Street throughout.

†Southgate Street, having been redeveloped in the 1970s, is due for redevelopment again, so that any attempt to indicate the location of lost pubs by reference to present-day landmarks will soon be overtaken by events. A few pointers have, however, been included, even though they will soon be rendered meaningless.

The Odeon is screening *The Lost Weekend* starring Ray Milland in this 1945 view of Southgate Street. Oliver's Wine Vaults is on the far right.

The same view today.

THE LOST PUBS OF BATH

On the east side of the street, the first pub we would have come to was the **Kettle & Pipes** (a reference not to domestic implements but to martial instruments – kettledrums and pipes). It was there by 1745, when the following announcement appeared in the *Bath Journal*:

> Stolen or Stray'd: A Black Horse ... from Timsbury. Give notice to the Kettle & Pipes, Horse Street.

Its name was sometimes shortened to the Kettle, sometimes to the Pipes. It was as the Kettle that it featured in an advertisement in the *Bath Journal* on 22 September 1760:

> To be sold, at the sign of the Kettle, by St James' Church, Bath, on Wednesday and Thursday next ... a large quantity of stale beer, and all sorts of brewing utensils, which will be found very reasonable.

Stale beer may sound about as saleable as a used firework, but in the eighteenth century it indicated beer that had stood long enough to clear and was free from lees. The Kettle & Pipes closed around 1793.

Just below the Kettle & Pipes, at No 4 or 5 (the numbering is not consistent) was the **Punch Bowl**, open from around 1782 to 1805.

Next door – or next door but one (again it is difficult to be sure) – was the **Oxford Stores**, at No 6. Its history encapsulates the problems of trying to trace the history of Southgate Street's pubs. It was first recorded as the Plume of Feathers on 19 August 1754, when it was announced in the *Bath Journal* that "last Thursday died Mr Richard Batchelor who kept the Plume of Feathers in Southgate Street in this city." It was still known as the Plume of Feathers when it was taken over by the Northgate Brewery in 1802.

Following Wellington's victory at Waterloo in 1815, in which General Blucher

played a decisive role, it was renamed the Blucher's Head, later shortened to the Blucher or the Blucher Inn. It was as the Blucher Inn that it appeared in a newspaper report concerning a missing coat on 2 November 1837:

> William Eyles, aged 19, who could read and write imperfectly, was charged with stealing a great coat, the property of John Shew, a fly driver, from the stables of the Blucher Inn ... After the robbery he took the coat to Mrs Litma, a dyer in Walcot Street, and wished it to be dyed a different colour.

William Eyles received two months hard labour.

Southgate Street in 1956. Curry's, formerly the Oxford Stores, is on the far right.

Around 1870 the memory of Blucher had faded somewhat and the pub was renamed the Gladstone Arms after the Liberal leader. It is astonishing how much political sensibilities have changed in the last 135 years. If you looked for a pub called the Blair Arms today you'd be out of luck: like the Saddam's Arms, it doesn't exist.

An inventory from the 1870s records that the Gladstone Arms had a bar, small parlour, tap room, skittle alley, drawing room, and six bedrooms, as well as a brewery, courtyard and stables. Around 1878 it changed its name again to become the Oxford Brewery or the Oxford Stores. The brewery closed around 1923 and the pub closed in 1927. Curry's later took over the building.

Naming pubs after political leaders such as Gladstone has fallen out of favour somewhat.

A little further down, on the west side of the street was a beerhouse called the **Silver Lion**. It opened as the Birmingham Tavern around 1833, changed its name around four years later and closed in the 1840s. If this report from 1838 is anything to go by, some of its clientele were exceedingly dubious:

> Caroline Johnson was indicted for stealing a shawl, the property of Elizabeth Keating of Monmouth Street ... It appeared Johnson slept in the same room with the prosecutor, and took the shawl from the bedroom. She afterwards went to the Silver Lion, and had some beer and gin, but not having money to pay for it got Harriet Willey to pawn it for 1/6.

The former Silver Lion is on the right of this picture. The building next to it with the elaborately painted walls was the Georgian Restaurant.

Back on the east side of the street, on the corner of Marchant's Passage, was the **Rose & Crown**, which first appeared as the Leek in a newspaper report on 5 March 1770:

> Last Monday ... Charles Jones, a labouring man of Bathwick, after carrying a truss of hay to Mr Sheppard's in Horse Street, went into the Leek public house, and after drinking a half pint of beer, complained of a pain in his stomach, and died instantly.

THE LOST PUBS OF BATH

Cater's Wine Vaults on the corner of Marchant's Passage, was the successor to the Rose & Crown.

Marchant's Passage in 1959, with the entrance to Cater's Wine Vaults indicated by the arrow above the archway.

In 1776 Martin Moger took the lease and renamed it the Leek & Crown. In 1778, Charles Dudden, a brewer from Warminster, acquired a cellar in the Ambury, and placed an advertisement in the *Bath Chronicle* announcing that his stock of strong beer could be tasted at the Leek & Crown. In 1801, Martin Moger changed the pub's name once again – to the Crown & Leek. Then, in what can only be described as a process of renaming by stealth, it became the Rose & Crown. But renaming is only part of the story.

Behind the Leek, in Marchant's Passage, was another pub called the Three Tuns & Crown, first recorded in 1776 with Samuel Jones as the licensee. By 1809, the licences of both pubs were held by Betty Russell. A couple of years later, the Three Tuns & Crown disappeared from the licensing records, and the two pubs were amalgamated as the Rose & Crown. The new Rose & Crown survived until 1875, when the renewal of the licence was refused. The contents, such as they were, were acquired by George Falkner, who owned a wine merchant's next door, for £34. The wine merchant's was later taken over by Cater, Stofell & Fortt, the entrance to whose wine vaults was in Marchant's Passage.*

A couple of doors along was the **Golden Lion Inn** at No 10. This opened sometime before 1776 and was rebuilt and set back between 1803 and 1806. It extended back over 130 feet and its stableyard looked over Ham Meadows.

An inventory prepared in 1885 shows it to have been an impressive establishment. In the inn was a tap room,

*The present Marchant's Passage is some way further down the street than the old one.

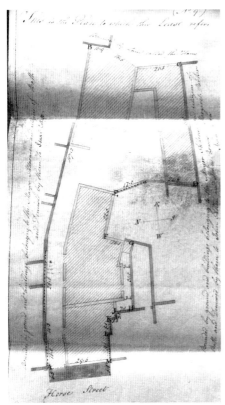

A plan of the Golden Lion from 1803 shows how far it extended back from the street.

The Golden Lion closed in 1923 and became Greig's grocer's.

bar parlour, bar, ten bedrooms, a small front drawing room (with turkey carpet and sofa), and a splendidly-appointed large drawing room, whose decorations included a japanned coal box, morocco-leather chairs, a rosewood chiffonier with a marble top, a glass epergne and inkstand, numerous ornaments and framed engravings including "The Dawn of Love," "The Blind Fiddler" and "Blind Man's Buff."

At the back of the inn was a brewery, cooperage and hop room, a harness room, an ostlers' lock-up, a three-stall stable, a seven-stall stable with loft, a fourteen-stall stable, a coach house with loft (containing a quantity of loose bedding for stable-hands), a pigeon house and a "fowl house fitted on beams." In the yard was a pump for draining the cellar in the event of flooding and a free-standing "spirit room" with a few chairs, and flags and pictures on the walls.

The Golden Lion closed in 1923 and the building later became Greig's Grocer's.

Over the road, where HSBC stands today, was the **New Inn**. Until the 1930s, Corn Street ran through to Southgate Street, and the New Inn stood on its northern corner. As part of the Forum redevelopment, the section of Corn Street between St James's Parade and Southgate Street was infilled. Although the buildings erected at the time have been demolished, the layout has survived.

William Taylor opened the New Inn as the Jolly Skinner in 1777 and renamed it the Jolly Taylor a year later. When Uriah Langley took over in 1782, he renamed

FREAK PIG- (Lived 12 Hours.) One of 11 farrowed at Mr. EMERY'S farm, Midsomer Norton, Som. Owned by Mr. GEO FEREBEE, NEW INN, SOUTHGATE ST. BATH,

A photograph of the original New Inn, taken in the 1850s.

George Ferebee, who kept the New Inn in the early 1900s, not only put this curious object on display; he featured it on a postcard.

it the Jolly Sailor, before changing his mind and calling it the New Inn in 1785. An advertisement from 1834 gives an idea of the facilities on offer:

> Families supplied with hay, corn and straw on the most reasonable terms. A constant supply of genuine Somersetshire Cider.

One hopes that the hay, corn and straw were not for sleeping on, but, with a constant supply of cider on tap, who knows? The only consolation would have been that, after drinking the cider, you would not have noticed.

Cider was still being made at the New Inn in 1885, when an inventory of the property listed a cider house in the yard. It also had five bedrooms, sitting room, bar, tap room, smoking room, skittle alley and saddle room in the yard.

The New Inn was pulled down and rebuilt in 1896-97. The new New Inn had one large bar divided into several compartments, one of which was used for lunches. When the eastern end of Corn Street was blocked off in the 1930s, Membery's Ironmonger's expanded into a new building to the south of the New Inn. The south-facing windows of the inn were blocked up.

On 1 September 1962, it was announced that

> the New Inn, Southgate Street is to be demolished if Bath City Council agree to proposals submitted by George's Brewery. A spokesman for the company said on Thursday, "we are considering redevelopment of the New Inn as two shops with offices over, and, to this effect, planning application has been made to Bath Corporation ... The New Inn was acquired by George's in 1923 from the old Bath Brewery and the public house has now a skittle alley which is the "home ground" of nine teams in the city. The landlord of the New Inn for the past six years, Mr Stanley George Maguire, is leaving the licensing trade.

Permission was granted and the New Inn was demolished the following year.

The New Inn as rebuilt in the 1890s. The similarities to the Old Farmhouse on Landsown Road, rebuilt at around the same time, are striking.

THE LOST PUBS OF BATH

Southgate Street under water in the early 1920s, showing the Picturedrome (later the Odeon) and Oliver's Wine Vaults.

On the southern corner of Southgate Street and Corn Street was a Post Office. Next to it was the **Somerset Wine Vaults**, which extended back round the Post Office to a side entrance in Corn Street. It was owned by Alderman Rubie, who also owned the Castle Inn and the Saracen's Head. It opened around 1894 and closed in 1932 when the licence was transferred to the newly-opened Englishcombe Inn. To give some idea of our bearings, McDonalds today covers both the Post Office and the Somerset Wine Vaults.

Facing the Somerset Wine Vaults was the **Exeter Inn** at 15 Southgate Street. It was first recorded in 1785 as the Chequers, and renamed the Hope & Anchor around four years later. In 1807, it was rebuilt by the Corporation and leased to the Oakhill Brewery. The lease described it as having "rooms over the gate or passage on the south side." This gate, which had a headroom of 10 feet 3 inches, led not only to the inn yard but also to tenements in Harris's Court, which bounded it on the north. It had a frontage of just over 32 feet and extended back 140 feet.

The Hope & Anchor became the Exeter Inn in 1811. An 1870 inventory listed a bar, bar parlour, sitting room, four bedrooms and a brewery. After it closed around 1911, the site was redeveloped. The left-hand side became Blacket & Baster's stationer's, the right-hand side became the Picturedrome Cinema, later the Odeon.

Behind the Exeter Inn, at the bottom of Harris's Court, was one of Southgate Street's most notorious pubs, the **Spread Eagle**, which opened around 1805. A tragic story from 1815 indicates the type of clientele it attracted. A woman named Mary Brown, who was "accustomed to being heavily intoxicated with liquor sometimes two or three times a day," turned up there one evening with a young man from the Wiltshire Militia. Although already the worse for wear, she managed to down six pints of beer, before taking him upstairs. Later she turned up in the Plume of Feathers, but

In the mid-nineteenth century, Bathe & Co ran the wine vaults later taken over by Oliver's. As this advertisement from 1858 shows, they also brewed their own beer.

Oliver's, renamed simply the Wine Vaults, in 1956.

The former Ship at 22 Southgate Street.

was so drunk she was asked to leave. At this, she became "very disorderly and abusive," and used "very improper language." She was finally removed from the premises, but that was the last time she was seen alive. Her body was later found in the river.

It is possible that Mary Brown lived in one of the 13 small tenements in Harris's Court, whose reputation was every bit as bad as that of the pub itself. The Spread Eagle was renamed the West of England in the 1840s and closed around 1852.

Next door but one to the Exeter Inn, at 17-18 Southgate Street, was **Oliver's Wine Vaults**, opened by Richard Bathe in the 1850s as the London Wine & Spirit Vaults, with a brewery and a small public bar. It was also known for a time in the late nineteenth century as Fuller's Wine Vaults. It was demolished in 1971.

Next to Oliver's, at 19 Southgate Street, was the **Bath Arms** (or the Old Bath Arms), which opened some time before 1776 and closed around 1837.

A little further down, at No 22, was the **Ship**, open by 1776, renamed the Ship & Nelson in 1805, and closed in the late 1820s.

Next door but one was the **Plough** at No 24. It first appears in a distressing report from the *Bath Journal* of 13 December 1773:

> Jane, the wife of Richard Hall, shoemaker of this city, is reduced by the most calamitous

The former Plough at 24 Southgate Street.

The Cliff View Hotel, on the corner of Southgate and Dorchester Streets, took over the upper floors of the adjoining buildings, including those of the former Plough, which can be seen on the extreme left of this picture.

circumstances to apply in this manner to the feelings of the humane. Within the space of six years she has been tapp'd for the dropsy 33 times (twice in childbed) and has been brought to bed only five weeks. Last Tuesday 20 quarts of water were taken from her, and she now lies very ill in bed, and is obliged to have a woman sit up with her all night. The water is saved for any person to see who chooses it.

She has with all these disadvantages several helpless children, which her poor husband by his wages is incapable of supporting. It is unnecessary to paint in a more lively manner their complicated distress, the sensibility of the humane will represent it.

She lodges at Mr Pitcher's at the Plough in Horse Street, where the contributions of the charitable will be received with the greatest gratitude.

In the mid-nineteenth century, the landlords of the Plough experimented with a couple of name changes – to the Nelson & Victory in the late 1840s and to the Southgate Hotel in the 1860s. By the early 1870s it was back to the Plough. The 1903 report on the property described it as having a bar divided into three compartments by partitions seven feet high, three bedrooms and an upstairs club room used by Druids. It closed in 1911 and the building became part of the Co-op. The Plough, along with the Ship, now lies under Boot's, which also covers the site of the Anchor Brewery and the South Pole pub, which was round the corner in Dorchester Street.

Before we look at the site of Southgate Street's most famous lost pub, here is a roll call of those whose exact locations are unknown:

The **Fountain** – also known as Sayce's Wine & Brandy Vaults – is listed in alehouse recognizances for 1776-80, with Samuel Sayce, of the Northgate Brewery, as licensee. All the indications are that it was a wine and spirit merchant's rather than a pub – witness this advertisement from the *Bath Chronicle* of 6 January 1778:

Sayce's Wine & Brandy Vaults
Horse Street
(opposite Bradley's Buildings).
Old Red Port, Wine, White Port, Mountain at 6/- a gallon
Madeira £1-12-0 Dozen bottles
Coniak Brandy 12/- a gallon
He begs to inform the public that his rums are really genuine
as they come from the planters, and of the finest quality,
at 10/- per gallon, or two gallons at 19/6, ready money,
in any quantity not less than one quart.
A trial may therefore be cheaply made
and the public not led away with the mistaken notion
that genuine rum is only to be purchased of
Messrs Collins, Evans, & Co.
or their country agents
as they seem to insinuate.

The **Joiner's Arms**, on the east side of Southgate Street, was open by 1745, when the following advertisement appeared in the *Bath Journal*:

> To be sold – The Joiner's Arms, situate in Horse Street, in the City of Bath, a good accustom'd inn, well tenanted, determinable on three good lives held of the Corporation. Enquire of Mr Purlewent, Attorney, or William Tucker in Abbey Church Yard.

Another announcement appeared in the *Bath Journal* in 1752:

> Stolen or strayed out of the grounds of John Tucker, between Bath and Twerton, on the 14th of this Instant October, a Brown Bay Gelding, six years old; the hair on one of his knees ruffled; a bar shoe on the off-foot before, marked with the letter T; about 15 hands high; his tail long in the dock, and nick'd. - Whoever shall give notice of the said Gelding, so that he may be had again, to John Tucker, at the Joiner's Arms Inn in Horse Street, Bath, shall receive a handsome reward, and all reasonable charges.

The Joiner's Arms, which had its own stables and brewhouse, closed around 1801.

Other Southgate Street pubs whose exact locations are not known include the **Beer Butt** (c1809-c1830), the **Coach & Horses** (c1776-c1778), the **Gardener** (c1776-c1781), the **Rummer** (c1776), and the **Still House** (c1776-c1811).

Finally, we come to one of the city's most famous lost pubs – the **Full Moon**. This stood near the Old Bridge on the site currently – but for how much longer? – occupied by Churchill House. It opened as the Gun sometime before 1703. In 1728, the year after the Avon Navigation opened, the lease was taken by Thomas Atwood, who renamed it the Ship. Around 1750, he changed its name once more, to the Full Moon. In 1770, the lease passed to his son, Thomas Warr Atwood, one of the biggest property developers in the city.

In 1791, Dr Graham from Edinburgh, presumably inspired by the legend of Bladud, turned up in Bath with what he claimed was a sure way of curing many

Above A counterpart lease of 1703 for the Gun Inn, later the Full Moon.
Left The original Full Moon can be seen in this eighteenth-century view of Broad Quay and the Old Bridge.

THE LOST PUBS OF BATH

illnesses – bathing in Bath mud. On 17 November 1791, the *Bath Chronicle* reported that,

> for the conveniency of emptying the warm Bath Water Mud Baths into the river
> every day, Dr Graham has removed his earth and mud baths from Kingston
> Buildings to ... the Full Moon in Horse Street next to the Old Bridge, where he is
> to exhibit them every day this week from 11 till 3.

Unfortunately, Bath mud seems to have lost its potency since Bladud's day, and Dr Graham soon disappeared from the scene.

The Full Moon's position made it an popular rendezvous for those trading on the river. In 1792, for example, when John Ricketts, a builder from Argyle Buildings, started running a weekly service between Bath and Bristol using a barge called the *Surprise*, he placed an announcement in the *Bath Chronicle*:

> A very sober and skilful person is engaged as master of the said vessel, who
> may be heard of at the Full Moon, Old Bridge ... where goods may be left to be
> conveyed by the said barge.

The use of the word "sober" to describe the master suggests it was a virtue that could not be taken for granted. Hardly surprising when boatmen conducted so much of their business in pubs like the Full Moon. Despite the master's capacity to resist temptation, however, Mr Ricketts' enterprise foundered when he fell victim to the slump of 1793. On 4 June 1793, another announcement appeared in the *Bath Chronicle*:

> For sale by auction, by order of the assignees of John Ricketts, bankrupt – at
> the Packhorse near the Old Bridge, two barges and an old hulk, with its inwork
> and materials, now lying under water, near the Full Moon at the Bridge Foot; the
> timbers of which would be valuable for paling in a gentleman's park or gardens.

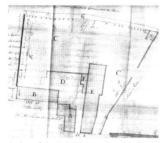

A plan of the Full Moon as it was in 1767. The river is on the right, Southgate Street at the bottom.

In 1807, the Corporation drew up plans to develop the riverside by creating a towpath, and announced that "no lease [was] to be granted of premises called the Full Moon." When the current lease expired in 1811, "the premises [would] be taken down and converted into a more useful purpose for the advantage of the city." James Grant Smith of the Anchor Brewery, who held the lease, did not want to see one of his top inns bite the dust. He had friends in high places and eventually persuaded the Corporation to agree to the Full Moon being rebuilt. In 1816, the Corporation appointed a committee "to consider a letter from Messrs Ward & Merriman, clerks to the Kennett & Avon Canal Company, regarding the proposed towing path from the old bridge to the lock and the rebuilding and setting back of the Full Moon Inn." Six years later, another committee was appointed "to consider a letter and plans left with the Mayor by J Grant Smith, of the proposed alteration of the line of the new street to be called Dorchester Street, leading from Horse Street to Lord Manvers' Estate called the Ham, and of the improvement of the Full Moon Inn." In 1823,

The Full Moon from the Old Bridge …

… and from Southgate Street.

Looking down Southgate Street towards Beechen Cliff a century ago.

The same view today – but how long before Churchill House follows the Full Moon into oblivion?

The Full Moon as rebuilt in the 1820s, with the railway in the background.

the City Architect, George Manners, was instructed to carry out work at the bridge "as recommended by Mr Telford," including "the removal of ground by the Full Moon." The Full Moon was rebuilt, in line with Smith's plans soon afterwards.*

The opening of the Great Western Railway dealt a serious blow to the coaching trade, but the Full Moon exploited its proximity to the new station, placing advertisements such as the following in local papers:

FULL MOON INN

Only 100 Yards from the GW Railway Station.

Edwin Bartlett begs to inform Commercial Gentlemen & Others

That they will find the above Establishment conducted

With every attention to Comfort, combined with Moderate Charges,

So as to deserve that Patronage he has hitherto received.

NB Good Stables and Lock Up Coach Houses.

The House kept open for the Reception of Passengers

By the Night Mail Train.

Well-aired Beds.

FULL MOON HOTEL, BATH,
(Near the Old Bridge and G. W. Railway Station.)

VISITORS will find good Accommodation at Moderate Charges.

WELL-AIRED BEDS & GOOD STABLING.

An advertisement from 1880.

In 1851, Stephen Burridge, the "boots" at the Full Moon, gave evidence at a robbery trial, which was reported in the *Bath Chronicle*. Unwittingly, he also left us with a vivid insight into life as an under-servant in a nineteenth-century inn:

The usual time of closing the inn is about one o'clock, but the gates of the yard are shut at nine in the evening. On Thursday morning … at one o'clock, he had let out a Bristol fly from the yard, and afterwards locked the gates … He then locked the doors of the house, and he and the under-ostler, who slept with him, proceeded to bed, which is in a room adjoining the hay loft, and to which the only access is by a flight of steps in the yard, commencing close by the back door of the house.

The Full Moon, one of Bath's best-known landmarks for over 200 years, closed in 1931 when the Ministry of Labour, in a bid to reduce unemployment, provided a grant for building an extension to the electricity works next door, which entailed the demolition of the inn. A spokesman for the electricity board said that, although there were plans to build an extension, they had not intended to start work on it for four or five years. The money from the Ministry, however, was given on condition that work started by 1 July 1931, so in late May the tenants of the Full Moon were given a month's notice.

*The old Full Moon had a frontage of 48 feet onto Southgate Street, stood next to the Old Bridge, and had houses adjoining it to the north. There was access to the river from the yard at the back of the inn, which extended 150 feet along the river bank. The new Full Moon was to the north of the old one, with no access to the river, but with a new street – Dorchester Street – running alongside it on the north. It was set back further than the old inn to allow for road widening. It had a frontage of 55 feet on Southgate Street, and 56 feet on Dorchester Street. The entrance to the yard and stables, formerly on Southgate Street, was in Dorchester Street.

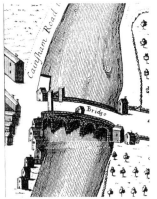

The Old Bridge in 1694 ...   ... and in 1964.

Had the Men from the Ministry not got involved, who knows – four or five years on from 1931, add another two or three years for official inertia, and we come to the brink of the Second World War, when most building projects came to an abrupt halt. And if the Full Moon had survived till 1945, perhaps it would still be there, the centrepiece of a very different – and much more attractive – riverside than the one we have today, with the best beer garden in Bath.

§

For centuries, Southgate Street led straight onto the Old Bridge. The earliest recorded bridge, built in 1304, had a chapel dedicated to St Lawrence halfway across, and a gate with a stone archway on the far side. It was rebuilt in the 1750s and again in the 1840s, before disappearing in 1964, when Churchill Bridge, fifty yards or so downstream, was built.

On the other side of the bridge, facing the Full Moon, was the Greyhound, the

The Engineer's Arms on the riverbank, a few yards up from the Old Bridge, in the floods of 1899.

starting point for our seventh excursion. For now, though, we will turn westward and head along the Lower Bristol Road. Two of the eleven pubs between the Old Bridge and Windsor Bridge Road have survived; the rest are long gone, bulldozed to make way for industrial and commercial developments.

On the riverside, between the Old Bridge and the Bath Brewery's maltings, was a beerhouse called the **Engineer's Arms**. It was first recorded in the 1866 *Postal Directory*, with William Troutt, a musician, as licensee. By 1871, he had

The Lower Bristol Road Tavern, on the corner of Union Terrace, in another picture of floods, from the 1920s.

been replaced by a weaver called James Reynolds. Later, it was kept for many years by Mary Ann Fishlock. The Bath Brewery Company closed the Engineer's Arms in October 1901 as part of the deal for getting a licence for the Moorfields Park Hotel.

A little further along, on the other side of the road, was Dagger's Newsagents at 13 Angel Place. Recently refurbished after long years of dereliction, it is the only part of Angel Place still standing. Next to it, at No 14, was the **Lower Bristol Road Tavern**, first recorded in the 1876 *Postal Directory*. In 1886, the Walcot Brewery, which owned it, seized the goods of the licensee (including a cradle, two stags' heads, a deal clothes box, two bedsteads, a bagatelle board and six cases of stuffed birds) in lieu of rent. The tavern consisted of a bar and a bar parlour. It had a side entrance to Union Terrace – the alleyway leading under the railway – and closed in 1931.

By the time the Stroud Brewery took over the Railway Tavern it had become the Railway Hotel.

A short detour up Union Terrace, under the railway line, and 50 yards along to the right brings us to the recently derailed **Railway Tavern** at 11 Prospect Buildings. Prospect Buildings date from 1824, when Samuel Orchard leased "a certain plot of land called Bayly's Close alias Westmead" to Humphrey Samuel, on which he "intended to form a certain row or pile of buildings called Prospect Place." The Railway Tavern actually predated the railway, being opened by Joseph Sydenham in 1836 or 1837 as the Railroad Tavern and

THE LOST PUBS OF BATH

catering for the navvies building the line. After the railway opened in 1840, it went through a variety of names -- the Railway Station Tavern (1852), the Sydenham Tavern (1856) (an appropriate choice, for not only was it kept by Sarah Sydenham, but it also overlooked Sydenham Fields cricket ground), and finally the Railway Brewery. It had its own brewery, which closed in the late 1920s. Part of Prospect Buildings, above the Railway Tavern, was destroyed by bombing in 1942. The Railway Tavern itself was so badly damaged it had to be rebuilt. In 1976, when Fred Pearce visited, it had a lounge with a real fire, a bird's-eye view of the railway and a public bar with darts, shove ha'penny, crib and dominoes. It has since been converted to flats.

Now we retrace our steps down to the Lower Bristol Road, where a turn to the left brings us to the Esso Garage, which stands on the site of Westmorland Buildings. In the 1850s you would have found a beerhouse there called the **Angel & Crown** – but you would have needed to be quick. The only reference to it we have found is in the 1854 *Postal Directory* with Thomas Harris as landlord.

Tokens bearing the name of the Gardener's Arms were issued by William Chidgey in the late nineteenth century.

Just before Oak Street, at 5 St John's Place, was the **Gardener's Arms**, which opened in the 1840s. At the time of the 1903 report, it consisted of a bar in two compartments, a tap room, a smoke room, a "small room," a skittle alley and a large club room on the first floor. In March 1900, a party of 60 people met there to form the Gardener's Arms Sick & Benefit Society. On 19 October 1923, the *Bath Chronicle* reported that

> last evening at the Gardener's Arms, Lower Bristol Road, a presentation of medals took place to the playing members of the Bladud AFC. In the Thursday league last year they won the silver cup for the first division and also the silver plate for the second division.

The pub closed when the renewal of its licence was refused on 18 July 1940.

The **Bell Inn** stood almost directly opposite the bottom of Oak Street. Immediately to the east, a row of cottages, called Bell Cottages, ran down to the river. First recorded in 1837, by 1879 the Bell had a bar, bar parlour, parlour, tap room, club room, skittle alley and three bedrooms.

Its end came suddenly, as a result of the floods of November 1894. The *Bath Herald* recorded its demise:

> The damage sustained by the inhabitants of the Lower Bristol Road through the flood is considerable. In almost every house in the buildings facing Collins's Mills [Camden Flour Mills, just east of the Bell], the floors of the rooms level with the street have been forced up by the water, and on Friday morning workmen were busily employed in relaying them. At the Bell Inn, the bowling saloon which runs

alongside of the house has been rendered a complete wreck. The wall, facing the stay factory, stood against the force of the current for some time, but about two o'clock on Thursday morning gave way, and the floor was carried by the stream some distance along the Lower Bristol Road. The current then washed against the wall of the house, and grave fears were entertained by the landlord, Mr P Barrett, as to the safety of the house, and it was deemed advisable to remove to other quarters. At this spot the current seems to have been exceptionally strong, and heavy stone walls and outhouses have been bodily removed.

The site of the Bell is now occupied by a car park.

A little further along is the Green Park Tavern. The building dates from around 1813, the pub from the 1840s, the Colony Room next door from 2004. Past the Green Park Tavern, past the cemetery, comes Brougham Hayes, where on the far corner, at 1 St Peter's Terrace, was the **Newbridge Hotel**. It was named after the nearby Victoria Suspension Bridge, built by James Dredge in 1836. The Newbridge Hotel first appeared – as the Bridge Tavern – in a newspaper report on 25 November 1841:

> On the night of Tuesday … some villain maliciously cut down the vines before the houses, Nos 10 and No 18 Brougham Hayes Buildings, near the Bridge Tavern, Twerton.

Five doors along, on the corner of Lorne Road, was the **East Twerton Hotel**, which opened in the 1870s as the Midland Arms. The first landlord was a butcher called John Butcher. He later handed it on to William Butcher, who was a butcher as well.

Yet another flood, this time in 1968 at the East Twerton Hotel on St Peter's Terrace.

Another view of the East Twerton Hotel, with the Newbridge Hotel on the far corner.

The same view today.

THE LOST PUBS OF BATH

It was rebuilt around 1894, with exuberant architectural flourishes, such as capitals and keystones with finely carved vegetation.

The East Twerton Hotel and the Newbridge Hotel survived until 1971, by which time they were both part of the Courage empire. Then the City Engineer decided that the whole block, which also included Hiscott's fishmonger's and Gray's butcher's, had to go to improve the junction of Brougham Hayes and Lower Bristol Road. Last orders were called and two pubs which had survived in friendly rivalry for over a century were razed to the ground.

A little further along, on the other side of the road, is the Belvoir Castle, opened around 1850, and, with its outbuildings, forming as instructive an example of nineteenth-century pub design as you are likely to find anywhere. Just past the Belvoir Castle, roughly where Stone's Coach Depot is today, were Hopmead Buildings, presumably named after a long-forgotten hop plantation. In the 1850s, William Holmes opened a beerhouse called the **White Lion** at 1 Hopmead Buildings. It closed in the 1870s and Mr Scobie, a stationmaster, moved in. By 1880, nine out of the ten houses in Hopmead Buildings were occupied by Midland Railway workers – two foremen, two porters, three signalmen and a guard. The terrace survived the Bath Blitz (although the old White Lion was seriously damaged) but has since been demolished.

A late nineteenth-century map showing the Royal Oak.

On the other side of the road, past Bath Press, past Brook Road, is the pub that came back from the dead – the **Royal Oak**. Dating from the mid-1790s, part of the building sits over a brook, which suggests it was a mill or even a brewery. It is first recorded as a beerhouse in 1839, and, although it may opened several years earlier, it would not have predated the Beerhouse Act of 1830. In the 1840s, the licensee was a cooper called Thomas Strange.

In 1874, the Somerset & Dorset Railway, swinging down from Devonshire Tunnel to join the Midland Railway line, crossed the Lower Bristol Road beside the Royal Oak. A detailed inventory of the Royal Oak was prepared in the same year. It had a bar (with a five-motion beer engine, four pewter beer engines, porter pull, partition and serving counter), bar parlour, back parlour (with chess table, ottoman, decanters and candlesticks), taproom, parlour, four bedrooms, workshop, brewery, skittle alley and club room.

Apart from its Somerset & Dorset connection, the Royal Oak was also famous for having one of the longest serving landladies in Bath. Alfred Beard had been at the Royal Oak for less than five years when he died in 1874. His widow, Eliza Beard, took over the pub and ran it until around 1930. The building was badly damaged in the Bath Blitz, with a large crack running right across the front of the building. The front wall was hastily rebuilt – unfortunately marring the appearance of the building in the process – and the pub reopened.

Early one Sunday morning in May 1957, with the Somerset & Dorset Railway closed for engineering works, a light engine crosses the Lower Bristol Road, en route for Midsomer Norton.

Fifty years later, and it is as though the railway never existed. All the buildings on the far side of the road have gone as well. The Royal Oak narrowly escaped demolition in 2002, and has now reopened.

THE LOST PUBS OF BATH

In 1976 Fred Pearce visited and found it

> an intimate and exceptionally pleasant well-kept house. The public (Oak Room) has black and white TV, matching wood panelling and tables, darts and shove ha'penny. Small compact lounge has flowering plants in the window.

In 1993 Courage's sold the Royal Oak to Moles' Brewery (who also owned the Hop Pole and the Old Crown in Twerton), but it closed in 1999. In 2002, it survived plans to demolish it and build a Jehovah's Witness Hall. Since then, extensive – and extremely sympathetic – renovations have been carried out. The front wall, in particular, now looks as good – if not better – than it did before the Luftwaffe left their calling card. In August 2005, it finally reopened, and looks set to be one of the top real ale pubs in the area.

§

After stopping for a celebratory drink in the Royal Oak, we step westward once again towards Twerton. Originally known as Twiverton, Twerton grew up around the weaving trade. There were once vineyards at Twerton as well. As late as 1743, a traveller reported seeing "Mr Cawley's vineyard, a fine plantation on the side of the hill [with] a good view of Bath"

In the late eighteenth century, weaving, traditionally a cottage industry, was mechanised. The opening of Twerton's biggest mill was reported in the *Bath Chronicle* on 1 November 1792:

> At the opening of the Worsted Spinning Mills at Twerton ... on Saturday last, an elegant dinner was given by the proprietors, Messrs Bamford and Cooke, to a party of gentlemen, and to the mechanics, woolcombers, and every other person employed about the mill, upwards of 280 in number. After dinner the tables were liberally supplied with wine, punch and strong beer.

Despite this gesture of alcoholic largesse, the mill owners found drinking an increasing problem as the nineteenth century wore on. The efforts of Mr Wilkins, who later acquired the mill, to curb drinking by fining workers found in public houses, is perpetuated today in the name of a local dance group, Mr Wilkins' Shilling.

In 1819, Pierce Egan described Twerton as "a neat, interesting looking village ... rather conspicuous for its large broad-cloth manufactory. This building, which is lofty and capacious, possesses all the appearance of an elegant mansion. It is the property of Mr Wilkins, who has erected, contiguous to his manufactory, a very handsome range of neat and comfortable dwellings, built of freestone, in the Gothic style, for his numerous workmen."

In 1840, the railway arrived. An early passenger has left us a vivid description of what Twerton was like at the time:

> We soon arrive at the village of Twerton with its huge factories and bustling inhabitants, many of whom bear token, in the blue dye which stains their faces and apparel, of the employment in which they are engaged – the manufacture of cloth ... The factories form almost the entire support of the village, and ... the large

number of persons employed in them have the great advantage of working under one of the best and most considerate of masters – Mr Charles Wilkins, Esq.

The coming of the railway had a devastating effect on Twerton's economy. Just eight years later, the *Bath Postal Directory* informed its readers that Twerton "was formerly noted for its extensive manufacture of superfine woollen cloth. As late as 1838, two mills gave regular employment to upwards of 700 persons; at present there is only one mill, the productions from which are very limited."

The railway had an even more devastating impact on the physical aspect of Twerton. It sliced through the village on a viaduct, high as a house, leaving a blot on the landscape which the passage of over 150 years has done little to soften. Twerton station, which closed in 1917, was a spur to development, and, despite the collapse of the weaving industry, Twerton grew rapidly in the late nineteenth century. The old village was swamped by new housing. When Mrs Wheatcroft wrote a book of picturesque rambles around Bath in 1897, she described Twerton as a "tremendous suburb, almost entirely populated by the working class, who are all more or less occupied in ministering to the wants of those on the other side of the water."

Mrs Wheatcroft's dismissal of Twerton has set the tone for later guidebooks to Bath. Few, if any, visitors venture out there, and most Bathonians know little of what is hidden behind Brunel's viaduct. The approach to Twerton, along the Lower Bristol Road, is hardly inspiring, so comprehensive has the process of demolition, dilapidation and uglification been. Twerton, too, has been ill served by the planners, yet it still has a scattering of interesting old buildings, some dating back to the seventeenth century. More to the point, it also has some old pubs. A reappraisal of Twerton's architectural heritage as part of Bath's urban landscape seems long overdue.

Before taking a stroll around Twerton, we will take a quick look at the lost pubs whose locations we have been unable to track down. These included the **Anchor** (c1858-c1880), the **Boot** (c1849), the **Clothier's Arms** (c1841-c1849) which had a malthouse, the **Rainbow** (c1892), the **Swan** (mid-nineteenth century), and the **Tanner's Arms**, which appears on an undated brass token. There was also an eighteenth-century inn called the **Coach & Horses**. The *Bath Chronicle* of 6 August 1761 advertised a cockfight, "to be fought at Mr Charles Smith's at the Sign of the Coach & Horses in the Parish of Twerton ... between the Gentlemen of Somerset and the Gentlemen of Gloucester." Lastly, there was the **Sword**, which featured in *Farley's Bristol Newspaper* in 1726:

> November 17th. We have an account for Bath, that yesterday was seven-night [ie a week yesterday], Mr Yeamans, the Sheriff's chiefest officer in that city, being out a shooting, went into the Sign of the Sword at Twerton, a mile off, and laying his gun on a table, the same went off, and shot him in the bowels, of which he instantly died.

Charles Ware's Morris Minor Centre on the Lower Bristol Road.

An early-twentieth-century plan of the Atlas Stores.

The Atlas Stores stood on the opposite corner of Fielding's Road to the Golden Fleece.

A tram trundles past the Seven Stars sometime before the First World War.

We start our pub crawl round Twerton on the Lower Bristol Road. Fielding's Place once stood opposite Jew's Lane, and was named after the novelist Henry Fielding, who wrote part of *Tom Jones* in a house nearby, which has also been demolished. A few doors back towards Bath one building survived in the face of official opposition, saved, like the south side of Kingsmead Square, by Charles Ware, King of the Morris Minors. It is a symbol of what was lost when they pulled down so much of old Twerton. On the corner of Fielding's Place was the **Atlas Stores**, which opened around 1880. When an inventory was carried out in 1906, it had a smoke room with a mahogany window screen, mahogany-topped drinking tables and a panelled partition, a bar with front and side counters, a private glass room, and a jug & bottle. The outside of the building was lit by gas. Even though it had been renamed the Atlas Brewery by this time, it does not seem to have had its own brewery. The Atlas Brewery closed on 6 December 1962 and has, like the house Fielding stayed in, been demolished.

This part of Twerton was lavishly provided with pubs. On the opposite corner was – and still is – the Golden Fleece. Next to it, at 4-5 Avon Buildings, was the **Seven Stars**. This opened as a beerhouse in the 1850s, and was rebuilt in the late nineteenth century. It was granted a full licence in 1951. In 1976, when Fred Pearce visited, it was a "versatile three-bar local." The public bar had a TV, juke box and fruit machine; the small smoking room had darts and another juke box; and the games room had pool and pinball. Fred made a point of referring to the "nice pub glass." In January 1990, most of the glass fell victim to rival soccer hooligans from Bristol Rovers and Bolton Wanderers who clashed in a "western-style brawl." After closing in the 1990s, the Seven Stars became the New Trams Social Club, which has recently closed.

Much of the rest of Avon Buildings has gone. Only No 11 (once Dillon's Butchers) and No 12 (Clark's Business Products) survive. Beyond No 12, however, was the **Railway Inn**. This opened sometime before

A railmotor pulls out of Twerton station for Bath around 1910. The station opened in 1840; the Railway Inn, on the left of the picture, opened shortly afterwards. The station closed in 1917, but the inn stayed open until destroyed by bombing in 1942.

1861, and was so badly damaged in the Bath Blitz of 1942 that it had to be demolished.

At the back of Avon Buildings was JD Taylor's malthouse, built in 1901, at a cost of £12,000, to replace one at the back of the Three Cups in Walcot Street which had been destroyed by fire. In March 1915, it too was gutted by a fire, described as the largest in Bath for several years, in which malt to the value of £12,000 was lost. It

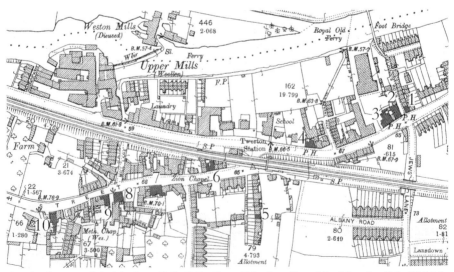

The pubs of Twerton: 1) the Atlas Stores; 2) the Golden Fleece; 3) the Seven Stars; 4) the Railway Inn; 5) the Woolpack; 6) the Ring of Bells; 7) the White Hart; 8) the George; 9) the Old Crown; 10) the Wheatsheaf.

THE LOST PUBS OF BATH

was rebuilt, with four floors instead of two, as an aircraft factory, which has also disappeared.

Across the road and under the railway bridge lies Twerton High Street. On the left, just past the bridge, was a row of houses called Prospect Buildings. At No 11 was a beerhouse called the **Woolpack**, which opened sometime before 1867. In 1906, the licensing authorities refused to renew its licence, justifying their decision as follows:

> This house is situated up a cartway or footway for some 16 houses about 35 yards from the High Street ... The house is kept in a dirty condition. The apparent trade done there is very little. There have been six transfers in the last ten years.

The premises consisted of "a bar, tap room, kitchen (the only living room downstairs),

 4 bedrooms (2 unfurnished), and wash house – WC and urinal in wash house for use by tenant and public." Today the site of Prospect Buildings is covered by modern housing.

On the north side of the High Street, at No 4, was the **Ring of Bells**. This opened in the late 1850s and closed in 1963. Today it has been converted to flats.

The Ring of Bells, now converted to flats.

A little further up, on the other side of the road, at 142-144 High Street, was the **White Hart**, which opened some time before 1767. In January 1798, when factory workers from Bradford on Avon, Trowbridge, Frome, and Beckington marched on Twerton intending "to demolish the works of Bamford and Co and Collicott and Co.," the White Hart was the headquarters of the local militia and those charged with "suppression of this violent outrage." Appropriately, Twerton's stocks stood across the road from the inn.

Around 1818, the White Hart was taken over by William Wiltshire. His tenure came to an abrupt and tragic end 14 years later, as reported in the *Bath Chronicle*

> On Monday evening, December 10th, about four o'clock, as Mr Wiltshire, of the White Hart, was returning from a friend's house beyond the Bear at Holloway, and was crossing the fields leading to Twerton Road, he was attacked by two ruffians, who with the most dreadful threats upon his life, fell upon him and beat him so cruelly as to leave him without the power of speech, and, in fact, with little signs of life. His clothes were torn from his body in tatters, and his pockets were rifled of 100 sovereigns, which he had that day drawn from the bank.

A salutary lesson of the inadvisability of going for a walk in the country with what, in today's terms, would amount to over £5,000 in loose change in your pocket. It is astonishing how often, in the eighteenth and early nineteenth centuries, men of property were robbed of vast sums of money, after taking unnecessary risks. Take this story of an innocent abroad from March 1787:

> Thursday last, a married farmer, at Bristol Fair, got among a room full of prostitutes at a public house, who eased him of 109 guineas [around £8,000 in today's terms]. Several of them were secured next day.

William Wiltshire's injuries were such that, although he survived, he had to retire. A few months later a notice appeared in the *Bath Chronicle*, advertising a sale of beer, casks, furniture, brewing utensils, a screw cider press, etc. "by Mr Wiltshire, who is quitting the Inn." It was taken over by James Collins.

When an inventory was carried out later in the century, the White Hart had a bar, a bar parlour (with a barometer, china ornaments, eight Windsor arm chairs, a Broadwood square piano and a glass showcase), a tap room, a sitting room (with a bagatelle table), a club room and a brewery.

The White Hart, taken over by temperance templars in 1899.

In 1899, the Bath Brewery Company closed the White Hart and transferred its licence to the newly-built Victoria Hotel in Oldfield Park. The inn was bought for £355 by the Twerton Lodge of Good Templars and turned into a Temperance Institute and Restaurant. At the opening ceremony on 16 May 1899, the Templars burst the old vats and broke "other things connected with alcohol." The Independent Order of Good Templars was a pseudo-masonic organisation of abolitionist zealots founded in the USA in 1851 and introduced into this country in 1868. The Bath branch was founded in 1873. Its extremism made it unpopular with other temperance campaigners. Thomas Whittaker, for example, a Methodist preacher who advocated teetotalism, declared:

> Good Templarism has always seemed to me a society set on foot to put little men into big places, and as there are so many little men, they cannot all be provided for.

Although the Templars have gone, the words WHITE HART TEMPLAR INSTITUTE AND RESTAURANT … TWERTON LODGE can still be faintly made out above the door, with the words they covered up – WINES & SPIRITS – coming through underneath.

Waterloo Buildings, once served by a beerhouse called the Queen's Head.

Just along from the White Hart was the **Queen's Head** beerhouse on Waterloo Buildings. When it opened in the 1850s, it was known simply as the Queen. It was renamed the Queen's Head in the 1860s and closed in 1913.

The **George**, facing the entrance to Mill Lane at 132 High Street, was first recorded in 1787, when John Bailey was the landlord. In the same year it was put up for sale, described as "that old accustom'd house … much the best house in the parish for entertaining travellers." We do not know how long it had been open, but the building appears to date from the seventeenth century, and may have been an inn from the start.

In 1832, the George was rebuilt and the entrance moved from the front to the side. The date of the rebuilding can still be seen above the new entrance. The George was last recorded in the 1878 *Postal Directory*, with John Cadby as landlord.

Looking down Twerton High Street a century ago, with the old George on the left and the Old Crown just beyond.

The Wheatsheaf on a map of around 1890.

Today, the Wheatsheaf, with all the buildings around it gone, sells carpets rather than beer.

Continuing up the street, past the Old Crown, still very much in business, we come to Jeffrey's carpet shop, now standing in splendid isolation, but once at the end of a row of buildings. This was the **Wheatsheaf**, opened as a beerhouse by Thatcher's of Welton around 1858. Although the building dates from the eighteenth century, the frontage was added later. From the appearance of the gable ends, it also appears that an extra floor was added at some time, possibly in connection with the establishment of a brewery.

The Wheatsheaf was closed by the licensing authorities in 1906. Thatcher's received £1,000 in compensation; the landlord, Edward Fulford, received £100. The magistrates made great play of the fact that there were so many pubs close by. They summed up the Wheatsheaf as follows:

Small bar, small tap room, smoking room, kitchen, cellars, skittle alley. Upstairs, sitting room and 3 beds, and 2 small rooms at back, not used. Urinals fairly good; WC bad. House kept in fairly clean condition. Apparent trade very little. Twelve transfers in ten years, or 21 since 1876 ... The licensee admitted that he desired to leave the house as soon as he could get out, and could not get a living.

There is one further lost pub in Twerton, but, as it is over a mile away uphill, you may decide it is time to head off in search of a non-lost pub instead. If you are determined to stick with the excursion to the bitter end, head back down the High Street, turn right up Shophouse Road, past the White Horse, and carry on up The Hollow until you reach the **Beehive**, one of Bath's unlikeliest lost pubs.

In 1939, as houses sprang up along Mount Road, Bass, who owned the Beehive on Walcot Street, obtained approval to transfer its licence to "premises … to be erected on land to be known as Whiteway Housing Estate." The war intervened; the Beehive on Walcot Street did not close until the mid-1950s and it was the licence of the Grove at Padley Bottom that was transferred to the new Beehive on Mount Road.

The Beehive, now a doctor's surgery.

Fred Pearce has let us a vivid record of what it was like when he visited in 1976:

> No less than two washbasins in the men's loo! Unheard of luxury! Could be that high unemployment has pushed up the lunchtime trade of some of these suburban pubs – certainly the Beehive was very busy on our visit. The large tatty 1950s public bar was packed with young (round the dartboard) and old (mostly engaged in a verbal dispute which led to one old guy walking out saying "he wouldn't accept charity in the form of a consolation drink"). Good beefburger rolls at 18p. Full Bass range of beers plus, unusually, Courage BA. Five bottled ciders available, piano accordion on a Saturday night and a lounge that is rather underused.

Despite the lack of any other pubs in the vicinity, the new Beehive, like the old, has closed. Since 1998, it has been home to the Beehive Surgery.

THE LOST PUBS OF BATH

EXCURSION THE THIRD

STEPPING EASTWARD

Our third excursion starts at the old North Gate and heads east, along what has always been the most important road into and out of Bath – the road to London. In 1749, 15 years before it was pulled down, John Wood wrote that the North Gate "seems, till of late years, to have been a noble work. [It] was, in effect, the Triumphal Arch of the

city; and the Kings, Queens, Princes, and Princesses that have honour'd Bath with their presence, were generally receiv'd at it by the Corporation in their Formalities." It was adorned "from the remotest ages … with a statue of King Bladud." By 1749, however, the gate had been hemmed in by buildings and the old statue of Bladud replaced by one which looked "more like a dressed puppet, seated in a ducking stool, than the figure of a famous king."

In 1707, Samuel Ditcher, a barber, paid £20 for a 99-year lease of "a messuage with appurtenances over the North Gate and two rooms adjoining." In 1764, with 42 years of his lease left to run, the North Gate was pulled down. It has left a powerful legacy behind it. The tradition of ringing a bell to warn readers in Bath Central Library (near where the old North Gate stood) that the doors are about to close, for example, perpetuates the old custom of a bellman warning stragglers, as nightfall approached, that the North Gate was about to close for the night. But a more tangible reminder is the Bus Gate which has recently been erected virtually on the site of the North Gate. Like much modern architecture, it has aroused strong feelings. Although it has many staunch supporters, many more want to see it demolished. Love it or loath it, there is no doubt that it is at the cutting edge of modern architecture. The most innovative thing about it is that it does not exist. It is a figment of its architect's imagination. It is a bold, even breathtaking statement which owes nothing to tradition – the architectural equivalent of John Cage's *4'33"*.

In John Wood's day, Northgate Street was known as Old Street. He described it as follows:

It is 44 feet in breadth, contains 25 houses, and by its being terminated at one end with a church, at the other with the principal gate of the city, we need only carry ourselves back in imagination to the time when all the buildings were in their original state, and the conduit ... rising up as a tower, or High Cross in the midst of them, to conceive this street as beautiful an atrium before the entrance into the city, as art itself could form.

It is not only the conduit which has gone. Today, there is not a single pub in Northgate Street, but at one time you would have been distinctly the worse for wear if you had tried getting round them all in an evening. And attempting to untangle their history is a bit like trying to solve Rubik's Cube wearing boxing gloves.

The only tangible reminder of the old Northgate Street is that most unlikely survivor among Bath's thoroughfares, Slippery Lane, formerly known as Alvord Lane. This ran outside the city walls from the river up to the North Gate. At one time the lane continued – as Barton Lane – on the other side of Northgate Street. There was a pub called the **Rose & Crown** on the corner of Barton Lane, which closed around 1780.

On the northern corner of Slippery Lane (where the Bath Rugby shop stands today) was the **Royal Oak**, which extended down to the river. The building was there by 1585, when Joan Wyatt leased it, along with

Slippery Lane, one of the few relics of pre-eighteenth-century Bath.

the "tann houses" next door. It became an inn sometime before 1707, when the lease was taken by John Stibbs, later Mayor of Bath.

In 1761, when Mary Hickes "and others" took the lease, the Royal Oak's address was given as Slippery Lane, even though it had a 38 foot frontage on Broad Street. It closed some time before 1776.

Next door but one to the Royal Oak was the **Three Cups**. In 1617, William Eveland received a licence from Sir Giles Mompesson for an inn in Bath called the Three Cups. However, this may have been somewhere else, for when Richard Shatford leased the building in Northgate Street in 1639 there was no mention of it being an inn. It was definitely an inn by 1655, however, when Robert Rogers took over a "tenement late

The east side of Northgate Street in the mid-nineteenth century, with Bridge Street on the right. Brooke & Bishop's, on the corner of Slippery Lane, was formerly the Royal Oak; next door but one is the Three Cups; next to that are the Unicorn and Packhorse.

Richard Shatford's and now called the sign of the Three Cups."

In 1681, the lease was taken by William Sherston. Other early leaseholders included James Baily, a saddler (1734), John Morley, a tiler (1746), and Thomas Selden (1765). We know that it was rebuilt around 1747, for a deed of that year describes it as "new erected." In 1758, its outbuildings included a brewhouse, three stables, a malthouse, a pigsty and a court.

The Three Cups' name came from the three cups on the coat of arms of the Worshipful Company of Salters, which suggests that its first landlord was a salt seller. It must have been a respectable establishment, for it was here, in 1739, that John Wesley spent his first night in Bath. In 1752 it was advertised for sale as "a well accustom'd inn … with good stables, cellars and malthouse, that will make about seven quarters per week."

On 5 January 1797, the following announcement appeared in the *Bath Chronicle*:

THREE CUPS INN & CHOP HOUSE

near St Michael's Church, Bath.

GARLAND (from Mr Lucas's, York House)

informs his friends and the publick that he has entered on the above inn,

where they may be assured of meeting with excellent beds,

good stables and comfortable accommodation at reasonable charges.

The continuance of the favours of Mr Morley's friends and

the old customers to the house is requested;

they may rely on particular civility and

attention being paid to their demands.

In 1805, the Three Cups was, in the words of the *Bath Chronicle*, "wholly taken down, set back and rebuilt at considerable expense, whereby the street [was] widened and the premises … greatly increased in value." In 1846, the Northgate Brewery was given permission "to discontinue the Three Cups in Northgate Street as a tavern and to use it as a shop." The name of the Three Cups was transferred to the Pelican in Walcot Street (of which more anon).

Next to the Three Cups were three more inns, the site of which is now covered by the Podium. Their history is a saga of openings, closures, reopenings and renamings, bound up with the story of Northgate Brewery, which lay behind them.

The three inns in question were the Three Horseshoes, the Boat, and the Packhorse. The Three Horseshoes, the southernmost of the three, was an inn as early as 1585. The Boat, next door, opened sometime before 1640. Both closed in the early to mid-eighteenth century, but were later reopened by the Northgate Brewery as a single inn called the Unicorn. A curious feature of the Unicorn was that, while the freehold of one part of it – the old Three Horseshoes – belonged to the Corporation, the freehold of the other – the old Boat – belonged to St John's Hospital. Next to the Unicorn was the Packhorse, dating from the early eighteenth century, or possibly earlier, and later taken over by the Northgate Brewery. The brewery closed in 1868; the Packhorse and the Unicorn closed shortly afterwards. The Unicorn had a brief renaissance as the Northgate Wine Vaults, but this closed in 1888. That is the history of this site in a nutshell. Here it is in a little more detail.

In 1585, Humphrey Paine was granted the lease of an inn called the Horseshoes. By 1671, when Humphrey Page took the lease, it had become the **Three Horseshoes**. Like the other inns along this stretch, the land attached to it extended down to the river. In 1674, the lease was taken by George Collibee, a maltster. In 1722, the lease passed to his widow and the inn closed.

Next door to the Unicorn was the **Boat**, first recorded in 1640, when George Middens took the lease. Its name suggests that it was connected in some way with the ferry to Bathwick. In some early documents, it appears (or seems to appear, such are the vagaries of seventeenth-century handwriting) as the Boot, but this is almost certainly a mistake, and one that would have been easy to make in those days of sporadic literacy and uncertain spelling.

In 1717, the lease was taken by Thomas Tagg. It later passed to his wife, and later still to an apothecary called John Ford, who handed it on to Thomas Warr Atwood. It closed sometime before 1766.

In 1768, William Pulteney leased the property. This raises some interesting

A plan of the Unicorn in 1778.

questions. The development of Bathwick was about to get underway. Did the Boat feature in his plans? Did he intend to knock the old inn down and make a road through to a bridge across the river? We will probably never know, for, a year later, the Corporation gave him permission to pull down old St Mary's Church inside the Northgate and get access to the river that way. The old Boat remained in the Pulteney family until the early 1800s, but by then it had reopened as part of the Unicorn.

It is unclear when the **Unicorn** opened. The first record of it comes in October 1773, when James Jones moved there from the Ring of Bells in the Orange Grove. However, it is possible that, at this stage, it only occupied the old Three Horseshoes. The logistics of opening an inn which incorporated two properties, owned by two different freeholders and leased to two different people would have been considerable. The first record of the Unicorn occupying the old Boat comes in 1791, which may be the year in which the Unicorn expanded into it.

The Unicorn also had a tap. In 1787, the *Bath Chronicle* announced that there was, "just arrived from Norwich, a choice collection of canary birds …

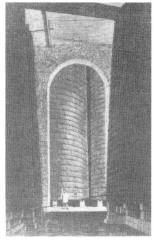

Three mid-nineteenth-century views of the Northgate Brewery, the biggest in the West of England.

now selling at Mr Needs's at the Unicorn Tap near St Michael's Church, Northgate Street, Bath. A cage of 400 birds – the finest, stoutest and richest Junks, Medies, Turn-Crowns, etc., that was ever brought into this city."

The Unicorn belonged to the Northgate Brewery, which had been built on the land behind it around 1770. It brewed porter, for which there was an almost insatiable demand, and, due to a combination of luck and astute management, it eventually became the biggest brewery in the West of England. When it outgrew its original site, a tramway bridge was slung across the river to Grove Street, so that it could continue expanding there. The aroma would have been inescapable and the brewery's pollution of the river was a constant cause for complaint. There were other problems as well. In November 1853, for example, the council fined the Northgate Brewery for using "the chimney flue of their brewing furnace without taking means to consume the smoke thereof." In June 1807, however, it was the council who had had to pay £44 in compensation "for damage done to the brewery in making the watering place near the Old Packhorse in Bath."

The entrance to the brewery from Northgate Street was through a "narrow gateway [leading] to a spacious, well-paved yard, with offices on each side, and at the further end spacious storerooms for hops, and a powerful crane by which the whole of the beer is hoisted from the different cellars and loaded on drays for conveyance to the railway station and elsewhere."

In 1868, two of the partners who owned the brewery died within a short time of each other, and the third, "a gentleman of large fortune," was "disinclined to carry it on." The brewery, together with 28 tied houses, was put up for sale, but, although most of the pubs were snapped up, there were no takers for the brewery, and the brewing equipment was sold off piecemeal.

The Unicorn closed shortly afterwards. In 1872, Hitchman's Brewery of Chipping Norton took over part of the old Northgate Brewery as a "wholesale brewery and wine merchant's." In the same year, Elias Hawking, a wine merchant, moved into part of the old Unicorn. By 1876 much of the old brewery was a builder's yard, but the wine merchant's had become a pub called the **Northgate Wine Vaults**. In 1878, Hitchman's left and the Northgate Wine Vaults was renamed the Unicorn. It closed in 1888.

Finally, we come to the **Packhorse**. Although the building was there by 1631, when William Elkington held the lease, the first record of it as an inn comes

A plan of the Packhorse in 1790. Part of the old St Michael's Church can be seen at the bottom.

in 1724. An entry in the 1755 *Bath & Bristol Guide* indicates why it was called the Packhorse:

> The Carrier for Exeter (thro' Wells, Bridgwater, Taunton, etc.) sets out every Tuesday from the Packhorse, near St Michael's Church; and comes in from thence Wednesdays. Also sets out from the said inn for Tetbury every Thursday and comes in Mondays … N.B. Mr Maggs keeps Waggons to convey heavy burdens that can't conveniently be carried by the Pack-Horses.

In 1749, an announcement that the Packhorse was to let included the information that it had been "kept for many years by John Scratchley, lately deceas'd, with good stabling, water, and all conveniences." Eleazer Pickwick was landlord for a short time around 1778, before moving to the Angel in Westgate Street, and later to the White Hart in Stall Street.

Eventually, the Northgate Brewery added the lease of the Packhorse to their portfolio. By the late eighteenth century, it stood in the way of civic improvements, and in April 1796, the Council instructed John Palmer to make "a plan and elevation … for the building of a new inn, etc., where the Old Packhorse stands near St Michael's Church." The plans were approved and two years later the Packhorse was described as "new built." A mere fourteen years later, however, the Northgate Brewery was instructed to rebuild the front of the inn and set it back in line with the Council's plan for widening the street.

The Packhorse's most enduring legacy is the part it played in the saga of Princess Caraboo. It was in April 1817 that a strange young woman turned up at Almondsbury in Gloucestershire. She had a turban on her head and spoke a language no one could understand. She was taken in by a wealthy couple, who, in an attempt to understand what she was saying, got hold of a Portuguese sailor who claimed to know several obscure eastern languages. After listening to her, he declared that she was a member of the Javasunean royal family called Princess Caraboo. Abducted from her native land by pirates, she had jumped overboard in the English Channel and swum ashore. Soon her story was national news. She was not Javanese, however, but a cobbler's daughter from Devon with a theatrical bent. All it needed to make her a celebrity was a sailor with a finely-honed sense of humour. The only problem was that, even in those pre-photographic, pre-televisual days, there were enough people around who were likely to recognise her from her description once it started appearing in the papers.

In order to stay one step ahead of the game, she had to keep on the move. And so she turned up, one June evening, at the Packhorse, where "considerable embarrassment was experienced from the inability of comprehending her language, but the landlady paid the kindest attention to her." When a gentleman by the name of Dr Wilkinson, who had already met Princess Caraboo and fallen hook, line, and sinker for her story, received news of her arrival in Bath, he followed her. Assuming that the longer people spent with her the more likely they were to see through the hoax, the last thing she wanted was people following her around the country. Dr Wilkinson, however, had no doubts about her authenticity. "Every circumstance," he wrote, "contributes to the proof that Caraboo is the character she represents herself to be;

Two views of the buildings once occupied by the Unicorn and Packhorse – in the 1920s and in the 1950s. The Podium now occupies the site.

THE LOST PUBS OF BATH

and those who have paid the greatest attention to her have no doubt, but that she is a native of one of the Japanese Islands, called Javasu, and that her father is Chinese! From some circumstances it would appear, that her mother was of European descent, probably Portuguese; she is evidently acquainted with the principles of Christianity; she described the crucifixion and resurrection … Nothing has yet transpired to authorise the slightest suspicion of Caraboo, nor has such been ever entertained, except by those whose souls feel not the spirit of benevolence, and wish to convert into ridicule that amiable disposition in others!" Nothing, that is, until Princess Caraboo, sensing that her luck would soon run out, owned up to the hoax a few days later. Dr Wilkinson's comments on the occasion are, unfortunately, not recorded.

By the 1860s, the Packhorse had a distinctly old-fashioned feel to it. Visitors entered a large lobby with an office desk and two plaster casts on brackets. It had eleven bedrooms, a commercial room with a loo table, a cloak room, a private room and a coffee room. There was also a bar, bar parlour, and parlour. A separate entrance led to the tap room. The Packhorse, like the Unicorn, closed soon after the Northgate Brewery. Much of the old brewery, along with substantial parts of the inns that stood in front of it, survived until the wholesale redevelopment of the area in the 1970s. Today the whole site is covered by the Podium Shopping Centre.

CASTLE INN, near St. Michael's Church, Bath.

A POST-COACH sets out from the above Inn, every Monday and Thursday morning, for LONDON, at half past seven o'clock; lays at Reading the first night, and arrives in London next day to dinner. The same Coach flies out of Bath on Tuesday, Friday, and Saturday afternoon, precisely at 4 o'clock, and arrives in London the next morning to breakfast.
The FLYING POST-COACHES, as usual, continue to set out for London, every morning at 4 o'clock, and every afternoon at 5, at the usual prices.
Also set out from the above Inn, The Exeter, Weymouth, Salisbury, Southampton, Gosport, Gloucester, Worcester, Shrewsbury and Holyhead Coaches.
Performed by HULBERT and Co.
No valuables will be accounted for, unless entered as such, and paid for accordingly.

Post-coach services from the Castle in 1780.

The Castle & Ball may sound like a couple of comedians, but for almost 200 years it was one of Bath's top inns. Sometimes known just as the Castle, it stood on the corner of Northgate and New Bond Streets. It was first recorded in 1746, when Posthumus Bush took the lease. An announcement in the *Bath Journal* in 1782 gives an insight into the intricate

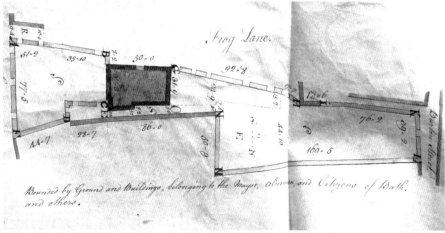

A plan of the Castle in 1794, with Northgate Street on the left, Frog Lane at the top, and Barton Street on the right.

The Castle in the 1840s.

relationship which existed between innkeepers and coachmasters. The Castle was to let, and interested parties were invited to "enquire of John Hulbert, Coachmaster, whose carriages will continue to set forth from the said inn." Mr Hulbert was running two coaches a day to London, two a day to Bristol, and three a week to Gosport and Holyhead. As a condition of the lease, John Hulbert undertook to "engage the tenant £25 a year for the profits of book-keeping the said coaches which may be done without an additional servant."

The inn was taken by Thomas Cook who ran it with his wife Eliza. One of the barmaids at the Castle was Sarah Arlott. Eliza Cook suspected her of pocketing "monies taken at the bar." When she mentioned her suspicions to her, the barmaid went up to her room in great distress. Mrs Cook ordered her to come down and get on with her work. Later, Mrs Cook, having "lost some edging, told the said Sarah Arlott that she would be guilty of one thing as she might of another and that she most likely had the edging but she denied any knowledge of it." This time, Sarah went and locked herself in the toilet. There they left her until, several hours later, they started to get worried. When they broke the door down they found her "with her throat cut and a large quantity of blood on the floor."

By 1806, Matthew Temple, the best-known of the Castle's many landlords, had taken over. In 1807, when New Bond Street was built, the inn was extended to take in the adjoining property. Two years later, the houses between the Castle and the corner of Green Street were "rebuilt and set back in line with the Castle." In 1826, Charles Westmacott (under the pseudonym Bernard Blackmantle) published *The English Spy*, a gentleman's *vade mecum* of major English towns and cities. He recommended visitors to Bath to take "a social pipe in the Sporting Parlour at the Castle," otherwise known as "Matthew Temple's snuggery":

> One of the greatest characters in the city of Bath is the worthy host of the Castle; at whose door stands the rubicund visage of our Cheltenham friend, Blackstrap, ready to give us a hearty welcome, and introduce us to Matthew Temple, who, making one of his best bows, leads the way into the coffee room, not forgetting to assure us that Mistress Temple, who is one of the best women in the world, will take the greatest care that we have every attention paid to our commands

THE LOST PUBS OF BATH

and comforts; and, in good truth, honest Matthew is right, for a more comely, good-humoured, attentive, kind hostess exists not in the three kingdoms of his Gracious Majesty George the Fourth. In short, Mrs Temple is the major-domo of the Castle, while honest Matthew, conscious of his own inability to direct the active operations of the garrison within doors, beats up for recruits without; attends to all the stable duty and the commissariat, keeps a sharp lookout for new arrivals by coach, and a still sharper one that no customer departs without paying his bill; and thus having made his daily bow to the *ins* and the *outs*, honest Matthew retires at night to take his glass of grog with the choice spirits who frequent Sportsman's Hall, a snug little smoking room on the left of the gateway, where the heroes of the turf and the lads of the fancy nightly assemble to relate their sporting anecdotes, sing a merry chaunt, book the long odds, and blow a friendly cloud in social intercourse and good fellowship.

The Castle even had a song written in its honour:

> Come all you gay fellows, so merry and witty,
> Ye Somerset lads of the elegant city,
> Ye sons of the turf who delight in a race
> And ye Nimrods of Bath, who are fond of the chase;
> Come join us, and pledge us, like true brothers all,
> At old Matthew Temple's the Castle & Ball.

An advertisement from 1846.

After Matthew Temple's death in the 1830s, his widow, and later his son, took over the running of the inn. Later in the century, it was taken over by Alderman Rubie, who also ran the Saracen's Head in Broad Street, the Bladud's Head in Walcot Street, and a wine merchant's next to the Castle in New Bond Street. In 1904,

proposals [were put] before the Corporate Property Committee on the part of a syndicate of leading citizens to take upon a lease of 75 years the large slice of Corporate property partly occupied now by the Castle Hotel and stretching round from the end of Mr Goldsworthy's shop in New Bond Street [No 21] to the first shop in Green Street, in consideration of their erecting thereon a fine commercial hotel ... That an ultimate settlement will be arrived at cannot be doubted, for the parties to the negotiations are, on the one hand, a company of public spirited citizens, and, on the other, the Corporation, who must realise, when they know the details, that the scheme is the greatest public improvement since the Empire Hotel was built. This is the impression left from the description of the plans which Messrs Silcock and Ray have prepared, which [are] as follows: The entire demolition of the existing property on the site mentioned is involved, and the structural outlay will probably be at a casual estimate of £20,000. With its commanding corner position (to be more prominent one day when Northgate Street is widened at its High Street end) and enormous frontage to two important thoroughfares, the architectural possibilities are exceptional. The architects have treated the building in quite the local style, showing scrupulous regard for local architectural tradition, and only at the corner of New Bond Street is the treatment rather more elaborate. This will be the feature of the great building, and to avoid technical detail for the present, there is surmounting the corner (which is circular in plan) a finely conceived stone turret, which serves to balance the whole composition. The corner will be greatly improved, no less than 220 superficial feet being given up to the pavement, and it may be added that the utmost harmony with St Michael's Church is assured.

The main entrance will be in the centre of the main frontage to Northgate Street, much where it is at present, and there will be a private passage for the admission of travellers' stock at the corner of Green Street, convenient for the eight or nine stock rooms which are to be an important feature of the building. On the ground floor of the New Bond Street frontage, from the end of Mr Goldsworthy's to where the Midland Receiving Depot now is [21-24 New Bond Street], will be a range of lock-up shops, the provision of which have an important financial bearing on the scheme. Six of them have a depth of 33 feet, and will be lit by large windows at the rear (good light on both sides is a rarity in business property in Bath) and the other three decrease in extent until the ninth will suffice only for a tobacconist's store, or some such purpose. A tenth shop is provided round the Green Street corner.

Avoiding detail also as to the interior, it may be said that the most striking feature of the hotel will be its lounge at the New Bond Street corner (where there will be no entrance as at present). This apartment, being 50 feet by 30 feet, will have nothing to approach it in the city, either in regard to dimensions or prospect, for the windows will, of course, command High Street and the Municipal Buildings. The lounge will have a bar counter running half the length of one side. The commercial room (36 feet by 28 feet) will be on the other side of the main entrance. The bedrooms on the first and second floors will number 40 to 45 … The dining room will be above the lounge, and of equal dimensions, and above that (on the second floor) will be in turn the billiard room … Internally as well as externally the building will be a great adornment to a city already rich in fine buildings.

But, of course, it never happened. The Castle closed in 1924 and was demolished to make way for the Post Office.* However, the layout of the Post Office not only followed that of the Castle – even down to the entrance into the courtyard – but has some of the old walls incorporated into the building.

The site of the Castle today.

---

*A sub post office had opened next to the Castle, in Alderman Rubie's former wine merchant's in New Bond Street, several years earlier.

And now, most noble boozers, and you my very esteemed and poxy friends, it is time to perambulate that paradoxical penumbra of preternatural potworthiness – the nobly caparisoned yet miserably de-pubbed Street of Walcot.*

The name of Walcot has a curious origin. After the Romans abandoned Aquae Sulis, the people left behind settled down, making the best of things and trying to stay out of the way of ravaging hordes. Eventually one ravaging horde – the Saxons – scored an overwhelming victory at the Battle of Dyrham in AD577, before moving on to Bath to destroy much of what remained. The city's desolation was later celebrated in a poem called *The Ruin*, but by then the Saxons had established a power base within the old ramparts. The bit inside the walls they called Akemancester, the bit outside, where the native population contrived to eke out a precarious existence, they called Walcot, meaning "place of strangers." They did the same elsewhere. There are Walcots in Berkshire, Lincolnshire, Shropshire and Warwickshire, a Walcote in Leicestershire, and Walcotts in Norfolk and Worcestershire. Walsall, Cornwall and Wales – all places beyond the Anglo-Saxon pale – have a similar derivation.

This means not only that the Saxons had the bare-faced cheek to call the people that were here before them foreigners, but also that Walcot probably has a longer continuous history of settlement than central Bath. And here's another thought. As the Saxon chieftains sat quaffing mead and reading *Beowulf* of a summer evening, and saw the sun sink over Akemancester, did they hear the noise of Celtic drums wafting up from Walcot Street, and think to themselves, "the natives are restless tonight?"

Today – unless we count the Ha! Ha! Bar and the back entrances to the Saracen's Head and the Pig & Fiddle – there is only one pub – the Bell – left in Walcot Street. There used to be over twenty. Walcot Street has always been the hub of Bath's commercial district. Until the railway opened, it was also the way most people entered the city, so there was plenty of passing trade. There were also hordes of people crammed into one-up, one-down hovels in the courts and alleys running off Walcot Street, in conditions we cannot even begin to imagine. As late as 1927, a family with six children hit the headlines when they were found living in a roofless hovel in Broad Street Place in the depths of winter. If that could happen in 1927 just think what people had to put up with in 1827 – or 1727. The pubs of Walcot Street – however grim they were – must have seemed havens of comfort compared with such squalor.

---

*The reference of course is to the opening of François Rabelais's *Gargantua and Pantagruel*, to which the earnest attention of students of binge is humbly directed.

There have been inns and taverns along Walcot Street for almost 2000 years, but the Roman and medieval ones are lost in the mists of time. The story of those we know about, from the sixteenth century on, is a rich and often bizarre one. And, as befits an area which has always been predominantly working class, it has little to do with the polite excesses of Beau Nash's etiquettopolis.

Today, Walcot Street has been tweely dubbed Bath's Artizan Quarter, but a century ago there was nothing twee about it. It was the workshop of Bath. There were gasfitters, shoemakers, printers, saddlers, carpenters, coopers, rag merchants, coach builders, tripe dressers, brass finishers, sign painters, basket makers, gunsmiths, bookbinders, cutlers, ironmongers, stone masons, auctioneers, builders, tinplate workers, and iron makers. It had a corn market and, after 1810, when it moved from the Sawclose, a cattle market. Farmers haggled over the price of grain, herds of cattle ambled down the street and sheep pens were set up against the walls of alehouses. Imagine what it smelt like on a hot summer's day – and what it was like when it rained. Slip in Walcot Street on market day and you'd almost certainly hope you wouldn't have a soft landing.

The Roman road leading out of the city lies buried some seven or eight feet below the level of today's street. Yet, despite the fact that nothing from Roman times survives above ground, Walcot Street displays an awesome continuity of function – a continuity which many fear is about to be broken as the pace of Walcot Street's gentrification gains momentum.

In the centuries that followed the departure of the Romans, Walcot Street shrank back towards the city. Although trade continued at the southern end, many buildings fell into ruin. It is likely that the Bell, if it existed as an inn before the sixteenth century, stood in open country on the borders of Walcot Parish. In the seventeenth century, as the population of Bath began to grow, large houses were built on Ladymead, with their gardens running down to the river, as part of a genteel

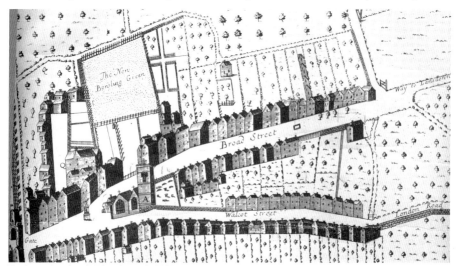

Northgate, Broad and Walcot Streets in 1694.

THE LOST PUBS OF BATH

suburban development. It was an idyllic spot. Vineyards covered the slopes above Walcot Street; above them sheepwalks led up to the grassy heights of Lan's Down. Across the river lay the water meadows and farms of Bathwick. Beyond Ladymead, a walk across fields where grass-grown mounds marked the remains of Roman buildings, lay the hamlet of Walcot, huddled round its ancient church.

By 1738, buildings once again stretched the length of the street. A few years later, John Wood wrote that, although Walcot Street had "one of the finest situations for building in, that nature is capable of producing … instead of finding it covered with habitations for the chief citizens, it is filled, for the most part, with hovels for the refuse of the people." Walcot Street's brief flirtation with gentility was, it seems, over.

A last echo of the rural haven created in Walcot Street in the late seventeenth century appeared in a newspaper report with a *Midsummer Night's Dream* quality from 1757:

> Numbers of people have for some time past resorted to a garden at Walcot near the riverside on the report of a very strange noise being heard there every night. It is a common saying, one fool makes many; this was verified one night last week, when near 200 persons went to hear this strange noise, many of whom were so credulous to believe that it proceeded from some invisible being. However, upon strict examination into the affair, it appeared to be no more than a screech-owl, which is kept in a barn at Bathwick, opposite the aforesaid garden.

By this time, Walcot Street was already acquiring a reputation for alternative lifestyles. Take this report of cross-dressing from the *Bath Journal* of 15 October 1744:

> As remarkable an affair was discovered here about three days hence, as is scarcely to be parallel'd in history, viz. last Friday morning died here a person call'd by the name of Sutton, who declared before death that she was a real woman, born at Rumsey in Hampshire, tho' have appear'd for many years in man's apparel; that her reason for so doing was an attempt offer'd her, at about the age of fourteen, to betray her virtue: after which she was hired into a gentleman's service, as a footman, with whom she liv'd five years; that soon after she enlisted herself into the army, as a drummer, and was in Scotland at the time of the rebellion, at the beginning of the reign of his late majesty, and behaved gallantly in his Majesty's Cause; that when part of the army were disbanded she had a new way of life to seek, therefore she betook herself to peddling goods, history books, etc, up and down the country for many years; that for fourteen years past she had lived with another woman, and passed as man and wife; but was always punctual and honest to every person she had any dealings with. The said Sutton have liv'd here for these three years past, rented a house of £10 a year in the Parish of Walcot and dealt in buying and selling old clothes. What is very remarkable, few or none suspected her, as above, she carrying the affair on with a great deal of art.

By the 1760s, Walcot Street had been changed forever by the monstrous erection that had arisen above it. Instead of vineyards climbing gently away towards Lan's Down, a cliff was built, a cliff called the Paragon. Looking at it today, almost 250 years later, it seems incredible that anyone believed it would ever stay up. But, unlike the

eastern part of Camden Crescent and the buildings which once covered the slopes of Hedgemead, it did. It is still there, a monument to human endeavour and the architectural equivalent of a two-fingered salute to the plebs below.

If the well-heeled residents of Ladymead needed any convincing that the area was going downhill, the building of the Paragon provided it, and Walcot Street soon acquired a reputation for rowdiness. This report, picked at random from the pages of the *Bath Chronicle* in 1828, suggests that a pub crawl along Walcot Street in the early nineteenth century was not for the faint-hearted:

A desperate riot took place on Wednesday evening among a set of dissolute fellows at the Fox & Hounds public house in Walcot Street and also at the Three Tuns; some of them were apprehended and [certain] individuals have been committed in default of bail for assaulting the tythingmen [parish constables] in the execution of their duty.

The part of Walcot Street which has been more or less continuously settled since Roman times is the stretch between Northgate Street and the Corn Market. There were several inns along this stretch, which, although less prestigious than those within the walls, were still respectable. They started to close shortly after the railway from London opened in 1841. Walcot Street's inns relied heavily on passing trade – especially trade connected with the market – and carrier traffic. Carriers to towns and villages outside Bath were based at inns which served as receiving points for goods and passengers. The railway did not kill this trade overnight – many

Sir Patrick Abercrombie's vision for Walcot Street.

THE LOST PUBS OF BATH

villages were miles from the nearest station and relied on carriers until the early twentieth century – but it fell off sharply. The demise of many of Walcot Street's inns was accelerated by the opening of a Cornmarket Hall in 1855, built with the express intention of providing an alternative to the pub as a place for market-goers to conduct business.

All the buildings on the east side of Walcot Street between Northgate Street and the Tramshed, including several historic inns and pubs, disappeared in the 1960s. If plans for postwar redevelopment had gone ahead, the whole of Walcot Street would be no more than a distant memory. The plans actually started before the war. In 1935, the council proposed demolishing all the buildings on the east side of the street between Northgate Street and Beehive Yard and building a bus station, with a bridge across to Grove Street. The Abercrombie Report, published in 1945, proposed the demolition of Walcot Street and its replacement by a pseudo-Georgian block stretching from St Michael's Church to Cleveland Bridge and a road and walkway alongside the river. The only parts of Abercrombie's grand plan for Bath to come to fruition were the bus station and the abattoir, which, between them, give us some inkling of what the new-look Walcot Street would have been like. Less than 20 years later, Colin Buchanan came up with a scheme to relieve traffic congestion by building a tunnel from Walcot Street to Royal Victoria Park. This, too, involved the demolition of vast swathes of Walcot Street, but, like Abercrombie's plan, it came to nothing.

The threat to what remains of Walcot Street's buildings seems, for the time being at least, to have receded. There is, however, a more insidious threat – not to the fabric of Walcot Street, but to its character, as increasing gentrification, with new residential developments secreted, Beverley-Hills like, behind electronically-operated gates, seeps in. The price of one of the apartments in the newly-refurbished Tramshed nudges £600,000, probably beyond the reach of even the most industrious of the artisans whose quarter (according to the signposts pointing Walcotwards) this is. But who knows what the future holds? For now, let us wander down Bath's most colourful street and drink in its alcoholic heritage.

Just past the back entrance to the Saracen's Head is the first of Walcot Street's lost inns, the **King's Arms** at No 5. It opened some time before 1776 and by 1833 had been taken over by Sainsbury's Brewery. It was a fairly substantial inn, with bar, bar parlour, two dining rooms, and a number of bedrooms. In 1840, GP Manners, the City Architect, valued it at £40. It closed around 1854, a victim of the loss of trade

The King's Arms as many still remember it – home of the Bath Bun Café.

caused by the coming of the railways. Its last landlord was Frederick Bowler, the father of JB Bowler. By the late 1850s, it housed Fletcher's Marine Stores and Parker's Furniture Store. By the end of the nineteenth century, Palmer's Antiques and Chorley's Grocer's-cum-Servant's Registry had moved in. Twentieth-century occupiers included the Merrifield Café, Weaver's Furniture Store, the Dolphin Grill, Homevac

Electrics, and the Bath Bun Café. Today the old King's Arms houses Knickerbean and Save the Children.

A few doors along, at No 13, Cooper's Electrical Superstore stands on the site of the **Hand & Shears**, which owed its name to the weavers and cloth merchants who once frequented it. It opened some time before 1776 and was later taken over by the Anchor Brewery. In October 1825, the landlord, John Cox, was fined £5 for keeping a "disorderly house." Nevertheless, the Hand & Shears, which had a courtyard and stables, still had some pretensions to respectability. Some of its customers, however, did not. In 1841, for example, the *Bath Chronicle* reported that

> a young man named James Goff ... has been lodging at the Hand & Shears public-house in Walcot Street ... On Saturday evening stewed eels were served up for supper, and Goff was supplied with a silver table spoon with which to eat his portion of the savoury dish. When dinner was over, he left the house with the said spoon in his pocket and went to the shop of Mr J Lawrence, Pawnbroker in New Westgate Buildings.

A plan of the Hand & Shears in 1838.

The upshot of this impulsive act was two months hard labour.

In 1840, George Trimby took over the Hand & Shears and renamed it the Nightingale. Perhaps he was hoping that his customers would be put in mind of the immortal lines of Keats' *Ode to a Nightingale*:

> O, for a draught of vintage! that hath been
> Cooled a long age in the deep-delved earth,
> Tasting of Flora and the country green,
> Dance, and Provencal song, and sunburnt mirth!
> O for a beaker full of the warm South,
> Full of the true, the blushful Hippocrene,
> With beaded bubbles winking at the brim,
> And purple-stained mouth;
> That I might drink, and leave the world unseen,
> And with thee fade away into the forest dim.

It is more likely, however, that they would have seen it as a knocking shop. In nineteenth-century slang, prostitutes were known as nightingales, presumably because they did most of their work at night. The Nightingale closed a few years later, and by the late 1850s was home to Brooke's Chemist's, which later produced mineral water.

A little further up the street, to the right of the steps leading to Broad Street Place, at No 35, was a beerhouse called the **Jolly Sailor**, open for a brief period in the 1830s. Today it is Pax Marice.

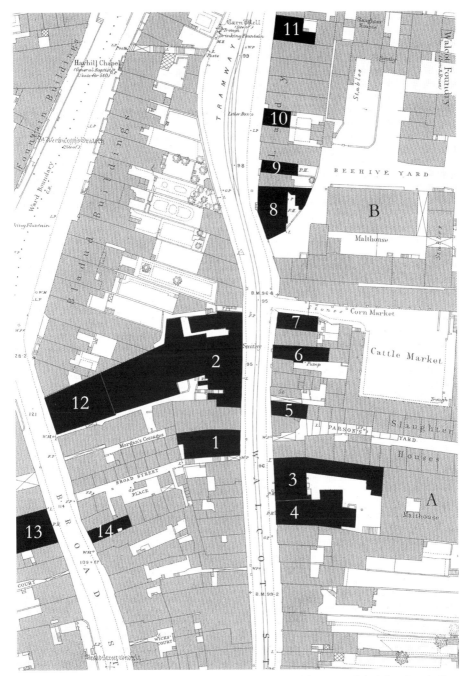

The lost pubs of southern Walcot Street and Broad Street: 1) the Jolly Sailor; 2) the George; 3) the Pelican (later the Three Cups); 4) the Fox & Hounds; 5) the Newmarket Tavern; 6) the Queen's Head; 7) the Duke of Wellington's Arms; 8) the Beehive; 9) the Catherine Wheel; 10) the New Inn; 11) the Duke of Edinburgh; 12) the Dolphin; 13) the Turk's Head; 14) the Wheatsheaf. A and B indicate malthouses.

STEPPING EASTWARD

Cockfighting was a gentlemen's pastime in the early eighteenth century, with large sums of money changing hands.

Moving along, we come to the site of the **George** – sometimes known as the George & Dragon – a fine old inn which, in the mid-eighteenth century, was equipped, for the entertainment of gentlemen, with a cockpit. In January 1747, the *Bath Journal* advised its readers that

a cock match will be fought at Mr Trueman's at the George in Walcot Street, between the gentlemen of Somerset and the gentlemen of Wiltshire ... To weigh Tuesday 13th, and fight the three following nights.

Some mid-eighteenth century amusements at the George were less barbaric. In July 1744, Mr Trueman held a "florist's feast" there. The *Bath Journal* reported that

there were a great many firm blossoms of carnation produced; the silver spurs were won by Mr William Harding; the gold ring by Mr George Allen, both of this city; the ordinaries and extraordinaries by Mr Holdstock of Walcot. There was a very elegant entertainment provided; and the whole was conducted with good order and decorum.

After cock fighting was outlawed, Mr Trueman's successors had to find a use for the cockpit. Travelling menageries were one solution. In 1820, Drake's Royal Menagerie was exhibited at the George. Its star exhibit was "the stupendous elephant which was overturned in coming down Lansdown Road."[*]

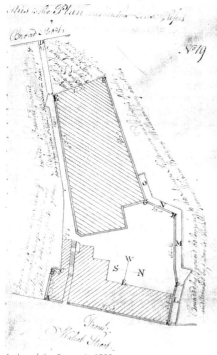

A plan of the George in 1788.

The George was a sizeable establishment. An old map shows a passageway leading through the middle of the pub and up a flight of steps to an alleyway at the back. This led to Morgan's Cottages, which backed onto Broad Street Place. When Richard Harford took the lease of the George in 1759, it stretched back as far as Bladud's Buildings, then less than five years old. In 1782, after John Hensley had acquired the lease, he built two houses fronting Broad Street, one of which became the Dolphin, almost certainly the tap for the George.

In 1818, the Corporation instructed John Hensley to set back the front of the inn so that the street could be widened. When he demurred, they gave him an ultimatum: if he did not agree to carry out the refronting, they would revoke his

*See *Awash with Ale*, p171

THE LOST PUBS OF BATH

lease. He complied, and, the following year, set about extending the premises. The Corporation ordered that "Mr Plumpton [should] be paid £20 for so much of his ground as may be required for continuing the improvement of Mr Hensley's premises in Walcot Street, the George Inn."

John Hensley sublet the George to Williams' Brewery in 1793. Later, Sainsbury's Brewery took over. The George called last orders around 1868, when the landlord, Worthy Baker (who had previously kept the Rose & Crown in Larkhall), crossed the road to become landlord of the Beehive. The old building was occupied by a variety

Harvest Wholefoods – all that survives of the George.

of tradesmen – a coachsmith, a drover, a horseclipper and a cooper – whose callings echoed the inn's traditions. In the 1890s it became Welch's veterinary surgery. In the twentieth century, Goddard's banana-ripening warehouse and Pickford's warehouse occupied the site. Part of the old stable block survives as Harvest Natural Foods. The entrance to the shop was the entrance to the courtyard and the alleyway leading to Broad Street Place. Most of the old George, however, was pulled down to make way for the YMCA, which sits almost exactly on its site. The kink in the building halfway between Walcot Street and Broad Street, for example, can be clearly seen in plans of the George.

On the other side of the road from the YMCA, stretching between the Hilton Hotel and the disused Corn Market, is one of the worst bits of streetscape in Bath. It would not be so bad if the area lacked potential, but it borders the River Avon, and could be transformed into a piazza and riverside walkway worthy of a World Heritage Site. The council planned a walkway along the river over two centuries ago; the wasteland we see today is both a tribute to and an indictment of official inertia.

Once, this area was a hive of activity. Turning the clock back to the mid-nineteenth century, the roll-call of businesses which operated from here was an impressive one. There was a seedsman, two tailors, an eating house, three grocers, a basket maker, a greengrocer, a dyer, two tinmen, three clothes dealers, a straw bonnet maker, two confectioners, three bakers, a gunmaker, a printer, a cabinet maker, a furniture dealer, a hairdresser, a currier, a bootmaker, an umbrella maker, a pork butcher, a well sinker, and a tripe dresser. There was also a Bethel Chapel, several courts of back-to-back tenements, and five pubs.

The most celebrated was the **Pelican**. This stood midway between Northgate Street and the Corn Market and opened around 1668. In the late eighteenth century a horse sale was held there every Saturday at noon, along with occasional auctions of farming stock.It was also the meeting place of the Amicable Bathonian Society.

In 1776 James Boswell, who had followed Dr Johnson down to Bath, stayed at the Pelican. Although he did not record his impressions of the Pelican, it was a different story when he moved on to Bristol with Dr Johnson :

> We were by no means pleased with our inn at Bristol. "Let us see now," said I,
> "how should we describe it?" Johnson was ready with his raillery. "Describe it,
> sir? Why, it was so bad that Boswell wished to return to Scotland."

Two years after Boswell's visit, Matthew Rood, the landlord of the Pelican, went bankrupt, and the inn was put up for sale. It was advertised with stabling for 40 horses, "proper coach houses," and a daily "flying machine and diligence" to London.

In 1781, two servants, Charles Hawkins and Thomas Huntley, went with their masters' horses to "the usual watering place at the bottom of the Pelican yard." Charles Hawkins rode one of the horses out into the river, unaware that there was a deep hole a little way out. The horse went under, he fell off and was drowned.

In 1799, the council instructed the Northgate Brewery, which held the lease of the Pelican, to "take down and set back the front" for road widening. They seem to have ignored the order, for, seven years later, they were again told "to take down and build a new front, setting back the same in a line with the messuage adjoining on the south." As no further instructions were issued, we can only assume they complied.

The Pelican survived as a successful coaching inn until about 1841. Then, following the collapse of the coaching trade caused by the opening of the Great Western Railway, it was taken over by Francis Norrison from the Three Cups in Northgate Street. He had been forced to close the Three Cups due to lack of trade, but brought its name with him, renaming the Pelican the Three Cups. It soon became

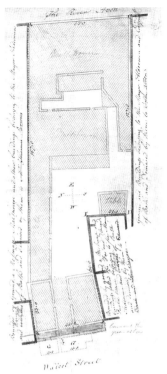

A plan of the Pelican in 1776.

The Three Cups in the 1930s.

The malthouse behind the Three Cups.

clear that the glory days of the old Pelican had passed, along with its name, and it started to acquire a rather unsavoury reputation. In 1858, for example, the ostler at the inn was summoned for "creating a nuisance in Walcot Street" by leaving a "quantity of dung" there.

A visitor to the Three Cups in the late nineteenth century would have found much of its eighteenth-century atmosphere intact, if a little ramshackle. It consisted of a bar, bar parlour, tap room with bagatelle table, club room, seven bedrooms, brewery, coach house, and yard. There was also a large malthouse at the back, owned by JD Taylor & Sons. In 1899 the malthouse burnt down, although the Three Cups was undamaged.

In 1923, GK Chesterton unveiled a tablet on the building to commemorate Dr Johnson's visit, even though Boswell, in his *Life of Johnson*, made it clear that it was he who stayed there, while Dr Johnson lodged with his friends the Thrales on South Parade. In June 1938 the Three Cups moved one last time. The *Bath Chronicle* takes up the story:

> Mrs Sarah Ann Burgess, licensee of the Three Cups, Walcot Street, applied to Bath Licensing Justices … for an order sanctioning the special removal of the Three Cups from 40 Walcot Street to 6 & 8 Walcot Street. Mr F Glover, making the application, said that Mr Burgess was tenant for some 20 years prior to his death in March and in May the licence was transferred to his widow. The house belonged to the Corporation. The site of the street on which the Three Cups stands was particularly involved in a big improvement scheme, and the City Improvements Committee were anxious to get on with the work. One of the chief obstacles to getting on was that licensed house. The Corporation were doing all they possibly could to help Mrs Burgess, and were giving 6 & 8 Walcot Street, formerly occupied by Mr Whiting [a cutler] and Eastman's Ltd [butchers], as temporary accommodation..

When the Chairman of the Magistrates asked whether the temporary transfer was to last for six or twelve months, Mr Glover replied that, "the future is rather in the lap of the gods about that. The licensed house will be re-established in some part of the new street, probably near its present site." He went on to explain that "one of the houses would be used as the licensed house and the other for lavatory purposes." Among the things in the lap of the gods, of course, was the Second World War, and this, combined with official procrastination, ensured that the Three Cups was never rebuilt near its old site. It remained at its new address, 8 Walcot Street, at the entrance to Hen & Chicken Court, until it closed on 21 August 1967. Its obituary appeared in the *Bath Chronicle* two days earlier:

> THREE CUPS TO GO DRY
>
> The Three Cups will serve its last customer on Monday. The pub, which has a closing order on it, is in a redevelopment area under the Buchanan plan. It is leased from Bath Corporation. The licence will change back to the brewery, Wadworth's of Devizes, who will hold it in abeyance until the council allocate a new site.
>
> Mrs Nesta Courtenay, the wife of the licensee for the past two years, explained, "the

ceilings in the bathroom, my bedroom and above the staircase have all collapsed. Although they have been repaired, the trouble is likely to keep on recurring."

The original Three Cups stood further up Walcot Street for more than 300 years before it was demolished in 1949. Known as the Pelican Inn until the end of the last century, it was probably the oldest tavern in Bath.

The site of the last Three Cups is now marked by the entrance to the Podium Car Park. As a footnote to the story, the tablet unveiled by GK Chesterton commemorating Dr Johnson's visit is believed to have remained on the old inn until it was demolished in 1956 (not 1949 as stated in the above report). Its current whereabouts are unknown.

There is, however, another footnote to the story of the Three Cups. Its final move – to the entrance of Hen & Chicken Court – revived, quite by chance, the fortunes of an inn whose very existence had been forgotten.

In 1763, Thomas Counsel leased "all that messuage or tenement ... in Walcot Street ... commonly called or known by the name or sign of the **Hen & Chicken** ... together with a brewhouse, five tenements, a garden and workshops behind the same." It was bounded on the north by "another tenement, brewhouse, court and garden of the said Thomas Counsel, on the south by a tenement and garden of Benjamin Wingrove, on the east by the River Avon, and on the west by Walcot Street."

This is the only reference to a pub called the Hen & Chicken, so presumably it closed shortly afterwards. Its memory, however, lingered on in the name of Hen & Chicken Court, a row of cramped, damp, eighteenth-century hovels that survived

The southern end of Walcot Street in the 1850s. Hen & Chicken Court can be seen directly below St Michael's Church.

Walcot Street in the 1930s: A) the Three Cups; B) the Fox & Hounds.

The same view today.

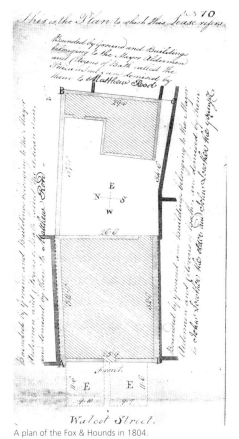

A plan of the Fox & Hounds in 1804.

until the mid-1960s. The Three Cups' final move was a revival – even though nobody realised it at the time – of an inn that closed almost two centuries earlier.*

Next to the Pelican was the **Fox & Hounds** (originally the Hare & Hounds), which may have started life as the Pelican's tap. It opened some time before 1776, when John Whittick, a victualler, took the lease. The terms of the lease stipulated that he had to give up the garden ground at the back of the inn if requested, so that the Corporation could build "a parade with a balustrade with rails" alongside the river. In 1794, however, when the Northgate Brewery acquired the lease, the "little garden behind" was still there, although the same proviso applied. Over two centuries later, the alluring prospect of a riverside walkway north of Pulteney Bridge, first mooted by the Corporation in the 1770s, and again in the 1970s, seems as far away as ever.

The Fox & Hounds was rebuilt and set back at the same time as the Three Cups. It had its own brewery and, although it was a respectable establishment, with clubs such as the United Brethren Society and the Society of Inhabitants meeting there, it had its livelier moments, such as the "desperate riot" mentioned earlier.

By the end of the nineteenth century, the lease of the Fox & Hounds, as well as that of the Three Cups, was held by Charles Stride. In 1915 the licensing authorities decided that the Fox & Hounds was redundant. George Davis, the licensee "said he did not object to the house being closed if he received compensation. He said he did not make a living out of the house, but simply made enough to live rent free. He was employed as a cabinet maker." After it closed, the Fox & Hounds became an antique shop.

There were three other pubs between the Three Cups and the Corn Market. Three doors along from the Three Cups (roughly where the plinth on the site of the old

*The Hen & Chicken or Hen & Chickens was a common pub name in the eighteenth century. It referred to the thirteen jugs or "hanaps" which all licensees had to have in case anyone queried their measures. The largest – the Hen – contained four gallons. The others – the Chickens – ranged in capacity down to a third of a gill. There are still 19 pubs called the Hen & Chickens in Britain, including one in Bedminster.

toilets is today) was a beerhouse called the **Newmarket Tavern**. It opened around 1860, having previously been Chapman's Pork Butcher's. When an inventory was drawn up in 1888, it had four bedrooms, a sitting room, a tap room, a bar parlour, and a bar with "a model of a cow." It closed in 1906 and later became Hope's Hairdresser's.

Four doors further up was another beerhouse opened as the Boar's Head around 1837, renamed the **Queen's Head** a couple of years later, and closed in the early 1850s. The building was then occupied by James Pratt, a confectioner, before being taken over by a tripe dresser called Thomas Glisson. It was a tripe dresser's until well into the twentieth century.

In April 1809, the council paid £500 for land "behind the houses in Walcot Street" to build a cattle market. Work started the following year and, in September 1811, the vaults under the market were let to a grocer called William Naish from New Bond Street. In January 1812, John Palmer, the architect, was asked to "examine the house in Walcot Street lately used as a poor house for St Michael's, and to report how it may be utilized for the accommodation of the persons attending the Cattle Market." Four years later, the council was still considering how "the ground and buildings near the Cattle Market, lately used as the poor house, should be disposed of." It was decided to demolish and rebuild, and in 1818 a "new public house in Walcot Street, next to the Cattle Market, [was] to let, with the stables under the market."

The pub was taken by Henry Mundy, who called it the **Duke of Wellington's Arms**. In 1819, a customer called James Gage came in to get warm and spent some time sitting by the fire in the tap room drinking dog's nose (gin and beer) and

Cattle Market Bath

THE LOST PUBS OF BATH

complaining of the cold. After he had finished his drink, he went on his way but got no further than one of the arches under the cattle market, where his body was found next morning.

In 1829,the name of the pub was changed to the Wellington Arms & Newmarket Tavern. The following year, the Corporation agreed to reduce the rent "at the request of Henry Mundy … in consequence of a considerable decrease in the business, especially that part of it which was derived from the market." Despite the reduction, Henry Mundy decided to quit; the following year an advertisement appeared in the *Bath Chronicle* announcing that the "Wellington Arms Inn & Tavern in Walcot Street, adjoining the Cattle and Corn Market, also several vaults under the said markets," was to let.

By 1833 the name of the pub had changed to the Newmarket Tavern (not to be confused with the Newmarket Tavern a few doors along, which opened around 1860). By 1837, it had changed back to the Wellington Arms, but business still failed to pick up. Eventually, in 1845, the council, "having considered the state of the Wellington Arms … and the great difficulty they have had in finding an eligible tenant for it in consequence of the number of public houses in the neighbourhood," decided "to divide it into two houses with shops." A month later an advertisement appeared in the *Bath Chronicle*:

> Builders disposed to contract for converting the Wellington Arms Inn, Walcot Street into two houses may see the plans and specifications at the office of Mr Manners, City Architect, No 1, Oxford Row … One of the intended houses and a long range of dry, healthy vaults under the Corn Market House, to be let.

After the conversion, half the property became Harrison's Grocer's, which survived until the early twentieth century. The other half, after a spell as an outfitter's, reopened, around 1870, as a beerhouse called the **Corn Market Tavern. T**his was a very short lived enterprise, lasting for only about five years. Nevertheless, its promoters obviously had high hopes for it. It had four bedrooms, a bar, a bar parlour and a concert room with a cottage piano in a painted case and a small stage. It later became the Cornmarket Coffee Tavern, and survived in this form until the 1930s.

Beyond the old Tramshed – now the Ha! Ha! Bar – lies the stretch of Walcot Street known as Ladymead, so called because it once belonged to Edith, wife of Edward the Confessor. The seventeenth- and early-eighteenth-century houses on Ladymead not only had gardens running down to the river; they also had gardens fronting Walcot Street. These disappeared in 1829 and "the accommodation of foot passengers was materially promoted by an excellent causeway, of fourteen feet, and the remainder of the ground [was] added to the carriage road."

At 66 Walcot Street, on the corner of Beehive Yard, was the **Beehive Inn,** which opened in the 1840s. It had two entrances from Walcot Street and an exit at the back into Beehive Yard, where there was a large stable and coach house. In 1939, Bass, who owned the pub, obtained approval to transfer the licence to "premises … to be erected on land to be known as Whiteway Housing Estate." This was the Beehive

Market day outside the Beehive in the early twentieth century. The iron sign-bracket of the piub is still there.

at Mount Road, Southdown, which, like the Beehive in Walcot Street, is now one of Bath's lost pubs. However, plans to build the new Beehive had to be put on hold because of the war and the old Beehive did not close until the mid-1950s. It was later taken over by Archway Garden Machinery; part of it now houses Domino Pizzas.

The Catherine Wheel occupied what is now the left-hand side of Shannon.

Next door but one to the Beehive, at 70 Walcot Street, was the **Catherine Wheel**. This opened some time before 1776 as the Orange Tree and became the Catherine Wheel around 1786. Compared with the Beehive, it was tiny. However, its upstairs extended over the shop next door (No 68), and "well-aired beds" were available for visitors. It had a bar with a zinc top counter, a bar parlour at the back and a small room partitioned off at the front. There was no rear exit. It closed around 1909. After being occupied by a horseflesh dealer called Joe Maris and a grocer called Walt Murray, it became a café, latterly known as the Pandora. Today it forms the left-hand side of Shannon. The stained-glass door may date from when the building was a pub.

Three doors along, at 76 Walcot Street, was the **New Inn**. Its story is a short yet tragic one. In 1837 John Grist was the landlord of the Catherine Wheel. Ten years later, the Catherine Wheel had been taken over by Richard Perkins from the Unicorn in

The former Catherine Wheel is on the extreme right of this photograph from the 1930s. The former New Inn is three doors along, with the blinds down.

Northgate Street, and John Grist had opened the New Inn as a beerhouse. The move had been forced on him by his financial situation; to make ends meet, he supplemented his income by working as a cobbler. This failed to solve his problems, however, and, on 4 May 1848, the following report appeared in the *Bath Chronicle*:

> An inquest was held on Friday evening … on the body of John Fletcher Grist, landlord of the New Inn, Ladymead, who committed suicide by cutting his throat the same morning with a broken knife used by him in his trade as a shoemaker. The deceased was a man of weak nerve, and for some time had been depressed and wandering in his mind, in consequence of pecuniary difficulties. He was also subject to epileptic fits, and had one after he inflicted the wound in his throat. The jury returned a verdict of "insanity." Grist has left a widow and three children.

His widow, Jeannette Grist, kept the New Inn going for a while, but soon gave up the struggle, and the inn closed.* The building was taken over by a tailor called James Descomb or Dascombe. Other occupiers have included a saddler and a baker. Since the 1960s, it has been a sewing machine shop.

In 1876, another shoemaker called James Cox opened a beerhouse called the **Duke of Edinburgh** at 86 Walcot Street. It was named after Prince Alfred, Duke of Edinburgh, the second son of Queen Victoria, who was a popular figure, especially around 1874, when he married a Russian princess. The beerhouse quickly

The former Duke of Edinburgh.

*It is not known if this was the same Jeannette Grist who ran the Crown Inn at Bathford from the 1850s to the 1870s. If so, she had achieved a remarkable turnaround in her fortunes.

passed through the hands of two other licensees – E Keevil and Albin Oram – until, at the 1883 licensing sessions, no application was made to renew the licence. It lingered on for a while as the Walcot Club, but this closed around 1886, and the building was taken over by Humphries' Outfitter's. Twentieth-century occupants have included the Horstmann Gear Company, Taylor's Confectioner's and James's Scalemaker's. Today it is Fast Signs.

At 90 Walcot Street, on the corner of Old Orchard was the **Bladud's Head**, one of Walcot Street's longest-surviving inns. Its opening, in November 1792, was marked by an advertisement in the *Bath Chronicle*:

> J Parker, late waiter at the New Rooms, respectfully informs his friends and the publick that he has opened a new inn in Ladymead, known by the sign of the BLADUD'S INN & TAVERN. The inn by its situation in the London Road leading from Walcot Street, will be very convenient for farmers, higglers, and persons that frequent Bath market with carts, having a large yard for carts, and good stabling for horses, with the best of hay and corn, and every other accommodation. Having laid in a stock of good wines and spiritous liquors, etc., he humbly hopes to merit the favours of travellers and his friends.

Four years earlier, Mr Parker had opened a "chop house" next to the tennis court in Morford Street (now the Museum of Bath at Work). His move to an inn and tavern in Walcot Street was a step up in the world, but he was there for less than three years, for in April 1795 the Bladud Inn was advertised to let.

By 1800 James Harris held the licence; a year later it was advertised for sale:

> To be sold by PRIVATE CONTRACT
> on Moderate Terms
> That Convenient, Newly-built, Roomy and Substantial
> INN and TAVERN,
> known by the name of the
> BLADUD'S INN, in LADY-MEAD,
> With ample Stabling, Yard and Coach-houses adjoining,
> Well adapted for the accommodation of
> Farmers and Travellers in general;
> and has the advantage of sufficient space
> for erecting a good private Brewery near the cellars.
> It is now lett to James Harris, as tenant at will;
> held on lease of three healthy lives,
> at a trifling quit-rent, and always renewable on easy terms.
> A purchaser may be accommodated, if required,
> With a desirable Piece of Garden Ground,
> Lying very near the premises,
> and most pleasantly bordering on the River Avon

By 1805, the inn was held by Thomas Linnell, who was not only an "importer and dealer in foreign wines and spirits (wholesale and retail)," but also bought and sold greenhouse plants.

Around this time, the name of the pub was changed to the Bladud's Head, and it was in this guise that it featured in the Poor Law Records for St Michael's Parish in 1817. A girl called Mary Bank from Batheaston had left home at 17 to work as a servant in the Bladud's Head. After she had been there for nearly a year she was dismissed because the landlady was "afraid she would come to some harm in her house and said that she was a good servant and would give her a good character when she could find a situation" This was not the real reason, however. If Mary Bank had stayed there for over twelve months, she would have established residency in St Michael's Parish and become entitled to poor relief. Employers were under pressure from parish authorities to ensure that servants from outside the parish moved on before the year was up. It was a brutal system, as the sequel to Mary's story shows. She failed to find another job, ended up pregnant, and, not being entitled to relief in St Michael's Parish, was forced to go back to Batheaston. She was 20 years old.

A story from 1826 provides a salutary warning of what can happen when you let the beer do the talking. William Gunn was drinking at the Bladud's Head with William Hicks, a pinmaker, when an argument broke out as to which of them was the best swimmer. As the river was at the back of the pub, they decided to settle the issue there and then. Wagers were taken and the two men strode down to the river bank and stripped off. They swam across with Hicks in the lead, but on the way back Gunn disappeared. His body was found later downstream.

A year later, the landlord of the Bladud's Head was the target of an unsuccessful scam:

> Thomas Powell of the Bladud's Head Public House in the parish of St Michael's ... maketh oath and saith that on Saturday the 13th day of January instant at about 12 o'clock in the forenoon, Thomas Sims came to deponent's house and after drinking a glass or two of beer told deponent that he expected a parcel of silver spoons from Bristol which he had sent there to be engraved and had ordered them to be left at deponent's house and requested deponent to pay the expenses attending the parcel. That about 5 o'clock the same day a parcel came to deponent's house directed to T Sims and for which the person who brought it demanded 8/6. That deponent suspecting that the parcel did not contain silver spoons but that the said T Sims was attempting to deceive and impose upon him opened it and found it contained only 3 iron spoons. That deponent in consequence had the said Thomas Sims taken into custody and prays that he may be dealt with according to law.

The main entrance to the Bladud's Head was in Walcot Street, but there were also two side entrances from Old Orchard – one to the malt house and brewery, the other to a yard with three five-horse stables.

In 1855 the City Fathers came to the Bladud's Head for a slap-up meal to celebrate the opening of the new market hall just down the street. It is ironic that one of the reasons for building the hall was to dissuade farmers from doing their business in pubs.

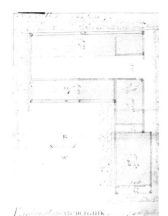

A plan of the Bladud's Head in 1794, with Old Orchard on the right.

By the early twentieth century, the Bladud's Head consisted of eight bedrooms, drawing room, dining room, breakfast room, commercial room (with bagatelle table), smoking room, bar, store rooms, and wine cellar. An inn sign stretched across the entrance to Old Orchard.

The Bladud's Head was the only building in the row north of Old Orchard to survive redevelopment in 1904. By 1932, however, it had fallen on hard times, and trade was very slack. On an average evening, while the Three Cups attracted around 84 customers, and the Bell and the Beehive each had around 55 people through their doors, the best the Bladud's Head could hope for was about 15. On top of that, it was in poor condition and had no ladies' lavatory. When the licensing magistrates decided that Walcot Street had too many pubs, it was a foregone conclusion which would be recommended for closure. The Bladud's Head closed on 3 November 1934 and is now the Sukhotai Restaurant.

The former Bladud's Head.

There were two short-lived beerhouses a little further along on the other side of Walcot Street. The **Red Lion** at No 87 Walcot Street was opened by William Curtis around 1837, but lasted for only a couple of years. Subsequently, it became a grocer's, a refreshment room, a bakers and a tripe dressers. Until recently it housed Walcot Pottery.

A couple of doors along, at 91 Walcot Street, was the **Rifleman's Arms**, opened in the 1860s by a coal merchant. This too only lasted a couple of years. Today it is Walcot Upholstery.

A little further along, we come to the only one of Walcot Street's numerous inns to have survived – the Bell. Across the road from the entrance to the Bell yard was the **Walcot Wine Vaults**, with its wonderful concave front. Around 1820, a perfumier called Edward Watts leased the property from St John's Hospital, slapped the elaborate frontage on, set his son up in business as a wine merchant on the right-hand side, and sublet the left-hand side to

Beer flows again at the Rifleman's Arms on Walcot Nation Day 2004.

THE LOST PUBS OF BATH

The former Walcot Wine Vaults in the 1930s …

… and in the 1950s.

ESTABLISHED 1798.

BAGGS AND SONS

(LATE E. WATTS),

WINE AND SPIRIT MERCHANTS,

WALCOT WINE VAULTS.

B. & S. beg to call attention to their STOCK of Very Choice Old WINES and SPIRITS.

SPECIALITE CROWN SHERRY (Pale)

24s. per Dozen.

FINE PORT   … … … … … … … 24/- Per Dozen.
OLD CRUSTED Ditto   … … … from 30/-   ,,
ORDERS RECEIVED FOR BAGGS'S FAMILY ALES.

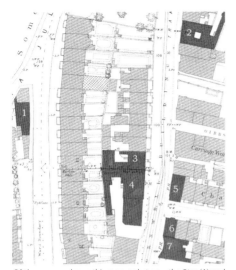

Of the seven pubs on this map, only two – the Star (1) and the Bell (4) have survived. Those that have gone include: 2) the Don Cossack; 3) the New Cornwell Brewery; 5) the Chatham House Tavern; 6) the Carpenter's Arms; 7) the Walcot Wine Vaults.

a grocer called William Goddard. The concave frontage came about because carts and carriages heading into the Bell yard needed a wide turning space. The entrance to the yard was on a slope, and drivers needed to take a run at it to ensure they did not grind to a standstill. Extending a standard bow window into the street would have seriously restricted their room for manoeuvre. One of Bath's most idiosyncratic architectural gems owes its genesis, therefore, to the exigencies of the nineteenth-century carriage trade

Edward Watts, Jr. was there until his death in 1878, when Mark Baggs from the Porter Butt took over and turned the Wine Vaults into a public house. It was later taken over by the Bath Brewery Company and closed in 1914. We have managed to turn up very little on the Walcot Wine Vaults – or the Walcot Spirit Vaults as it was sometimes known – but a 1903 report on its sanitary arrangements is worth quoting:

> No sanitary accommodation for public except WC in cellars, approached by trap
> door in bar.

Which is probably not the sort of thing you'd want to try after a few beers.

The former Carpenter's Arms.

Next to the Walcot Wine Vaults was the **Carpenter's Arms**, on the corner of Chatham Row. When Chatham Row was built in 1762 it was called Pitt Street in honour of William Pitt, Bath's MP. He became Earl of Chatham four years later. However, the street does not seem to have been renamed immediately. In 1777, for example, an alehouse called the **Gallon Can** was licensed in Pitt Street. By 1782, however, the **Chequers** – possibly the former Gallon Can – was licensed in Chatham Row.

In 1800, the Carpenter's Arms – possibly the former Chequers – opened at 14 Chatham Row. It was not only run by a carpenter, it was the venue for meetings of the Union Society of Carpenters & Joiners. In 1819, it was taken over by Sainsbury's Brewery. It made the papers at least once with a haunting story from December 1840:

On Tuesday an inquest was held at the Carpenter's Arms public house on the body of Benjamin Stoneman, aged 20, a Polish Jew. It appears that the deceased, who was a very poor man, had been lodging at the Carpenter's Arms for a few days, and during that period had continually complained of illness. He was occasionally attended by a medical man from the United Hospital. On Saturday morning he was seized more violently than before; he remained in bed the whole of the day, and in the evening expired. The medical gentleman ascribed the cause of death to apoplexy.

It closed in the early 1840s and later became a grocer's, the current shopfront being added in the late nineteenth century. Until quite recently, it boasted some impressive writing on its walls. To the left of the Venetian window facing Chatham Row was the slogan:

TOWER TEA

AGENT R STONE

TOWER TEA

On the right of the window was:

MOTHERS DIADEM

HIGH GRADE

DOUBLE EXTRA

SELF RAISING FLOUR

Unfortunately these have now been well and truly scrubbed off, another bit of Bath's history gone for ever. Today the old Carpenter's Arms houses Bath Women's Aid.

The former Chatham House Tavern.

On the opposite corner of Chatham Row, still looking very much like a pub, was the **Chatham House Tavern**, which opened in the early 1840s. A report in the *Bath Chronicle* from 1849 gives a harrowing insight into the grim reality of life in Bath's courts and alleys a century and a half ago:

An inquest was held on Friday evening … at the White Horse Cellar, Walcot, on the body of Emma Brockenbrow, an illegitimate infant, nine days old, lying dead at No 6, Hooper's Court [at the bottom of Guinea Lane, where Hedgemead Park is today]. The reputed father, whose name is George Saunders, and the mother cohabit, and they were drinking in the tap room of the Chatham House Tavern on Monday, when they quarrelled and struck each other, and the child was taken from the mother's arms. The next morning the child died, but notwithstanding this the man and woman went out together for the whole day, and acquainted none of the inmates of the house with the death of the child until their return at night, when they were asked concerning the baby by some of the people in the house, whose suspicion had been aroused.

The report went on to say that "considerable excitement was created in the neighbourhood" when the baby's death was discovered.

In addition to the tap room, the Chatham House had a main bar with a separate entrance. There was also another door in Chatham Row for the jug & bottle department. The Chatham House Tavern closed in 1908.

The three lost pubs at the top of Chatham Row are a striking example of the piecemeal way in which Georgian Bath was built. The Carpenter's Arms and the Chatham House Tavern were the first parts of Chatham Row to be built. They formed an impressive entrance to the street, almost like eighteenth-century showhouses, tempting property developers to put their names down for plots further down the row. In the case of Chatham Row, this was only partially successful. The northern side of the row was completed, but the southern side petered out a few doors down, leaving the toothstones of the end house waiting for a house which was never built.

The Carpenter's Arms also displays another way in which eighteenth-century developers operated. When it was built, instead of following the line of the street established by the building next door, it was extended outwards in the street, thus giving it greater prominence, and, no doubt, upsetting the people next door. Eventually, as we have seen, a concave bow window was slapped onto the front of the building next door to bring its frontage forward.

Next door to the Bell, on the site now occupied by Aqua Glass, was the Cornwell House, also known as the **New Cornwell Brewery**. Until the eighteenth century, the Walcot Parsonage Barn stood roughly on this site. In 1830, when Charles Robinson of Weston leased it, it was described as a "messuage, garden, etc., on the west side of Walcot Street, bounded on the south by the Bell Inn and west by Axford's Buildings, also court of area belonging." By the 1860s it had become a pub and brewery. In the early 1870s, the licensee, Uriah French, had a smithy there. The New Cornwell Brewery closed in January 1875 and later became a dye works and a mattress workshop. The building was demolished after being damaged in the Bath Blitz.

Further along, on the east side of Walcot Street, was the **Don Cossack** at No 132. The building no longer exists, but in its day it was one of the biggest pubs in the area. It had a smoking room, bar, sitting room, tap room, three bedrooms, drawing room, bathroom, and brewery. Around 1900 it was "practically all rebuilt" internally and a long club room put in on the first floor. It extended back some distance, curving round the buildings to the east, and had a side entrance near the entrance to Walcot Chapel.

It opened some time before 1824, and, although it was also known as the Cornwell Brewery from about 1854 to 1870, was generally known as the Don Cossack. It was named after the cossacks who forced Napoleon to retreat from Moscow in 1812. The only story associated with it comes from 1846 when two men and a ten-year-old boy entered the pub and stole "three decanters, a copper warmer

Porter's Fish & Chip Shop, formerly the Don Cossack.

and two screws of tobacco." The Don Cossack closed in 1907 and became Ridout's (later Porter's) Fish & Chip Shop.

Despite all appearances to the contrary, the row of buildings on this stretch of Walcot Street is among the most modern in Bath. The old row, including the old Don Cossack, disappeared years ago. About fifteen feet below the present buildings lies the site of a Roman pottery, uncovered during an archaeological dig when the site was redeveloped. It achieved national fame when it featured on TV's *Meet the Ancestors*, in which it was suggested that the body of a man buried nearby probably came from Syria.

So much for the lost pubs of Walcot Street whose locations are known. There were at least three others: the **Mug**, which closed around 1786, the **New Inn**, on the east side of the street, which closed in 1778, and the **Thatched House**. It is the name of this last pub that makes it especially interesting, and all the more galling that we do not know where it was. Assuming it was thatched, it would, by the time it appeared in the alehouse recognizances in 1776, have been an extremely rare survival. The only other building in Bath known to have been thatched by the 1770s was the Bathwick Poor House, which burnt down in March 1773. The Thatched House closed by 1786, and was probably re-roofed before a similar fate befell it. Thatched houses in heavily built up areas were, as the great fires of London, Northampton, Warwick, Marlborough and many other towns and cities had demonstrated, not a desperately good idea. Southgate Street had experienced a similar fire in 1726, but Bath within the walls, with a preponderance of stone-built, tiled roofed buildings, seems to have avoided such a conflagration, thanks to the Corporation, which, in the early seventeenth century, passed an edict "that every person that hath a thatched house shall not mend his house with thatch or newe thatche his house, but shall repair it with tyle or slate."

The alehouse recognizances for 1776-7 also list an establishment called the **White Swan**. Despite its name, this seems to have been a grocer's that sold alcohol, rather than a pub, as this advertisement, from the *Bath Journal* for 6 September 1762, indicates:

> William Lewis, the White Swan (near St Michael's Church); who sells the best French brandy, Jamaica Rum and all other sorts of spiritous liquors, at the lowest prices. Great allowance to those who sell again. Devizes Snuff, London Tobacco of each sort, and the best Farnham hops. Likewise fine Welsh butter. – He has just entered into the cheese trade, and has a large quantity of fine Gloucestershire cheese of the first make, which will be sold very reasonable.

§

Beyond the Don Cossack, Walcot Street turns into London Street, home of the late lamented Hat & Feather. At the other end of the block to the Hat & Feather was the **Three Crowns**, which first appears on a map of 1740. In 1755, the *Bath & Bristol*

The former Three Crowns (on the far left) and the former Hat & Feather (on the far right).

THE LOST PUBS OF BATH

Guide informed readers that "a waggon sets out from the Three Crowns at Walcot, Wednesdays and Saturdays; in Tuesdays and Fridays – tho' not always certain."

In 1757, the *Bath Journal* reported the death of "Mr Caple, who kept the Three Crowns at Walcot." Two years later, on 19 Match 1759, it carried another announcement:

A main of cocks to be fought at the Three Crowns at Walcot – to weigh the sixteenth of this instant and fight the two following days.

The presence of a cockpit at the Three Crowns indicates that, like the George, it was a cut above the average inn.

In March 1779, the contents of the brewery was sold off. The auction catalogue gives a good idea of what constituted a well-appointed brewhouse over two centuries ago:

To be sold by hand at the Brew House behind the Three Crowns Inn at Walcot on Tuesday the 30th of March instant. A quantity of very good brewing utensils; consisting of a large copper furnace, a large piece holding 30 barrels, a mash tun holding 30 bushels, some butts holding 140 gallons each, puncheons, hogsheads, kilderkins, firkins, large coolers, a copper pump, etc.

Eighteenth-century buildings at the back of the Three Crowns.

The Three Crowns had a lot of land attached to it. In 1771, when Peter Hooper took over the lease, it included a "stable, garden, orchard and pasture called Highmeer running down to the River Avon." Peter Hooper developed the site, and by 1786, when Sainsbury's Brewery took over, there were "several messuages and buildings to the rear." A deed of 1794 indicates the extent of the development – "two messuages adjoining; three messuages behind with three coach houses, two stables and buildings; six messuages and coach house, two stables and buildings." This range of buildings even had its own name – St Swithin's Court.

Several of the Three Crowns' landlords were stonemasons, and for many years the Loyal Society of Masons met there. In 1833, there was a special meeting to discuss forming a trade union. Unions had been legalised in 1825, but many people still regarded them as dangerously radical. The *Bath Chronicle*, when it heard of the plan, declared that "we have every reason to suppose that the operatives of Bath will not suffer themselves to be duped by idle and itinerant bloodsuckers, calling themselves delegates." Despite this, the union went ahead. The Three Crowns was the venue not only for union meetings, but also for an annual Whitsuntide rally. We are fortunate to have an eyewitness account of one of these rallies, written by George Smith in 1898:

Each of the members wore a short, clean leather apron, and on the top of their club sticks were the several emblems of their trade. On one was a trowel, on another a plumb rule, then a square, another a mallet, then dividers, etc.

What with the large bow of satin ribbons secured at the side of the tall hat, the big bunch of flowers fastened in the coat – or an enormous bloom of double stock – and the clean aprons, these masons appeared very attractive and felt uncommonly proud of their Society and their own imposing appearance. After the service was concluded at church, and a special club service had been preached to them, they would, headed by the band, perambulate the chief streets of the city before they sat down to partake of their annual club dinner, which was of a most substantial character. Then a little club business would be transacted at the conclusion of which the club room would be thrown open for the admission of friends, who, together with the members, would give themselves up to pleasure and enjoyment all night, for the law as to the closure of public houses did not interfere if publicans kept customers in their houses all night as long as the house was quietly conducted.

When an inventory of the Three Crowns was carried out in 1889, it had a bar, bar parlour, tap room, club room, drawing room, four bedrooms and a brewery. In 1901, however, the building was pulled down to widen the street and the licence was transferred to recently-built premises next door at No 18. However, some of the buildings at the back of the pub, put up by Peter Hooper in the 1770s, survived the redevelopment, and can still be seen today. A report on the new Three Crowns in 1903 concluded that its accommodation was very good, with a bar in three compartments and a spacious billiard room. Which makes it all the more surprising that it closed in 1917. Today it forms part of Hayes' Furniture Store.

The lost pubs of Lower Hedgemead: 1) the Hat & Feather; 2) the White Horse Cellar; 3) the Hope & Anchor; 4) the Gloucester Inn; 5) the North Pole.

On the other side of the road, where Hedgemead Park is today, were four more lost pubs. In the mid-nineteenth century, this whole hillside was covered by rank upon rank of terraced houses. They disappeared in a series of spectacular landslips at the end of the nineteenth century; all that survives is a row of four cottages called Gloster Villas.

The first of the four pubs – the **White Horse Cellar** – stood opposite the entrance to Walcot Church. When John Shepherd leased it off Sir Peter Rivers Gay in 1784, it was known as the Full Moon. When John Shepherd died in 1788, he stipulated in his will that his wife should only receive 1/- because she had run off leaving him to look after their children. It was taken over by James Lilley, who renamed it the White Horse Cellar.

THE LOST PUBS OF BATH

The following description of it appeared in the *Bath Journal* on 5 March 1898:

No 14 was the White Horse Cellar held by Jabez Hunt for many years. The entrance door to this inn was directly opposite the front entrance to the parish church on the right-hand side of which stood that bygone implement of punishment, the old parish stocks, silently cautioning the patrons of Jabez to keep within bounds, for there was their instrument of chastisement and degradation if they so offended against the statutes of society. This inn was a quaint looking old building, the most ancient in all the neighbourhood, and, no doubt, at one time stood alone in its glory, forming an old wayside hostelry, with the parish church for its only neighbour. It was very low, and the walls were rubblework and very thick, and plastered and cemented over, and then coloured with a pale yellow wash; dormer windows, gable shaped.

From this description of it, it is clear that the building dated back to the days when

Walcot was a village. As late as 1743, an unknown traveller could record that he had walked "upon the hill which is very delightful to the village of Walcot from whence we had a fine prospect of the city, the river and the country about" The White Horse Cellar survived the development of Hedgemead, but closed around 1873, and disappeared in the landslips a few years later.

The site of the White Horse Cellar.

To the left of the steps that now lead up through Hedgemead Park was a beerhouse called the **Hope & Anchor**. It opened around 1837 and closed in 1881.

Opposite the Hat & Feather was an inn with a variety of names. Generally it was known as the **Gloucester Inn**, but among its other titles were the Gloucester & Oxford Inn (1794), the Gloucester Inn & Commercial Tavern (1826), the Gloucester Inn & Agricultural Tavern (1834) and the Gloucester Hotel (1852). It was built in 1792 by Peter Hooper, who "took down an old messuage," together with "a little tenement and cellar," a barn, granary, stables and garden to build the Gloucester Inn & Coffee House. He sold it to the Northgate Brewery, who in 1812 sold it (together with "all the coach houses, stables, offices and erections") to Williams' Brewery for £2,500.

An 1849 auction notice described the Gloucester Inn as

so well known as to require but little description. The house has been lately put into a complete state of repair by the present tenant, and contains, on the ground floor, a capital bar, bar parlour, commercial room, tap room, kitchen and scullery; four large drawing rooms, with patent water-closet on the same floor, and ten excellent bedchambers; good cellarage, a nine-stall stable, and large coach house and other outbuildings, in addition to which there has been erected, at great cost, by the tenant, one of the MOST CONVENIENT & COMPACT BREWERIES IN THE CITY; the produce of which has attained such deserved celebrity that the worthy and respected host can hardly supply the demand. A very superior skittle

The Hedgemead landslips: looking up towards the Star, with the same view today.

THE LOST PUBS OF BATH

Looking down towards Walcot Church.

alley has also been lately built by the tenant, 60 feet long. The premises have a frontage to the London Road of about 34 feet, exclusive of the side entrance to the stables, and a depth altogether of about 150 feet by 78 feet wide.

The brewery was later converted to an organ factory. A reminiscence of the old days at the Gloucester Inn appeared in the *Bath Journal* on 27 August 1898:

> This was one of the old well-conducted hostelries in Bath where tradesmen and artisans met and rubbed shoulders together in the large smoke room, to enjoy their long clay and social glass, and to improve each others' minds. The custom was to sit behind a long pewter pint, with a long spiral glass, perhaps six or eight to the pint, moistening the alderman every once now and then with a sip from the vessel, and converse with one another on the political and social events of the day. If the pint was not sufficient to last out the evening, our old fathers would have another half-pint put in the cup, and rarely, if ever, would they exceed this.

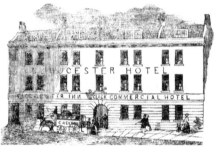

The Gloucester Inn or Hotel, built in 1792 and burnt down in 1901.

TR Hayes' Carpet Shop on the site of the Gloucester Inn.

Gloster Villas, all that is left of the Hedgemead development.

With customers like that, it is not surprising that so many pubs went out of business. The Gloucester Inn went out more dramatically than most, however. Having survived the Hedgemead landslips, it burnt down on 1 December 1901. The site is now occupied by Hayes' carpet store, some of whose external walls incorporate parts of the old building. The only other reminder of its existence is the row of cottages called Gloster Villas on the hillside above.

Opposite the old Three Crowns, at 5 Margaret's Buildings, was the **North Pole** – or to give it its full name, the North Pole Brewery Inn. An advertisement from 1832 gives a detailed description of it:

> To let ... that capital and well-accustomed PUBLIC HOUSE, now in full trade, known as the North Pole near Walcot Church ... lately fitted up at considerable expense [consisting of] a convenient bar, tap room, and kitchen on the first floor; two excellent smoking rooms above, and five good bedrooms. There is a most capital and well-arranged

brewhouse, well supplied with water, with facilities for brewing to a great extent, with little expense of labour, communicating with two large cellars, capable of containing 16,000 gallons of beer.

A dispute in the brewery was reported in the *Bath Chronicle* in 1851:

Joseph Primme and Henry Primme, brothers, were charged with being drunk and creating a disturbance at the North Pole Public House on Monday evening. It appeared that Joseph had been employed by Mr Miller of the North Pole to grind some malt, and when he was finished he was told that it was not ground fine enough, and he must therefore do it over again; he however thought he knew better than his master, and refused to do so, insisting on being paid for the work he had done, and, becoming very abusive, a policeman was sent for to turn him out of the house. He refused to go quietly, but with his brother became so abusive that both were obliged to be taken to the station house.

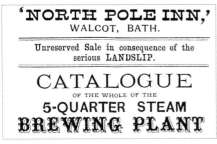

The equipment from the North Pole Brewery was sold off after the landslip of 1889.

The licensing register records that the North Pole was "pulled down in consequence of being dangerous by reason of the landslip, October 1889."

Fifty yards up Margaret's Hill, on the northern corner of Lower Hedgemead Road, was the **Barley Mow**. It opened around 1792, and was the meeting place of the Prince Regent Benefit Society. An inventory drawn up in the early 1930s shows that it was a centre for sporting activities, particularly boxing. In addition to the bar, where there were six framed photographs of football teams, and the smoke room, with a piano, a shove-halfpenny board and table skittles, it had a training room with "nine various baths, four collapsible deal forms, four running boards, a punch ball, a mangling machine, a pair of six tread steps and a sanitary dustbin." It closed in 1938 and has since been demolished.

We now make our way down Pera Road and into Clarence Street, passing an old malthouse, now converted into offices. This was attached to Walcot Brewery, on the London Road. After the brewery was taken over by the Anglo-Bavarian Brewery of Shepton Mallet around 1887, the main building became a warehouse, while the offices of the brewery were demolished and Anglo Terrace built in their place. Past the malthouse, Clarence Street runs into Thomas Street, built around 1830. At 25 Thomas Street – two doors up from the chapel – was a beerhouse, open for a few years in the late 1840s.

At the bottom of Thomas Street is the King William. On the opposite corner was another beerhouse called the **Queen Adelaide** after King William's wife. Like the King William, it opened around 1830; unlike the King William it closed around 1841.

Left Clarence Street Malthouse, now converted to offices.
Below The former Queen Adelaide.
Below right Queen Adelaide.

Thomas Street has survived more or less intact, but, as we turn left and walk along the north side of London Road to Long Acre, we enter the Snow Hill redevelopment area, where virtually nothing from before the 1960s is still standing. When Pierce Egan passed this way in 1819, Long Acre consisted of three small buildings, two of them occupied by coach makers. A few years later, two pubs opened. One – the Long Acre Tavern – still survives, although it has been completely rebuilt. The other is not even a distant memory. The **Globe** at 1 Long Acre was opened by Fred Ryall as a beerhouse in the 1840s. It closed in the late 1860s and became part of Vezey's Coach Builders.

Opposite Long Acre, at 4 Walcot Buildings, was the **Black Dog**, which opened around 1840 as the Walcot Porter Stores. It consisted of two rooms – a bar and a parlour

The old Long Acre Tavern, demolished in the 1960s.

An Usher's Brewery lorry outside Long Acre Hall in November 1956. Around 17 pubs in Bath were owned by Usher's. The brewery closed in 2000, its location in the centre of Trowbridge being deemed too desirable to be given over any longer to the brewing of beer. It is currently awaiting redevelopment.

The former Black Dog.

with a bagatelle table – and closed in 1917.

We now come to Snow Hill. With the exception of a solitary beerhouse near the top of the hill (which we will visit in the fourth excursion), no trace is left of any of Snow Hill's pubs, nor of the streets they stood in.

On the corner of Snow Hill and Berkeley Street, roughly where the second row of flats stands today, was the **Coachmaker's Arms**, which also had its own

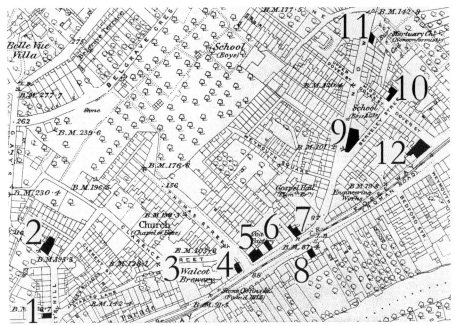

Only two pubs on this map have survived – the King William (4) and the rebuilt Long Acre Tavern (7). The nine that have gone include: 1) the Barley Mow; 2) Gay's Hill Tavern; 5) the Queen Adelaide; 6) the Globe; 8) the Black Dog; 9) the Coachmaker's Arms; 10) the Berkeley Arms; 11) the New Inn; 12) the Traveller's Rest. Also shown is the former Walcot Brewery (3).

brewery. The last reference to it in the licensing records reads "Licence in suspense 1955."

Further along Berkeley Street was the **Berkeley Arms**. Built in the 1790s, it was originally known as the Half Moon and stood in Half Moon Street. When the street became Berkeley Street in the 1880s, the pub was renamed as well. It had three

Looking up Snow Hill, with the Coachmaker's Arms just visible on the corner of Berkeley Street.

An advertisement from 1858.

bars and a brewery, which closed in 1893. The pub survived until the area was redeveloped; the last reference to it in the licensing records reads simply "Licence in suspense 1962."

The children's playground, a little further up the hill, stands on the site of Juda Place. At 8-9 Juda Place was the **New Inn**, which opened around 1850. It also had its own brewery, which closed when the pub was taken over by Oakhill Brewery. Last orders were called on 31 March 1966, when the New Inn's regulars presented the landlord, Frederick Kean-Lowe, with four brandy goblets.

There was also a beerhouse at 1 Juda Place for a brief period in the 1840s.

The Traveller's Rest.

The footpath to the right of the playground leads down through a car park to the London Road. Near the bottom, on the right, roughly where the entrance to the flats is today, was a beerhouse called the **Traveller's Rest** on the corner of Lower Dover Street. It opened around 1841 and quickly gained an unsavoury reputation. On 7 August 1856, the *Bath Chronicle* reported that

> Benjamin Bailey, keeper of the Traveller's Rest, Dover Street, was summoned for having, on Sunday last, allowed drunken and disorderly persons in his house, and for having his house open between three and five o'clock for the sale of beer.

Benjamin Bailey seems to have been a peripatetic soul – perhaps because he needed to stay one step ahead of the law. In 1855 he was at the Norfolk Tavern at 7 Albion Place; by 1858 he had moved to the Oddfellows' Arms at 10 Albion Place. The Traveller's Rest was also known for a short period around 1854 as the London Tavern.

By 1934, when George Yates took the licence, the Traveller's Rest was a much more respectable establishment. He was there until 1952, when his son Charles took over. In September 1956, with the Snow Hill clearances already under way, Bath Corporation acquired the pub from George's Brewery for the nominal sum of £1, and it closed. It was demolished two years later.*

In the 1850s, there was a beerhouse known as the **Californian Tavern** in Dover Terrace, which now lies under the Esso Garage.

*For this information, and for the photograph of the Traveller's Rest, we are indebted to Charles Yates' grandson, Simon Newton, who lives in Australia. Further information and photographs can be found at www.bristolslostpubs.com/html/travellersrest.htm.

THE LOST PUBS OF BATH

The former Wiltshire House.

Across the road, between the Porter Butt and the old Walcot Poor House, was the Kensington Brewery, which closed in 1889. The building now houses a furniture store.

Brunswick Street, opposite the Porter Butt, once had a beerhouse called the **Wiltshire House** at No 12. It opened around 1835 and closed around 1850.

§

At the top of Brunswick Street a flight of steps leads to Kensington Gardens. Here, a right turn, followed by a left at the end of the road, takes us along to Upper East Hayes. There are no lost pubs up here, but coming this way gives us a chance not only to see a hidden corner of Georgian Bath but also to avoid the traffic on the London Road while enjoying some stunning views across the valley. At the end of Upper East Hayes, turn right and take the first left into Belgrave Road. Turn right at the end of Belgrave Road, walk to the bottom of the hill (where you'll find the back door to Filo's – a pub that is very much alive) and turn left into St Saviour's Road.

The former Queen.

St Saviour's Church was built around 1830 and set the seal on Larkhall's development. Across the road from the church, on the corner of Malvern Terrace, is an elegant little building which, in 1854, opened as a beerhouse. Originally called the Worcester Tavern (after Worcester Buildings on the London Road), by 1860 it had been renamed the Worcester Arms. Soon afterwards it became the **Queen.** In 1903, it had a bar with a jug & bottle and a tap room. A chairman called Mr Edwards was allowed to keep his wheelchair in the yard and helped out in the beerhouse in return. The Queen closed in 1928 and the building is now a private house.

Larkhall originally consisted of a large eighteenth-century house called Lark Hall. The hall, long since converted to the Larkhall Inn, now stands in the middle of a bustling community, but in the late eighteenth century it was in the middle of the country. A nearby bridge over the Lam Brook gave the area its original name – Lambridge. By 1819, when Pierce Egan passed through, Lambridge was "a neat row of houses … with long gardens tastefully laid out in front of them … giving this part … the air of a delicate village." The area around Lark Hall remained largely undeveloped until 1832, when Mr

Left Larkhall in the late nineteenth century: 1) the Spa Rooms; 2) the Spa Gardens; 3) the Bladud's Head; 4) the Wagon & Horses.
Below The former White Lion.

Blackwin, who was sinking a well for a brewery on the eastern side of St Saviour's Road, hit a spring. The water tasted so foul, he sent it away for analysis. The results showed that he had discovered one of the most potent chalybeate springs in the country. So, instead of a opening a brewery, he built a Greek Revival Spa over the well. This catered for visitors until the 1930s, when the spring dried up.

Facing the Larkhall Inn, at 1 Lambridge Buildings, was the **White Lion**, opened by George Hansford around 1839. In 1885, when it was bought by William Mortimer of the Park Tavern in Park Lane, it consisted of a tap room, parlour, bar, bar parlour, club room, skittle alley, brewery, hop room, fermenting room and cooperage. It was an unusually well-appointed establishment, as the 1903 report indicates:

> Exit at back into stable yard with exit into Brookleaze Gardens. WC in passage for females. Very good. Long bar on right of entrance and glass room on left, bar parlour beyond bar with bagatelle table. Brewery at rear.

LARKHALL OMNIBUS "VICTORIA."

Leaves White Lion, Larkhall, at	9.45	11.30	2.0	3.30
,, Gloucester Inn,	,, 10.0	11.40	2.10	3.40
,, Bond Street,	,, 10.5	11.50	2.15	3.45
Arriving at G.W.R. Station in time for Trains due at	10.15	12.0	2.40	4.0
Leaves G.W.R. Station for Larkhall, at	10.30	12.40	2.55	4.20
,, Bond Street, at ...	10.35	12.45	3.0	4.25
,, Gloucester Inn, at ...	10.40	12.50	3.5	4.30

In 1880, the Larkhall Omnibus ran from the White Lion, calling at the Gloucester Inn on its way into town.

When it closed in 1959 and became a butcher's, its licence was transferred to the Rose & Crown in Brougham Place, which till then had only held a beerhouse licence. The White Lion's impressive sign bracket can still be seen mounted on the wall above the entrance to the butcher's.

Around 1854, John Osborne, the landlord of the White Lion, opened a beerhouse-cum-grocer's called the **Lamb** behind the Larkhall Inn, at 1-2 Brookleaze Place. It

The Larkhall Inn (1) is still open, but the White Lion (2) and the Lamb (3) have both gone.

closed in the mid-1870s and the site is now covered by a car park.

Lambridge Street, facing the Larkhall Inn, once had two beerhouses. The **Ring of Bells** at No 3 was opened by a grocer called Luke Flack in the late 1830s and closed a few years later. The **Lambridge Tavern** at Nos 7-8 opened around 1840 and closed around 1854. The row in which they stood, dating from around 1819, has been demolished and replaced by modern housing.

Continuing along St Saviour's Road past the Larkhall Inn, the first turning on the left leads to Dafford's Buildings. Around 1840, William Abraham opened a beerhouse called the **King's Head** at 1 Dafford's Buildings, which closed sometime before 1850.

Further along St Saviour's Road, the next turning on the left takes us along Dafford Street to the Brain's Surgery – formerly the Royal Oak. On the far side of the road is Eldon Place, a row of modern buildings standing where a earlier terrace once stood. Around 1840, a beerhouse called the **Victoria Arms** opened at 26-27 Eldon Place. The 1903 report described it as consisting of a bar, glass room and tap room, with an "arbour in front of the premises." It closed in the 1930s.

Our last lost pub isn't really a lost pub at all. At the far end of St Saviour's Road is the Bladud's Head at 1-3 Catsley Place, which opened as a beerhouse at No 1 in the 1840s. In the 1870s, another beerhouse – the **Wagon & Horses** – opened next door at No 2. It survived until 1890, when it was absorbed into the Bladud's Head, which later took over No 3 as well. We have strayed a little beyond the borders of Bath here, for Catsley Place lies not in Walcot parish, but over the border in Swainswick. Ending at a lost pub in which you can still get a drink seemed ample justification enough for overstepping the mark. Swainswick's other lost pubs, however, along with those in Bailbrook, Batheaston and Bathford, are covered in the tenth excursion.

EXCURSION THE FOURTH

THE NORTH-EASTERN SLOPES

Our fourth excursion starts just outside the old North Gate, at the bottom of Broad Street. Broad Street was so called not for its breadth but because of the broadloom weavers who lived along it in the middle ages. Chaucer's Wife of Bath, a weaver who lived "beside Bath" (in other words, outside the city walls) may have been based on a real-life character who lived in Broad Street over 600 years ago. That said, Broad Street was much broader before eighteenth-century developers started whacking classical frontages onto sixteenth- and seventeenth-century houses. Go down any of the alleyways on the west side of the street and you can see where they joined them on – and while you are there marvel that at one time there were at least 14 pubs along this short street.

The former King's Arms from the courtyard.

The Saracen's Head Inn is justly celebrated for its early eighteenth-century façade. Just across the road is another inn which, externally at least, has survived almost intact. The passageway to the Moon & Sixpence restaurant was once the entrance to the coachyard of the **King's Arms**. Walter Wiltshire got his hands on this piece of real estate in 1762, tore down the existing building and built an inn.

He quickly established it as an important coaching inn, with a twice-weekly service to Oxford. On 23 May, 1765, the Rev James Woodforde recorded in his diary that "we got into Bath this evening about seven o'clock, and we put up at the King's Arms in Broad Street, where I supped and spent the evening and laid." As Woodforde generally stayed at one of Bath's top inns, such as the Christopher or the Angel, this indicates that the King's Arms was a well-appointed house. And the area was coming up in the world. The year after Woodforde's visit, the foundation stone of the Octagon Chapel was laid on land behind the King's Arms.

The King's Arms closed around 1776. This may have been due to lack of trade, although it is more likely that Walter Wiltshire wanted to expand his carrying business, based next door in what is still known as Shire's Yard. The yard and

The entrance to the King's Arms yard.

A unique survival: half timbering next to the old King's Arms.

outbuildings could be more profitably employed as holding areas, warehouses or workshops, while the inn could be let out as shops and lodgings. The building continued to be known as the King's Arms, however. In 1800, when Walter Wiltshire's son, John, took over the lease, it was described as "a messuage called the King's Arms on the west side of Broad Street," although, when he renewed it in 1813, it was described as "a messuage formerly the King's Arms, now a private house in the possession of Mr Watkins, cheesemonger."

Today the ground floor of the building is occupied by a mobile phone shop; the Bath Festivals Office is on the upper floors. The stable block is now the Moon & Sixpence. Although no trace of the building that Walter Wiltshire pulled down in 1762 survives – at least externally –the buildings on either side give some indication of what it may have looked like. Walking through the archway from Broad Street, a blocked-up seventeenth-century window can be seen on the right-hand side; at the top of the steps that run up the other side of the King's Arms can be seen a unique survival of the half-timbered buildings that once lined the street.

The story of the Black Horse, which once stood on the site now occupied by the old King Edward's School, can be found in *Bath Pubs*. On the other side of Broad Street, at No 27, was an eighteenth-century alehouse known as the **Wheatsheaf**. In 1790, the landlord was involved in an unpleasant incident involving a drunken bill poster. One January evening about seven o'clock, John Denbury strolled into the Unicorn in Northgate Street, where he saw Hopton Haines and asked him if he wanted a drink. Haines, who had already had more than enough, jumped at the offer. While they were downing their pints, he asked Denbury to help him stick some bills up. Denbury agreed and they wandered up Broad Street towards the York House stables. As soon as Haines started trying to stick posters up, however, it became clear that he was "so far intoxicated" it was pointless continuing. Denbury suggested they come back in the morning. Haines agreed and went across the road to the Wheatsheaf for another drink. There he saw some friends of his eating veal. They asked him if he

The east side of Broad Street in the 1840s: 1) the Wheatsheaf; 2) the Saracen's Head.

The former Wheatsheaf, the gable visible in the previous picture hidden by infilling.

wanted some, but soon regretted it, for, no sooner had he swallowed a couple of mouthfuls, than they came back up, along with the beer he had downed at the Unicorn. The landlord chucked him out. A few minutes later, a passer-by stuck his head through the door and announced there was somebody lying on the pavement outside in a bad way. The landlord went out and, with the passer-by's assistance, carried him into Gracious Court and left him at the top of the steps leading down to Walcot Street. He later admitted that he had intended to carry him further but had to give up because "he had so offensive a smell." He realised that all was not well, however, and, a short time later, had him removed to the casualty hospital where, despite a surgeon being called, he died.

Three years later, Domani Kleiser displayed a "most curious collection of musical clocks" at the Wheatsheaf. Admission to the exhibition cost 6d (3d for children and servants). There was a clock which played "six tunes upon the dulcimore," one representing "harlequin dancing on a stage, with his five companions, upon one leg," one representing a singing canary, and one representing John the Baptist losing his head.

In the late nineteenth century, the Wheatsheaf boasted a bar, bar parlour, sitting room, bagatelle room, skittle alley and brewery. By 1903, the licensee, Tom Moore, lived in Bristol, where he brewed the beer for the Wheatsheaf. He visited the pub once a week, on Mondays. The rest of the time it was in the hands of a manager. The Wheatsheaf closed in 1908 and was taken over by a printer. On 16 November 1929, the following report appeared in the *Bath Chronicle*:

> The emblem of the old Wheatsheaf Inn, 27 Broad Street, Bath, has been presented to the Municipal Art Gallery by Mr J Grant Melhuish. The inn, according to the great authority the late Rev CW Shickle, was one of the oldest public houses outside the ancient city walls, the honour being shared by the Old Farm House and the Britannia, Walcot. The Wheatsheaf was noted for its skittle alley and was much frequented by the tradesmen of the city, and the servants of the gentry, who were sent to post letters when the Post Office was in Broad Street. It was closed some years ago on the grounds of redundancy, after having existed for upwards of 300 years.

Perhaps when that gap in the city's celebration of its heritage – a museum devoted to its history – opens, we will get to see the old sign, along with other long-hidden and forgotten treasures.

The former Turk's Head.

The Turk's Head expanded into No 14 in the late nineteenth century.

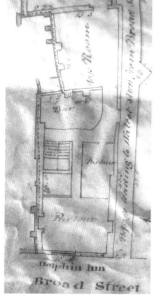
A plan of the Dolphin in 1840.

Gracious Court, where Hopton Haines's night on the town came to a tragic end, is today known as Broad Street Place, although its old name can still be seen painted on the wall. The developer who built it, Gracious Stride, originally called it Gracious Street. There was even a pub down here, the **Crown & Raven**, which closed around 1780.

Back on the other side of Broad Street, at No 15, was the second of Broad Street's pubs with a Moorish connection – the **Turk's Head**, which opened some time before 1776. In 1827, the fire which seriously damaged the York House Hotel also spread to the Turk's Head, destroying nearly all the furniture in the house.* Even worse, "some seven or eight pieces of strong beer, containing from 2,000 to 3,000 gallons each, which were in [the] cellars, burst, and of course the contents were lost."

In 1838, with the railway about to bring the coaching era to an end, the licence of the Turk's Head was taken by one of Bath's most famous coachmen, William Clark. In 1899, George Smith recalled seeing him standing outside the Turk's Head, the embodiment of a bygone age:

> Whilst Mr Clark kept the Turk's Head he continued to handle the ribbons, and many a time and oft I have seen him emerge from the door of this hostelry, when I was a youth, with his whip in his hand and his mackintosh or great coat, according to the season of the year, on his arm. He was not a big framed man like many of the old stagecoach men were, but he was well put together, and the essence of smartness, with the type of his occupation stamped plainly upon his appearance.

In the late nineteenth century the Turk's Head was extended into No 14 Broad Street, previously a chemist's. The newly-enlarged Turk's Head had two main bars. The larger of the two was divided into three compartments, with an oil painting of a Turk's Head taking pride of place. A panelled and glazed door led into the parlour. The Turk's Head also had a sitting room, drawing room, dining room and billiard

*See *Bath Pubs*, pp170-71.

THE LOST PUBS OF BATH

The effects of the Dolphin were put up for auction before it was demolished.

room. There was a brewery at the back, which by 1903 was described as "ruinous." In 1907, the lease of No 15 was given up, but the Turk's Head continued operating from No 14 until it closed in 1935.

Across the road, at No 20, was the **Dolphin**. This was built in 1782 by John Hensley on land belonging to the George Inn in Walcot Street. It adjoined the entrance to the upper yard of the George, and was almost certainly intended as its tap. It survived the closure of the George, finally being demolished in 1883 to make way for the YMCA building.

The York House Hotel opened in 1769, but the **York House Tap** on Broad Street opened around 25 years later. The original York House Tap was on Lansdown Road, probably in what is now Mandalyns'.* Once it moved, the York House Tap, later known as the York House Vaults, had a long and colourful history. In the early 1840s, one of its landlords (according to George Smith) was Dan Weller, previously head ostler at the York House Hotel. The tale of how he came to take over the York House Tap is a cautionary one:

> At this time, Daniel was a widower, and the York House Tap was kept by a widow who had twice before entered the holy bonds. Being in the habit of taking his daily glass here, he became somewhat enamoured, and cast a "sly glance" at the widow, which was cordially reciprocated, the natural consequence of which was a match. Dan congratulated himself that he had made a good bargain, but no sooner had the marriage taken place, and he had become the landlord of the Tap, than he discovered that he had made a very unprofitable venture. The widow, who was supposed by Dan to be in comfortable circumstances, was found to be similarly situated to a man wearing a hat he had never paid for – i.e. over head and ears in debt, and the newly espoused widower had all his work cut out to keep himself out of the debtors' apartments of Grove Street Prison ... Dan was an uneducated man, yet interesting in his conversation, communicative, and fairly spoken. His occupation as ostler at the York brought him into the company of many travellers, and Dickens, being then a frequent visitor to the "City of Palaces," as Sam Sly, then a resident here, designated Bath, and the unlucky Dan, it is not improbable, might have got into conversation with each other, and the unfortunate and unhappy position of Dan disclosed by his own statements, hence the solemn caution of the "old 'un," "Be wery careful o'widders all your life, Sammy."

Another cautionary tale, from 1841, concerns the perils of purloining beer glasses:

> On Friday ... Frederick Dixon ... went into the York House Tap and sat for a long time over one glass of beer. Whilst in the tap room he was seen to shift one of the

*See *Bath Pubs*, pp119-20

Fuller's, formerly the York House Tap.

glasses from a shelf and secrete it behind a curtain. He was afterwards seen by the landlady putting it under his coat, and walking off with it. She immediately told her husband, who followed the thief and deposited him at the station house. He was committed for trial on Saturday.

Somehow you feel Mr Dixon was not cut out for a life of crime.

In the late nineteenth century, the York House Tap was taken over by Messrs Fuller & Hicks who converted part of it to a wine merchant's and renamed it Fuller & Hicks' Wine Vaults. At the beginning of the twentieth century, the conditions of its licence stipulated that it had to close between 8.30 and 9.00 each evening and could not open on Sundays.

In 1976 (by which time it was known simply as Fuller's) Fred Pearce visited and described it as follows:

> Single modern large split-level lounge. Low lighting except for horrible glaring bulbs over the main bar. And to add to the visual assault course the far wall is one big disconcerting mirror. It's a young pub – "Only Sixteen" sings the jukebox, and a lot of them look it. Double Diamond and Ind Coope Special won't please the beer connoisseur. A high capacity pub with a second serving area at the lower level.

Today it is Ask restaurant.

There were seven other alehouses on Broad Street to which we cannot ascribe a precise location. These were the **Artichoke** (c1776), the **Old Bell** (c1779-82), the **Black Horse** (c1776-78), the **Chequers** (c1786), the **Green Man** (c1776), the **Porter**

THE LOST PUBS OF BATH

Vaults (c1811), and the **Rodney** (c1785). There were also a couple of short-lived nineteenth-century beerhouses – one recorded in 1874 at 10 Broad Street and one in 1874 at 26 Broad Street.

§

Fountain Buildings, at the bottom of Lansdown Road, stand on the site of a spring that ran down from St Swithin's Well, below Camden Crescent, and was piped to the upper part of the city. There was once a chapel dedicated to St Werburgh over the fountain, which may have stood on the site of a nunnery founded by King Osric in the seventh century. When the chapel fell into disuse after the Reformation it found a new use as an alehouse, which was still in business, according to John Wood, in the mid-eighteenth century.

This part of Bath has another alcoholic connection, for there was a vineyard nearby. In 1670, Edward Brimble, a weaver, leased a plot of ground with "the vineyard on the south, the way to Walcot on the east, and the road to Lansdown on the west." In 1704, William Newman "paid £4 for lease of 99 years of a plot of garden ground called St Walborow Chapel, near the said city abutting on a piece of ground called Vynyard." The houses built on the site in the eighteenth century are still known as the Vineyards today. Fountain Buildings were also home to the **Fountain Wine Vaults**, a wine merchant's which opened around 1806 and closed in 1883.

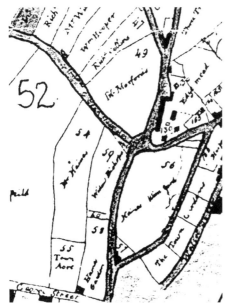

On this 1740 map, the Hand & Flower ground – with the lease held by "Widow Bishop" – is indicated by number 59. The Vineyards ("Haine's Wine Yard") can be seen on the other side of Lansdown Road.

On the northern corner of Alfred Street was a tavern and pleasure garden called the **Hand & Flower**. In July 1747, an advertisement in the *Bath Journal* invited

> all florists … to meet their brethren at the Sign of the Hand & Flower on Lansdown Road, on Wednesday, the 29th of this instant July, and to bring with them their choicest carnations. He that shows the best will be entitled to a silver cup.

Its grounds extended north almost as far as Julian Road and east to where Saville Row and Russell Street run today.

With few buildings to spoil the view, it would have been a wonderful spot. It fell victim to the northward expansion of

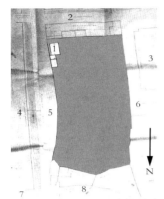

The Hand & Flower ground (shaded) shortly before the site was developed: 1) the Hand & Flower Tavern; 2) Alfred Street; 3) the New Assembly Rooms; 4) Belmont; 5) Lansdown Road; 6) Bennett Street; 7) Guinea Lane; 8) Montpelier.

the city in the 1770s. But, if John Wood's plans for this area had been realised, it might still have been there.

In Tobias Smollett's *Humphrey Clinker*, published in 1771, that archetypal grumpy old man, Matthew Bramble, writes to a friend from Bath:

> The same artist who planned the Circus has likewise projected a Crescent; when that is finished, we shall probably have a Star.

This has always been treated as a joke. But was it? Smollett knew and admired John Wood, who designed the Circus, as well as his son, John Wood the Younger, who took over the project after his father's death in 1754. What if there were plans to build a star? And where would it have been?

There are three exits from the Circus. The first leads to Queen Square, the second to the Royal Crescent; the third – nowhere in particular. Shortly after leaving the Circus, Bennett Street kinks to the right and runs along to a T Junction with Lansdown Road. It has been like that for so long, nobody asks why the Woods – those masters of the grand gesture – came up with something so banal.

The likely answer is that they intended the street to lead to an architectural showpiece to rival Queen Square or the Royal Crescent. If the street had continued in a straight line, it would have met Lansdown Road at its crossroads with Julian Road and Guinea Lane, so creating a five-pointed star. The distances from the Circus to Queen Square, the Royal Crescent, and the Lansdown Road crossroads are roughly the same, which suggests that this was planned from the start. And it seems more than coincidence that the pub built just below the crossroads in the 1760s should have been called the Star.

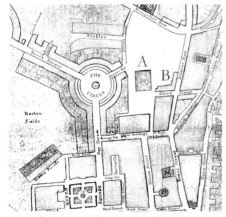

A map from around 1772, showing the New Assembly Rooms (A) and the Hand & Flower (B). Even at this stage, there was nothing to prevent Bennett Street being extended to the Lansdown Road crossroads to form a star.

Finding a location for John Wood's Star is one thing; trying to imagine what it would have looked like is more difficult. The chances are that, like the Royal Crescent, it would have had extensive views. Which brings us back to the Hand & Flower grounds. John Wood the Younger may have had his eye on this for building, but it is far more likely that he wanted to keep it – as well as the land on the other side of the road – as an open space.

It was surely with this in mind that he planned his Assembly Rooms. The *Pevsner Architectural Guide to Bath*

THE LOST PUBS OF BATH

The southern part of Oxford Row, built on the Hand & Flower ground in 1773.

echoes the prevailing view when it describes the Assembly Rooms as "a large and noble block, tucked away behind the Circus in an unimaginative urban arrangement." It was not John Wood the Younger's imagination that was deficient, however. He designed his Assembly Rooms to be viewed from the east. Take away the card room he stuck onto the east end when his grand design had been hemmed in by buildings and you have a truly imposing building.

It was John Wood the Younger's arch-enemy, Thomas Warr Atwood, who scuppered his plans. Unlike the Woods, Atwood knew how to work the system; he was not only a councillor, but also the city architect.

Between 1755 and 1775, he built Bladud's Buildings and the Paragon. Although visible from the Hand & Flower grounds, they did not stand in the way of John Wood the Younger's plans.

However, between about 1770 and 1773 a new terrace – Belmont – was built on the east side of Lansdown Road, blocking the view east from the Hand & Flower grounds. Nobody knows who built it, but on stylistic grounds alone it is likely to have been Atwood.

Atwood's next move put paid to John Wood the Younger's plans altogether. The council owned the freehold of the Hand & Flower. In March 1773, Atwood persuaded them to dispossess the leaseholder, Mr Rogers, and transfer the lease to him. Within weeks, the grounds were transformed into a building site. Oxford and Saville Rows, the north side of Alfred Street, the east end of Bennett Street, and the east side of Russell Street were the result. All John Wood the Younger could do was follow the lines Atwood had laid down, continue Bennett Street towards the Circus, and build houses on the south side of Alfred Street and the west side of Russell Street.

Today, this area, although full of perfectly respectable Georgian buildings, lacks the visual excitement of Queen Square, the Circus, or the Royal Crescent. It is, simply, unimaginative. And while praise for the interior of the Assembly Rooms is matched by lack of enthusiasm for its exterior, its intended façade is hidden away down a narrow alley. How different it could have been if the Woods' scheme had not been scuppered by eighteenth-century insider dealing.

Although the Hand & Flower disappeared over two centuries ago, some of its walls may have been incorporated into boundary walls in the new development. The courtyard behind 3 Saville Row, for example, over ten feet below the level of the garden of 3 Oxford Row, which it abuts, appears to have an earlier wall built into its retaining wall.

Guinea Lane, one of the streets leading off John Wood's Star, once had two pubs. The Star is familiar to every beer-lover in Bath, but the **Darby & Joan**, which once occupied No 16, is totally forgotten. It opened in 1784, shortly after the row it stands in was built.

It was at the Darby & Joan that one of Bath's most notorious criminals was arrested after a long police investigation. Charles Hibbert was a well-known and well-respected figure in Bath, having worked his way up from a tenement in Gallaway's Buildings to a house on Grosvenor by virtue of his skill as an engraver. But it was this skill which undid him, for he used it to forge bank notes. His local was the Darby & Joan and he was arrested there in August 1819.

The Darby & Joan's most famous landlord was Joseph Davis, who fought in the Battle of Alexandria in 1791, was six feet four inches tall and "grandly proportioned." After his death in 1825, he was buried with military honours, but, as he was such

The former Darby & Joan.

a fine figure of a man, members of his family had to keep watch over his grave for several days to prevent him being dug up. This was not paranoia. In 1826, a man called William Clark, who lived in a house overlooking Walcot churchyard, confessed that he had dug up 45 newly-buried bodies there over a five month period and sent them to London by stagecoach (suitably boxed) for anatomical study. As each body was worth up to ten guineas, the fine of £100 and one year's imprisonment seems, given the draconian sentences meted out to petty criminals at the time, very lenient.

Nefarious activities of a more amusing kind were also associated with the Darby & Joan, as the following story from the *Bath Journal* shows:

Although Bath was an inland town, there was contraband business and some amount of smuggling carried on within its precincts, and the old chairmen, whose avocation, of course, called them out at all hours of the night, were the chief offenders in this illicit traffic. Peter Glass was one of the greatest, if not the greatest, wag of the whole confraternity, who then numbered ... some 400, and was licensed to the "stand" connected with the Darby & Joan. The kegs of spirits were in the town, but the difficulty was to get them to their destination in the upper part of the city, and the hero of my narrative was deputed to use his own stratagem. He started from a given point late at night, when the old night watchmen were on duty – under the cover of the dim light emitted from the oil lamps – with a keg on his shoulders uncovered and exposed. Near the bottom of Lansdown Road, between Mr Gould's stables and Mr Stuckey's back entrance is ... what was once a doorway, but is now filled in with stone. This was a watchman's box, and when Peter reached here he was challenged and brought to bay by the "Charley" in occupation ... Peter cautiously feigned obstreperousness when the watchman vehemently sprung his rattle. This, of course, brought other "Charleys" on the scene and the prisoner was taken in triumph to the watch-house, the "Charleys" carrying the keg, which Peter put on the ground when challenged and resolutely refused to carry. The prisoner

THE LOST PUBS OF BATH

was placed in a cell, which, in those days, was not like the cells in modern police stations, for he could hear distinctly the conversation taking place between his captors. A proposition was made to spile-hole the keg, with a view to tasting the contents, which was immediately agreed to. One tasted and pronounced the liquor tasteless, a second expressed a similar opinion, and after all the "Charleys," who had been summoned together from off their several beats by the vigorous springing of the rattle, had held consultation, they came to the conclusion that they had wrongly apprehended Peter as the keg contained nothing but water. The prisoner was summoned from his cell, and after expostulating with his captors for apprehending him and locking him up for carrying a keg of water, threatened them with all kinds of proceedings, and parleyed with them as long as suited his purpose. Whilst this little episode was being enacted the blockade was safely run by Peter's accomplices and the cargo of real Cognac safely and securely landed at its destination. There were high jinks at the Darby & Joan for several evenings after the occurrence. Peter lived many years after to tell the amusing tale, "how he tricked the Charleys."

The name of the pub, incidentally, is not unique. At least two other Darby & Joans are still in business – at Crowle in Lincolnshire and Abington Pigotts in Cambridgeshire. The name originated with a ballad published by Henry Woodfall in 1735, and was later applied to happily-married elderly couples. Bath's Darby & Joan closed around 1850 and became a shoemaker's.

§

Retracing our steps up to Lansdown Road, we continue uphill, past the entrance to Hedgemead Park, past the alleyway running down beside Curry Mahal – both of which were once streets leading into the warren of tenements on Hedgemead – to Caroline Place. In the 1840s and 1850s, there was a beerhouse called the **Belvedere Tavern** or Belvedere Arms at 6 Caroline Place.

The former Belvedere Tavern.

At the bottom of Caroline Place, the road curves into Ainslie's Buildings. The buildings, however, have long gone, victims of the Hedgemead landslips. At the end of the road, where it turns into a footpath, were two beerhouses. The first was the **Crown & Anchor**, which opened around 1837 and closed a couple of years later. The second was the **Oddfellows' Arms**, which was kept by a greengrocer called Henry Bush. It opened around 1854 and closed around 1870.

Its licence was transferred to a new **Oddfellows' Arms** at 1 Gloucester Place, further down Hedgemead. This survived until it was pulled down as part of a general clearance in 1883.

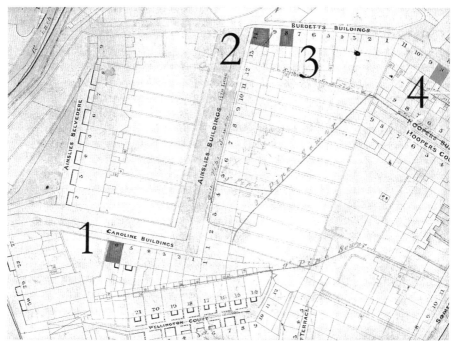

Upper Hedgemead in the 1850s: 1) the Belvedere Tavern; 2) the Oddfellows' Arms; 3) the Crown & Anchor; 4) William Cooper's beerhouse.

The footpath running down from Ainslie's Buildings once led past Burdett's Buildings to a brewery and beerhouse set up by William Cooper around 1840 and closed around ten years later.

Rows of houses once covered this area: two beerhouses – the Oddfellows' Arms and the Crown & Anchor stood on the far side of this path.

William Cooper's beerhouse stood on the left of this path.

Entering Hedgemead Park through the gate at the end of Ainslie's Buildings, take the left-hand path, climb the steps to the road, turn right and walk downhill until the road (and the double yellow lines) swings to the right. A little way up the hill on the left was an exceedingly short-lived beerhouse called the **Prince of Wales** at 12 Camden Cottages, open for a few years in the early 1860s.

Carry straight on between the houses to Gay's Hill. The electricity sub-station facing you at the end of the alleyway marks the site of a beerhouse called the **Gay's Hill Tavern**, which opened in the 1840s as the Crooked Fish.

In the 1940s and 1950s, the Gay's Hill Tavern was at the centre of the local community. Mr & Mrs Warner, the licensees, regularly put on children's parties and ran coach trips to the seaside. Sadly, the

200   THE LOST PUBS OF BATH

Gay's Hill Tavern in happier times ...

... and with demolition already under way.

A children's party in the yard of Gay's Hill Tavern around 1950, with Mr Warner standing in for Father Christmas. If ever there was a community pub, this was it.

THE NORTH-EASTERN SLOPES

community it once stood at the heart of is no more, having been pulled down in 1964 to make way for Alpine Gardens. The pub lingered on for a while, and in September 1964 the *Bath Chronicle* reported on its unlikely survival:

> They might rewrite a famous song about it one day and call it, "The lament of John Watt and his pub with no customers and almost no beer." The customers have all gone. Not surprisingly, seeing that the houses they once lived in have gone too. The pub, lighthouse-like, commands the scene on the hill at Hedgemead, while all around it what were houses lie in a sea of rubble, having been demolished to make way for new. The pub, the Gay's Hill Tavern, is to stay, however, under the redevelopment scheme, and while the bulldozers do their work outside, life goes on as normal at the pub – well, almost. Licensee Mr John Watt … opens the doors regularly each night. Then he waits, usually the whole evening. The last time a genuine customer came in was three months ago … Before the evacuation of the area, the pub had three darts teams … "It was like a ghost town when all the people went, but now the houses are down, it's not so bad," says Mrs Watt.

But, while they waited "for the day when the new houses go up and the customers return," there was a change of heart. The Gay's Hill Tavern closed in 1965 and was, like the houses that once stood around it, demolished.

Continuing up Gay's Hill, past the former ASYLUM FOR TEACHING YOUNG FEMALES HOUSEHOLD WORK, we come to Camden Road. A few doors along on the left was the **Rivers' Arms** at 25 Camden Place. This first appeared in the 1841 *Postal Directory* and for a brief period in the 1840s was also known as the Brewer's Arms. It closed on 18 February 1970 and is now a private house.

To find our next lost pub, we walk east along Camden Road, turn down Bennett's Lane, take the second left up to Highbury Cottages, and turn right at the top into Highbury Terrace. The house at the bottom of Highbury Terrace, on the corner of Snow Hill, was the **Highbury Arms**. It opened around 1830 and was originally called the Hooper's Arms, after the property developer, Peter Hooper.

The Rivers' Arms.

The Hooper's Arms had two rooms for customers – a bar and a tap room – as well as a brewery. Around 1898 it was acquired by the Bath Brewery Company and renamed the Highbury Brewery. Charles Harvey held the licence from 1898 until around 1912, when it was taken over by George Wells, who renamed it the Highbury Arms. In 1917, he handed over to Daniel Pritchard, who was there until the Corporation closed it down in 1928 as part of their drive to reduce the number of pubs in the city.

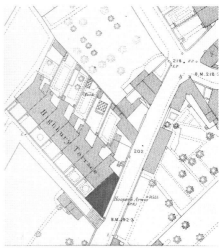

The Highbury Arms occupied an imposing position on the corner of Highbury Terrace.

A short way up Snow Hill – which soon turns into Tyning Lane – is a sealed-up horse trough on the left, with a weathered biblical text extolling the virtues of water. Just past it is a sealed-up doorway. This was the entrance to an alleyway which led to a row of tenements called Lucklom Buildings. These, along with the other buildings

The Rising Sun (1) is still open, but the Mason's Arms (2) and the Crown (3) are long gone.

on the left-hand side of Tyning Lane – including two beerhouses – have gone. In their place is a block of flats and a health centre. The beerhouses were the **Crown** at 15 Claremont Row, which opened in the early 1850s and closed in 1888 when its licence was transferred to the Fairfield Arms, and the **Mason's Arms** at 11-12 Claremont Row, which opened in the 1870s. The 1903 report described it as follows:

> Entrance from Tyning Lane. Door at top of steps at rear to Lucklom Court. Bar with serving window for jug & bottle and drinking bar. Also glass room with bagatelle table and tap room. Skittle alley at rear.

It closed in 1959.

Carrying on to the top of Tyning Lane, crossing the road and continuing along Fairfield Road for a few yards, we come to Claremont Buildings, a modern development that stands on the site of a nineteenth-century terrace with three pubs.

At 6-7 Claremont Buildings was a beerhouse called the **Old Standard** which opened in the 1850s and closed in 1885. In the 1870s, it was kept by a painter and decorator called John Fletcher.

At 16-17 Claremont Buildings was a beerhouse that never got around to acquiring a name. It was opened around 1860 by Thomas Ascott, a shoemaker. At the time of the 1903 report, it consisted of a "shop with drinking counter" in No 16 and a tap room in No 17. Trade was "principally off." It closed in 1917.

At the top of Claremont Buildings, in splendid isolation, was the **Claremont Arms**. It opened in the 1850s and was extended in 1898 when "Mr WG Reynolds of Winchester House, Oldfield Park, owner of the Claremont Arms … applied that the licence at present held by Samuel Hughes … should be extended to certain additional buildings erected on the front or east side of the Claremont Arms."

At the time of the 1903 report, the bar was in four compartments with a tap room at the side. Later patrons may also remember the tip-up cinema seats which stood in the bar. The Claremont Arms closed in the 1960s and the site is now occupied by garages.

The footpath on the left-hand side of Claremont Road leads up through the woods to Richmond Place, built in the early 1800s. Initially, many of the houses in Richmond Place were occupied as country residences by well-to-do tradesmen in the city. Before long, however, they were sliding ever so discreetly downhill. By the end of the nineteenth century, the residents included grocers, carpenters, stonemasons, laundresses, bootmakers, porters, waiters, stokers, basketmakers, warehousemen,

The Claremont Arms.

THE LOST PUBS OF BATH

The pigeon club at the Rising Sun in Richmond Place.

coachmen, labourers, and gardeners. Not surprisingly, there were three beerhouses as well.

At 39 Richmond Place was a beerhouse called the **Rising Sun**. It was opened in the 1840s by William Miles, a baker. In 1903, it consisted of a small general provision shop and a tap room at the back with a bagatelle table. It closed in February 1936.

At 37 Richmond Place was a beerhouse called the **Lansdown Arms**, first recorded as a retail brewery run by Thomas Pinnock in 1837. It closed around 1856.

The third – the Richmond Arms – survives as a bright and lively gastropub, and a handy place to celebrate the end of this excursion.

EXCURSION THE FIFTH

THE UPPER ROAD TO BRISTOL

The fifth excursion begins, like the previous two, outside the North Gate. This time we head west, down New Bond Street, or, as it was once known, Frog Lane. According to John Wood, it got its name "from the spring of mineral water in it." The entrance to

Frog Lane in 1694, with the Unitarian Chapel marked with a Q. The Bowling Green to the north disappeared under Green Street about 20 years later.

Frog Lane was through an archway from Northgate Street. It was first recorded in 1617, when John Waterford leased a tenement and garden there. In the early eighteenth century, Walter Wiltshire's father, William, built a malthouse there. On the north side of the lane was a Unitarian Chapel, where Samuel Taylor Coleridge preached in 1795.

By the 1760s, with the city walls tumbling and streets being built to the north, the council decided that Frog Lane had to go. The first stone of Old Bond Street, at the far end of Frog Lane, was laid in April 1769, but Frog Lane croaked on for another 37 years. In 1800, there were plans, which came to nothing, to create a circus on the site. Eventually, in

BATH, July 10, 1780.

PUBLICK-HOUSE.

TO be LETT, and Enter'd on Immediately, A Well-accustom'd and very Convenient PUBLICK-HOUSE (having three different Ways to it) in the Centre of this City, and near the Markets.

☞ Enquire at the Chequers in Frog-Lane.

The Chequers in Frog Lane advertised to let in 1780.

April 1806, Frog Lane was cleared away to make way for New Bond Street. Although New Bond Street has never had a pub, Frog Lane had three.

The **Chequers,** which closed around 1784, had two addresses – "Brooms Court, near Boro Walls" and Frog Lane.

The **Joyner's Arms** opened around 1780 and closed shortly afterwards.

The only pub that survived until Frog Lane was redeveloped was the **Three Blackbirds**. In 1772, William Harding was granted "liberty to make a way into the sewer in Broad Street from the Three Blackbirds in Frog Lane." When it closed in 1806, its licence – and its name – was transferred to the Three Blackbirds in Little Stanhope Street, which opened in April 1807.

Heading west out of New Bond Street, we come to another street noted for its shops rather than its pubs. There was a pub of sorts in Milsom Street at one time, however, or at least Fred Pearce thought there was when he compiled his *Critical Guide to Bath Pubs*. This is what he to say about **Fortt's**, wedged between the Lotus Shoe Shop and Boot's Chemist's at 4-5 Milsom Street:

> Follow the arrows through the Fortt's restaurant complex; persevere and you'll eventually stumble on the Kitchen Bar. Now why you'd want to go there at all unless you were eating in the place I can't imagine – but a lot of youngsters do.

Fortt's in the 1960s.

THE LOST PUBS OF BATH

They find plenty of space, seating divided into bays, cream painted brick walls – the combined effect is very bare. A few lads play darts and occasional couples roll their hands over one another in the corner. Beer is DD and Special. Very dead.

Quiet Street is publess today, but was once home to the **Raven**, which was on the north side at No 4. It opened in 1778, when John Fox moved there from the Raven in Abbeygate Street. When his widow, Hannah Fox, took over after his death, she renamed it the Fox & Raven. In the 1820s (by which time it had reverted to the Raven) the landlord was Alexander Snodgrass, who later moved to the Caledonian Tavern in Trim Street. In its later years the Raven acquired a dubious reputation. In 1838, for example, Mark Shore, the landlord, was fined £5 and costs for allowing gaming in the house. It closed in the 1850s and, in 1871, the block in which it stood was refronted by Major Davis. The old pub is not entirely forgotten, however; round the corner in Queen Street, the pub formerly known as Hatchett's has been revamped and renamed the Raven, with some of the best beer – and pies – in the city.

In 1776 there were four other pubs in Quiet Street – the **Plume of Feathers**, the **Queen Charlotte**, the **Roebuck** and the **Three Crowns**. All closed in the early 1780s.

A left turn at the end of Quiet Street brings us to Queen Street, built by John Wood around 1730, and home to an eighteenth-century alehouse called the **Chequers**. This also closed in the early 1780s, after having its name changed twice – to the Coach & Horses and the Horse & Jockey – in its final months.

The loss of five pubs in Queen Street and Quiet Street during the Corporation's crackdown on licensed premises in the wake of the Gordon Riots indicates that they were seen as hotbeds of sedition. The patrons of these houses were not, by and large, the sort of villains and ne'er-do-wells who frequented the alehouses in the rougher parts of town. They were servants and tradesmen associated with the gentry who lived nearby. Clearly the Corporation saw them as just as much of a threat – and probably more so – than the army of the dispossessed in the lower part of the city. John Butler, the scapegoat for the Gordon Riots in Bath, for example, was in the service of the City Architect, Thomas Baldwin, and lived in the Circus.

It is tempting to see eighteenth-century Bath divided into two camps – the haves in the elegant squares and terraces to the north of the city, and the have-nots in the sinks and squalor of the lower town. It was not so clear cut. Quiet Street and Queen Street, in the heart of the new town, must have been pretty rough. Why else would the Corporation have wanted five out of their six pubs shut down?

Rough in eighteenth-century terms was relative. What passed for polite society may have been regulated by strict rules of etiquette and decorum, but when it let rip, it was with all the abandon of modern-day Brits on a booze-fuelled holiday bonanza. The Assembly Rooms – Upper and Lower – were the epitome of gentility, but when disputes arose between them, they were settled, not by tête-à-têtes over a dish of hartshorn jelly, but by bodice-ripping, wig-seizing brawls between opposing factions.

If the servants kicked up the odd disturbance now and again, they were only aping the manners of their masters. The difference was that, whereas their masters – and mistresses – could get away with it, they – like the unfortunate John Butler – were punished. The Assembly Rooms carried on regardless, but many of the pubs and taverns they frequented were shut down.

At the bottom of Queen Street is Trim Street, built by Councillor George Trim after he breached the city wall and bridged the ditch in 1707. Originally it was known as Backward Buildings. Construction was piecemeal; twelve years later, Dr Claver Morris rode over from Wells "to see the manner and proportion of the battlements of a new house … in Trim Street."

In the early 1730s, when John Wood started developing the area to the north, an archway was knocked through the north side of Trim Street to provide access to Queen Square. Although Trim Street started off upmarket, and boasted General Wolfe's parents among its residents, by the early nineteenth century it was decidedly frayed at the edges; by 1845, there were "several poor inhabitants there." Some of the houses were converted into workshops or manufactories. Inevitably, alongside the cardboard-box makers, bookbinders, and stay makers, there were pubs.

The former Cabinet Maker's Arms (on the left of the archway) after absorption by Lee's.

THE LOST PUBS OF BATH

A pub called the **Post Boy** was recorded in Trim Street in 1776, but closed around 1780.

At 4 Trim Street, on the left-hand side of the archway, was a cabinet maker called James Hawkins who branched out into beer selling around 1837, and called his pub the **Cabinet Maker's Arms**. Later landlords kept up the tradition of subsidiary occupations. In the 1870s, for example, it was kept by a painter and decorator called John Morley, who resisted the temptation to rename it the Painter & Decorator's Arms. The Cabinet Maker's Arms had a single bar, divided in two by a partition, and a tap room. It also had a brewery at the back which closed around 1914. The pub closed in 1920, when the premises were acquired by JJ Lee & Sons (Cardboard Box Makers & Wholesale Paper Merchants), who also owned 2, 2a, 3, 3a and 4 Trim Street, and 2, 3 and 3b Harington Place. The bar of the Cabinet Maker's Arms was turned into an office and print composing room. The block was later redeveloped.

At 16 Trim Street was the **Caledonian Tavern**, which opened in the early 1830s. Many years later, it featured in an article in the *Bath Journal*:

> In July 1897, an old landmark was removed from Trim Street, in the demolition of a porch or projection at No. 16, when the premises were absorbed into the Stay Manufactory of Messrs. Drew & Co. In my school days, at the old Blue Coat School, this was a public house known as the Caledonian, which had been carried on for some years by a Mr A Snodgrass, and the little square building, about eight or ten feet high, and no larger than the smallest room in my cottage, formed the bar of this tavern, where the liquors and beer were served from; and, at the windows, on three other sides of the square, were the various coloured bottles of spirits characteristic of inns and taverns. This house was very liberally patronised by the class of smaller tradesmen as well as by the more respectable of the artisan and working class, for it was the chief Friendly or Benefit Society house of meeting in Bath. I don't know whether the Bath City Lodge of Oddfellows commenced their prosperous career there, but in July 1838, they held their ninth anniversary and dined there. The Hearts of Oak Society held their meetings there, and in 1843, the Patriarchs, afterwards called the United Patriots, opened their first Bath branch there. It was at the period of the tenancy of Snodgrass at the Caledonian that Dickens ... was in the habit of frequently visiting Bath, meeting literary friends, and picking up some of his amusing, aye, and even detestable objectionable personages. Not only did he visit the Caledonian, but also the Marlborough Tavern and the New Inn, Rivers Street, licensed houses of the old sedan chairmen, and the St James's Hotel, St James's Square, and the Beaufort Arms, Princes Street, houses patronised by the coachmen and flunkies of the gay families then residing in this city.
>
> Snodgrass, host of the Caledonian, was an intellectual, matter-of-fact, hard-headed Scotchman, with the initial A signifying not Augustus but Alexander. The company who smoked their long clays at this hostelry were men who met

together to glean information and instruction from each other. No youths or hobble-de-hoys were admitted at this tavern.

The last recorded landlord of the Caledonian was Charles Frankcom in 1854. The old entrance to the Caledonian is now a window between 15 and 17 Trim Street with the dates 1724 and 1897 above it.

A westward stroll along Trim Street brings us to Barton Street. John Wood built the first house in this street – which later became "coach houses and granaries" – in 1728. The names of the two pubs in Barton Street at the end of the eighteenth century – the Horse & Jockey and the Coach & Horses – provide ample evidence of the occupations of the people who drank in them.

The **Horse & Jockey**, sometimes known as the Horse & Groom, was at 2 Barton Street, one door up from the corner of Beaufort Square. It was first recorded in 1800, when Mary Doveton was the licensee. It was badly damaged by fire in January 1845. According to the report in the *Bath Chronicle* the pub was "occupied by Mr Kelson, whose mother-in-law, Mrs Cross, for a long series of years the keeper of a notorious brothel in this city, perished in the flames … The materials of the internal part of the house being very old, the devastation went on rapidly." The report went on to say that, because of illness, Mrs Cross had moved into the Horse & Jockey from her house in Trim Street. The pub was rebuilt and taken over by a new licensee,

The fire at the Horse & Jockey in 1845.

THE LOST PUBS OF BATH

Henry Coplestone. Charles Kelson moved to another house in Barton Street, which he opened as a pub called the **Fleur de Lis**. It lasted for only a couple of years, and its location is unknown.

For anyone familiar with Bath's brewing history, the name of Kelson in the above report may come as a surprise. Messrs Sayce & Kelson were, until their partnership was dissolved in 1809, the proprietors of the Northgate Brewery, and two of the most prosperous men in town. One of their pubs was the Horse & Jockey, which they leased from St John's Hospital. The Mr Kelson who kept the pub in 1845 was probably a descendant or relative of the brewery's erstwhile owner. For the *Bath Chronicle* to feel free to disparage him at a time of personal tragedy, albeit only by association, not only indicates the low esteem they must have held him in, but also hints at a significant reversal in the family's fortunes.

After a couple of years at the Coach & Horses, Henry Coplestone renamed it the **Queen Square Tavern**, perhaps in a bid to exorcise its unsavoury reputation. However, it continued to attract the wrong sort of clientele, and in October 1850 Mr Coplestone was brutally attacked by one of his lodgers. Ogle Wallis, 57 years old, followed no occupation and described himself as a gentleman who had formerly held a commission with the 12th Dragoons. One day, Mr Coplestone met him coming downstairs with his bag packed. As he had not settled his account, he tried to prevent him leaving. Mr Wallis responded by assaulting him, first with a stick and then with a razor. When Mr Coplestone's screams brought his wife running, Wallis attacked her as well.

Looking down Barton Street with the former Queen Square Tavern – advertising Teas – on the right.

Leaving his two victims seriously injured, Wallis set off in the direction of the Upper Bristol Road with his stick under his arm and his blood-stained hands in his pockets. A boy working for Mr Drew, a staymaker in New Bond Street, raised the alarm, and Wallis was arrested outside Lansley's Riding School on the Upper Bristol Road. The newspaper report, which said that Mr Coplestone and his wife were both likely to recover, albeit with terrible scars, concluded with a damning description of their assailant:

His beard was unshorn and his attire that of a careless dissipated man. His general appearance is that of a foreigner rather than that of an Englishman.

When an inventory of the Queen Square Tavern was carried out in 1887, it had a drawing room, tap room and bar, with a partition creating a bar parlour. There was, perhaps unsurprisingly given the attack on Mr Coplestone, no mention of rooms to let.

In February 1913, the magistrates proposed closing the pub on grounds of redundancy. The police, they pointed out, had kept a watch on the Queen Square Tavern for a whole week, and, during that time, only 122 people had used it. In reply, the licensee, Elizabeth Lloyd, said that she had "no objection to the house being closed. Recently the trade done was not worth speaking of. The average weekly takings were about £2-10-0." And so, the Queen Square Tavern slipped, without a murmur of protest, into history. The site has since been redeveloped.

At 11 Barton Street, on the north corner of Harington Place was the **Coach & Horses**. This had a longer, albeit less colourful, history than the Horse & Jockey, being first recorded in 1779 and closing in 1926. It was tiny, the public accommodation consisting of a bar and one other small room. There was also a skittle alley in the basement, but the 1903 report on the property said that this was "seldom if ever used, being very wet." Today it is the Walrus and the Carpenter Restaurant.

Finally in Barton Street was the **Crown & Thistle**, with a solitary reference in the 1782 alehouse recognizances.

The former Coach & Horses, now the Walrus and the Carpenter.

Beaufort Square – sometimes called Beauford Square – was built by John Strahan around 1727 as lodging houses for fashionable visitors. Even John Wood, Strahan's greatest critic, was forced to admit that the houses in Beaufort Square had "a sort of regularity to recommend them," even though, he added, they were examples of "the piratical architecture of Mr Strahan." As Charles Robertson says in his architectural guide to Bath, the square gives "a vivid impression of the small-town atmosphere which characterized pre-Wood Bath." Beaufort Square must have been even more atmospheric before the Theatre

THE LOST PUBS OF BATH

Royal was built on its south side in the early 1800s. By then, Beaufort Square had gone down in the world. In 1819, Pierce Egan wrote that, "as a place of residence, it has no pretensions whatever, the houses being small and irregularly built, and the inhabitants chiefly tradespeople." It also had a number of pubs.

In 1778 a pub called the **Tankard** opened on the corner of Barton Street. It closed around ten years later.

Even shorter-lived was the **Fox & Hounds**, which was first recorded in 1781, but closed by 1786. There are no clues as to whereabouts in the square it was. There was also a Chequers in 1776, but as this was the only year it was recorded, it probably became the Tankard or the Fox & Hounds.

We are on much firmer ground with the third of Beaufort Square's pubs, which opened some time before 1776. This was at No 3, on the north-east corner of the square. It was known as the **Prince Frederick** (except for a short period between 1800 and 1805 when it became the Duke of York). It was named after Frederick, the eldest son of George II, whose visit to Bath in 1738 was commemorated by the obelisk in Queen Square. The pub probably dated from around the same time. Prince Frederick never became king; he died in 1751 after an accident playing tennis, and his son succeeded to the throne as George III.

By the late nineteenth century, the Prince Frederick had three bedrooms, two parlours, smoking room (with Broadwood grand piano and mahogany card table),

Beaufort Square, with the former Prince Frederick on the corner.

The former Tankard on the corner of Beaufort Square.

THE LOST PUBS OF BATH

and bar. The bar had a panelled, pewter-topped counter, with a glass-panelled partition at the end of it, oil paintings on the walls, three fancy baskets on a shelf, and an ornamental fixture (with turned pillars and silvered backs) behind the bar. There was also a skittle alley.

It closed in 1909. Its last landlord, Ernest Thorp, was described in the *Postal Directory* as an electrical engineer. It later became lodgings and, despite, John Wood's grudging acknowledgement of its architectural merit, was pulled down in the 1960s to make way for a car park. They also pulled down the house next door and were about to start on the one next to that when the resultant outcry not only stopped the bulldozers in their tracks but led to Nos 3 and 4 being rebuilt. Despite appearances to the contrary, the present building on the site of the Prince Frederick is less than 50 years old.

There were also two short-lived beerhouses, at 14 and 15 Beaufort Square, which appeared in the 1837 *Postal Directory*, but closed by 1839.

Princes Street, which dates from the 1730s and runs between Beaufort Square and Queen Square, once had two pubs - the Horse & Groom at no 9 and the Beaufort Arms at no 8.

The **Horse & Groom**, at 9 Princes Street, was open by January 1761, when the *Bath Chronicle* reported that "last Sunday morning early a fire broke out at the Horse & Groom in Princes Street, but timely assistance being given, only the furniture of one of the rooms receiv'd damage thereby."

Given its name, it is not surprising that many of the pub's regulars were connected with livery stables. Horse sales were also held in the inn yard. In the early nineteenth century, it was renamed the Farrier's Arms. In 1842, it was advertised for sale, along with

> a private dwelling house adjoining, containing together a frontage of 57 feet 9 inches. This Public-house has been established nearly a century, the premises in the rear are sufficiently extensive for a small brewery, and, from its situation, is sure to command a good share of business. It is held under St John's Hospital on three lives.

Its share of business could not have been that good, however, for it subsequently closed and became a lodging house.

The **Beaufort Arms** was next to the Horse & Groom at 8 Princes Street. It was first recorded in 1777, and, apart from a brief change of name to the Bird Cage in 1805, remained the Beaufort Arms – or the Beaufort – to the end. In the late nineteenth century, one of its rooms was a minor tourist attraction, because of a belief that it was the one supposedly visited by Sam Weller in *Pickwick Papers* on the night of the "swarry." In fact, the fictional "swarry" did not take place in a pub at all. The story was invented by an acolyte of Dickens called Percy Fitzgerald, whose bust of Dickens can still be seen in the Pump Room.

The Beaufort Arms when it was owned by the Bear Brewery.

THE LOST PUBS OF BATH

Ernest Mills was landlord of the Beaufort Arms from 1924 to 1958. During his tenancy, he extended the pub into No 9, the old Horse & Groom. In the Second World War, the cellars were an air-raid shelter for local residents. By 1976, when Fred Pearce visited,

> successive destruction of inside walls [had] left the serving area entirely surrounded by lounge. Slightly Edwardian decor, predominantly red, with subdued red lighting, lots of space, lots of seats and lots of custom … Some old pub glass denoting bars that no longer exist.

Since then the Beaufort Arms has joined the ranks of Bath's lost pubs. Although threatened with demolition in the late 1980s, it has survived and, although it still looks like a pub, it is now an office.

§

Monmouth Street, at the southern end of Princes Street, is not high on most visitors' must-see list. The history of the inns and pubs which once stood there, however, is one of the most fascinating in the city. Two of them – the Seven Dials and the Bell – appear in *Bath Pubs*, under the entries for Pulp and the Raincheck Bar, as does the Griffin, which still bears the name it had in the eighteenth century.

In his *Description of Bath*, John Wood described Monmouth Street as "a new-built street, of 22 feet broad, [containing] 31 houses, among which there is one that makes a handsome appearance, and the rest are not inferior to those in any other out street of the city." As he rarely praised the work of other architects

The Seven Dials, with the Westgate Tavern (visited in the first excursion) on the right.

working in Bath, his enthusiasm for Monmouth Street suggests he may have had a hand in its development.

On the south side of the street were two beerhouses. At No 8, opposite the Ustinov Theatre, was the **Old Monmouth Arms**, which opened – and closed – in the 1850s. It later became a fish and chip shop.

At 11 Monmouth Street, opposite the Raincheck Bar, was the **Times Tavern**, also known as the Bath Tavern and the Freeman's Arms. It opened around 1840 and closed less than 20 years later. It became a billiard saloon and, like the Old Monmouth Arms, was destroyed in the Bath Blitz of 1942.

On the corner of Monmouth Street and St John's Place was the **Theatre Tavern**. It was first recorded as the Bolt & Tun in 1792, but changed its name to the Theatre Tavern after the Theatre Royal moved next door in 1805. In 1825, its stock in trade, "comprising several thousand gallons of strong beer, a quantity of spirits and wine, a large quantity of casks in excellent condition, a complete set of brewing utensils, [and] about 16 hundredweight of hops," was offered for sale. In 1843, when it was advertised to let, it was described as "that well-accustomed, home-brewed Inn & Tavern with spacious yard and stabling." It also had a skittle alley and a meeting room capable of holding at least 200 people. Like the nearby Garrick's Head, it was a meeting place for radical groups. In 1847, for example, the club room was "tolerably well filled" by a Chartist rally.

In 1815, David Hughes, a lodger at the Theatre Tavern, met with a horrific end. After going to bed somewhat the worse for wear, screams were heard coming from his room. James Chapman, another lodger, rushed in to find him engulfed in flames. He tried to help him onto the bed but his skin came off in the attempt. Hughes managed to tell him that he "had put the candle on the chair and having taken off my small clothes the tail of my shirt caught fire while I was making water." Nothing of the shirt was left except the wristbands. Hughes later died, in great agony, of his injuries.

Forty-seven years later, on the morning of Good Friday 1862, another fire broke out at the Theatre Tavern. The landlord heard a peculiar crackling sound outside, which he took to be rain. When the noise grew more persistent, he went into the yard to investigate, and was horrified to see smoke billowing from a window in the theatre. He raised the alarm, but, by the time the fire brigade arrived, it was too late. Before long, the theatre was gutted. The cause of the blaze was never established, but, as the building had not been used since the previous Wednesday, it was thought that a spark from a flue in the brewery of the Theatre Tavern, which backed onto the theatre, was probably to blame.

The Peep O'Day, on the corner of St John's Place, faced another of Bath's lost pubs – the Garrick's Head.

Ironically, the Theatre Tavern was largely untouched by the fire and stayed open till 1888, when its licence was revoked. Shortly afterwards it was pulled down to make way for St Paul's Parish Hall and Church House. This later became a cinema and is now the egg theatre.

At the other end of St John's Place, past the old Garrick's Head, was a beerhouse called the **Peep O'Day**. It stood on the corner opposite the Theatre Royal and was one of the most notorious pubs in the area. On 21 December 1903, for example, the landlord was fined for refusing to admit a police constable to the premises. Those who did manage to get in would have found a bar with a small enclosed compartment and a smoke room at the back. One thing they would not have found, however, was a toilet. Customers either had to use the public urinal in the Sawclose or keep their legs crossed.

The story behind the pub's name is an intriguing one. The last play to be performed at the Theatre Royal before it burned down in 1862 was *Peep O'Day* by Edmund Falconer (aka Edmund O'Rourke). Its story concerned a member of a band of Irish Protestant rebels (known as "peep o'day" men because of their habit of visiting

THE LOST PUBS OF BATH

St Paul's Church Hall, built on the site of the Theatre Tavern, now houses the egg theatre.

Ellen Terry, Queen of the Fairies.

their victims' houses at daybreak), who is saved after being buried alive, and wins a pardon from the British military and the hand of the heroine. It was the first time a play had been staged at the Theatre Royal during Holy Week, and many saw the fire as a judgement by the Almighty on its blasphemous proprietors.

Be that as it may, the theatre was rebuilt and reopened less than a year later with a production of *A Midsummer Night's Dream*, starring a 16-year-old Ellen Terry as the Queen of the Fairies. If they thought that Shakespeare's magic would dispel the memory of the terrible fire, they had not counted on the tenant of the shop at the top of New Westgate Buildings who, to celebrate the reopening of the theatre, opened a beerhouse and called it the Peep O'Day. To have had your theatre burnt down by one pub was bad enough. To have the event celebrated by the opening of another was really rubbing salt into the wound.

The Peep O'Day closed in 1906 and became the Peep O'Day fish and chip shop.

At 34 Monmouth Street is the Raincheck Bar, once the Bell Inn, whose history is traced on pages 142-43 of *Bath Pubs*.

The **Victoria Wine & Spirit Vaults** at 29 Monmouth Street opened some time before 1830, later changed its name to the Victoria Tavern, and closed in 1851. An almost miraculous survival from over 150 years ago is the decorative ironwork above the frontage, liberally adorned with casks and bunches of grapes, the symbols of the vintner's trade.

At 25 Monmouth Street was the **Midland Arms**, which opened as a beerhouse around 1868. It consisted of a single bar, part of which was partitioned off to

Far right The former Midland Arms.

Right The former Victoria Wine & Spirit Vaults.

Below Casks and grapes still adorn the Victoria Wine & Spirit Vaults, over 150 years after it closed.

A plan drawn by Edward Davis in 1830, showing the location of the Elephant & Castle.

form a smoking room. It closed in 1910, and today the building is used by Future Publishing. It is still recognisable as a pub with a hanging sign and a decorative feature similar to that on the Porter Butt on London Road above the cornice.

Finally, we come to Monmouth Street's *pièce de resistance*. The **Elephant & Castle** is not only one of Bath's most irrevocably lost pubs but also one of its most fascinating. The only known picture of it is a small engraving on a trade card in Bath Central Library, which is reproduced in James Lees-Milne's *Images of Bath*. Even in this – the only book which seems to mention it – the author admits he is at a loss as to its exact location. Postal directories are of little help. The directories for the first forty years of the nineteenth century assign it a range of different addresses – Monmouth Place, Monmouth Street, Upper Bristol Road or "near Queens Square" – and none of them include a street number.

Fortunately, there is one map which shows it – a plan of the future Royal Victoria Park prepared by the architect Edward Davis in 1829 – where it is shown occupying the position on the corner of Chapel Row and Monmouth Place now filled by Holy Trinity Church.

The Elephant & Castle was not just another street corner beerhouse which disappeared in the name of road improvements or to make way for a church. It was known as the Elephant & Castle Inn or the Elephant & Castle Inn & Tavern and it was a well-designed and well-proportioned four-storey classical building.

On 12 June 1794, an advertisement appeared in the *Bath Chronicle*:

ELEPHANT & CASTLE, Monmouth Street:

Robert Tanner begs leave to inform his Friends and the Publick that he has taken and fitted up in a genteel manner the above elegant and commodious house which he has opened as an inn and tavern.

Mr Tanner was a perfumier who had held the lease of King James's Palace Pleasure Gardens at Widcombe between 1791 and 1793. At the time, this was one of the most fashionable venues in Bath, with musical breakfasts twice a week, gala nights and firework displays. Unfortunately, Robert Tanner fell victim to the financial crash of 1793, which also claimed John Eveleigh, the architect and presiding genius of Grosvenor Gardens, as well as two of Bath's six banks. In the sale which followed his bankruptcy, even the plants in the greenhouses at King James's Palace went under the hammer.

Despite this setback, Robert Tanner bounced back less than a year later to open an "elegant and commodious inn." Why he chose to call it the Elephant & Castle – the emblem of the Cutlers' Company – is not known, nor do we know what happened to him after he gave up the lease around 1801. He was succeeded by William Springford, who had previously kept the King's Arms in Monmouth Place. He died in 1812, and his widow, Emma, took over the business. When she died in 1838, it passed to her son, John Springford. It is probable, although not certain, that this was the same John Springford who, in 1828, placed an advert in the *Bath Postal Directory* for the Bath Arms Inn & Tavern at Warminster, from whence coaches ran daily to Bristol, Bath, Salisbury, Romsey, Southampton, Brighton, Gosport and Portsmouth. In the 1822 edition of *Paterson's Roads*, an indispensable handbook for travellers in the pre-railway age, the Elephant & Castle is one of only six inns listed for Bath.

In 1830, the promoters of a Bath & Bristol Railway proposed to bring their line across Lower Common to terminate at a station in Stable Lane (now Palace Yard Mews), directly behind the inn. The scheme foundered when a number of local landowners got together and resolved that

> the land and water communications now existing between the cities of Bristol and Bath are fully sufficient for all purposes of conveyance and that the proposed railway is uncalled for upon public grounds which would alone justify the inroad it will make upon private property and the rights and comforts of individuals.

Ironically, it was the opening of the Great Western Railway from Bristol to Bath ten years later, with a station on the other side of town, that led to the collapse of the Elephant & Castle's business. As late as October 1839, when it was described as a "family hotel," it was one of only five Bath hotels (along with the York House, the White Hart, the White Lion, and the Castle) listed as having received fashionable visitors the previous week. On 12 August 1841, just over a month after the railway from London opened, it was advertised for sale in the *Bath Chronicle*. It was described as a "well known and desirable inn and commercial tavern, standing in one of the most commanding entrances to the city of Bath." Since the opening of the railway, it was an entrance which had seen passing trade – or at least the sort of passing trade which it needed in order to survive – dwindle almost to nothing. The advertisement went on to say that "the building, which is detached, is a handsome freestone elevation, and possesses an admirable frontage towards Green Park." The basement (or what would be referred to today as the ground floor) contained a bar, coffee, smoking and two retirement rooms, a good larder, a waiters' room, and "a well-sequestered water closet." The first floor had five "superior sitting rooms," two bedrooms and another water closet. The two upper floors contained "17 sleeping apartments." In the yard there were stables for 30 horses and a tap room with two bedrooms over it.

Nobody seems to have been interested in taking it on as an inn, and on 23 February 1842, the following notice appeared in the *Bath Chronicle*:

> The premises, so long known as the Elephant & Castle Inn, have been taken by Dr Hillcoat, with the intention of converting them into an establishment, supported by voluntary contributions, for the relief of 50 poor persons or upwards.

Applicants had to be "beyond labour" and have "seen better days." The Elephant & Castle became, in other words, an old people's home. The entry in the 1846 *Postal Directory* describes it as "St Mary's Establishment for aged females, supported by voluntary contributions."

But, even though it ceased to be an inn, its subsequent history is, if anything, even more interesting. To understand it, however, we must sketch in a bit of ecclesiastical history. The Dr Hillcoat who bought the Elephant & Castle had been the minister of Queen Square Chapel since 1817. This chapel was behind the Elephant & Castle on the north side of Chapel Row. It came under the Rector of Walcot, whose own church, St Swithin's, was in a rather more unfashionable part of town, directly opposite the notorious Hat & Feather Yard. It was not unknown for respectable churchgoers to be heckled by disreputable characters hanging around St Swithin's waiting for the pubs to open. On at least one occasion they even had "dirt" thrown at them. Not surprisingly, the majority of people living in Queen Square preferred to use Queen Square Chapel instead of trekking all the way down the Paragon to have things thrown at them. And, naturally, they left any legacies or bequests to the minister at Queen Square rather than the Rector of Walcot. All of which caused a most unholy row to break out, involving the Bishop, threats of deconsecration, and, ultimately, the imprisonment of Dr Hillcoat in Lancaster Castle for debt. At issue was the question of whether baptisms and marriages could be held in Queen Square Chapel. The Rector of Walcot insisted they could not but Rev Hillcoat took no notice and carried on regardless. Hence the court case, which the Rev Hillcoat lost, leaving him to pay the costs of the action, which, despite the money left to him, he was unable to do.

The Rev Hillcoat's successor was Rev Loughnan, who agreed to lease the chapel in 1852. Things turned sour the following year, however, when he announced that he was unable to come up with the money as he had been let down by a lady who had promised to lend him £1,000. He was saved – although not before his possessions had been seized by the bailiffs – when an appeal, orchestrated by the *Bath Chronicle*, raised £1,163 to buy him a "life-interest" in the chapel.

Whether the old people's home at the Elephant & Castle survived the storm-tossed seas of religious infighting is not known, but its days were now numbered, due to another railway scheme. The Midland Railway planned to build the terminus of its branch from Mangotsfield just south of the Elephant & Castle, on Seymour Street. The Act of Parliament authorising construction of the line stipulated that the Midland Railway had to build streets wide enough to carry the anticipated traffic from the terminus to the town centre. One of the streets that needed widening was Chapel Row, then no more than a narrow alley. The original plan was to demolish the houses on the south and east side of Chapel Row, leaving the Elephant & Castle and Queen Square Chapel untouched. On 13 December 1866, however, the *Bath Chronicle* reported that, at a meeting of the City Act Committee,

THE LOST PUBS OF BATH

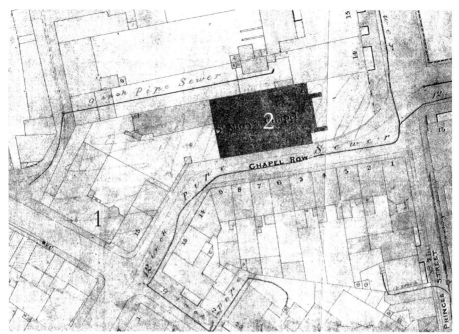

A map from around 1850 showing the former Elephant & Castle (1) and Queen Square Chapel (2), both demolished to improve access to the Midland station.

the Clerk reminded the board that a parliamentary notice had been issued by the Midland Railway Company in reference to the approaches to the terminus of the line in course of construction and said that he had inspected the plans which were deposited with the clerk of Walcot parish, and he found that the company intended to abandon the widening of the left-hand side of Chapel Row going towards Charles Street, which they proposed to do by their act of 1864, and instead thereof to take down the chapel on the north side of the row, and the large building at the end, formerly known as the Elephant & Castle. He had consulted with the surveyor when he inspected the plans and Mr Parfitt was of opinion that the present plan of widening on the north side was much the more preferable.

If Rev Loughnan was going to lose his chapel, he wanted to make sure he got adequate compensation. He put in a claim for £7,984 – equivalent to around £400,000 today. The Midland Railway, having examined his stipend (£100 a year plus half the pew rents) and the sum he had paid for a "life interest" in the chapel (£1,163), declared this to be "a most exaggerated claim." Not so, replied Rev Loughnan, if the value of the gifts and legacies received from wealthy members of the congregation was taken into account. But, even though he took them to court, he ended up with a mere £4,151.

Columns and other architectural features from the chapel went to the gardens of a house next to Cleveland Bridge and a house above Camden Crescent. The reredos in the Masonic Hall in Old Orchard Street, attributed to John Wood, may also

The west side of Queen Square as originally built. Queen Square Chapel can just be seen on the extreme left.

have come from the old chapel. However, we do not know if anything was saved from the wreck of the Elephant & Castle.

After Chapel Row had been widened, a new church, St Paul's, was built on part of the site once occupied by the inn and consecrated in 1874. But, even though the Elephant & Castle passed into history at the behest of the Midland Railway, we cannot leave it without a last look at the picture on the Springfords' trade card. It was indeed an "elegant and commodious house," so elegant and commodious, in fact, that it looks remarkably like the two buildings by John Wood on the east side of Queen Square which were later linked together to form a complete row. Given its location, it seems probable that, like Queen Square Chapel, it was built by John Wood.

There is no way of proving this – but remember John Wood's description of Monmouth Street:

> It is a new-built street, of twenty two feet broad, contains thirty-one houses, among which there is one that makes a handsome appearance, and the rest are not inferior to those in any out street of the city.

The only building which stood out in any way in Monmouth Street was the one which later became the Elephant & Castle. Even if he did not have a hand in the rest of Monmouth Street, but decided, most uncharacteristically, to praise its builders, surely the one building he singled out for especial praise would have been by him. His account of the building of Queen Square Chapel is also suggestive:

> Upon the 3rd of February 1731, I made a proposal to Mr. Gay, the Patron of the Rectory of Walcot, to build a chapel in that parish ... After this I declared publickly my resolution of erecting a handsome chapel by Queen Square, which raised such a spirit in people to build near the place where the chapel was to stand, that I had an immediate application made to me for ground for no less than seventeen houses! And so eager were the people for it, that though I was not possessed of the land myself, yet they entered into a conditional contract, bearing date the 26th of February, 1731, to take it of me when I should. Accordingly I procured, by the 8th of March following, a lease of as much land as was necessary to supply this great demand, as well as to build a chapel upon.

THE LOST PUBS OF BATH

The former Queen Square Wine & Spirit Vaults.

It seems likely that the Elephant & Castle was one of the buildings designed by John Wood to meet "this great demand." The only clue to its use before Robert Tanner opened it as an inn comes from a plan in Bath Record Office, drawn by John Wood the Younger in 1766, on which it is identified as "Jennings' Stables." Who Mr Jennings was, and quite why such a palatial building was used as stables are just two of the mysteries surrounding one of Bath's most fascinating lost inns.

On the side of Chapel Row which escaped demolition, at no 11, was a pub called the **Queen Square Wine & Spirit Vaults**. It opened around 1856 as an agency for the Southstoke Brewery and closed in 1912. It had a drawing room, bar parlour, shop and three bedrooms to let.

§

A short walk down Monmouth Place brings us to the New Inn, opened in 1837 and still in business. Cumberland Row, facing it, once had two pubs. The **Heart & Compass** opened some time before 1747, when an advertisement appeared in the *Bath Journal*:

> A cart and horses sets out every morning from the Heart & Compasses in Monmouth Street without Westgate, Bath and will carry to and from Bristol all manner of goods, under two tons weight at a very reasonable fee.

The Heart & Compasses was one of many variations on its name. "Heart" sometimes became "Hart" and, for long periods, it was known, not as the Heart & Compasses but the Heart Encompassed, and even, on one occasion, the Old Heart Encompassed. It closed in the 1850s.

There was also a beerhouse called the **Wheelchair** in Cumberland Row. In 1834, the landlord, James Hartery, was fined £5 for "allowing gaming in his house." It closed shortly afterwards. Both the Heart & Compass and the Wheelchair were destroyed in the Bath Blitz.

At the bottom of Cumberland Row is New King Street, which, despite its length, has never had any pubs. This is curious, because, according to a report in the *Bath Chronicle* for 24 January 1771, there were certainly brothels there. But, as we are not on the trail of Bath's lost brothels, we will take a left and pass quickly on to Charles Street. At one time we could have crossed the road and carried straight on down Kingsmead Street to Kingsmead Square, but offices and flats now block the way. The

The corner of Kingsmead Street and Charles Street around 1910. On the corner is Matthews' Bakery. Next to it, bearing the name of the Anglo-Bavarian Brewery, is the Kingsmead Wine Vaults. Three doors down from the corner is the Gloucester House. Kingsmead House now occupies this site.

The only pub on this map to have survived is the New Inn (5). Those that have gone include: 1) the Victoria Wine & Spirit Vaults; 2) the Midland Arms; 3) the Elephant & Castle; 4) the Queen Square Wine & Spirit Vaults; 6) the Gloucester Inn; 7) the Railway Hotel; 8) the Kingsmead Wine Vaults; and 9) the Red Lion.

watering holes in Kingsmead Street will be covered in the eighth excursion. For now, we will content ourselves with the two that once stood in Charles Street.

On the other side of the road, a few yards further down, at No 10, was the **Gloucester House**, which opened around 1864 as a Bottle Ale & Porter Store. From about 1878 to 1908 it was described as a wine & spirit merchants, but it also seems to have served as an unofficial refreshment room for railway travellers. The 1903 report records that cold meat, bread and cheese were available. The bar was divided into four compartments with moveable partitions and a had smoke room behind. It lost its licence in 1919 but remained a restaurant, later becoming the Albion Private Hotel.

At 16 Charles Street, on the corner of James Street West, where the entrance to

THE LOST PUBS OF BATH

The corner of James Street West and Charles Street today.

Kingsmead House is today, was the **Railway Hotel**, which opened around 1868 as a Cider, Ale & Porter Stores and was renamed when the Midland Railway station opened in 1870. The 1903 report describes it as having a back exit to James Street West, an enclosed bar with a smoke room behind, and a club room upstairs. It closed around 1960.

A right turn along James Street West brings us to the car park of Avery, Knight & Bowler's. This is the site of the **Edinburgh Arms**, a substantial three-storey building, with three steps up to the front door, and a room either side. The three windows on the first floor had ornamental balconies, and there was a court – known as Dane's or Dance's Court – on the western side. Built sometime before 1776, it was first recorded as the White Hart in 1805. It changed its name to the Midland & Derby Tavern in 1869, and later became the Edinburgh Arms. It consisted of a bar with a painted panelled counter and marble top, back shelving with turned pillars and cornice, a four-motion beer engine, a gilt-frame chimney glass and eight spittoons, and a tap room with a settle, two tables and four deal forms. It was open all day for meals. No doubt it was a cheap and convenient alternative to the buffet on the station, and much missed when it closed in 1918.

A westward stroll along James Street West, following the road round into Stanhope Place, brings us back to New King Street. Here a short detour eastward brings us to St Ann's Place. In the 1960s, this area was earmarked for demolition. Somehow, it managed to survive, and, today, immaculately restored, it is one of Bath's best-kept secrets – a world away from what we generally think of as Georgian Bath,

The back entrance to the Royal Oak in St Ann's Place.

but exuding a strong sense of what the city was like in the eighteenth century. At the end of the court, its crazily-angled roofs clearly indicating building work of different periods, is the back entrance to the old **Royal Oak**. When it was being restored after the threat of demolition had been lifted, it was discovered that it had originally been thatched. It is likely that it dates from the seventeenth century or even earlier, with later additions.

Turning to its history as a pub, there is no evidence that it was licensed before the 1840s. The first reference we have found to it is in the 1848 *Postal Directory*, when Ann Davis held it as a beerhouse. It had only one bar, but a parlour at the

The former Royal Oak still boasts its nameboard.

back, used by the family, was also open to selected guests. When an inventory was drawn up in 1886, the bar had a four-motion beer engine, a two-light gasolier and smoke consumers, two drinking tables on iron stands, fixed seating round the wall and nine spittoons. Among the furnishings in the parlour were a mahogany drinking table, two Windsor chairs, a box of dominoes and a copper beer warmer. In 1903, when few pubs served food, the Royal Oak sold bread and cheese to its customers.

It closed in 1961, but a walk round to the front of the building reveals that its nameboard, now weathered and faded, is still there above the door. Although not a thing of any great beauty and next to worthless if removed, it is nevertheless a unique part of Bath's heritage and gives the building a tangible link with the past that no amount of restoration or makeover could achieve. Although it has only been closed for just over 40 years, already it seems to belong to the dim, distant past.

Across the road, at the bottom of Charlotte Street, where the last house in Crescent Gardens stands today, once stood a beerhouse called the **New Inn**, opened by a coal merchant called Charles Davis in the late 1840s and closed a few years later.

At 1 Little Stanhope Street, on the corner of the Upper Bristol Road, was the **Three Blackbirds**, which opened in 1807. Its licence was transferred from the Three Blackbirds in Frog Lane, which closed when Frog Lane was pulled down to make way for New Bond Street.

The King's Arms (4) is still open, but the Three Blackbirds (1), the Royal Oak (2), and the New Inn (3) are long gone.

Inquests were frequently held at the Three Blackbirds on bodies dredged from the river. In 1833, for example, an inquest was held on Elizabeth Pearce, age 19, of 2 Nelson Place, who drowned while collecting a can of water from the river for her mistress. In March 1842, an inquest was held on Thomas Mulligan, the editor of the *Bath Herald*. The last person to see him alive was Mr Manners, a music professor, at whose house he

THE LOST PUBS OF BATH

had spent the evening. He was worried by the failure of the Monmouthshire Iron & Coal Company, in which he had invested a good deal of money, but the jury found there was insufficient evidence to return a verdict of suicide.

That same year, the Three Blackbirds was advertised for sale. It was described as "the corner house of Little Stanhope Street and the Upper Bristol Road, with two frontages of 27 feet and 24 feet 6 inches. The house is admirably situated for business, has long been established, and is now in the occupation of Mr Eustace, as yearly tenant, at the rent of £35." It closed in 1961.

Before we head west along the Upper Bristol Road, here – as an aperitif – are three Upper Bristol Road beerhouses whose exact locations are unknown: the **Belle Vue Tavern**, Belle Vue Cottage (c1837-c1849); the **Mackworth Tavern**, Mackworth Place (c1860-c1864); and the **Mason's Arms**, 3 Park Place (c1860-c1864).

The former Robin Hood.

Just past Nile Street, at 1-2 St George's Place, was the **St George's Brewery**. In 1837, Amelia Perris was recorded as a brewer at 2 St George's Place. Four years later, Thomas Cook opened a beerhouse there. This soon closed, but, around 1880, Henry Arnold opened a beerhouse at Nos 1 and 2. It consisted of a bar, parlour, shop, and brewery. It was later taken over by the Bath Brewery Company, but closed in 1904. The building was destroyed in the Bath Blitz.

A few doors along, at 8 St George's Place, was a beerhouse called the **Robin Hood**. It opened around 1870 and closed in 1931. It consisted of a small bar with a tap room behind. It is now Mr D's takeaway burger bar.

Beyond St George's Place comes Albion Place, most of which lies under Hinton Garage. In the early nineteenth century, however, it boasted two breweries and a pub. In 1800, Richard Brooke, a brewer, leased a plot of land in Albion Place. Nine years later, he went into partnership with John Phillips and opened the Albion

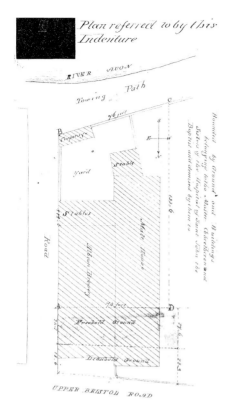

Reference The yellow colour and letters ABCD circumscribe the plot of Ground hereby demised. The Hatched lines shew the Buildings.

A plan of the Albion brewery in 1825.

Brewery, which was impressive enough to receive a special mention in Pierce Egan's 1819 guidebook to the city. It is likely, judging by the style of the houses in Albion Place (two of which remain), that they were built around the same time as the brewery. By 1819, the partnership had been dissolved and Richard Brooke held sole control. In 1825, he leased the brewery to George Alcock, a wine and spirit merchant, who later entered into partnership with John Bond. Bond later bought out Alcock, and, in the 1840s, the brewery was sold to Messrs Symes & Harman. It closed in 1854.

In 1826, James Dredge opened the Norfolk Brewery on Albion Place. It burnt down in July 1832, but was soon rebuilt. Dredge, who built the suspension bridge nearby in 1836, stayed at the brewery until 1849, when it was taken over by King & Co. It was acquired by Strange & Son around 1860, and closed a year later. It was converted to a staymaking factory, and later became a cabinet works.

At 7 Albion Place was the **Albion Tavern**, which opened in the early 1820s. A few days before the licensing session in 1828, the magistrates received an anonymous letter:

Honor'd sir

Please to excuse my boldness in taking the liberty of writing to you on such a subject but obligation forces me to inform you of the circumstance it is concerning of the Albion Tavern now kept by Mr Liquorish (late Mr Evans) he has had a skittle alley made in his under kitchen and it so annoys we neighbours that we can get no rest untill 12 or 1 o'clock at night owing to its being under ground and back no eye or watchman can see or hear them and the Landlord lets them play so long as they please and of a Sunday he puts them in the alley during the whole of divine service and oftentimes we are awaked up 2 & 3 in the morn by the noise of those drunkards just come out of the above Inn & Sir! I trust, tomorrow being Licence day that there will be a stop put to that Alley.

> I am Sir
> Your Obedient & humble servt.
> A Tradesman residing near the above Inn.

After making further enquiries, the magistrates decided to revoke the licence. A few months later an auction was held at the Albion Tavern. Among the items on offer were "an elegant three-motion beer engine and pipes, mahogany drinking tables, several single and double settles, form, stools, pewter, cups, cans and measures, draining trough, cupboards and silver ... the property of Mr Liquorish, leaving the house."

The Albion Tavern stood empty for a couple of years, until, in January 1831, "Albion House, Upper Bristol Road, with a licence for a tavern ... situated in the intended new line of road leading from Bristol by Newbridge to Bath," was advertised to let.* This suggests the magistrates had had a change of heart. They had not. The Beerhouse Act had come into force a year earlier, enabling householders to take out a beer licence without recourse to the magistrates. The licence referred to in the advertisement was a beer licence.

The Albion Tavern was reopened as a beerhouse by James Dredge of the Norfolk Brewery, who changed its name to the **Norfolk Tavern**. It survived the demise of the brewery in 1861, and was taken over by Spencer's Brewery of Bradford on Avon, eventually becoming part of Usher's empire in 1913. By the time of the 1903 report, it had become the Norfolk Arms, and consisted of a bar with a jug & bottle department and a tap room. The premises were in a very good state of repair "except at the rear." The report spelt out the deficiencies: "WC at rear, used also as a urinal, but with no proper seat accommodation."

Sometime after 1903, the Norfolk Arms was upgraded to a fully licenced house. It survived until 1942, when it was destroyed in the Bath Blitz. Its licence was held in abeyance until 1955, when it was transferred to the Quiet Street Wine Vaults (now the Raven), which until then had only held a beer and wine licence.

At 10 Albion Place from around 1858 to 1862 was a beerhouse called the **Oddfellows' Arms**. Like the Norfolk Tavern, it now lies under the Hinton Garage.

A little further along we come to Albion Buildings. There were once two beerhouses here: one – the Hop Pole – is still very much with us; the other is closed, bombed and forgotten. The **Caledonian** at 1 Albion Buildings opened as a beerhouse around 1872. The 1903 report described it as a "very small house," consisting of a "bar used as a provision shop with a room behind used by public and family jointly."

The furnishings of the front bar were simple and functional – a deal counter, two sets of scales, a set of brass weights, a set of iron weights, a back counter, ten tea canisters, a four-motion beer engine, three beer measures, two tin funnels, eight cups, eight glasses, eight tea caddies, two biscuit tins, half pint, pint and quart measures, an old glass case, a vinegar cask and a gas stove.

The back room was where customers who wanted more than a swift half or a few groceries ended up. Its furnishings included a deal table, a mahogany table,

---

*In the early 1830s, the Upper Bristol Road was improved, Newbridge Road built, and the New Bridge widened by the Bath Turnpike Trust.

The gentleman with the bowler and brolly lends a Magritte-like quality to this photograph of the Norfolk Arms.

THE LOST PUBS OF BATH

eight chairs, a long stool, six spittoons, four prints, an eight-day clock, a brass fender, two fire irons and a chimney glass.

Although the Caledonian lost its beer licence in 1909, it stayed open as a grocer's until it was destroyed in the Bath Blitz of 1942.

A brisk walk along the Upper Bristol Road brings us to the **Windsor Castle**, on the corner of Windsor Bridge Road. Its current appearance is, of all Bath's lost pubs, perhaps the most bizarre. It opened as a beerhouse around 1837, was subsequently granted a full licence, and was substantially rebuilt in 1920.

In 1967, the son of the landlord dug up an enormous millstone in the backyard. Although its origin was never explained, it suggests that the Windsor Castle may have started life as a mill. In 1976, when Fred Pearce visited, the Windsor Castle had just been extensively renovated. The public bar had been renamed the Castle; the lounge was the Windsor Bar, with wood panelling, padded loo doors, brown-tiled ceiling, black and orange carpets, fancy lighting and horse brasses galore. Less than a year later, it was revamped again. The alterations prompted an article in the *Bath Chronicle* which covered a good deal of the Windsor Castle's history (even though it stated it was 30 years younger than it was):

> The last of the tiny holes and corners, which characterised the century-old pub has been straightened out in a conversion costing several thousand pounds. Landlord Ray Cook decided the old off-licence and a corner of the public bar would have to go. In the process he has extended the saloon bar and enlarged the bar counter itself. The Windsor Castle, built as a cottage style pub about a century ago, originally boasted a back garden which ran to the River Avon. Today all that is covered in factories. Although it looks out of place in an area of high walls and terraced houses, the squat and solitary Windsor Castle depends for its trade on the local industry and workforce. At one time even the lounge bar was flagged and the locals talk half-jokingly of the sawdust and spittoons. Today, with newly-fitted carpets, nobody need get cold feet about dropping in for a drink. The latest building work is more a rationalisation than anything else. For instance, there was an odd corner of the public bar which few people used because it was three or four steps down from the rest. By a stroke of good fortune the builders have been able to incorporate the wasteland into the lounge bar just by shifting a wall a few feet. Demolish a partition between the lounge and the "bottle and jug," turn the bar through ninety degrees and hey presto! – customers are presented with a spacious and comfortable pub which belies its outer appearance. Another innovation Mr Cook has made: real beer (Bass Charrington flavour) dispensed through a hand-pump, proudly resurrected on the lounge bar counter.

Today, all that is left of the pub is the front wall, with a massive archway driven through it, leading to a business and residential development. The words WINDSOR CASTLE INN, incised in letters several feet high, can still be seen above the first-floor windows.

So ends our fifth excursion, although it can be extended to take in the site of Bath's biggest lost brewery. To find it, continue along the Upper Bristol Road and take the first left into Locksbrook Road. Eventually you will pass the Dolphin Inn on your left. Carry on and turn right into Avondale Road. Carry on up the hill until you come to a bridge carrying the road over an old railway line. This was the Midland line from Green Park to Mangotsfield. In the old quarry on the left-hand side – now the site of Hartwell Motors – was the Bath Brewery, opened in 1896 and taken over by George's of Bristol in 1923. In 1930, the brewery was sold to JD Taylor & Sons of Twerton, who converted it to maltings.

EXCURSION THE SIXTH

THE JULIAN WAY TO WESTON

Once again our excursion starts at the old North Gate, outside which, in former times, was a bowling green. In 1716, the green was grubbed up to make way for Green Street; the old green tree that shaded the bowlers was commemorated in the name of one of Bath's most famous pubs. There was another licensed establishment on Green Street in the early eighteenth century. Although it would be stretching a point to call it a pub, it is worth including on the strength of an advertisement that appeared in the *Bath Journal* on 25 May 1747:

> The **Bath Punch House**, kept by James Morse, Chymist and Distiller of Rich Cordial Waters in Green Street ... where punch is made to the highest perfection in several quantities of Batavian Arrack, Jamaican Rum, Coniac Brandy, or Shrub ... viz Brandy & Rum made into Punch at 4/- per quart, and so in proportion right down to the half quarters for 3d; right citron and usque baugh.*
>
> NB Any gentleman that is willing to advance a sum of money in a genteel and

---

*Usque baugh (water of life) was the original Gaelic name for whisky; arrack (an Arabic word meaning sweat-juice) was distilled from the fermented juice of the coco-palm.

Paint removed from the walls of the Assembly Rooms in June 1961 revealed signs for nineteenth-century shops, including Lawson Howes' wine merchant's, where India Pale Ale was on sale. The workmen paused long enough for them to be recorded for posterity; then they were removed as well.

profitable business, there is a person lately arriv'd from abroad that can instruct them in the best manner; to be spoke with at the aforesaid place.

Green Street had been there for around 45 years before the first houses in Milsom Street were built. Originally intended as a quiet residential development, Milsom Street soon became Bath's most fashionable street. The closest it ever got to having a pub (until the Litten Tree opened in the former Lloyds Bank in the 1990s) was Fortt's, visited in the fifth excursion. Walking up Milsom Street and crossing George Street, we come to Bartlett Street, where the House of Bath department store marks the site of the **King's Head**.

Bartlett Street dates from the early 1770s, and the King's Head was a pub from the start. As the closest pub to the New Assembly Rooms, it was doubtless popular with sedan chairmen waiting for custom. Its history seems to have been uneventful. In July 1836, two police constables were dismissed when they were discovered taking an unofficial break there at 10.30pm one evening, but that is about all. It consisted of a bar, parlour, tap room, and dining room. In the yard was a brewery and a toilet house with a bucket. It closed in 1866 and the site was redeveloped by Evans & Owen, who already had a store on the other side of the street.

We continue up Bartlett Street and into Saville Row, with the old Hand & Flower ground on our right. At the end of Saville Row, a left turn takes us along the northern portico of the Assembly Rooms, which once housed a variety of shops, including a wine merchant's. At the end of the portico, we head across the road and into Circus Place. After a few yards, the street swings round to the left, revealing a vista that is overwhelmingly modern, the legacy of heavy bombing in 1942. It is difficult to imagine what this street was like in its heyday. Even as late as the 1920s, it

still echoed to the shouts of liverymen and hummed with the pungent aroma of steaming horse exhaust. There were two beerhouses as well. To find them, we need to walk down to Catherine Cottage, on the left-hand corner near the end of the street.

On the opposite corner was the **Circus Brewery**, first recorded in 1837 as the Jolly Coachman and renamed the Country House Tavern a couple of years later. By 1852, it was the Circus Tavern. It became the Circus Brewery in 1880. It had a bar in two compartments, with a glass room on the right, a bagatelle room on the left and a brewery at the back. It received a direct hit on the second night

The pubs of Circus Mews: 1) the Rising Sun; 2) the Circus Brewery.

THE LOST PUBS OF BATH

of the Bath Blitz. The licence was later transferred to the Wansdyke Inn. A modern building now occupies the site.

The former Rising Sun.

Next door but one to Catherine Cottage, in the cul-de-sac leading to the back of Brock Street, was the **Rising Sun**, which opened around 1846 and consisted of a bar and bagatelle room. By 1913, its trade had fallen to such an extent that

> Chief Inspector Bence said the house was not required for the needs of the neighbourhood. There were very few people living there. After about seven o'clock in the evening the place was practically deserted. The trade done there was very small indeed. It was practically a one-man house for six nights, the same man going in each time.

The licence was not renewed. The building is still there, its ground floor converted to a shuttered garage.

Rivers Street Mews, facing Catherine Cottage, leads to Rivers Street, built by John Wood the Younger in the 1770s, and with a pub – the New Inn (now the Chequers) – there from the start. There was also a pub called the **Bristol Arms** in Lower Rivers Street, but it closed in the aftermath of the Gordon Riots in 1780.

The expanse of grass at the west end of Rivers Street marks the site of a large church – St Andrew's – whose spire once dominated the whole of this area. It was destroyed, along with many other buildings in the Julian Road area, in the Bath Blitz.

St Andrew's Church dominated the area.

Julian Road was originally known as Cottle's Lane, but was renamed in the nineteenth century after Via Julia, the Roman Road whose course it followed.* Publess today, it has a rich history of alcoholic imbibification, as do the streets on either side of it. This area, wedged between ghettoes of conspicuous gentrification – the Circus, the Royal Crescent, Belvedere, Camden and Lansdown Crescents – was packed with the tradesmen necessary for maintaining the lifestyles (and the buildings) of those around them. While their houses were not showpieces, neither were they slums, which makes it even more of a pity that, after being knocked about by Hitler's bombs, they were comprehensively cleared away in the 1960s, with only a few fragments left to remind us what they were like.

---

*The Victorians decided it was the Via Julia, although the Romans knew it as Highway 14.

Looking towards St Andrew's Church after the raids of April 1942 …

… the same view today.

The view from Northampton Street in April 1942 …

… the same view today.

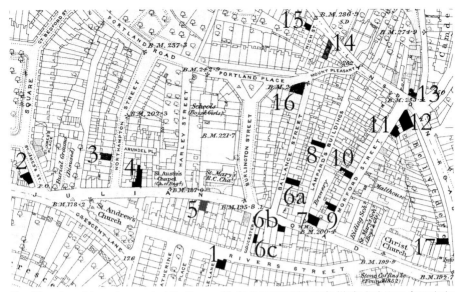

Five of the pubs on this map have survived: the Chequers (1); the St James's Wine Vaults (2); the Dark Horse, formerly the White Horse (3); the Belvedere (12); and the Old Farmhouse (13). Those that have gone include: 4) the Oxford Tavern; 5) the Weymouth Arms; 6a) the Bell (c1790-c1830); 6b) the Bell (c1850-64); 6c) the Bell (c1864-1960); 7) the Manage Horse; 8) the Live & Let Live; 9) the Rose; 10) the Dorset House; 11) the Bunch of Grapes; 14) the Lansdown Brewery; 15) the Adam & Eve; 16) the Portland Arms; 17) the Beehive.

Abingdon Buildings, on the north side of Julian Road between Harley and Northampton Streets, were built by John Pinch in 1795-97. Facing the top of Upper Church Street was the **Oxford Tavern** at 7 Abingdon Buildings. It was opened around 1841 by Sainsbury's Brewery, and consisted of a bar, parlour, kitchen, dining room, four bedrooms, and brewery. The bar had a four-motion beer engine, a one-motion beer engine, five spirit crutches and taps, and a four-tap spirit fountain.

Above John Pinch's drawings for 6 and 7 Abingdon Buildings. No 7 later became the Oxford Tavern.

Right An urgent request from the Oxford Brewery in 1916.

Around 1879, it was renamed the Oxford Brewery. By 1903, the bar had been divided into three compartments (one very private), with a glass room at the side. It survived until 1942, when the front part of the building was destroyed in the Bath Blitz. The rest of the building was demolished shortly afterwards.

Walking eastward along Julian Road, we come to St Mary's Roman Catholic Church. Opposite the steps leading to the church, at 6 Burlington Place, was the **Weymouth Arms**, originally the Duke of Weymouth's Arms. It was built in 1791, and seems to have been a pub from the start. In 1806, Thomas Edwards took the lease; it remained with his family for over 60 years. It was clearly a good investment, for in March 1845 Henry Edwards, who had taken over in the late 1820s, built a large house on Weston Lane.

In 1819, the Weymouth Arms was the setting for a tragedy which gives some inkling of the desperate circumstances of many working class people at the time. Ann Edwards – possibly one of the landlord's in-laws – was a widow with six children and no means of support except for the pittance she earned as a servant at the Weymouth Arms. She married a man called Govey in Bristol and brought him back to Bath to live with her at the pub. Her first husband's family were incensed by this, letting it be known that "she had done a very wrong thing." She was, by all reports, "very low and unhappy" and eventually cut her throat.

The Weymouth Arms was one of the best-known pubs north of the city. In July 1837, JA Roebuck, Bath's famous radical MP, addressed a meeting there. The pub hit the headlines five years later when a fight got out of hand:

> On Tuesday night, two men named Edward Cains, a clipper of horses, and William Bushell, a plumber, were drinking together at the Weymouth Arms public house, in Cottle's Lane, when a quarrel arose between them and blows followed. After beating each other for some time Cains went out and returned with a large clasp knife with which he inflicted a fearful wound on the side of Bushell's neck, from which the blood flowed copiously. Surgical assistance was procured and the wounded man was taken to the hospital, where he lies in a precarious state.

The business continued to expand, and the brewery became one of the most popular in Bath. An 1860 advertisement for the "Burlington Brewery, near St James's Square, Bath," offered "Pale Ale at One Shilling a Gallon in Casks of All Sizes, Brewed Upon the Burton-on-Trent Principle, Expressly for the Use of Private Families."

In 1870, George Edwards went bankrupt, and the pub and brewery were advertised for sale:

> Burlington Brewery, Burlington Place.
>
> To be sold by private contract this freehold brewery (eight quarter plant) with full licensed house adjoining, situated in one of the principal thoroughfares of the city, now in full working order. The brewery is fitted throughout with steam power and all modern appliances. The fully licensed house known as the Weymouth Arms is an old-established business, doing a large trade.

It was bought by Morgan Bracher of the nearby Portland Brewery. He leased the pub to Charles Kidner, a builder from Ballance Street but retained the brewery for his own use. Mr Kidner passed the lease on to Morgan Blake, a plumber from Dover Street, the following year. It passed through a number of hands, until, in 1887, no application was made to renew the licence.

The 1887 sale notice for the contents of the Weymouth Arms – "in consequence of converting the premises into other uses" – gives a detailed description of what was left when last orders were called. In the bar was "a capital seven-motion counter beer engine with extra lead piping and unions, metal-top panelled counter and fittings, copper muller, painted oak spirit cask, plated tankards, measures, cups, glasses, mahogany shelving with silvered glass back, eight-day dial, glazed doors, lobby, and useful partitioning." The smoking room had "a valuable mahogany billiard-bagatelle board," "three fine old sporting pictures," and stuffed seating, while the club room had "a capital set of mahogany telescope dining tables."

The pub became a greengrocer's. It was demolished after being badly damaged in the Bath Blitz.

The former Bell in Rivers Street Place (slightly retouched).

Continuing eastwards along Julian Road, we come to 2a Rivers Street Place, between the Smile Store and Julian Road Stores. In the early 1850s, Edward Bowler opened a beerhouse here called the **Bell**. It quickly passed though the hands of two more licensees – Elizabeth Laidler and James Grotton or Gorton – before Edwin Bright took over around 1862. A couple of years later, he moved the beerhouse round the corner to 5 Gloucester Street, where it stayed for the best part of a century. When the Oakhill Brewery took over in 1897, it had a serving bar, a bar with seats, and a small tap room. It closed in 1960.

Before either of these two Bells, however, there was another. Ballance Street, which now lies under the flats which bear its name, was built in the 1780s; at No 6 was an inn called the **Bell**. It was the meeting place for the Amicable Belvedere Society, and closed in the 1830s, John Sumsion, a mason, being the last landlord. Christ Church Infants' School was later built on the site.

The former Bell in Gloucester Street.

A little further along Julian Road, opposite the Domestic Appliances Shop, was a street originally called Crooked Lane, and later renamed Lampard's Buildings after the landowner. On the eastern corner of Lampard's Buildings was the **Manege Horse** or the Managed

Lampard's Buildings today.

BATH POLICE.—Guildhall.

SATURDAY.—Chas. Stockman was ordered to find bail—himself in £10, and two sureties in £5 each, for using threatening and abusive language to Mr. J. Bence, of Twerton.

Charlotte Sargeant, Sussanna Potter, and Susan Dyer, were brought up on remand, and committed on a charge of stealing a quantity of print from the shop of Mr. Jones, of Union-street. There was another charge against them on which they were further remanded.

MONDAY.—Two sailors, named Nichols and Chappel, were charged with drunk and riotous conduct and damaging a pair of trucks, the property of Wm. Deverill, of Lampard's-buildings. The prisoners, from the evidence, seem to have got very drunk yesterday morning, smashed the trucks in Mr. Deverill's yard, damaged a fence in Hedge-mead, and broke three lamps in Tyning-lane. They were apprehended at their residence, in Viner's-court, Lampard's-buildings, after the occurrence. Nichols, on being taken hold of by P.C. Sealey, took up a knife from the table, at which they were sitting at breakfast, and cut the officer on the hand. Chappel tried to trip up the constable who had him in charge. They were fined 14s. and costs or seven days for the damage done to the trucks and assaulting the officer; Chappel was further fined 10s. and costs or seven days for breaking the three lamps. There was a third man, named Edwin Hopton, included in the charge of damaging the fence, but the owner did not appear and the case was dismissed.

Edward Trainer was charged with begging in Southgate-street and using abusive language to Mrs. Ponting. Discharged with a caution.

TUESDAY.—A man named John White, brought up for being drunk and incapable, in Bath-street, was dismissed with a caution.

Joseph Johnson was charged with being concealed in a garden at the back of No. 9, Dunsford-place, for an unlawful purpose. The prisoner, who described himself as a discharged soldier, was committed for 7 days, with hard labour.

The dangers of 24-hour drinking, from the *Bath Chronicle* of December 1857.

Horse. It was first recorded in 1789 when No 12 Lansdown Crescent (newly built) was sold there by auction. It took its name from the *manege* or riding school nearby. *Maneggiare* was an Italian word for the training of horses; a *manege* was where the training took place. Later, *maneggiare* came to mean not just the training of horses, but skilful handling of musical instruments, weapons, or whatever took your fancy. In the sixteenth century the word entered the English language as "manage." So it is that management, one of the buzz words of twenty-first century corporatism, originally referred to the training of horses.

We digress. In the 1840s the Manege Horse was kept by Simeon Reynolds, who was also a coal merchant. In 1846, his son had a salutary if somewhat brutal lesson of the perils of cherry-knocking:

> Mr WA Cox, Surgeon of 54 New King Street, was summoned to answer the complaint of William Reynolds, son of Mr S Reynolds of the Manege Horse public house, Cottles Lane, for an alleged assault, The complainant is a youth about ten years of age … He stated that on Saturday, as he was returning from school, he rang Mr Cox's doorbell. A gentleman, whom he supposed to be Mr Cox, came to the door and laid hold of him, took him downstairs into a room, and there, by force, extracted one of his teeth.

It turned out that the assailant was an assistant of Mr Cox's called Henry Price, who was dismissed because of the incident. In his defence, however, Mr Cox said that, "with regard to the assault itself, the annoyance from schoolboys frequently ringing the doorbell for mischief was so provoking that some means was necessary to put a stop to the practice, though he did not justify the act complained of." This Marathon-Man treatment seems to have had no long-term ill effects on young Master Reynolds. By the end of the century he ran a string of pubs and was a director of the Bath Brewery Company.

The Manege Horse had three bars – a main bar, a bar parlour, and a tap room. After it closed in 1893, John Webb reopened it as the Manege Horse Coffee & Dining Rooms. When he retired in the late 1920s, it was taken over by Mrs Withers, whose family ran it as a butcher's-cum-dining rooms. It was demolished around 1970.

Halfway up Lampard's Buildings, on the left-hand side at No 14, was a beerhouse called the **Live & Let Live**. It was opened by Thomas Bush around 1858 and closed on 13 October 1934. It consisted of a bar, bar parlour and tap room with a serving window.

There was also a beerhouse recorded next door but one, at No 16, in 1841.

There were three other pubs in Julian Road, when it was still known as Cottle's Lane, whose exact locations are unknown. The **Mason's Arms**, the **Punch Bowl**, and the **Old Darby** all closed around 1780, more victims of the Corporation's clean-up campaign after the Gordon Riots.

East of Lampard's Buildings was – and still is – Morford Street. Most of the frontages on the west side of the street have survived, although Morford Street's best-remembered pub, the **Rose** at No 3, has not. It was first recorded in 1830, with James Dunn, a brewer, as the licensee. In 1903, it had a bar in two compartments, with a glass room behind. It closed in 1971.

On the other side of the street, an archway leads to one of the oldest – and largest – buildings in the area. Built as a Real Tennis court in 1776, and later put to a variety of uses, including a spell as a malt house, the Museum of Bath at Work is an essential

port of call for anyone interested in the history of Bath's pubs, or any other aspect of the city's social and industrial history. The nucleus of the museum's collection is a Victorian mineral-water manufactory and engineering works, moved here from its original home in Corn Street when the site was redeveloped. Much of the original equipment survives and some can be seen working.

A little further up Morford Street, at No 9, was a beerhouse called the **Dorset House**. Originally known as the Fox & Hounds, it opened around 1837 and closed in the 1850s.

On the other side of the road, at the back of the Belvedere Wine Vaults, was the **Bunch of Grapes**. Originally the tap for the Belvedere, it was licensed

The Rose in Morford Street.

The former tennis court and maltings before conversion to the Building of Bath Museum.

The former Bunch of Grapes in Morford Street.

separately from around 1840. In 1886, it consisted of a bar, glass room, tap room, brewery, hop room and cooperage. It closed in 1907.

Heading up Lansdown Road, we come to two more pubs that have totally disappeared. Just past the Chinese takeaway is a house where Thomas Gainsborough once lived. Facing it, where the

The Lansdown Brewery, demolished to build Ballance Street Flats.

THE LOST PUBS OF BATH

High Street Lansdown: the Adam & Eve was the second house down.

entrance to Ballance Street flats is today, was the **Lansdown Brewery** at 6 Belle Vue Buildings. It opened in the 1840s and consisted of a front bar, bar parlour, tap room and back room. It closed on 14 December 1968 and was pulled down shortly afterwards.

A little further up, on the same side of the road, is a driveway with WHEEL CLAMPS IN USE. It was once a street of eleven two- and three-storey houses, one room

High Street today.

wide, with square-headed Venetian windows on the first floor. It had two names, being known as both High Street and Hill Street. At No 10 was the **Adam & Eve** beerhouse, which opened in the early 1830s, but closed by 1840. The building, like the rest of the street, was demolished in 1969.

The site of the Portland Brewery.

Down the hill, opposite the Chinese takeaway, is a footpath which follows the course of a street called Mount Pleasant. It leads to Portland Place, the one bit of this area that was so posh they could not pull it down – apart from the pub at No 12. This stood on the south side of the road, east of what is now the last house. In 1830, Richard Betteson was listed as a wine and spirit merchant at 12a Portland Place. Later, the

Portland Brewery was established at the same address. The **Portland Arms** opened next door in the 1870s. It consisted of a bar, parlour and "small room." The brewery was acquired by Bathwick Brewery in 1877 and closed down. The pub closed in 1957 and its licence was transferred to the Old Farmhouse, which had survived on a beer licence up to then. It was demolished in 1969.

At the end of Portland Place, we carry on into Portland Road, turning, at the top of Great Park Street, into Park Street Mews. Continue into Cavendish Road, turn right, and walk uphill, past Cavendish Crescent, to the crossroads. Behind Somerset House, the large building with a bow front on the north-east corner of the crossroads, was the **Somerset Arms**.* It was first recorded as a beerhouse in 1854, although there had been a brewery here since around 1840. In 1888, the pub was acquired by the Morford Brewery and the brewery was closed. The description of the premises in the 1903 report underlines the hilly nature of the site:

> One entrance from Winifred's Lane. Ascent by steps from back of premises to loft opening into large garden on level of first floor of premises, and door from garden opening into Winifred's Lane above pub. Serving bar with glass room on right, with bagatelle table and tap room on left.

It closed in 1914.

---

*Although there is no record of Somerset House being part of the pub, it must have been connected with it, because until recently the letters …ND BEERS were visible on its wall until they were scrubbed off.

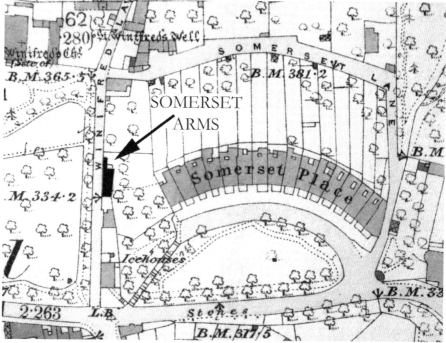

Had the Somerset Arms survived, it would have been ideally placed for students at Bath Spa University.

THE LOST PUBS OF BATH

The left-hand fork at the crossroads below Somerset House leads west along Sion Hill to Summerhill Road, and to a footpath leading down to Primrose Hill. Around 1850, Thomas Vincent, a plasterer from Milk Street, moved to Primrose Hill and opened a beerhouse called the **Summerhill Tavern**. A couple of years later, he renamed it the Sion Hill Tavern. It was last recorded in the 1868 *Postal Directory*. There is no record of which number it was, but it is likely that it became one of two pubs on Primrose Hill recorded in the 1872 *Postal Directory*.

The Gardener's Arms at Primrose Hill, on the left.

The first was the **Gardener's Arms** at No 7, which closed in 1917.

The second was the **Retreat** at No 5, which stayed open until 1975. This is, almost certainly, Bath's most missed pub. Even those who only went there once have fond memories of this magical spot. Here, to set the scene, is a list of some of its contents from an inventory of 1879:

SMOKING ROOM Engraving of "The Battle of Waterloo," three framed engravings of dogs' heads, six coloured prints of race horses, an oil painting, "The Copper Smith."

BAR PARLOUR Chiffonier, tapestry carpet, china sardine box.

GARDEN Double light cucumber frame, greenhouse with grape vine, 36 currant trees, 7 fruit trees, 2 rows of raspberries, heap of manure, shrub and rose trees, rustic stones forming edging to garden, two large forms.

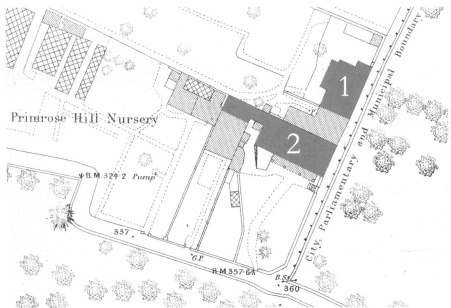

The Gardener's Arms (1) and the Retreat (2) could only be reached down a narrow footpath.

In May 1974, an article on the Retreat appeared in the *Bath Chronicle*:

> The Retreat is far from the madding crowd. It is concealed by trees and shrubs behind a high stone wall, to be reached only by those prepared to abandon their cars in Sion Hill and venture down a footpath which looks as if it leads nowhere. Landlord Richard Gawith has been there for 25 years. The pub has been in his family since the turn of the century. And its charm is that not much appears to have happened to the place during that time. Which, ironically, may spell final closing time for this outpost of the pub-crawler's dwindling empire. We may like the Retreat, but the city's public health inspectors are not happy with its facilities. So

Up the garden path to one of Bath's most missed pubs.

Courage's are now looking into the cost of bringing the place up to their standards. It sounds as if they could be thinking of modernising it beyond recognition -- or closing it. A brewery spokesman said, "our architects and surveyors are studying it to see what is involved and we cannot say anything about the future of the Retreat until they have made their report." With the brewer's well-known passion for shutting my sort of pub, that strikes me ominously like beating the retreat.

The Retreat closed a year later. Dick Gawith died two days before it closed, at the age of 69, and Nora, his widow, had to move into her new home at Meadow Gardens on her own. The Retreat was bought by an antique dealer called Rae Harris and became a private house. But that was not quite the end of the story. Seventeen years later, in the summer of 1991, Geoffrey and Pauline Roper, who had bought

the old Retreat, reopened it for one day for charity. Mrs Gawith, now 84, visited it for one last time to meet many of the old regulars. For a few hours, it was possible to think that old times had returned and the Retreat would once again be one of Bath's most cherished institutions. But it was not to be. As darkness fell, last orders were called for the very last time, the lights were extinguished, and the doors were locked on the past. Two days later, having seen the brief renaissance of the pub she had lived in for so long, Mrs Gawith died.

Tokens bearing the name J Markey were issued at the Retreat in the late nineteenth century.

THE LOST PUBS OF BATH

We have already crossed the border into Weston here. To reach the centre of the old village, we have to continue down the path beside the Retreat, turn left at the bottom, and then right into Weston Lane. We are following in famous footsteps. On 21 May 1801, Jane Austen wrote to her sister that she had gone with Mrs Chamberlayne for

> a walk up by Sion Hill, and returned across the fields – in climbing a hill Mrs Chamberlayne is very capital; I could with difficulty keep pace with her – yet would not flinch for the world – on plain ground I was quite her equal – and so we posted away under a fine hot sun, she without any parasol or any shade to her head, stopping for nothing, and crossing the churchyard at Weston with as much expedition as if we were afraid of being buried alive.

Jane Austen seems to have walked to Weston regularly, although, in another letter to her sister, she pointed out that it was the walk, rather than the destination, that appealed to her:

> We walked to Weston one evening last week, and liked it very much. –
>
> Liked *what* very much? Weston? – no – *walking* to Weston.

John Wood was not that struck with Weston either, describing it as "one long street with a brook running down the middle of it." It has had its supporters, however. The 1848 *Bath Postal Directory* stressed that "the admirer of rural scenery should not forget to visit this retired spot. Leaving Bath by way of Victoria Park, you proceed along a paved footway, having on each side a string of delightful villas; a few minutes bring you, shoe-dry, even in winter, to the quiet little village, where the antique cottages contrast agreeably with the more modern villas just left behind." Even though many of the antique cottages have disappeared, Weston still has its share of historic buildings, including three old pubs – the Crown, the King's Head, and the Crown & Anchor.

We start our tour of Weston's lost pubs outside the Crown on Crown Hill. According to Joan Hargood-Ash, Weston's historian, the **White Lion** beerhouse was on the other side of the road from the Crown, just west of Prospect House. In 1837 it was kept by John Usher, who was described as a brewer rather than a publican. By the 1850s it had been taken over by Mark Barnard, but it closed when he moved to the Queen's Head around 1864.

The **Mason's Arms** at 34 High Street opened as a beerhouse sometime before 1858. It consisted of a bar, jug & bottle and tap room. It was kept by at least two masons – John Cutler, who was there in 1858, and James Podger, who was there in 1878. In 1914 it came under the scrutiny of the magistrates. They argued that, as it was only 22 paces from the Crown and 60 paces from the Queen's Head, it was surplus to requirements. It was also dilapidated and did very little trade. The licence was revoked and the building was later demolished.

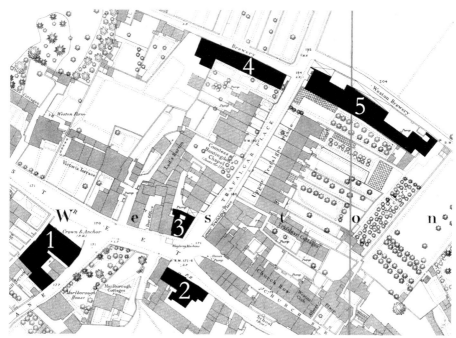

The Crown & Anchor (1) and the King's Head (2) are still open, but the Queen's Head (3) is long closed, as are Weston's two breweries – Pointing's (4) and Edgecumbe's (5).

Opposite the King's Head, at 1 Trafalgar Road, was the **Queen's Head** beerhouse. Originally known as the Queen Victoria Inn, it opened sometime before 1842. By 1861, when Mark Barnard was the licensee, it had become the Queen's Head. It consisted of a bar, tap room, smoke room and jug & bottle on the ground floor, with a "large public sitting room" on the first floor.

In February 1914, Frank Helps, the landlord, was summoned "for keeping a skittles instrument for public use without a licence." The case was dismissed "due to the licensee's ignorance of the law." Later the same year, when the licence came up for renewal, the magistrates informed Mr Helps that, after due consideration, they had decided that the Queen's Head should close. They admitted it was a "well-conducted house" in "very good condition," but pointed out that, as there was a pub for every 216 people in Weston, one of them had to go.

The former Queen's Head.

Further up the High Street, at No 82, was the smallest beerhouse in Weston, and probably the smallest in Bath. The **Globe** was first recorded in 1852, with Charles English, an omnibus proprietor, as landlord. According to an inventory drawn up in 1883, when Charles English's widow, Matilda, transferred the licence to Isaac Smith, it had a bar, parlour and tap room.

THE LOST PUBS OF BATH

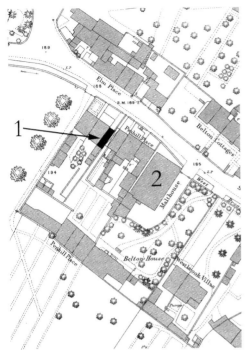

The diminutive proportions of the Globe (1) can be seen on this map from the 1880s. Note also the malthouse (2) a few doors along.

Septimus Smith behind the bar of the Globe.

It stayed in the Smith family for the next 83 years, but by 1944, when Isaac's seventh son, Septimus, took over, it had shrunk to a single bar, a mere three feet wide. Septimus had run the Shamrock in Avon Street from 1908 to 1914, when he left to serve with the North Somerset Yeomanry on the Western Front. He was a noted pugilist in his youth, but by the time he took over the Globe, he had acquired an impressive girth. Once installed at the Globe, he continued to grow, eventually tipping the scales at 21 stone. Not only was there no room for anybody else behind the bar once he was behind it; there was no room for a till. He solved the problem by wearing a multi-pocketed apron, each pocket holding coins of a different value. Sadly, this Weston institution closed on 31 March 1966, its passing marked by a report in the *Bath Chronicle*:

> The Globe Inn, Weston, went out with a bang on Thursday night. There were so many people at the pub for its closing night that some of its customers drank out of bottles because there were not sufficient glasses to go round. There was a presentation to the landlord, Mr Septimus Smith, who is 82 and retiring. The inn had been run by Mr Smith's family all his life. Mr V Vowles handed him a box of cigars and a bottle of brandy from the customers and Mr Smith's friends. There was also a bouquet for his daughter and a gift for his grandson.

There was also a beerhouse called the **Bladud's Head** somewhere in Weston High Street. It was opened around 1864 by Lescombe Hawkins, a cabinet maker, and closed in the early 1880s when he moved to 3 Church Row (now 11 Church Street).

No, there are no lost pubs in the Royal Crescent or Brock Street. We just couldn't resist sharing these two pictures with you.

THE LOST PUBS OF BATH

EXCURSION THE SEVENTH

WIDCOMBE

Although Widcombe has only been part of Bath since 1836, its history stretches back centuries. It was once one of the most important weaving centres in the West of England. In 1831, the only parish in Somerset with more textile workers was Frome. Naturally, with all that work going on, there were a lot of pubs.

Lying outside the jurisdiction of the city, Widcombe was also the haunt of all the ne'er-do-wells who found life too hot for them in Bath. Holloway was particularly notorious. Until the city's policemen extended their beats across the bridge in 1836, it was a breeding ground of criminality.

Much of old Widcombe has gone and now it is almost impossible to believe that it was once a major industrial centre. Virtually all of Holloway, much of Claverton Street and all of Dolemeads has disappeared. Some losses – especially that of Dolemeads – were an unmitigated blessing, but the destruction of some of the seventeenth- and eighteenth-century buildings on Holloway and in Claverton Street was one of the worse excesses of the Sack of Bath. Although few people counted them among the architectural highlights of Bath, some did appreciate their

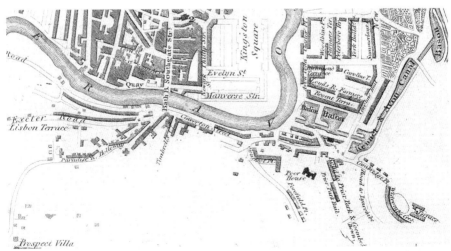

Widcombe in the early nineteenth century, showing the Dolemeads development, along with the planned development on the other side of the river that was never realised.

worth. As long ago as 1883, Charles Davis wrote that "Holloway contains many buildings that are despised, but none the less picturesque, that a visitor may have seen in 1675."

Looking across from Widcombe to Bath, with the Greyhound on the right and the Full Moon on the far side of the bridge.

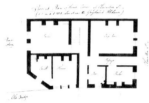

A plan of the Greyhound next to the Old Bridge shortly before it was demolished.

Our excursion round the lost pubs of Widcombe starts at a lost bridge. The Old Bridge was for centuries the only way across the river except by boat. It stood to the west of the Southgate Foot Bridge and was pulled down in the 1960s. Next to the Old Bridge was the **Greyhound**, a three-storey alehouse that probably served as a tap for the **Packhorse Inn** next door. The Packhorse was there by 1735 and had not only a courtyard and stables, but also a brewery and malthouse. Barges or wherries could be hired at the Packhorse for pleasure trips or for carrying goods to Bristol.

According to Sturge Cotterell, the Packhorse was the "headquarters of the Jacobean conspirators in the West of England in the eighteenth century." Supporting the Old Pretender – or the Young Pretender – was a risky undertaking. In July 1726, for example, the *Bath Journal* reported the case of William Sparks, who was sentenced to transportation for seven years for "breaking open and robbing the house of William Bellamy, and for drinking a health to King James III."

In 1755, the Packhorse changed its name to the Admiral Vernon. The admiral had become a national hero after capturing Portobello in Panama from the Spaniards in 1739. The following year, he earned himself a more lasting place in history by trying to reduce drunkenness in the navy. In the mid-seventeenth century, Admiral Blake had decided that, because of the difficulties of keeping beer fresh on board ship, sailors should have a pint of brandy a day instead. Following the conquest of Jamaica, rum was substituted for brandy. It was issued twice a day, half a pint at a time.

Knocking back half a pint of rum twice a day certainly made life on board ship a good deal more bearable. The problem was that many sailors took to saving up part of their ration, so that they could go on a bender a couple of times a week. Getting blind drunk on board ship was not only dangerous; if it happened to coincide with an enemy ship hoving into view, it could be a recipe for disaster. In 1740, Admiral Vernon ordered the daily rum ration to be mixed with a quart of water "in one scuttled butt kept for that purpose, and to be done upon deck, in the presence of the Lieutenant of the Watch, who is to see that no man is to be cheated of his proper allowance." The point of this was not to cut the amount sailors drank, but to stop them saving it up. Once mixed with water, the rum would not keep, so they had to drink it there and then.

THE LOST PUBS OF BATH

Admiral Vernon did not bother to come up with a name for the rum and water mixture, but, as he was known as Old Grog because of the grogram cloak he habitually wore, it did not take long for the new drink to become known as grog. In 1756, it was adopted throughout the Navy. In 1824, the ration was halved, and, in 1850, it was reduced to a gill (an eighth of a pint) a day. It survived until 30 July 1970, Black Tot Day, when the last pipe of "up spirits" was heard in the navy.

There are still seven pubs called the Admiral Vernon in Britain, but Widcombe's only kept its name for about 15 years before reverting to the Packhorse. In March 1774, it was the scene of a tragic accident, when a ten-year-old boy who lived and worked there slipped off the steps leading to the river and drowned before anyone could save him.

In 1823, the Corporation notified the Anchor Brewery, which held the lease of the Greyhound and Packhorse, that both properties were going to be demolished for road widening. They disappeared a couple of years later, and, although old prints suggest they had a certain elegance, Captain Mainwaring was overjoyed at seeing them go. "In 1825," he wrote, "the unsightly houses, on the Widcombe side of the Old Bridge, were levelled to the ground, and a commodious footpath formed on their site."

A few doors along was the **Jolly Sailor**, a beerhouse which opened in the 1840s, and was pulled down for further road improvements in 1856.

At 10 Claverton Street, a few doors further on, was a beerhouse called the **William IV**, which opened in the early 1830s and was demolished when the railway was built.

At 24 Claverton Street was the **Malakoff Tavern**, which opened around 1855 to celebrate the taking of Malakoff Tower during the Crimean War. The Bath Brewery Company closed it in 1901 as part of the deal for licensing the Moorfields Inn. It later became Crook's Butchers & Greengrocers and was demolished in 1966.

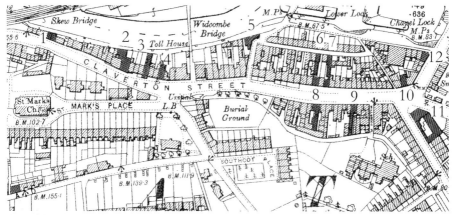

Three of the 12 pubs on this map have survived – the Ram (7), the Ring of Bells (9) and the White Hart (11). Those that have gone include: the Malakoff Tavern (1), the Claverton Brewery (2), the Cooper's Arms (3), the Lyncombe Brewery (4), the Boatman's Arms (5), the Greyhound (6), the Stag's Head (8), Prior Park Tavern (10), and the Canal Tavern (12).

The **Claverton Brewery**, at 33 Claverton Street, was opened around 1850 by George Lush, a brewer and wine merchant. The brewery, alongside the river, closed sometime before 1900. The pub closed on 23 June 1964 and was demolished two years later.

The **Cooper's Arms**, at 37 Claverton Street, opened sometime before 1792, when John Gardiner (who later moved to the Old Green Tree in Green Street) held the licence. In addition to a public bar, it had a bar parlour and club room, with a skittle alley and brewery at the back. It closed on 25 February 1965 and was demolished on 5 September 1966.

The Claverton Brewery shortly before demolition.

At 40 Claverton Street was a beerhouse called the **Lyncombe Brewery**, which opened around 1870. Brewing ceased around 1914 and the pub closed in 1920. It later became Dingle's Butchers and, before demolition, was Bowsza's delicatessen.

Twelve doors up from the Lyncombe Brewery, we reach the part of Claverton Street that is still standing, with Claverton Buildings on the north side and Widcombe Parade on the south. On the end wall of the first house in Claverton Buildings, the words Spring Gardens Road can still be faintly descried. Spring Gardens Road once ran alongside the river to Grove Street. A few yards along Spring Gardens Road was a beerhouse called the **Boatman's Arms**, which opened around 1839. In 1849, the son of Mr Trimby, the landlord, went missing and was later found drowned in the river. When the council inspector called in 1903, the pub was more or less moribund. There were no customers, the glass room had been taken over by the landlord's family, and they would not let the inspector use the toilet. He summed it up – rather charitably, considering the circumstances – as "indifferent." It closed in 1907.

The former New Greyhound.

THE LOST PUBS OF BATH

There were two pubs on Claverton Buildings. One – the Ram – is still open. The other was the **Greyhound** at No 18. It opened around 1825 as the New Greyhound to replace the old Greyhound near the Old Bridge. It closed in 1908 and is now a veterinary surgery.

Claverton Buildings was also home to several extremely short-lived beerhouses. In the mid-1830s, two opened at Nos 5 and 11. By 1839, these had closed and been replaced by one at No 6 called the **Seven Stars**. A news item in the *Bath Chronicle* for 5 March 1840 indicates the probable reason for its demise:

> On Monday night after the family had retired to bed, a fire broke out under the stairs in the Public House called the Seven Stars, in the occupation of a person called Paget, and situated in Claverton Buildings. The flames were observed by the policeman who was on duty at the time.

Another beerhouse opened at No 10 in the mid-1840s, but had closed by the time another, called the **Bell**, opened at No 14 in the mid-1850s. This too closed within a few years. The ephemeral nature of the beerhouses of Claverton Buildings (with the honourable exception of the Ram) is unusual, even by the standards of the mid-nineteenth century. It is likely, however, that those at Nos 5,6, and 11 were opened to cater for navvies building the railway and were not intended to be permanent.

Opposite Claverton Buildings is Widcombe Parade, with the Ring of Bells at Nos 9 and 10. There were two other pubs along here. At No 4 was a beerhouse called the **Stag's Head**, opened by George Lanham around 1837, and closed in 1854.

Next to it, at No 5, was an even shorter-lived beerhouse called the **Mason's Arms**. The only reference we have discovered to it comes in the 1854 *Postal Directory*. Curiously, the 1792 licensing register and the 1793 *Universal British Directory* also list a Mason's Arms in Claverton Street, but there are no records of it between then and 1854.

The Baptist Church complex, opposite the White Hart stands on the site of two more lost pubs. Around 1868, John Tiley from the Rose & Crown in Southgate Street opened a one-bar beerhouse called the **Prior Park Tavern** (also known for a time as the Horse & Groom) at 2 Coburg Place.

On the corner of Coburg Place and Ebenezer Terrace, where the entrance to the Baptist schoolroom now stands, was another beerhouse called the **Canal Tavern**, first recorded in 1837. It predated the Baptist Church, which opened in 1849, and was a fairly opulent establishment, with its own brewery. As early as 1862, the bar had a six-motion beer engine and a pewter-topped counter, while the bar parlour boasted no less than 24 spittoons. The facilities on offer in the bar parlour included a bagatelle table, two card boards, two crib boards and table skittles. A sporting theme was continued on the walls, which were decorated with hunting prints, a stag's head and a pair of horns. When the council inspector visited in 1903, he criticised the sanitary arrangements, which consisted of a "WC and open urinal in skittle alley." This suggests that, if there were any ladies' skittle teams in 1903, they must have been particularly broad-minded.

The skittling, bagatelling and cribbing (not to mention the urinalling) came to an end in 1908, when the Baptists bought the Canal Tavern – along with the Prior Park Tavern – and pulled them down. "Instead of the thorn shall come up the fir tree, and it shall be to the Lord for a name" was the unequivocal message carved over the door of the schoolroom they built on the site.

§

North of the canal lies an area of Widcombe once stacked with pubs – five along Pulteney Road and eight between Pulteney Road and the river. Today, only one remains – the Royal Oak on Summerlay's Place.

Setting out along Pulteney Road, the first pub we would have come to was the **Packhorse** on the corner of Albert Terrace. Albert Terrace was built around 1825

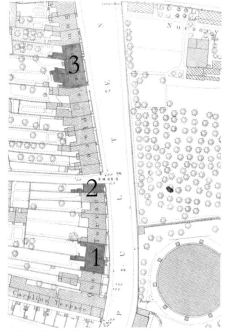

as Farmer's Buildings and later renamed in honour of the Prince Consort. The Packhorse, which had its own brewery, was a replacement for the old Packhorse near the Old Bridge. It closed in 1938 and was demolished in the late 1960s.

Prince's Buildings, just north of Albert Terrace, also had a pub on the corner. This was the appallingly short-lived **Joiner's Arms**, which only appeared in the 1841 *Postal Directory*. Prince's Buildings have, like Albert Terrace, been razed.

North of Prince's Buildings was Queen's Terrace. Nos 1-9 Queen's Terrace (including the Kozie Café) have been demolished, but the old **Golden Fleece** at Nos 10-11, has survived. Henry Amor opened this as a beerhouse around 1837 and was later granted a full licence. By

Pulteney Road, with a gasholder and nursery on the right and the Golden Fleece (1), the Widcombe Brewery (2) and the Royal Oak (3) on the left. Only the Royal Oak survives.

The Golden Fleece, still advertising Lamb Ales & Stout.

1903 it was in a poor state of repair, with "only one room exclusively for the public." It later improved somewhat, and by 1976 had three small bars (public, smoking room and lounge), although when Fred Pearce visited he found it deserted except for a collection of decorative dolls above the bar. Today it is quieter still, plans to reopen it as a restaurant having so far come to nothing.

At the far end of Queen's Terrace was the **Widcombe Brewery**, open by 1837 and closed around 1864.

Now we venture into an area whose pubs are not even a distant memory. The pubs of old Dolemeads may have gone, along with all trace of the streets they stood in, but that is a matter for celebration rather than regret. Walking the quiet, tree-lined streets of Dolemeads today, it is hard to imagine how grim this area once was.

Until the late eighteenth century, the Dole Meads was a riverside meadow. There was a ferry from South Parade, and footpaths across the fields to Bathwick and Widcombe. In summer it was a delightful spot, away from the bustle of the dusty

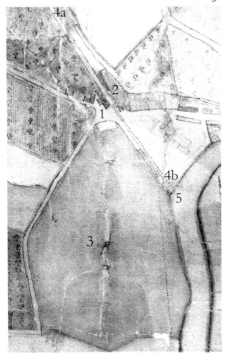

Dole Meads (3) in the mid-eighteenth century, with Ralph Allen's tramway (4a-4b) running down to the wharf on the Avon (5), between the White Hart (1) and Prior Park Cottages (2).

city, but in winter it was often under water. There were no houses because nobody had been stupid enough to build any. John Wood had built some on the other side of the river, it is true, and had plans – which came to nothing – to build on this side as well, but his houses stood on embankments high above the floods.

The Dole Meads was still pastureland in 1788, when the following advertisement appeared in the *Bath Chronicle:*

> To be lett, a meadow called DOLEMEAD, adjoining the River AVON and nearly opposite the South Parade, containing about 18 acres.

It did not stay a meadow for long. Bare-faced greed, taking advantage of the explosion in Bath's working-class population, saw to that. In 1821, Captain Mainwaring wrote of "those miserable abodes recently built on that low, swampy spot of ground, called the Dolemeads, and its immediate vicinity … To thread the mazes of those wretched dwelling places, became really a work of danger, whether from the difficulty of approach, or from the doubtful characters that inhabited them."

The worst problem with Dolemeads was its tendency to flood. In November 1823, for example,

> the poor people in the Dolemeads were soon obliged to take to their upper rooms; and their distressing cries were distinctly heard … Several of those houses appeared with little more than their roofs above water … In some instances, the water had actually entered the bedrooms of the poor sufferers who, as night approached, were seen with lights (beacons of their distress), and heard to call loudly for assistance … One poor person, being confined to his bed by a paralytic seizure, was drowned as he lay in that situation.

There was another severe flood in January 1841, the year after the railway viaduct had been pushed through the area. According to the *Bath Chronicle*,

> the effects of the flood were … the most severely felt in the Dolemeads, where, in consequence of the poverty of the inhabitants, houses with four rooms very generally contain as many families. During the recent severe weather, much misery has been experienced by this part of our population. In many of their dwellings there was neither food nor fuel, and but a very scanty supply of clothes and bedding. The aggravation of their condition, occasioned by the flood, may be easily imagined. On Monday, after the water had left their houses, the inhabitants were seen occupying them, wet as they were, without a spark of fire and exposed to the cold wind, making its way through the broken windows, from which the rags which had stopped them up had been washed by the flood. We regret being

The Mason's Arms, on the corner of Ferry Lane and Spring Gardens Road, had already closed by the time this photograph of the Avon in flood was taken in 1925.

THE LOST PUBS OF BATH

obliged to add that many of the inhabitants of the Dolemeads had gone to bed the previous night in a state of intoxication habitual to them, and had they not been roused by those differently situated, we should not now be able to announce that no loss of human life took place.

A sketch of Dolemeads in 1897, with the Mason's Arms on the left.

There were two fully-licensed pubs and five beerhouses in Dolemeads in the late nineteenth century, most of them along Spring Gardens Road near the river. At the bottom of Ferry Lane, near the starting point for the ferry to South Parade, was the **Mason's Arms**, which opened in the 1850s. This was the most upmarket pub in the area. The bar had a barometer, a desk, prints on the wall, and ornaments on the mantelpiece. There was also a parlour, reserved for customers who were particularly favoured, and a tap room for those who weren't. There were four bedrooms, a brewery, and a small shop for the sale of sweets and provisions. The Mason's Arms closed around 1914.

Five doors down from the Mason's Arms, at 2 Charles Place, was a beerhouse called the **Bird in Hand**, which opened around 1866 and closed in 1901.

Just south of the Bird in Hand was the **Oddfellows' Arms** at the bottom of Middle Lane. It opened around 1848 and closed around 1871.

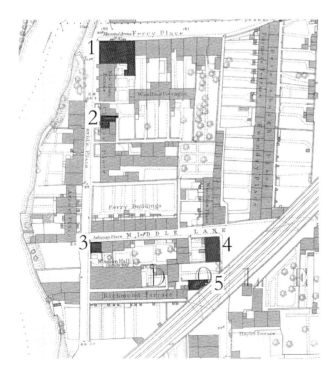

Left The lost pubs of North Dolemeads: 1) the Mason's Arms; 2) the Bird in Hand; 3) the Oddfellows' Arms; 4) the Lion Brewery; 5) the Olive Branch.

Further up Middle Lane, just west of the railway viaduct, was the **Lion Brewery**, a shop-cum-beerhouse with a brewery at the back, first recorded in 1870. In 1913 the licensing magistrates questioned the need for the continued existence of the Lion Brewery and asked the landlord, William Newman, if he did much business. He answered, "none

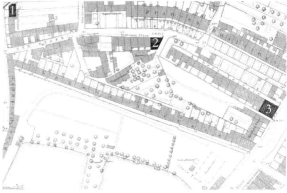

Above The lost pubs of South Dolemeads: 1) the Smith's Arms; 2) the Somerset Arms; 3) the Packhorse.
Top left The site of the Olive Branch.
Left The site of the Smith's Arms.

at all," adding that he had had no beer to sell for the past three weeks. Not surprisingly, his licence was revoked.

Next door to the Lion Brewery, on Richmond Terrace, hard up against Arch 24 of the viaduct, was a beerhouse called the **Olive Branch**, which was open between 1870 and 1888.

On the other side of the viaduct, down near the river, was the **Smith's Arms** at 1-2 Winifred's Terrace, open between 1841 and 1919. The high wall running alongside the footpath marks its site.

Dolemeads' other fully-licensed pub – the **Somerset Arms** on Pulteney Place – stood roughly where Widcombe Infants' School stands today. It was open from around 1850 to 1920.

Dolemeads from Beechen Cliff. The Smith's Arms can be seen just south of the bridge.

THE LOST PUBS OF BATH

There was also a beerhouse in Dolemeads called the **Roaring Cannon**, which was open between 1839 and 1841 for the navvies building the railway. Such temporary beerhouses were common, often being run by one of the navvies. At Box Tunnel, for example, was the Box Tunnel Inn, run by John Wilkins, a miner working on the tunnel.

Dolemeads was redeveloped in the early twentieth century as a model estate. In 1910, an official report on the area declared that, "whereas a man used to spend 3/6 a week in 'drink' and 3/6 a week in rent, he now spends 5/- a week for rent and 2/- for 'drink.' Formerly the wretched houses drove the men and women to public houses, now they live at home."

§

A brisk walk back to the White Hart and up Widcombe Hill as far as its junction with Church Street brings us to the site of the **New Inn**. It was there by 1747, when it was advertised for sale "with the malthouse thereto belonging." In 1751, a rather brutal contest was advertised:

> To be played for at Backsword on the Monday next, the tenth of June, at the New Inn at Widcombe near Bath … a gold-lac'd hat, value one guinea – To begin in the forenoon and leave off at sunset. The first man that breaks a head shall be instituted to the favour.

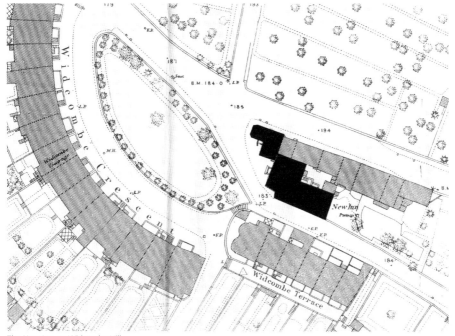

The New Inn on Widcombe Hill.

The Old Malt House above the New Inn.

The New Inn was also the venue for less energetic gatherings. In the early nineteenth century, for example, the Lyncombe & Widcombe Society of Tradesmen held their meetings there. By 1867, it consisted of a bar, smoking room, long room, tap room, sitting room, small room, skittle alley, brewhouse, cooperage and malthouse. When the inspector visited in 1903, however, it had seen better days. The accommodation had shrunk to a bar with a tap room on one side and a glass room on the other. There were also, he noted, "a number of old buildings at rear with skittle alley."

In 1913, the landlord, Ernest Thorpe, failed to appear before the magistrates to renew his licence, sending a friend along instead. It transpired that Mr Thorpe was in Guernsey and had been there for the last twelve months. The magistrates were surprised to discover that the pub had been closed for the whole of that time. Mr Thorpe's friend said that he was keen to keep the licence so that the pub could be sold as a going concern. Chief Inspector Bence of the Bath Constabulary, called upon to give his opinion of the matter, said that a pub that had been shut for a year was hardly a going concern. He added that the New Inn had seen little trade for years. The magistrates refused to renew the licence.

The New Inn never reopened. The building lingered on for another ten years until, on 23 January 1923 the following notice appeared in the *Bath Chronicle*:

> The old New Inn on Widcombe Hill has been demolished and the removal of the long derelict property – where fortunes had been made in previous times – is a distinct advantage. The entrance to Church Street is widened, but it seems a pity that the widening could not be continued further along that narrow street.

Today, little remains of the New Inn save for a bit of cornice and a few roof marks on the adjoining building, although a couple of doors up Widcombe Hill, the old malthouse survives as a private house.

There was another pub nearby called the **Hare & Hounds**. In March 1763 this notice appeared in the *Bath Chronicle*:

> There will be a Cock Match fought at Widcombe near Bath, known by the name of Mount Pleasant. To shew 31 cocks one each side in the main, for four guineas a battle, and £40 guineas the odd battle. The gentlemen of Wiltshire and Gloucestershire against the gentlemen of Somersetshire. To weigh on Saturday the second day of April, and fight the Monday and Tuesday following.

The Trafalgar Tavern on Calton Road.

In 1787, Samuel Saunders, the landlord of the Hare & Hounds, left to take over the Golden Lion in Horse Street, but unfortunately died less than three months later. His departure may have coincided with the closure of the Hare & Hounds, because there are no subsequent records of it. Although its exact location is not known, it may have been at 11-12 Church Street.

Further along Church Street, beyond the church, there is believed to have been another long-lost pub called the **Ring of Bells**, possibly the predecessor of the present Ring of Bells on Widcombe Parade.

Another lost Widcombe pub was the **King's Arms**. In 1649, when Elizabeth Coulthurst was the landlady, Thomas Gibbs was indicted for breaking into the premises. However, there is no record of where the King's Arms was.

Retracing our steps down Widcombe Hill and along Claverton Street, and turning up Lyncombe Hill, we come to Calton Road. A little way along, opposite the children's playground, was a beerhouse-cum-grocery called the **Trafalgar Tavern**, which opened in the 1850s. The 1903 report described it as having a "general shop with bar which serves as counter for shop. Very nice smoke room behind." It closed in 1935 and all trace of it has disappeared.

§

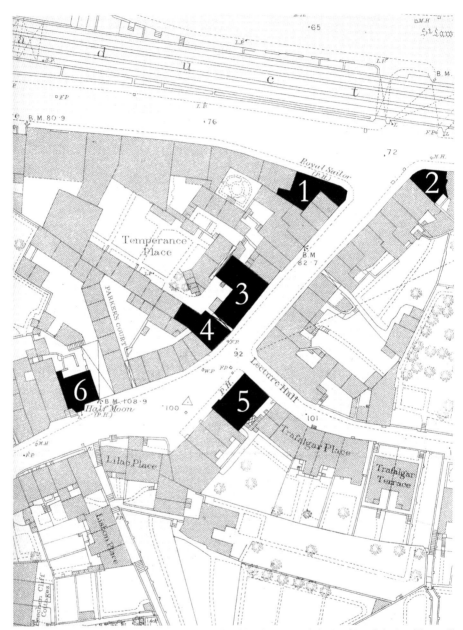

The lost pubs of Lower Holloway: 1) the Royal Sailor; 2) the Old Bridge Tavern; 3) the Angel Inn; 4) the Angel Tavern; 5) the Old Fox; 6) the Half Moon.

THE LOST PUBS OF BATH

Now it is back to the foot of Holloway for an excursion into one of nineteenth-century Bath's most notorious enclaves. Sadly, it will be an imaginary journey, for the maze of buildings that once covered this hillside has virtually disappeared. All that is left, halfway up the hill, is Paradise House, St Mary Magdalen's Church and the old Leper Hospital. The pubs and inns which served the thousands of people who lived and worked on this north-facing hillside are no more than a distant memory. Like the Avon Street and Snow Hill areas, it has been airbrushed out of history.

The road leading down Holloway dates back at least to Roman times. When John Leland, chaplain to Henry VIII, visited Bath in 1540 he recorded his first impressions of the place:

> Before I arrived at Bath Bridge over the Avon I descended past a craggy hill full of fine springs of water; and on this craggy hill a long street has been built as a suburb of Bath, with a chapel dedicated to St Mary Magdalene.

Over a century later, the traveller Celia Fiennes described Holloway as "a very steep hill and stony a mile from the town scarce any passing and there descends a little current of water continually from the rocks."

In the centuries that followed, the land on either side of Holloway was covered by a maze of alleyways and courts. Being outside the jurisdiction of the city, Holloway was a magnet for the criminal underclass. A rhyme on Bath's beggars published in 1836 identified their lodgings as "Holloway's garrets and cellars." Another writer declared that "Holloway was distinguished for two things – well-kept mendicants and ill-kept donkeys."

THE BEGGARS OF HOLLOWAY
From the *Bath Chronicle*, 17 October 1805

To be added to the list of Bath arrivals ... Fourteen of the accustomed beggars who have for more than twenty years regularly exercised the charity of this place during the season. They are returned from their former rambles to their watering places in different parts of the Kingdom ... One on crutches is arrived from Scarborough. A blind man has found his way from Harrogate, accompanied by three leprous children. Five cripples arrived from Tunbridge Wells. A St Vitus dancer from Margate. A woman troubled with convulsions from Brighton. A woman without a tongue from Weymouth. A man without legs who has visited Exmouth, Sidmouth, Dawlish and Teignmouth, and travelled as far as Mount's Bay in Cornwall and returned along the northern coast of Devon. The little black-bearded man, apparently deranged in mind, from Cheltenham, with two venerable dealers in ballads and pincushions. They have all taken their old lodging in Holloway and expect to be followed soon by the rest of their merry brother and sisterhood. – The blind sailor with pigeons on his head, the man with balls on every joint, and a Scotch bagpipe player are expected in the course of the ensuing week.

At a meeting of the fraternity held at a long-established lodging house in Holloway the following resolutions were proposed and agreed:

That our respectable fraternity hath existed from time whereof the memory of man runneth not to the contrary.

That the King of the Beggars is of much higher antiquity than the King of Bath.

That our fraternity is properly appendant on, appurtenant to, and connected with the Bath establishment.

The **Royal Sailor** stood on the corner of Wells Road and Holloway. It was named after William IV, who was an admiral before becoming king. Built in the 1820s, it opened as a beerhouse around 1834. It was built, like many of Holloway's buildings, of lias stone rendered to look like ashlar. It closed on 20 August 1963 and was demolished the following year.

On the opposite corner was a beerhouse called the **Old Bridge Tavern**, which opened in the 1850s. Around a hundred years ago, the landlady was Ruth Watts, whose husband ran the butcher's next door. It consisted of a bar divided in two and a parlour. It closed in 1930.

Because he was king when the Beerhouse Act was passed, William IV had hundreds of beerhouses named after him. He was also commemorated, as the Royal Sailor, in the name of a pub at the bottom of Holloway.

On the west side of Holloway, a few doors up from the Royal Sailor, was the **Angel Inn**. It was first recorded in 1747, when an auction was held there, but it was almost certainly much older. In 1749, a criminal trial was held there, suggesting that it was not only Widcombe's principal inn, but also its principal public building.

In 1766, the landlord of the Angel gave an ex-employee one of the worst references imaginable, and, to ensure it came to the attention of any potential employers, published it in the *Bath Chronicle*:

The Royal Sailor on the right, with the former Old Bridge Tavern on the opposite corner.

A Caution to the Public – Stephen Taylor, who lived with Mr Windsor at the Angel at the Bridge Foot, a month and four days only, by his drunkenness, obstinacy and negligence, occasioned the following accidents:

1) Broke the shafts from a chaise;
2) Broke down a chaise, the work of which was lost for three days, besides the expense of repairing;
3) Broke a perch, the repairing of which cost 30/- besides losing the work of the chaise for three days;
4) Broke a new pair of shafts;
5) Broke two glasses of a chaise;
6) Broke the body of a chaise all to pieces so that it cannot be repair'd.

He was likewise very barbarous to his horses, driving them excessive hard and not taking proper care of them afterward.

In 1780, the Angel Inn was taken by Thomas Lockyer from the Crown at Keynsham, in partnership with Ludford's Brewery of Romsey. The partnership was dissolved in 1782 and the Angel was advertised to let the following year.

In 1804, an accident that highlighted the dangers of old Holloway occurred outside the Angel:

At the moment Mr Parsons, London and Bristol carrier, was mounting his horse a few evenings ago, at the door of the Angel Inn over the Old Bridge, a tilted wagon turned the corner, at which his horse started and threw him, and from the narrowness of the place the wheels must inevitably have run over his body, had not his son, from great presence of mind, dragged him from that dangerous situation, though not so effectually that one of his thighs was dreadfully grazed by the wheels. The Commissioners of the Roads have had it some time in contemplation to widen this dangerous entrance into the city; and we trust it will be speedily carried into effect.

Next to the Angel Inn, with its own brewery, was the **Angel Inn Tap**. This was the setting for a fatal accident in 1816, when John Kite, a drayman from Williams' Brewery on the Quay, was delivering beer. One of his horses kicked him into the path of a four-horse coach, which ran over and killed him instantly.

The Angel Inn closed after the railway opened in 1841 and the Angel Inn Tap changed its name to the Angel Tavern. Tenements were built in the courtyard of the old inn, which was renamed Temperance Place. The temperance movement was clearly eager to celebrate the demise of one of Holloway's drinking dens. However, the celebrations were somewhat muted, as the only entrance to Temperance Court was through a covered alleyway beside the Angel Tavern, while the back door of the pub opened into the court.

The Angel Tavern was eventually taken over by the Welton Brewery and the pub's own brewery was closed. In 1911, the Angel Tavern's landlord, John Richardson, joined the long roll call of those who disappeared and was later found in the river. It nearly closed in 1916 when the licensing magistrates decided there were too many pubs in the area. The Welton Brewery put up a strong defence, saying it was their only outlet in Bath. Several customers appeared before the magistrates, saying they had a particular liking for Welton beer and would miss it if the Angel Tavern closed. The magistrates gave in, although regulars only had two years left to enjoy Welton beer, for the brewery was bought up by George's of Bristol in 1918. The Angel Tavern eventually closed in 1958.

Opposite the Angel Tavern was the **Old Fox**, first recorded in 1784. Originally just the Fox, it became the Old Fox in 1807 when the landlord, Paul Scudamore, left to open the Young Fox further up the hill.

It was a three-bayed stucco building on a corner site. When an inventory of the Old Fox was drawn up in 1879, the accommodation consisted of a bar parlour, tap room, sitting room, drawing room with grand piano and telescopic dining table, bedroom "with japanned bath as fixed with length of supply pipe and tap," and brewery. There were also around 500 brass checks in the bar parlour with "stamps for making same."

The Old Fox shortly after closure.

THE LOST PUBS OF BATH

In 1901, the pub was taken over by WG Reynolds, who installed a new four-quarter brewery at the back at a cost of around £1,200 – a considerable outlay considering that the pub's weekly turnover was less than £30. It was a poor investment, for the pub – and the brewery – closed a mere seven years later, in 1908.

Back on the west side of the street, a few doors further up, was the **Half Moon,** opened by the Northgate Brewery in the early 1790s. It soon established a tradition of landlords with exotic names. One of the earliest licensees was Zachariah Washbourne; in the 1820s the pub was run by Hezekiah Clark.

Holloway was not only a pretty lawless place; it was also the place where country met town. Take this story from 1837 of an out-of-towner falling victim to the wiles of a lady of the night:

> Margaret Manning was charged by a countryman with picking his pocket of £4.13s at the Half Moon, Holloway, last evening. The woman was not taken into custody until this morning, when nothing was found upon her; and on the examination, as there was a want of legal evidence to substantiate the charge, she was liberated.

When an inventory of the Half Moon was carried out in 1880, it consisted of a bar parlour with sofa, hunting prints and an engraving of William IV, a tap room, three bedrooms and a garden. The 1903 report on the property went into somewhat greater detail, and gives a good idea how steep the site was:

> Two entrances. Stable yard communicates with highway by large gates. Door used for admission of beer into stable yard; two doors from first floor into stable yard. Two doors from first floor into open yard. Steps from this down to stable yard. WC and urinal at rear of premises (dirty and unventilated). Bar with glass room at side.

In 1915, a private in the 4th Somerset Light Infantry stationed at Prior Park was given a month's hard labour for striking the landlady after she refused to serve him. A year later the licensing magistrates tried to close the pub down. They pointed out that there were several other pubs in the area, the accommodation was poor, average takings were only around £40 a month, and, during seven nights' observation, only 44 customers passed through the doors. The landlord, an old soldier called Henry Farmer, replied that, despite being almost 60, he had put in twelve month's military service since the start of the war, and had recently been invalided out of the army. He had been at the Half Moon for 15 years, made a comfortable living out of it, and was dismayed to find that, having served his King and Country, he was now being turned out of house and home. Despite his pleas, the magistrates referred the Half Moon to the compensation board. They took a more lenient view, however. The Half Moon survived, only to be destroyed 26 years later in the Bath Blitz.

Just up from the Half Moon, on the corner of Old Orchard, was Holloway's best-known and best-remembered pub, the **Young Fox**. It was opened in 1807 by Paul Scudamore from the Old Fox, and taken over by Sainsbury's Brewery in 1832. It had

The view from Beechen Cliff, with the Young Fox indicated by a star. Apart from those in the far distance, virtually all the buildings in this photograph have been demolished.

a bar with a room either side, a long club or smoke room, stables and a brewery. The bar, with a mahogany-topped counter, was plainly decorated, but the bar parlour was much more lavish, with a pair of horns and seven framed pictures on the walls. There was a ship in a glass case, stuffed seating in American cloth, a diapered-glass panelled door leading from the bar, a diapered-glass serving sash with half circular head, a mahogany serving flap and two trusses. In the club room were a cottage piano, two large cases of stuffed birds and a stuffed fox. According to Meehan, "in the old coaching days the landlord had frequently to go to the assistance of family and other coaches that got stuck in the mud and ruts of the Holloway as they were trying to enter the city. The newer Wells Road was not then in existence."

A plan of the Young Fox in 1842.

The Young Fox was badly damaged in the Bath Blitz, but stayed open until 28 September 1967. Demolition followed a few months later. It was a sad loss. A mish-mash of buildings on various levels, some dating from the seventeenth century, it would have been one of the showpieces of Bath had it survived. Vandalism is too mild a word to describe what happened to it.

THE LOST PUBS OF BATH

Just below the Young Fox was the entrance to Barton Place, where there were two beerhouses – the **New Inn** at No 19 from around 1860 to 1899, and the **Royal Marine** for a short period in the early 1840s.

Other pubs on Holloway whose exact locations are unknown included the **Three Blackbirds** (c1746-c1759), and four beerhouses – the **Smith's Arms** (c1833), the **Lord Melbourne** (c1841), the **Roebuck** (c1837-c1841), and the **Beehive** (c1864).

§

The number on the gateway of one of Holloway's lost houses.

The former Nelson Arms.

The former Pelican.

Just past the church of St Mary Magdalen, garden walls and steps leading to long-vanished front doors can be seen on the left-hand side of the road. Somewhere hereabouts was **Beechen Cliff Cottage**, which opened as a beerhouse around 1840 and closed soon afterwards.

There is also a footpath, which takes us up past Magdalen Park to Beechen Cliff. Just before the toposcope, installed in the 1920s and indicating features of old Bath that fell victim to the Bath Blitz, a path on the right leads to Beechen Cliff Road. Here, a couple of doors up to the left, is one of Bath's most tantalisingly lost pubs, the **Nelson Arms**, opened by John Skelton in 1844, with a pleasure garden looking over the city. It only had a beerhouse licence, and, after several unsuccessful attempts to upgrade it to a fully-licensed house, it closed around 1850. The old Nelson Arms is still there – now called Nelson House – but with no indication of its alcoholic past.

Beechen Cliff Road leads down onto Bear Flat, where, a hundred yards or so past the Bear, we come to the old **Pelican** beerhouse at 4 Bloomfield Terrace. It was opened in the 1830s by John Pasmore from the Star & Garter in Lilliput Alley. He closed it around 1840 and moved back into town to open the Porter Stores (now the Porter) in Miles's Buildings. The building now houses the Pure Health & Beauty Centre.

From here, it is an easy stroll along Bear Flat and back down Holloway to our starting point. For the intrepid lost pub spotter, however, there is one more pub to

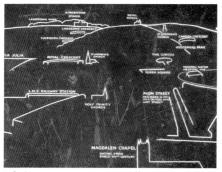

Left The toposcope on Beechen Cliff, indicating such long-gone sights as Holy Trinity and St Andrew's Churches, and the old Avon Street.
Right The view from the toposcope today.

be crossed off the list. Carry on up Wellsway, past the Devonshire Arms, and along the dual carriageway, until an electricity sub-station hoves into view on the left-hand side of the road. In 1832, St John's Hospital leased this plot of land to the Anchor Brewery to build a beerhouse called the **Plough**. It seems to have been the sort of place most people went out of their way to avoid. The following report, from the *Bath Chronicle* of 12 August 1869, gives an idea what its clientele was like:

> William Clifford (on remand) was charged with unlawfully assaulting Jane Knight. Mr JK Bartrum defended the prisoner. On the night of the 28th ult. the prosecutrix (who is the wife of the baker at the Union Workhouse and lives on Rush Hill) was on her way home accompanied by her four children and a little girl named Dowding. When passing the Plough public house the prisoner came out and joined them. He asked her to send the children on by themselves, and then put his arms round her, lifted her up, tried to kiss her, and otherwise misconducted himself. She ordered him to behave himself and he desisted but walked on by her side, and presently he put his arms round her again and tried to kiss her several times. When she got home Mrs Knight told her husband what had occurred, and he next day saw the prisoner and asked him to apologise and he would not be hard with him; but he would not do so ... Mr Bartrum addressed the Bench at some length and said that the prisoner was drunk at the time the offence was committed. As their Worships knew drink acted differently on

The Plough Inn on Wells Road.

THE LOST PUBS OF BATH

different people – some it made quarrelsome and some loveable. Drink made the prisoner very affectionate, and as on the day in question he had been drinking hard, when he saw the prosecutrix he put his hand round her and tried to kiss her. He pointed out the prosecutrix could not have been much frightened at what had occurred, for she passed several houses without giving any alarm, which she would have done had she thought the prisoner had intended seriously to assault her. The magistrates having deliberated in private, Colonel Ford said that the Bench looked on the case as proved, and drunkenness being no excuse they sentenced the prisoner to six weeks' hard labour.

A letter published by the *Chronicle* a year later suggests that the Plough was a popular rendezvous for recalcitrant coachmen:

Sir, This afternoon, about three o'clock, I was driving with my daughter along the Wells Road, and when near the Plough public house I saw an open double carriage at the door, and no one with the horses. Another vehicle was behind; and both coachmen were just issuing from the door of the public house, when the horses of the first carriage started off at a quick pace whilst the two coachmen were talking to each other, and the pace rapidly went into a furious gallop. I saw little more for nearly half a mile, when, coming up, I found the carriage smashed, one part lying in the road, and several men, apparently carters, holding down the heads of the horses, one of which was kicking; and both were much agitated. I asked the coachman, who had come up to the wreck, whose carriage it was, but he persistently refused to tell me, and I therefore deem it right to give the circumstance publicity, that the culpable driver may not conceal from his master the real cause of the damage. Most providentially, the runaway steeds, though flying past several vehicles, did not strike any of them, so far as I could see for the distance and the dust; but had my carriage been half a minute earlier, and we had passed instead of being a yard or two behind, I do not see how we could have avoided being run into and probably upset. Nothing can be more culpable than for a coachman to leave his carriage and a pair of high spirited horses at a public house door without any one to hold them, whilst he is drinking and gossiping within, and it is a mercy that in this case no one was killed. I observe from the papers that some time ago a man left a carriage at a public house door in a northern town; the horse ran away and killed a woman, and the driver has very properly been committed for manslaughter. I enclose my card, and will give the owner of the carriage further details if he requires it.

In 1883, the freehold of the Plough was transferred from St John's Hospital to Magdalen Hospital, who closed it down. The building was renamed Upper Magdalen Cottage, and it was there that a reporter from the *Chronicle*, on the trail of the Plough, called one day in 1932:

Definite information was difficult to get until I called at a house now known as Upper Magdalen Cottage on Wellsway. The occupiers told me that they had heard that the cottage was an inn more than 40 years ago and it had the nickname of

Hole in the Wall. I was shown the back kitchen, which was obviously used for storing the barrels of beer, and the hole in the wall was, I was told, probably a little window at the rear, which was an informal jug & bottle department.

EXCURSION THE EIGHTH

THE LOST QUADRANT

This excursion requires a great deal of imagination, for much of the area it traverses was comprehensively redeveloped in the twentieth century. Hitler's bombs accounted for some of the devastation, especially in the eastern sector; the town planners accounted for the rest. Only a few fragments remain to give an insight into what this forgotten area of Bath was like.

Southgate Street, which we explored in the second excursion, was the only significant development south of the city walls before the eighteenth century. There was a good reason for this: the whole area formed part of the Avon flood plain. Willow-fringed water meadows, such as King's Mead, Ambury Mead, and the Ham, were fine to graze horses and fatten cattle on, but totally unsuitable for building. Every winter they turned to a quagmire. After heavy rain or when the snows melted on the hills around the city, they disappeared under fast-flowing water.

Why developers such as John Strahan chose to build elegant lodging houses here, with only the merest of nods in the direction of flood prevention, is still a mystery. But they did, and the elegant lodging houses flooded, with the result that they did not stay elegant lodging houses for very long. The only developer who seems to have had the right idea was John Wood, whose North and South Parades, built high above the flood plain, were the opening sallies in a bid to create a Royal Forum of terraces on both sides of the river. It never came to anything and he turned his attention to the higher land north of the city, well above the flood plain, setting a trend for northward expansion which culminated in the high crescents of the late eighteenth and early nineteenth centuries.

What the flood-plain developers unwittingly created was a large area of housing which, because of its situation, was effectively sub-standard. The cellars were always damp; drainage and sewage were constant problems. On top of that was the ever-present threat of serious flooding. As the population of Bath boomed in the mid-eighteenth century, the area south of the city walls went rapidly downhill. And, of course, where there was poverty, deprivation and crime there were, inevitably, loads of pubs. Virtually all of them have gone, but we should not shed too many tears over their loss. Instead, let us think, as we embark on our virtual pub crawl, of the lives most of their customers had to endure, lives of back-breaking toil, of hunger, sickness

Of the 61 pubs on this map, only three are left – the Trinity (12), the Bath Tap (formerly the Devonshire Arms) (36), and the Hobgoblin (formerly the Talbot) (38). Those that have gone include: 1) the Kingsmead Wine Vaults; 2) the Coachmaker's Arms; 3) the Red Lion; 4) the Bath Arms; 5) the Times Tavern; 6) the Garrick's Head; 7) the Old Monmouth Arms; 8) the Theatre Tavern; 9) the Peep O'Day; 10) the Seven Dials; 11) the Westgate Tavern; 13) the Black Horse; 14) the Wheelchair; 15) the Globe; 16) the Rose & Crown; 17) the White Lion; 18) the Lord Nelson or Pig & Whistle; 19) the Fountain; 20) the Garibaldi; 21) the Oddfellows' Arms; 22) the Smith's Arms; 23) the Shamrock; 24) the Lamb; 25) the Jolly Sailor; 26) the Duke of York; 27) the Waterman's Arms; 28) the Rose & Crown; 29) the Chequers; 30) the Bacchus: 31) the Plasterers' Arms; 32) the Heart in Hand; 33) the Bird in Hand; 34) the Malt & Hops; 35) the Corn Street Brewery; 37) the Masons' Arms; 39) the St James's Tavern; 40) the French Horn; 41) the Bell (formerly the Crispin Tavern); 42) the White Swan; 43) the Somerset Arms; 44) Robert Baggs' beerhouse; 45) the Hole in the Wall; 46) the Crown Brewery; 47) the Kettle & Pipes; 48) the Punch Bowl; 49) the Silver Lion; 50) the Oxford Stores; 51) the Rose & Crown; 52) the Golden Lion; 53) the New Inn; 54) the Somerset Wine Vaults; 55) the Exeter Inn; 56) the Spread Eagle; 57) Oliver's Wine Vaults; 58) the Bath Arms; 59) the Ship; 60) the Plough; 61) the Full Moon.

and poverty, lives whose only highlight was a visit to some ramshackle alehouse.

And think that, if wiser counsels had prevailed, the area between the old city and the river could – with the exception of Southgate Street – have been something akin to Christchurch Meadows in Oxford, a pastoral retreat bordering the city, and providing the perfect foil to its Palladian splendours. Sadly, it was not to be, and the gallimaufry of lost buildings through which we now take our course stands as an indictment of the unbridled greed and lack of judgement of eighteenth-century speculators.

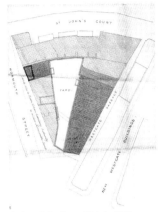

A plan of the Seven Dials in 1883.

We start this excursion outside the old West Gate, a part of the city that has changed beyond all recognition. The Seven Dials development, on the west of the Sawclose, stands on the site of an inn, originally called the Londonderry, then the Globe, and finally the Seven Dials, which was demolished in 1931.*

King's Mead was originally a meadow owned by the Abbey, where Bathonians were allowed to graze their cattle on payment "for each head of cattle having a tooth one penny, and for every one not having a tooth a halfpenny." In the late seventeenth century, it was developed as a pleasure ground. When Celia Fiennes visited the city in 1687 she described King's Mead as "a pleasant green meadow, where are walks round and cross it, no place for coaches ... There

*A full history of the Seven Dials can be found in *Bath Pubs*, pp138-40.

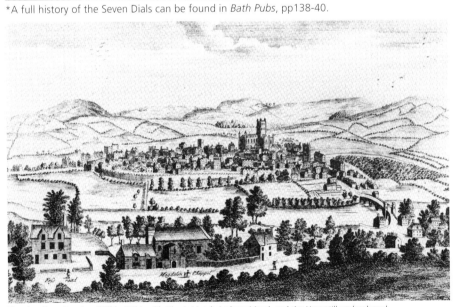

The view from Beechen Cliff in 1724, with King's Mead, Ambury Mead, and the Ham still undeveloped.

THE LOST QUADRANT

are several little cake-houses where you have fruit syllabubs and summer liquors to entertain the company that walk there."

King's Mead was one of the first places outside the city walls to be developed as the early eighteenth-century building boom got under way. John Strahan started building Kingsmead Square, which he originally called Westgate Square, in 1727. John Wood was not impressed. "The houses in King's Mead Square," he wrote, "have nothing, save Ornaments without Taste, to please the Eye." Over two centuries later, in 1967, the planners agreed with him, and the houses on the south side of the square were earmarked for redevelopment as part of a complex extending back to James Street West. Shops, a pub, a ten-pin bowling alley, a YWCA, a covered arcade, an underground car park, and car showrooms, were among the proposed delights. Had it been built, the chances are that today we would be discussing what to put in its place. Fortunately, Charles Ware, whom we encountered on our second excursion, orchestrated a campaign to save the south side of Kingsmead Square. Major refurbishment in 1975 managed to retain not only its frontage but also much of its character. It is a useful benchmark for what the planners were prepared to pull down in the 1960s and 1970s.

Even after Strahan had built Kingsmead Square, however, much of the surrounding area remained semi-rural. As late as 1755, the *Bath & Bristol Guide* could inform visitors that, "after passing down Kingsmead Street, the Nobility, Gentry, and Others, have delightful and pleasant walking, in fine weather, into the Town Commons, or round the King's Meadows, or to Weston Lock, about a mile from the City, where you walk along by the side of the River Avon, which affords a very agreeable amusement." There was always a faintly raffish air about this end of town, however, compared to the more refined delights of Spring Gardens. In 1775, when Sheridan set the abortive duel in *The Rivals* in Kingsmead Fields, it is unlikely that his audience was too surprised at his choice of venue. By then, like Avon Street, Kingsmead Square was on its way down in the world. Naturally, it soon acquired more than its fair share of pubs.

In 1736, nine houses were occupied in Kingsmead Square. One of the householders was John George, the innkeeper of the **Mitre**. Nine years later, the Mitre was put up for auction, "with good coach houses, stables, and all other conveniences, the bidding to start at £600." It was still there in 1747, but that is the last we hear of it. It is possible that it became the **New Inn**, which featured in a brief item in the *Bath Journal* on 3 March 1762:

> Last Friday died Mr Jeremiah Dimsdale, who for many years kept the New Inn in Kingsmead Square.

A couple of months later, Mr Dimsdale's widow, Elizabeth, placed an advertisement in the *Journal*:

> Elizabeth Dimsdale at the New Inn, Kingsmead Square, continues on the business of letting coaches, chaises and horses (with careful drivers) to any part of England, as in her husband's lifetime; and humbly entreats the continuance of her friends' former favours.

THE LOST PUBS OF BATH

Four years later, the Rev John Penrose, after visiting friends in Kingsmead Square, and "to avoid passing through Avon Street, a street of ill fame … went through an inn at the south-west corner of the square into King's Mead, then down to the river, along the quay to the bridge." This must have been the New Inn, and it is lucky that Penrose was so precise, for it is the only clue we have to its location.

In 1773 the New Inn was taken by James Matthews, for whom innkeeping seems to have been a secondary activity:

> James Matthews, Butcher, Stall Street, having taken the New Inn in King's-mead Square, with the Meadows adjoining thereto, the better to carry on his present business as well as that of a victualler; humbly begs leave to inform the Nobility, Gentry, etc, whom he has the honor to serve, that by the advantage arising from such a quantity of fine pasture land so near the city, he shall be enabled to sell all kinds of butchery much better and cheaper than any other person in the trade …
> The false insinuation propagated that he was going to quit his present business was spread with a manifest design to injure him, he having been very near losing many of his good customers thereby. He intends continuing his old shop in Stall Street for some time longer and will give the public notice of his removal to another. NB Cattle will be taken in as usual.

The pastureland was still there six years later, when James Matthews' successor, John Hucklebridge, placed an advertisement in the *Bath Journal* informing the public that "the King's Meads" were "open for the reception of cattle."

By this time, Bath was expanding rapidly. It was only a question of time before pastureland so close to the city centre fell into the hands of property developers. On 13 September 1785, a gentlemen called Henry Fisher drew up an agreement with two stonemasons called Thomas and Robert Lidiard, and a tiler and plasterer called Giles Fisher regarding "two meadows called King's Mead and the New Inn in Kingsmead Square and several other plots of ground with premises and appurtenances surrounding and adjoining King's Meads." Soon the "fine pastureland" had disappeared under housing. The New Inn seems to have closed at the same time, for that is the last we hear of it. Perhaps, once the land had gone, it was not worth keeping open.

The building seems to have survived, however. Forty years later, in 1825, the council was asked to contribute "to removing a ruinous house at the south-western corner of Kingsmead Square" – the same position as the inn John Penrose walked through in 1766. The council refused to help, and no more was heard about the proposed demolition until, in 1870, the whole south-western corner of the square was swept away when New Street was built by the Midland Railway to give access to its station at Green Park.

The row of houses saved by Charles Ware on the south side of Kingsmead Square once included three pubs. At No 9 was the **Black Horse**, which opened around 1841. It had a bar in four compartments with a smoke room behind. There was a small "snuggery" at the top of the steps leading to the yard, and a brewery and skittle alley at the back. The bar had a panelled circular-fronted counter with a mahogany top,

There were once three pubs on the south side of Kingsmead Square.

and a rosewood and gilt console table with a marble top. There was an oil painting of a black horse on the wall. An embossed glass panel on the door read "Foreign Wines and Spirits." There was a refrigerator under the counter and lino on the floor. The smoke room had two pairs of buffalo horns on the wall, a mahogany bagatelle table on a slate bed and a stuffed fox with a stuffed duck in a glass case.

Much of the Black Horse's stock of spirits was kept at the bonded warehouse underneath the Midland Station and duty was paid as it was redeemed. In 1883 the stock held at the station included 26.5 gallons of rum, 55.6 gallons of whisky and 26.8 gallons of brandy.

The Black Horse closed in 1908. The building was badly damaged in the Bath Blitz of 1942, but later restored. In the 1950s and 1960s, Leakey's fish and chip shop occupied the premises.

At No 7 was the **Wheelchair**, which opened in the 1850s as a meeting place for Bath Chairmen. It was later renamed the Clarence. In 1882, a change of ownership saw it transformed into the Clarence Temperance Hotel. Around 1900, part of the hotel was turned into a Post Office. The hotel and the Post Office both closed in the 1930s. The building was later occupied by Wing Yung's Chinese Laundry. Later, the Moody Goose restaurant opened in the basement. After the Moody Goose moved out to Midsomer Norton in 2005, a new restaurant, Mezzalune, opened.

The former Globe.

On the south-east corner of the square, at No 5, was the **Globe**, which opened when the Globe in Monmouth Street closed in 1770.* Eight years later, the Globe Inn & Excise Office in Kingsmead Square was advertised to let, but, apart from an appearance on a map of 1779 (which handily gives its location), that is the last we hear of it.

The building later had a variety of uses – a tallow chandlery (one of the smelliest businesses of all) in the 1850s, a steam saw mill in the 1860s, and a temperance dining room in the 1880s. In the mid-twentieth century, it housed Brook's (later Maidment's) General Stores. Today it is the home of Video South.

There were at least two other pubs in Kingsmead Square, but their exact location is unknown. The first was the **Black Boy**, which was there in 1776, but closed soon afterwards. Then there was the **Distill Head**, also recorded for the first time in

*The history of the Globe in Monmouth Street appears in *Bath Pubs,* p139

1776, with Gerrard Farrell as the licensee. Three years later, in 1779, the Distill Head had gone, and Philip Lynch was running a pub called the Gallon Pot in Kingsmead Square. The following year, Philip Lynch was running a pub called the Blue Mug in Kingsmead Square. By 1806, however, Gerrard Farrell was running the Gallon Pot; he stayed there until 1811. We could be looking at three different pubs here, we could be looking at two, or we could be looking at one. But, whatever the case, we have no idea where they – or it – were (or should that be was?).

Kingsmead Street today.

We now walk to the opposite corner of Kingsmead Square, past Rosewell House, and down what is left of Kingsmead Street. There isn't much. After a few yards we come up against a brick wall and a flight of steps leading down to a car park at what was once basement level. At one time, Kingsmead Street linked up with New King Street to form one of the major routes out of the city. Trams to Weston came this way, and, although it was not particularly glamorous, Kingsmead Street was one of the busiest streets in the city for about 200 years. In 1749, John Wood noted that it "contains 36 houses, some of which are extreme good ones; but for the rest little can be said to draw one's notice, except a very great irregularity in them should happen to do it." In the early twentieth century, it had two schools, a carriage works, tailors, butchers, greengrocers, laundries, cobblers, garages, printers, coal merchants, hairdressers, and fish and chip shops. Then, in 1942, the Luftwaffe came. Many of the buildings in the street were destroyed, many more were pulled down as

Kingsmead Street cleared for redevelopment, looking towards Monmouth Street.

unsafe. In the 1960s, the few that remained were cleared – all apart for a few at the east end – to make way for flats and offices.

Kingsmead Street in April 1942, with the Red Lion on the left.

There were at least six pubs in Kingsmead Street. On the north side, at No 33, six doors along from what is now the last house, was the **Bath Arms**, originally known as the Chequers and first recorded in 1776. One night in 1779, a customer called Michael Hood, "a little but not much disguised with liquor," was told to take himself home by the landlord, Henry Hawkins. On his way through the darkened city, he passed along Wood Street, on the south side of which stood Northumberland Buildings, half built, with no railings round the areas. He fell into the area of No 2, bringing his night on the town to an abrupt and tragic end.

In 1835, William Pinch built a large brewery – called the Bath Brewery – at the back of the Bath Arms. While sinking a well at the brewery, he tapped into one of city's hot springs. Although this was unfortunate for him, as the water was no use for brewing, it was even more unfortunate for the Corporation, who were faced with the prospect of the hot springs drying up. They had dried up 25 years earlier, and William "Strata" Smith had had to dig down and seal off the newly-formed channels into which the water was running. The Corporation took Pinch to court, where the case rumbled on for over two years, until, in September 1838, the hot spring in Kingsmead Street was ordered to be capped.

When the Bath Arms was advertised for sale in 1889 it consisted of front and side bars, parlour, kitchen, drawing room, four bedrooms and a brewery. It closed in 1919 and was destroyed in 1942.

Six doors down from the Bath Arms – its site now covered by flats – was the **Red Lion** at No 27, which opened sometime before 1776. An early newspaper cutting gives details of the sort of entertainment on offer there:

> To all Gentlemen, Ladies and Others, Lovers and Fanciers of Birds:
>
> There is to be seen at any time of the day, in a dining room at the Red Lion Inn in Kingsmead Street, a curious aviary of English birds flying within the compleatest piece of wire work ever made, being the whole bigness of the room; likewise a choice collection of beautiful perspective views, which for the elegance of taste are (by the judicious) deemed to exceed any of the kind; also a beautiful piece of grotto work, with a collection of sea shells; a collection of large fossils, and small ones, fitting to complement a small grotto with the shells; also a collection of sea weeds and sea sponges.
>
> Any of these things to be sold, with a great many other curiosities too tedious to mention.

THE LOST PUBS OF BATH

The Kingsmead Wine Vaults.

When an inventory of the Red Lion was carried out in 1869, it consisted of a drinking room, bar, tap room, parlour and brewhouse. The brewery closed around 1921, and the pub was destroyed in 1942.

Opposite the Red Lion on the south side of the street was the **Coachmaker's Arms** at No 12. This was first recorded in 1781 and closed in the late 1830s. It became a butcher's and later a greengrocer's.

Eight doors down from the Coachmaker's Arms, near the far end of the street, was the **Kingsmead Wine Vaults** at No 20. It first appeared in a newspaper report in 1843, concerning a man who called in one night, drank two pints of cider, and helped himself to the contents of the till while the landlord was otherwise engaged. It consisted of a bar and smoke room, with a club room on the first floor, and was owned by Smith Bros. of Westgate Buildings. It survived the Bath Blitz, finally closing on 30 November 1961.

There were two other pubs in Kingsmead Street whose locations are not known. A house "known by the name of the **Old Jolly Footman**, in Kingsmead Street, Bath" was advertised to be let or sold in 1746. On 19 November 1752, the *Bath Journal* announced that

> yesterday morning died Mr George Fear, who, a few years since, kept the Jolly Footman Publick House in Kingsmead Street; but having acquir'd a competent fortune, retir'd from business.

How long it took him to acquire his "competent fortune" we do not know, but it is clear that the Jolly Footman was there for some time before Mr Fear decided to dispose of it in 1746. It probably opened shortly after Kingsmead Street was built in the 1720s.

It came on the market again in 1754, when it was described as "a noted and well-accustom'd Publick House, known by the Jolly Footman (late George Fear's) situate in Kingsmead Street, [with] very good cellarage for holding a stock of beer, brewing utensils and all other conveniences." That is the last record we have of it. It may have closed, although it seems more likely that it was renamed and became either the Red Lion or the Bath Arms.

In the early 1830s, the Anchor Brewery opened a beerhouse called the **Devonshire House** in Kingsmead Street. Robert Griffin, the first tenant, soon found it was not the goldmine he had been promised. He struggled on for a time, getting more and more indebted to the brewery, and hoping that business would pick up. Then, in 1834, Mr Smith, the owner of the brewery, threatened him with legal action unless he repaid his debts. This was the last straw. From being a happy-go-lucky character, Robert Griffin took to sitting silently in the empty tap room with his head in his hands. Finally, one night, he told his wife to take over in the bar while he went down to the cellar to change a barrel. When he had not returned eight minutes later, she went downstairs and found he had hanged himself with a black silk handkerchief. She cut him down and caught him in her arms, but was not able to revive him. The Anchor Brewery decided to cut their losses and closed the Devonshire House down.

We now head south through the car park towards Bath's newest pub, the King of Wessex, before turning east along James Street West, past the Trinity, to Milk Street. Milk Street once ran down to the river, but has been blocked off part way down to make way for the Avon Street Coach Park. Only one of Milk Street's eighteenth-century buildings – housing the Ralph Allen Press – is left, stranded in a sea of modernity.

The only pub in Milk Street which anyone is likely to remember is a beerhouse called the **Rose & Crown** on the east side, three doors down from the old Mission Chapel. It opened around 1841 and closed in October 1938. The entrance to the Technical College Car Park stands on the site.

There was another beerhouse in the part of Milk Street now lying under the coach park. This was the **White Lion**, next to Sant's Pottery and Pipe Factory, which was open for a short time around 1837.

Three other pubs on Milk Street were all victims of the crackdown on dubious licensed premises in the wake of the Gordon Riots. The **Chequers**, the **Crown & Cushion**, and the **Crescent** were all there in 1776, but all closed in the early 1780s.

The Rose & Crown (indicated by a cross) was at 10 Milk Street, two doors along from the Mission Hall.

THE LOST PUBS OF BATH

We now retrace our steps to the top of Milk Street and turn right down James Street West towards Avon Street. Originally, James Street West ended at Milk Street. The section between Milk Street and St James's Parade, cutting through Avon Street, was built in the early twentieth century. Avon Street, the most notorious street in Bath, ran without a break from Kingsmead Square down to the river, its rows of terraced houses broken only by narrow alleyways and courts.

Today, Avon Street is not only publess, it is anodyne almost to the point of invisibility. A couple of hundred years ago it was a very different story. Built as fashionable lodging houses in the 1730s by John Strahan, on land owned by St John's Hospital, it went downhill fast. In 1749, John Wood wrote that, "from a regular and tolerable beginning [it has] fallen into an irregularity and meanness not worth describing." You did not go down Avon Street unless you had to, and if you had to there was a fair chance you were up to no good. Avon Street was the heart of Bath's red light district. In 1762, Henry Penruddocke Wyndham, an antiquarian and travel writer who was also High Sheriff of Wiltshire, visited Mother Addam's brothel there and wrote warmly of its charms.

By 1820, Avon Street was the home of "at least 300 people who obtain a living by begging, thieving or on the miserable wages of prostitution." Alongside them lived over a thousand others struggling to survive as best they could. At the time of the 1821 census, 1,500 people – over 5% of Bath's population – were living in Avon Street's 88 houses. When you consider that many of these houses doubled as pubs, shops, or workshops, you begin to get some idea of how overcrowded it was. When you add rudimentary or non-existent sanitary facilities, endemic drunkenness, prostitution, crime, hunger, lack of education, flooding, and disease, you come up with a cocktail of human misery that we cannot even begin to comprehend.

In 1819, Pierce Egan described Avon Street as a

receptacle for loose women [but] although it may be termed the Wapping of Bath, it is but common justice to observe, that it is far removed from the disgusting scenes which are so publicly witnessed at this memorable place at the East End of the Metropolis. With all the vigilance of the police of this elegant city, and its active Corporation towards removing public nuisances, Bath, in the height of its season, has its share of the frail sisterhood; but their language, manners and demeanour, are not of that very obtrusive nature which characterise these unhappy females in London, Liverpool, and Dublin.

Which is a roundabout way of saying that Bath had a better class of prostitute.

An official report on the city, written in 1842, pulled no such punches when it came to Avon Street:

Everything vile and offensive is congregated there. All the scum of Bath – its low prostitutes, its thieves, its beggars – are piled up in the dens rather than houses of which the street consists.

As if that were not enough, its smell was overpowering. In 1786, it got so bad that Mr Mansford, a local resident, complained to the council:

Avon Street looking towards Kingsmead Square.

I am sorry that present circumstances makes your attention necessary in Avon Street, which with the quantities of all kinds of nastiness thrown out by its inhabitants for a whole week together and the interspersion of here and there a group of pigs makes a perfect dung muckson from one end to the other. Because 'tis Avon Street once a week is thought sufficient for the scavenger to clean it but from the disorderly practices of most of its inhabitants makes it necessary it should be swept, etc., every day, which I shall leave to your consideration.

Because Avon Street was built on the flood plain, its cellars flooded regularly. It was not just water the residents had to worry about. Effluent from sewers, pigsties, and slaughterhouses washed back into the cellars. Think of the flies. Think of the mosquitoes. Think of the fleas. Think of the rats. It is hardly surprising that, in the cholera outbreak of 1831, 27 out of the 49 people who died in Bath came from Avon Street. Its reputation as a breeding ground for infection spread far beyond the city's boundaries. In September 1832, the Rector of Camerton

made a point of going to the shop, the public-house, and several of the colliers' residences to caution them against receiving mumpers or beggars coming from other parts, especially from Avon Street, Bath, into their houses, since by this means the cholera might be brought into the parish.

Many of Avon Street's residents were short-term, either passing through or using it as their first port of call in the city, before getting a job and moving on to better accommodation elsewhere. As a report from 1845 makes clear, its lodging houses would have looked in vain for a Tourist Board rosette:

During the season in Bath, when there is a considerable influx of visitors, the vagrants are the most numerous, and it is to be feared that indiscriminate charity somewhat prevails at this place. A large proportion of these vagrants is represented to be of the worst kind. They pay about 3d per night for their beds, placed in small, ill-ventilated rooms. The beds are usually occupied by two, but occasionally a larger number is crammed into them, without much respect for sex or age ... To relieve deserving poor travellers, a gentleman [of the Monmouth Street Society] attends daily (Sundays excepted) to hear the applications of poor travellers. He gives them (if considered deserving) a loaf of bread and some soup, under promise to leave the town.

Imagine you were one of the thousands of unfortunates who had to lodge in Avon Street. Having found your way there, you would have wandered down the street, past knots of idlers standing outside alehouses, picking your way past crowds of children playing in the gutter and piles of gently steaming excrement. Finding a likely-looking lodging house, you would have wandered in and been shown up to a room on the first-floor. This – unless you carried on up to the old servants' quarters – would be no ordinary room, but a large apartment, designed for wealthy visitors, long departed. Crumbling plasterwork on the ceiling, an ornate, but hacked-about fireplace, draped with scraps of clothes, and lavishly decorated alcoves would have

These houses on the west side of Avon Street were pulled down to extend James Street West. The group standing outside the door of one of Avon Street's many lodging houses includes a member of Bath's black community, whose story is a forgotten part of the city's heritage. Scenes such as this show that, even in a street with such severe social problems, people still managed to live lives of decency and dignity.

spoken of its former glories, as flies buzzed in cracked yellow window panes. Many panes would be missing, the gaps stuffed with rags.

Into this once elegant apartment would be crammed as many as 15 beds, with little room between them. The residents' few belongings would be stuffed under the beds, hung from makeshift hooks on the wall or piled on shelves in the alcoves. Some of the lodgers would be in bed, snoring off last night's excesses or simply lying there because they could think of no good reason to get up. Others would be sitting on their beds, staring at the walls, chatting idly or indulging in a game of cards. It is unlikely that any of them would be reading; learning to read was a luxury their childhoods had not included. Lack of any other forms of entertainment that we take for granted – radio or television, for example – meant that their lives had an emptiness and lack of stimulus that we would find terrifying. All they had, apart from talking, singing and playing a few rudimentary games, were drinking and sex.

Only a few traces of the wallpaper that once covered the walls would be left; the cracked and peeling plaster underneath would be smeared with filth and adorned with the initials of previous residents and crude, probably obscene, drawings. The stench would have been appalling. Under most of the beds would be a chamber pot, surrounded by a rich legacy of spillages and imperfect aims.

Then you would be shown your bed. Its blankets and sheets – if there were sheets – would almost certainly not have been changed since the departure of the bed's last occupant. Whatever he or she had done or left in the bed would still be there. Fleas, lice and enough assorted wild life to keep David Attenborough busy for weeks would be everywhere. Looking at your bed and around the room, thinking that this was all you were worth in the great scheme of things, must have been dispiriting beyond all measure. Hardly surprising that so many people who ended up in Avon Street drank themselves into a stupor or threw themselves into the river.

Conditions like these were a breeding ground for every kind of sexual licence, abuse, and deviance, often – though by no means always – accompanied by an exchange of money or other favours. Bullying and a primitive form of gangland rule, often organised by extended families, would have been a feature of community life. The arm of the law was rarely long enough to stretch down Avon Street, most of whose residents were united in their hatred of the police.

All cities had their slum quarters, although possibly not in such formerly lavish surroundings. And Bath, with its large immigrant population, had at least one advantage over many other cities. The endemic, generation-on-generation inbreeding that was a feature of life in places with more settled populations was much less apparent in Bath.

Life, however, was not unrelievedly grim for the residents of Avon Street, as this report from the *Bath Chronicle* of 6 May 1852 indicates:

> The "Merrie Month of May" was welcomed with the usual din of drums, and discordant sounds and capering of the sooty fraternity, decked in gaudy and absurd attire, issuing from the classic region of Avon Street. Why sweeps

THE LOST PUBS OF BATH

should rejoice on the day on which many persons sound the curfew, as far as their parlour fires are concerned, and thus curtail "Othello's occupation," might puzzle the world; but the gentlemen of the black robe, on this occasion, kindly informed Her Majesty's public of their reasons by a blue banner emblazoned with the following legend in bright letters:

IN REMEMBRANCE OF LADY MONTAGUE'S SON
WHO WAS STOLEN BY THE GIPSIES
& SOLD TO A SWEEP
& FOUND ON THE
1ST OF MAY

Which part of the pageant was intended to bring to "remembrance" the fair son of Lady Montague was very doubtful, nor could enquiry of the "mummers" elucidate the mystery.

Inevitably, there were loads of pubs in Avon Street. In 1776 there were eleven – one for every eight houses. By 1806, a clampdown by the Council had reduced this to three, but after the 1830 Beerhouse Act the number shot up to seven. Six managed to hang on till the beginning of the twentieth century. Two closed in 1901; a third in 1906. The remaining three closed in the 1930s, and today all trace of them has disappeared.

At the top of Avon Street, opposite the Globe, was the **Lord Nelson**, which opened as the Crown sometime before 1776 and became the Crown & Thistle around 1790, before being renamed around 1811. It was commonly known, however, as the Pig & Whistle. When Charles Westmacott published *The English Spy*, a *vade mecum* for gentlemen of independent means, in 1826, he included a vivid description of the delights of "the long room at the Pig & Whistle":

The house was formerly, it would appear, known by the sign of the Crown & Thistle, and was at that time the resort of the Irish Traders who visited Bath to dispose of their linens. One of the Emeralders having lost his way, and being unable either to recollect either the name of the street or the sign of his inn, thus addressed a countryman whom he accidentally met:

"Sure, I've quite forgotten the sign of my inn."

"Be after mentioning something like it, my jewel," said his friend.

"Sure, it's very like the Pig & Whistle," replied his enquirer.

"By the powers, so it is – the Crown & Thistle, you mean"; and from this mistake of the Emeralder the house has ever since been so designated.

Upon our visit to this scene of uproarious mirth, we found it frequented by the lowest and most depraved characters in society; the mendicants and miserable of the female sex, who, lost to every sense of shame and decency, assemble here to indulge in profligacies, the full description of which must not stain the pages of *The English Spy*. A gallon of gin for the ladies, and a liberal distribution of beer and tobacco for the males, made us very welcome guests, and insured us, during our short stay, at least from personal interruption. It may be asked why such a house is licensed by the magistracy; but when it is known that characters of this sort will always be found in well-populated places, and that the doors are regularly closed at eleven o'clock, it is perhaps thought to be a measure of prudence to let them continue to assemble in an obscure part of the suburbs, where they congregate together under the vigilant eye of the police, instead of being driven abroad to seek fresh places of resort, and by this means increase the evils of society.

Westmacott's vignette gives us an insight into a side of Bath that other commentators chose to ignore. It also underlines the extent to which Avon Street was, as much as anything else, a rich man's playground, with prostitution the driving force of its economy A cartoon by Robert Cruickshank of the "Buff Club at the Pig & Whistle, Avon Street, Bath" accompanies Westmacott's description and hints at some of the profligacies he disdains to mention.

Westmacott's view that it was better to keep places like the Pig & Whistle open so that the police could keep an eye on them may have been shared by the Corporation, but it was not one to which the government were amenable. The same year that Westmacott's book appeared (possibly as a result of the interest generated by it), Sir Robert Peel, the Home Secretary, contacted the Mayor to ask why the Pig & Whistle's licence had not been revoked. The Mayor sent back an evasive reply which failed to give the main reason for the pub's survival – it was owned by John Grant Smith of the Anchor Brewery, who had influential friends on the council.

The Pig & Whistle not only survived; it consolidated its reputation as Avon Street's top knocking shop. When the railway came to Bath, it did not take Brunel's navvies long to discover its charms. One Sunday afternoon in 1841, for example, a police inspector stuck his head round the door to be confronted by around 20

The Buff Club at the Pig & Whistle.

THE LOST PUBS OF BATH

railway navvies and a similar number of prostitutes in various stages of undress and intoxication. If that could happen on a Sunday afternoon, imagine what Saturday night was like.

By the time of the 1903 report, things seemed to have quietened down somewhat. The inspector described it as consisting of a bar with a small tap room beyond. There were "a few edibles for sale such as eggs, pickles, etc." It closed three years later; today the Technical College's Westgate Building stands on the site.

Next door but one to the Lord Nelson was the **Fountain**, which opened some time before 1792 and was the largest pub in Avon Street. The following newspaper report, describing a midsummer Sunday afternoon at the Fountain in 1849, gives some idea what the landlords of the time had to put up with:

> On Sunday afternoon last, through the outrageous conduct of a man named James Tiley, Avon Street was the scene of one of the most disgraceful episodes that can render a locality disgraceful. It appeared that this man had been drinking at the Fountain public house, where he conducted himself so offensively that the landlord was obliged to eject him by force; but in doing so he was much resisted and abused by some of Tiley's acquaintances who came to his aid. After the fellow was eventually expelled, he deliberately smashed about 20 panes of glass in the windows of the house, one after another, with his fist ... The police were sent for and on their appearance Tiley bolted down the street, sheltered by a group of his friends, and being closely pursued, he entered the house of a woman named McDonald, where the policemen met with the most determined resistance in attempting to capture him. The inmates assailed them with all kinds of abusive epithets, and threatened to attack them with pikes and other such weapons, while a large mob outside joined in abetting the outrages within. The officers were at last obliged to give up the contest, and to leave Tiley behind. They succeeded, however, in taking the woman into custody for aiding in resistance. She was bailed to appear when Tiley may be brought up, a warrant against him having been applied for.

Less than three years later, the windows of the Fountain were smashed again, this time by a mob baying for the blood of an Irishman who had taken refuge in the pub.[*]

The landlord of the Fountain at this time was William Chancellor. He left sometime in the 1850s and was succeeded by George Neil. He died in 1878 and his widow, Mary Anne Neil, took over the pub. By the time she handed over the licence to her son-in-law, Martin Harris, in 1891, she was the oldest licensee in Bath. The Fountain closed in 1901, but reopened as a club the following year. The club closed sometime before the Great War and the Fountain became a lodging house. It was pulled down in the 1930s to make way for a Co-op. The Co-op building is now Choices Video Superstore.

---

*The full story can be found in *Awash With Ale*, p66.

The Fountain, with the landlord, Martin Harris, at the door.

THE LOST PUBS OF BATH

Above Garibaldi made such an impression on his visit to Bath in 1864 that a pub was named after him.
Right The Oddfellows' Arms patriotically bedecked for the Coronation of George V in 1911.

Six doors down from the Fountain, at No 10, where the Games Workshop on the corner of James Street West now stands, was the **Garibaldi**. John Baker, who was a greengrocer there from around 1856, opened it as a beerhouse in 1864, the year of Garibaldi's visit to Bath. It was a single-roomed pub with a brewery and stable yard at the back. The brewery kept going until around 1921; the Garibaldi closed in 1933 and was demolished shortly afterwards.

Twelve doors down from the Garibaldi, at No 22, was the **Smith's Arms**, which dated from before 1776 and closed in the 1850s. The small piazza in front of the Technical College's Macaulay Building marks its site.

Opposite the Smith's Arms, at No 70, was the **Oddfellows' Arms**. This was a single-barred beerhouse with a shop and tap room at the back. Opened by Charles Gibbs by 1839, it closed in 1939.

Back on the east side of the street, ten doors down from the Smith's Arms, at No 32, was a beerhouse called the **Shamrock**. It opened around 1839, and had a back entrance leading past the Jewish Synagogue into Corn Street, which was originally a cul de sac. In the late nineteenth century, Corn Street was extended through to Avon Street, and several houses south of the Shamrock were demolished. The new

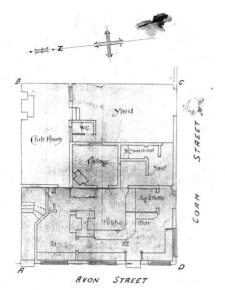

A plan of the Shamrock.

section of road, with the Shamrock on the corner was known for a time as New Corn Street. The 1903 report noted that one of the Shamrock's windows displayed sweets, tea and other groceries, and that children were served with these items at the jug & bottle entrance in Corn Street. It closed in 1938.

Ten doors below the Shamrock, at No 42, was the **Lamb**, a beerhouse-cum-grocer's next to the Bath City Iron & Brass Foundry. It opened around 1839 and closed in 1901. A multi-storey car park now covers the site.

At the bottom of Avon Street, on the corner of Narrow Quay, was the **Duke of York**, which opened around 1800. It was named after the Duke of York who commanded the English army in Flanders in 1794-95 and was immortalised in the song about marching 10,000 men to the top of the hill and marching them down again. Sometime after 1833, its licence was withdrawn by the magistrates, but it continued trading as a beerhouse until 1869. A newspaper report from 1851 indicates that it was a hotbed of criminal activity: a gang of pickpockets – John Skeates, John Curtis, Ann Harris and Mariah Green – were run to earth "at the Duke of York beerhouse on the Quay ... all sleeping in one room." Today, Green Park Road runs through the site.

Across the street, one door up from the end house, was a beerhouse called the **Jolly Sailor**. It was open from around 1837 to around 1848, with John Sumner as licensee.

So ends our virtual crawl of the pubs in Avon Street whose locations are known. There were many more. Eight were recorded in 1776 – the **Bird Cage**, the **Chequers**, the **Gallon Pot**, the **Hole in the Wall**, the **Lamb**, the **Rose**, the **Spread Eagle**, and the **White Hart**. All closed in the wake of the Gordon Riots in 1780, and most have left nothing but their names behind them. Advertisements featuring two of them, however – the Rose and the White Hart – have survived from the mid-eighteenth century. In February 1748, the house next to the Rose was advertised for sale; in 1771, "a modern Cassapus, or wonderful Giant," who had been entertaining visitors at the Three Cups in Northgate Street, "removed to a more genteel and airy room at the Rose in Avon Street." In November 1756, James Costard from London announced that he was staying at the White Hart in Avon Street, and teaching "the German Flute by the Month or Lesson on the most reasonable terms."

The former Jolly Sailor can be seen on the extreme right of this picture of flooding in the 1920s.

One pub did not even make it to 1776. The **Wheel** was open by 1746, when an advertisement appeared in the *Bath Journal*:

> Stables to be let; or horses' stand at livery, at 6d a night. Likewise good grass for horses at 2/- a week. Enquire of Absalom Fuller at the Sign of the Wheel in Avon Street, Bath.

It closed in 1763, when the house was advertised to be let, and "the Beer Casks, Brewing Utensils and Part of the Household Goods" were sold.

Finally, mention must be made of two more unlocated (and very short-lived) pubs – the **Bath Arms** (c1792) and the **Can & Bottle** (c1781).

§

We now walk east along Green Park Road to the corner of the Ambury. It is difficult to believe that, until the mid-twentieth century, this was the heart of Bath's dockland. Broad Quay (so called to distinguish it from Narrow Quay at the bottom of Avon Street) was built, according to John Wood, "in the year 1729, for the purpose of landing goods brought into the city by water." It was "480 feet in length by 97 feet in breadth" and contained "eleven houses; most of which were contrived by Mr Strahan." It always seems to have been something of a backwater. In 1819, for example, Pierce Egan wrote that, "notwithstanding the important name of Quay

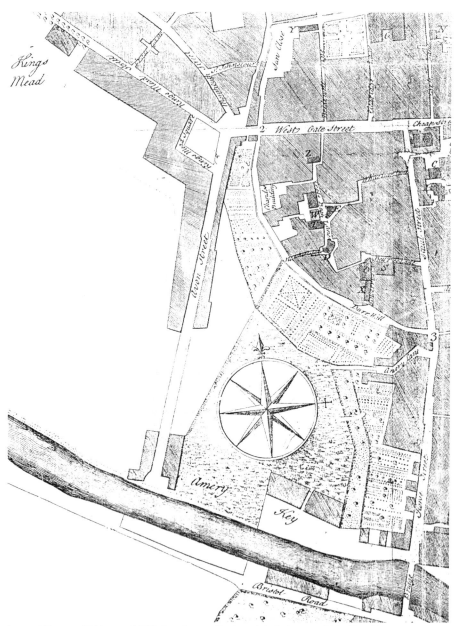

A map of Kingsmead Fields around 1755: Avon Street, still only partly built, has open fields either side.

THE LOST PUBS OF BATH

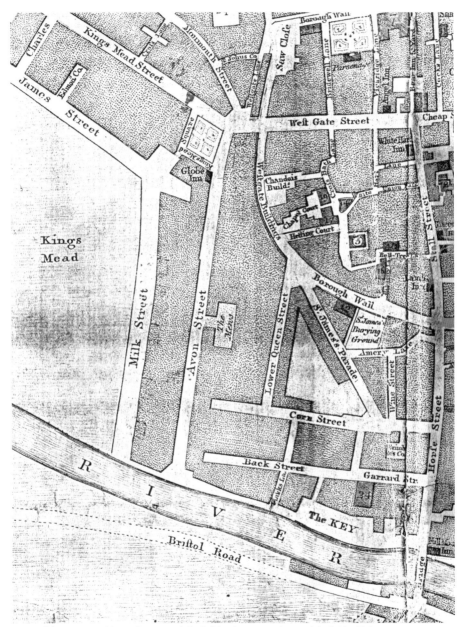

A map of the same area 30 years later: speculative builders have covered most of the fields with houses.

is attached to it, no bustle is experienced at this place, and it might be termed a river without any business; as merely a few stones lying on the ground from the different quarries, with not above a straggling solitary barge or two … seems the principal feature of traffic, which occupies the inhabitants of a few little houses situate alongside of the water."

Yet Broad Quay did have its moments of excitement. In 1795, at a time of national famine, 200 women boarded a barge loaded with grain intended for export to prevent it sailing. Despite singing "God Save the King" to indicate they were not republicans, they were dispersed by troops. Five years later, as food shortages continued, Williams' Brewery on Broad Quay was burnt down in protest at the hoarding of grain, with losses of around £20,000. Just in case anyone was tempted to think it was an accident, an anonymous letter was dropped into the Post Office, addressed to the Mayor and Corporation:

> Peace & a Large Bread or a King without a Head.
>
> As we can't make a rick, we'll do things more quick,
>
> As provisions get higher, the greater the fire.

Generally, though, Broad Quay seems to have been a fairly sleepy, if somewhat disreputable, place, only enlivened by the travelling fairs which set up there a couple of times a year. One of its star attractions, in the early twentieth century, was a chair-o-plane that swung its riders out over the river.

There were two pubs on Broad Quay. The **Chequers**, also known as the Jolly Angler, opened sometime before 1776. One day in 1783, Thomas Durrell spent a jolly afternoon and evening there, downing several quarts of strong beer. Unfortunately, on the way home, he fell into the river and drowned. The Chequers closed soon afterwards.

Broad Quay in the mid-eighteenth century.

THE LOST PUBS OF BATH

Broad Quay under water in January 1925.

The former Waterman's Arms, on the right.

THE LOST QUADRANT

The **Waterman's Arms**, which stood roughly where the south-west corner of the Ambury is today, opened as a beerhouse sometime around 1840. In 1915, the police opposed the renewal of its licence "on the grounds of redundancy," pointing out that there were seven other licensed houses within a radius of 250 yards. Not only was its accommodation "very poor," but it did "a very poor class of trade." All it had was one large bar with a window at the end of the passage for the jug & bottle trade.

The landlord admitted that he could not make a living out of the house and occasionally had to work as a coachman. However, a representative of the beerhouse's owners, Ruddles' Brewery of Bradford-on-Avon, argued that the pub was unique, being "more like a little country inn than any other house in Bath." The licence was grudgingly renewed and the Waterman's Arms struggled on for another 17 years, before closing in 1932.

Little Corn Street: the Rose & Crown stood roughly where the payment point is.

Fifty years ago, this would have been the view up Peter Street.

We now walk back along Green Park Road to the exit from Avon Street Car Park. This was once the entry to Little Corn Street, originally known as Clark's Lane. Its nickname was "Little 'Ell," and it had the reputation of being the worst street in Bath. By the payment point at the south-east corner of the multi-storey car park was the **Rose & Crown** at 16 Little Corn Street. It was opened as a beerhouse by Anthony Stidworthy in the 1830s and closed around 1869.

Just past the Rose & Crown, Back Street ran from east to west across Little Corn Street. Back Street also had a pub, the **Three Blue Posts**, open for a short time in the late eighteenth century.

On the north side of the car park, Little Corn Street met Corn Street. Corn Street still survives, but the street that continued on to the north has disappeared under the Technical College car park. The ramp up to the car park marks the approximate site of Peter Street, built in the 1770s and originally known as Lower Queen Street. On its left-hand corner, at No 14, was the **Chequers**, also known for a time as the Grapes. It seems to have attracted women of a certain disposition. In March 1837, for example,

> Elizabeth Webster was charged by Samuel Bailey, policeman, with striking him when he was called upon by the landlord of the Chequers in Peter Street, to turn her out of his house, she being in a state of intoxication.

Five years later, Anne Stephens was given six months hard labour for stealing a shawl off Mary Allen, a servant at the Chequers.

In the mid-nineteenth century, it was renamed the Old Chequers Brewery, and, around 1864, Charles Cavill, from Banwell in Somerset, became the landlord. He was

No photograph of the Chequers, on the south-west corner of Peter Street, has so far been found; this picture of the south-east corner of the street in the 1920s gives an idea what it may have been like.

there for over 20 years, and established something of a pub dynasty, four of his sons becoming publicans in Bath. In 1903, the premises, which consisted of a bar, tap room, bar parlour and an old brewhouse, were reported to be "very dilapidated." The Chequers closed ten years later. Its signboard was rescued, however, and can still be seen in the Museum of Bath at Work.

Corn Street dates from the 1770s, but has changed beyond all recognition. Not only have most of its original buildings gone; its layout has been radically altered. As we have already seen, the west end was a cul de sac until it was pushed through to Avon Street in the late nineteenth century. At the other end, Corn Street extended as far as Southgate Street until the section beyond St James's Parade was blocked off in the 1920s.

Although Corn Street today is a shadow of its former self, this is probably just as well. Take this newspaper report of forcible cross-dressing from October 1869, for example:

> George Hill, William Boodle and Joyce Powell were summoned – Hill for being disorderly in Margaret's Passage and the others with interfering with a police officer in the execution of his duty. On Tuesday afternoon ... there was a great

Two distant views of the Plasterer's Arms (indicated by a cross): from the west and from the east.

THE LOST PUBS OF BATH

disturbance in Corn Street and the neighbourhood and Hill was running attired in women's clothes. About 5.30 PC 50 (Weaver) took a woman named Taylor into custody when Boodle and the woman Powell tried to rescue her. Hill assured the magistrates that the woman's clothes were put on him against his will and that he was dragged to the top of the court. An alarm was raised that a policeman was coming and then Mrs Taylor and the man who had hold of him let him go and he at once took the things off. The other defendants denied having interfered with the police constable. Hill was discharged, and the other defendants were fined 10/6 and costs each or in default of payment 14 days hard labour.

Or this sorry tale of a mangle from February 1852:

A woman named Ross was summoned by William Newman for assaulting him on the evening of the 24th inst and a woman named George for inciting the defendant and using threatening and abusive language towards the prosecutor. All the parties are neighbours and reside in Baldwin's Court, Corn Street. A short while ago the complainant's wife died, and it was alleged that on her death bed she besought her husband not to sell her mangle, as the bread of the family depended on it. No heed was taken of this, but the mangle was sold, and a new lady-love was brought home, which proceeding very much incensed the neighbours, who thought a dying woman's words ought to be have been attended to. They were bound over to keep the peace for the space of three months.

At 22 Corn Street, just west of Little Corn Street, was a beerhouse called the **Bacchus**. It opened in the 1840s, was renamed the Traveller's Rest in the 1850s, reverted to the Bacchus in the 1860s, and finally became the Sumsion Brewery when Mary Sumsion took over in 1888. It consisted of a tap room and a bar in two compartments, with a brewery at the back. In the 1870s, the landlord, William Phipps ran a wood and coal dealer's business from the pub. It was closed in March 1934 under the Bath Corporation Improvement Scheme.

One of the few old buildings to have survived on Corn Street is the Mission Hall, now the Mission Theatre. Facing it, at No 16, was a beerhouse called the **Plasterer's Arms**, which opened around 1854. It was renamed the Hope & Anchor around 1860 and closed around 1869. JB Bowler, who owned several other premises in Corn Street, bought the old Plasterer's Arms in 1905.

Continuing east along the street, we come to the north end of the Ambury, that short stretch of road wedged between an office block and a car park, where you can pretend you're abroad, as you drive on the right hand side of the road (with bollards down the middle in case you decide you don't like it halfway along). The houses that once lined the Ambury, built in the 1760s by Thomas Jelly, Henry Fisher and Richard Jones, have gone, but in the mid-nineteenth century you would have found

The Ambury in the floods of February 1937.

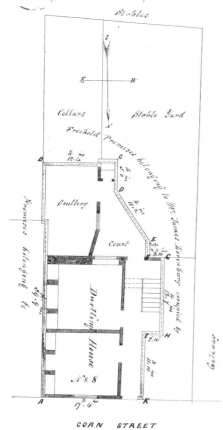

CORN STREET

A plan of the Bird in Hand in 1861, shortly before it was renamed the Albion Brewery.

a beerhouse down there. The **Heart in Hand** stood on the west side of the street at No 5. In October 1834, "the landlord of the Heart in Hand beerhouse, in the Ambury [was] fined 20/- and costs for allowing tippling in his house after 11 o'clock at night." Two hands holding a heart is an ancient sign of fellowship, and the name of the pub suggests that it was the meeting place of a friendly society. As well as a bar, bar parlour, and tap room, the Heart in Hand had a shop, bakehouse and brewery.

Around 1870 it changed its name to the Ambury Brewery and was acquired by John Davis of the Bear on Wellsway. In 1896, JB Bowler bought it for £150 and closed it down.

On the other side of the Ambury lies the old Forum – a lost cinema converted to a church. The back doors of the Forum mark the site of the **Bird in Hand** at 8 Corn Street. The building, although not the pub, dated from 1782, when Owen Batchelor leased a plot of land from St John's Hospital to build a dwelling house. The lease stipulated that the building could not be used by a "butcher, slaughterman, poulterer, tallow chandler, maker of tallow, soap boiler, distiller, vintner, victualler, farrier, blacksmith, brazier, coppersmith, pewterer, baker, leather dresser, currier, founder or plumber ... or any other noisome, offensive or troublesome trade or calling." The implication is clear. Corn Street was to be a street of respectable lodging houses, with nothing allowed to mar the residents' quiet enjoyment of their secluded backwater. With the great flood of 1774 fresh in the memory and the stews of Avon Street a stone's throw

THE LOST PUBS OF BATH

away, the developers were either wildly optimistic or out to make a quick killing from those whose knowledge of Bath was based on guidebooks rather than experience.

Not surprisingly, Corn Street went downhill faster than a steamroller without brakes. In 1795, Owen Batchelor went bankrupt, and St John's, despite the caveats of 13 years earlier, leased the building to a victualler called Thomas Humber, who opened it as a pub. In 1815, the Bird in Hand was taken over by the Anchor Brewery, who gave up the lease of the Bell (now the Raincheck Bar) in Monmouth Street in exchange.

Some of its customers, as might be expected, were a little dubious. One Saturday night in 1829, for example,

> the landlord of the Bird in Hand Public House in Corn Street, on retiring to bed between eleven and twelve o'clock, found that the lock of his bedroom door had been picked and his writing desk ransacked of £47 in sovereigns and silver. The robbery is thought to have been committed by three men who supped at the house.

A display of patriotic enthusiasm outside the Albion Brewery.

Nevertheless, the Bird in Hand, which was renamed the Albion Brewery in the 1860s, was quite an upmarket establishment. It had a bar, tap room, parlour, sitting room, long room, skittle alley, brewery, and four bedrooms. In the late nineteenth and early twentieth century the licensee was Thomas Stride. It closed in 1924.

Although most of old Corn Street, including JB Bowler's works and the Jewish Synagogue, disappeared years ago, one of its old pubs is still standing, although the pumps ran dry almost a century ago. On what was once the eastern corner of Corn Street and St James's Parade, before the way through to Southgate Street was blocked off, stands the old **Malt & Hops**, now the Lombard Money Shop. Today its address is 30 St James's Parade; it was originally 37 Corn Street.

The former Malt & Hops, the only one of Corn Street's pubs still standing.

The Malt & Hops opened some time before 1826. Its bar was divided into three compartments, one of which was a jug & bottle. At one side was a smoking room with a mahogany centre table and eight Windsor chairs. It closed in 1911, the renewal of its licence being refused "on the grounds of the house being ill-conducted," and became a pawnbroker's.

Corn Street from Southgate Street, showing the side entrance to the former Somerset Wine Vaults (1) and the former Corn Street Brewery (2).

On the south side of the section of Corn Street between St James's Parade and Southgate Street was a beerhouse called the **Corn Street Brewery**. It was one door along from Southgate Street and opened around 1837. The 1903 report on the property described it as follows:

> No back door. Bar with seats. Private bar on right and smoke room behind. Club room upstairs seldom used.

It closed in 1906 and later became Littlejohn & Owen's Dining Rooms. It now lies under McDonald's.

Fifty years ago, this would have been the view down Peter Street.

A stroll up St James's Parade, past the Bath Tap, opened in 1824 as the Devonshire Arms, brings us to what was once the north end of Peter Street, facing the Hobgoblin pub. Just before Peter Street was built, in 1780, the site was used for the execution of John Butler, the Gordon Rioter.* A century ago, Peter Street boasted two greengrocers, a dressmaker, a pork butcher, a coal merchant, a grocer, and two pubs, both of which opened shortly after the street was built. We have already seen the site of one pub – the Chequers – at the southern end. Three doors down from the northern end, on the west side, was the other. In the early nineteenth century, the **Mason's Arms** was the meeting place of a benefit society called the

*His story appears in *Awash With Ale*, pp 72-80.

THE LOST PUBS OF BATH

Looking down Peter Street towards Corn Street after the area had been cleared.

Old Bath Society. It had its own brewery, and three bars – parlour, bar parlour, and tap room. The bar parlour was quite select, boasting a musical snuff box, paintings, barometer, brass tobacco box, draught board, brass dominoes, a *Bath Directory* and a four-motion beer engine. The 1903 report found the pub "fair at front, dilapidated behind." It closed in 1924.

Walking back down the east side of St James's Parade, we pass the Lounge Bar at No 43. This was a short-lived real-ale pub called the **Heath Robinson**, which opened just in time for Fred Pearce to file a report on it in his 1976 *Critical Guide to Bath Pubs*:

> Brand new real ale bar set up to take advantage of the boom. Still perhaps without a true character of its own; it's just a bit like drinking in a shop front. But it's nice to see darts and shove ha'penny installed in such a small bar. On sale are 6X, Worthington E and South Wales Club Best Bitter (its only Bath outlet) all at 26p and Wadworth's Old Timer at 33p ... The bare unpolished wood tables and kitchen chairs bar decor is enlivened by brewers' publicity posters and some Heath Robinson manic machine drawings. Radio One is the only music. Our tip for the top.

33p for a pint of beer - even very strong beer - was steep in 1976, but if it had risen in line with inflation it would still be less than £1.50 today. Instead, the price of a pint of strong beer now stands at around £2.60. If the same rate of increase continues – which all those experts who once thought endowment policies a good idea tell us cannot possibly happen – we will be paying £20.50 (or its equivalent in euros) for a premium pint by 2036.

The Heath Robinson later became the Beau Nash Tavern, later still Mother's, before being reinvented as the Lounge Bar.

At the southern end of the block was a beerhouse called the **St James's Tavern**. It opened around 1830 and closed in 1879.

A left turn into Amery Lane brings us into one of Bath's least known thoroughfares, Wine Street. On the east side of the street, now lined with service areas for shops in Southgate Street, were three short-lived pubs.

First was the **Chequers**, which was there by 1776 and disappeared around 1809.

Then there was the gloriously styled **Leg of Mutton & Cauliflower** (a mouthful in more ways than one) which was also there by 1776 but which disappeared shortly afterwards. And, in case you are thinking its name must have been unique, there is still an eighteenth-century inn called the Leg of Mutton & Cauliflower at Ashtead in Surrey.

Finally, there was the **Isabella**, a beerhouse which opened in the 1830s and closed in the 1840s.

At the bottom of Wine Street, we pass the old Malt & Hops once again before turning left, crossing the road and walking down to the main entrance to the Forum,

Wine Street in 1963: at least three of the buildings on the right-hand side were former pubs

THE LOST PUBS OF BATH

on the corner of Somerset Street. A century ago, a beerhouse called the **Somerset Arms** stood on this spot. It opened in the 1850s and closed in 1909.

On the other side of Somerset Street, facing the Somerset Arms, was a short-lived beerhouse called the **Hole in the Wall**, which opened – and closed – in the early 1830s.

West of the Hole in the Wall was a Plymouth Brethren Meeting House. Beyond that was Mawer & Tanner's Malthouse, which dominated the whole area, and was demolished with explosives in 1974.

On the north side of Somerset Street (which, incidentally, was originally called Garrard Street after its developer), just where the wall of the Forum curves to the right, was another beerhouse. It was opened by Robert Baggs in the 1830s, but closed before he got round to naming it.

Somerset Street was not always a cul de sac. Once you could continue westward, along Back Street. Now, at the end of one of the shortest streets in Bath, a flight of steps leads down to the Ambury, and on into Avon Street car park. We will turn our back on this scene of devastation, however, to find another one, on the far side of Southgate Street.

Most of the lost pubs we have visited so far closed so long ago, few will remember them. Many we will encounter in the latter part of this excursion, however, closed much more recently.

§

There is not much left of Dorchester Street; what there is will soon be swept away by the new Southgate Development. Although few people will shed tears for one of Bath's busiest and least-loved thoroughfares, some still have fond memories of two pubs that once stood on the north side of the street.

Just along from Southgate Street was the **South Pole**. It opened around 1837, and was at one time known as the South Pole Brewery & Hotel. In its heyday it had nine bedrooms, a drawing room, a private bar, a bar parlour (with three stuffed settees), a serving bar, a tap room, and a brewery. It closed around 1970 and the site is now covered by Boots the Chemist.*

On the western corner of Newark Street was the **Great Western Hotel**. When it opened around 1850, it was known as the Railway Tavern or the Railway Station

---

*As with the excursion down Southgate Street, we have tried to indicate where lost pubs stood by reference to present-day landmarks. However, the proposed redevelopment of the Southgate area is likely to render many of these directions meaningless.

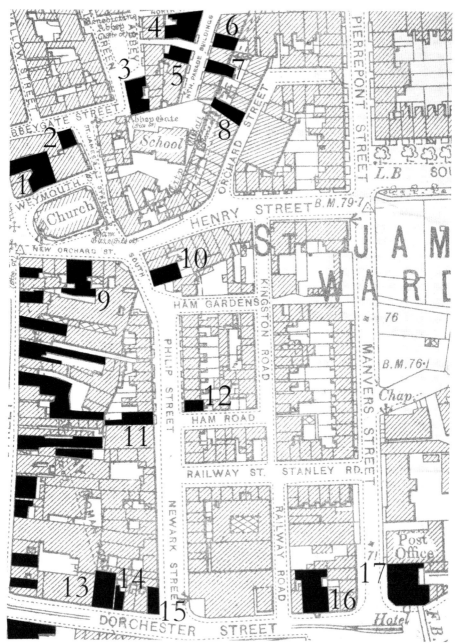

The eastern sector of the lost quadrant: 1) the Golden Lion; 2) the Talbot; 3) the Raven, later the Freemasons' Tavern; 4) the North Parade Brewery; 5) the Woodman; 6) the Waterloo; 7) the Queen's Arms; 8) the Shakespeare; 9) the Crown Brewery; 10) the Ship; 11) the Edinburgh Castle; 12) the Manvers' Arms; 13) the South Pole; 14) the Paul Pry; 15) the Great Western Hotel; 16) the Railway Hotel. The Royal Hotel (17) alone survives.

THE LOST PUBS OF BATH

Two views of the South Pole.

The Great Western Hotel.

Tavern. It was renamed when the Midland Railway opened a station at Green Park in 1869. It closed around 1971. It stood roughly where Somerfield's is today, although somewhat further forward.

Next to the South Pole was a pub that no one will remember, the **Paul Pry**. It opened as a beerhouse in the early 1830s and closed around 1840. *Paul Pry* was a play by John Poole, first produced in 1825, which featured a character who meddled in other people's affairs. So popular was the play that several pubs were named after him, including one still open in Peterborough.

The site of the Railway Hotel.

Further along Dorchester Street, a row of red telephone boxes stands on the site of the **Railway Hotel**, which opened as the Manvers' Arms in the 1840s and was renamed in 1861.* The history of the Railway Hotel was uneventful. Not so its demise. The licensing register brings down the curtain on it with the terse entry, "destroyed by enemy action, 1942."

We now retrace our steps to the bottom of Newark Street and walk up past the bus station. On the west side of the street was the **Edinburgh Castle**. This opened in the 1840s and, for a brief period around 1900, was known as the Newark Brewery. Brewing ceased around 1921, but, although the Edinburgh Castle was badly damaged in the Bath Blitz, and had to be closed while repairs were carried out, it survived until 1971, when the town planners completed the job started by the Luftwaffe.

---

*In a move designed to confused future pub historians, the Druids' Arms in nearby Philip Street was renamed the Manvers' Arms around 1870.

Looking up Newark Street towards the Abbey in the 1920s ...

... the same view today.

The Edinburgh Castle in the 1950s.

THE LOST PUBS OF BATH

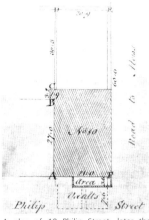

A plan of 10 Philip Street, later the Manvers' Arms, in 1812.

Opposite the Edinburgh Castle, on the corner of Philip Street, the entrance to the multi-storey car park stands on the site of the **Manvers' Arms**. It was built in 1812 by John Allen, one of Bath's biggest property developers, as his private residence. Allen was also one of the city's most famous radicals. At the time, Bath had a population of 38,000, but only a handful of people, nominated by the Corporation, were entitled to vote. Allen, despite being one of the richest men in the city, was not among them. In a curious echo of Henry Chapman's alternative election of 1661 (see page 29), he offered himself as a parliamentary candidate in opposition to those selected by the Corporation and organised a ballot. After achieving a comfortable majority, he declared himself MP for Bath. The Corporation was not impressed, and arrested him as he was making a victory speech outside the Guildhall. A major riot ensued, in which many of the Guildhall's windows were smashed and troops had to be called out to restore order. Although the Corporation's candidates took their seats, Allen's alternative election was an important step forward on the road to electoral reform.

Allen's house in Philip Street was the nerve centre of his campaign for parliamentary and local government reform. Once reform had been achieved and Allen elected an alderman, he moved to Hanover Square, off the London Road, and the house became a pub. Whether this was his idea, or whether its original name – the Druids' Arms – indicated his membership of a druidic order, is unknown. The Druids' Arms consisted of a main bar, bar parlour, tap room, drawing room, sitting room (with a stuffed squirrel in a glass case), and brewery. It was renamed the Manvers' Arms in 1874 and closed in 1911.

North of the Manvers' Arms, Philip Street led into St James's Street South. On the right-hand side, just before New Orchard Street, was the **Ship**, which opened as a beerhouse around 1837. It later became the Old Ship or Ye Olde Ship and closed in 1957.

The Bath Bacon & Sausage Factory stood opposite the Ship, with its main entrance on the corner of St James's Street South and New Orchard Street. Next to it, on New Orchard Street, was the **Crown Brewery**. Built around 1850, at the same time as the Bacon and Sausage Factory, it was an imposing exercise in Victorian Palladianism, possibly modelled on an early eighteenth-century building in St James's Street South. Sadly, this early example of neo-classicism has disappeared, along with the building that may have inspired it. The Crown, originally a beerhouse, obtained a full licence in 1876, and at one time brewed beer for the Old Farmhouse and the White Horse (now the Dark Horse) in Northampton Street. Although they are both still going, the Crown closed on 6 December 1967 and was demolished shortly afterwards.

New Orchard Street in the 1930s, with the Bacon & Sausage Factory on the corner and the Crown Brewery (with triangular pediment) next to it ...

... the same view today.

THE LOST PUBS OF BATH

The Crown Brewery can just be seen on the right of this photograph of St James's Church.

THE LOST QUADRANT

Where St James's Church once stood: redevelopment under way in 1957.

THE LOST PUBS OF BATH

An early eighteenth-century house in St James's Street South: the inspiration for the Crown Brewery? Incredibly, this building fell victim not to Hitler's bombs but Bath's bulldozers.

The former Shakespeare Tavern.

After all these vanished pubs, we head for Old Orchard Street to find one that is still there, even though it has been dry since 1917. Originally plain Orchard Street (so called because it stood on the site of the Abbey Orchard), this quiet backwater was once one of the busiest and most fashionable streets in Bath. From 1750 to 1805 what is now the Masonic Hall was the Theatre Royal, one of the most celebrated playhouses in the country. On the other side of the road – now the Bath Spiritualist Church – was the **Shakespeare Tavern**.

It was built around 1748, probably by Thomas Jelly, at the same time as Gallaway's Buildings, to which there was an exit through the yard at the back.* At the time, Orchard Street led directly into Ham Gardens and commanded "a delightful prospect of the Avon and fields and woods opposite." Not until 1806 – after the theatre had moved to its present site – was the first stone of Henry Street laid, beginning the process of turning Old Orchard Street into the claustrophobic, hemmed-in backwater it is today.

The Shakespeare was originally known as the Pineapple. It probably opened at the same time as the theatre, although the earliest record of it comes from December 1762, when the *Bath Journal* reported the death of "Mr Wild who kept the Pineapple in Orchard Street." The sign of the pineapple usually denoted a confectioner's and the earliest instances of it are generally supposed to date from around 1770. The early use of the name in Bath suggests a possible link to the pineapple pits at Devizes which were developed by Adam Taylor in the mid-eighteenth century. Such a delicacy would have been much sought after by fashionable society and the tavern across the road from the Theatre Royal would have been an ideal place to sell it. And Mrs Malaprop's famous gaff in Sheridan's Bath-based play *The Rivals* – "he is the very pineapple of politeness" – was the kind of in-joke fashionable audiences would have lapped up.

Perhaps there was also a hidden barb in the juxtaposition of the words Pineapple and Politeness. If the tavern had started to be shunned by polite society because of unseemly goings-on, then "the Pineapple of Politeness" may have been just the sort

*The head of the sealed-up archway that led to the Shakespeare can still be seen at the south-east end of Gallaway's Buildings.

of ironic label that stuck. And this in turn may explain why in 1776, the year after *The Rivals* was first performed, the tavern was renamed the King's Arms. It changed its name once again – to the Shakespeare – in 1805, the year that the Theatre Royal moved to its present site in the Sawclose.

Once the theatre had gone, Old Orchard Street – and the Shakespeare – went rapidly downhill. In 1851, it was one of seven pubs which the police wanted to close because they opened on Sundays and were frequented by "prostitutes and other bad characters."

By 1917 the landlord of the Shakespeare was Albert Ash. A report from the *Bath Chronicle* of 17 February indicates it was not an orderly house:

The adjourned meeting of the Bath Licensing Justices was held on Friday morning ... Mr FE Weatherly [a local barrister who also wrote the words of *Roses of Picardy* and *Danny Boy*] said he was present on behalf of Mr Ash to apply for a renewal of the licence of the Shakespeare Inn.

Mr JB Ogden of the Town Clerk's department said that in this case the Chief Constable had served a notice of objection on Mr Albert Ash, who was the licensee of the Shakespeare Inn, Old Orchard Street, a fully licensed house. The objection of the Chief Constable to the renewal of the licence was twofold – first, that the premises had been ill-conducted; and second, that Mr Ash was not a fit and proper person to hold the licence. The licensee had been convicted of five offences during the past 15 months. On December 23rd 1915 he was convicted of selling intoxicating liquor to a drunken person, and also permitting a soldier, who was an inmate of a military hospital, to be on his premises. The two offences related to the same person. On January 25th this year Mr Ash was convicted of three offences for giving more intoxicating liquor to customers than was demanded ... On January 25th the chairman of the magistrates remarked that he considered the cases of Mr and Mrs Ash very bad cases, and that the house was apparently very badly conducted, as according to the statement of their own witnesses, both the licensee and his wife were often away from the premises at the same time. On that occasion Mr Ash went into the witness box and gave what can only be described as a most lamentable exhibition of silliness and irresponsibility. He was asked questions with regard to the way he conducted the house, and his demeanour in the box was such as to convince everybody he was not fit to control other persons on licensed premises. On January 16th PC Jones called at the house to make enquiries in reference to the long pull cases, and he was greeted by Mrs Ash with very strong language, which showed that, at any rate, she was not fit to be the partner of a man who held a licence. In June and September 1913, police were called into the premises in consequence of disturbances between the licensee and Florence Ruth Giles, the barmaid. Again in March 1916, Sergeant Horler received a complaint from Mr Ash that he had been assaulted by Florence Ruth Giles. According to his instruction, the barmaid, Miss Giles, was the woman who was now passing as Mr Ash's wife. On March 26th 1916, Miss Giles came to the police station and complained of being assaulted by the licensee, with whom she was cohabiting, and she had a black eye, which she said had been caused by Ash striking her with a flower pot. It appeared that the relations between Ash and the woman with whom he was cohabiting were not of a happy character ... Chief Inspector Beamish gave evidence as to Mr Ash's demeanour and statements in the box on January 25th. Mr Ash did not seem to be responsible for his statements or actions. He appeared to be steeped in drink, and the Chairman said he did not believe the statements he had made in the box.

Sergeant Hembury said he was present in Court when Mr Ash was convicted of the offences in December 1915. Witness took down a statement from Mr Ash who struck him as an irresponsible person. He seemed to be not drunk, but soaked in drink. That was witness's impression then and on subsequent occasions.

Mr Weatherly: "Do you know he has been ill for some time, and was confined to his bed?"

"No, sir."

PC Horler stated that on March 18th last year he received a complaint from Mr Ash and accompanied him to the house. There Mrs Ash said to Mr Ash: "You know when you had the accident in the leg with the pistol how it occurred – what you were going to do with me. So you had best hush up"

Sergeant Maynard spoke to a complaint made by Miss Giles of Mr Ash having assaulted her by throwing a flower pot in her eye, and on that occasion witness and PC Hembury visited the inn, and found the drawing room in great disorder.

Mr Weatherly said that taking the licence away would be too severe a punishment as it would significantly reduce the value of the property.* "The business," Mr Weatherly continued, "has been in the same family, father and son, since 1832, and up to December 1915 nothing was known against the licensee of the house." He was clearly unaware of the police's attempt to have it shut down in 1851.

Despite Mr Weatherly's plea, the application for the renewal of the licence was refused. After it closed, the Shakespeare was a Centre for the Blind before being converted to a Spiritualist Church.

There was two other pubs in Old Orchard Street. The **Duke of Cumberland** was listed in the alehouse recognizances for 1776, but closed shortly afterwards. Its exact location is unknown.

In the early 1860s, a beerhouse called the **Prince of Wales** opened at 19 Old Orchard Street. It closed less than ten years later, and was forgotten about until almost a century later, when the stonework on the building was cleaned and the name of the pub, in letters extending the length of the building, between the first- and second-

---

*How times have changed: today, many pub owners are fighting to close pubs so they can realise the residential or commercial value tied up in them.

floor windows, was revealed once more. A photograph was taken before work recommenced and this last legacy of the Prince of Wales was obliterated forever. And on that sobering note, our excursion through Bath's lost quadrant comes to an end.

Words on walls: the Prince of Wales in Old Orchard Street.

THE LOST PUBS OF BATH

EXCURSION THE NINTH

BATHWICK

In 1743, Bathwick was described as

> a place for the people of Bath to walk to … Many of them has gardens with
> pleasure houses to which they resort. It also has a small number of inhabitants
> who are gardeners which supply the Bath with greens and roots.

Six years later, John Wood wrote that "many of the citizens of Bath have already
beautified the village by their little places of retirement in it."

The village of Bathwick lay round the old church, the forerunner of the present
St John's. It was an isolated spot. To get to Bath, most people took the ferry across
to Boatstall Lane. The only alternative was a long detour through Widcombe, across

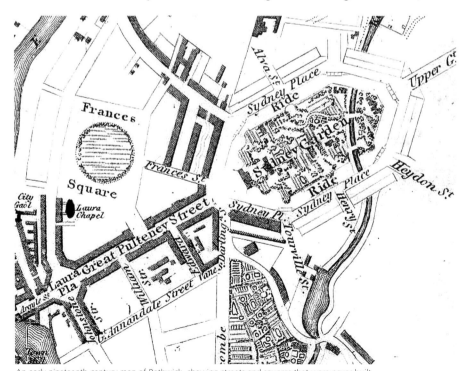

An early nineteenth-century map of Bathwick, showing streets and squares that were never built.

the Old Bridge and up Southgate Street. All this changed in the 1770s when William Johnstone Pulteney, whose wife had inherited the Bathwick Estate, decided to build a New Town there.

The first thing William Pulteney had to do was build a bridge across the river. He engaged Robert Adam to come up with a design, and the result is one of the most famous pieces of urban landscape in the world. Pulteney Bridge dates from the early 1770s and, although one of its piers collapsed less than 30 years later, it still survives today, despite the procession of double-decker buses trundling over it.

The unusual thing about Pulteney Bridge is that, like the Ponte Vecchio in Florence and the Rialto in Venice, it has shops on it, so that the unsuspecting visitor can wander across it without realising he has crossed a river. In the early nineteenth century this was seen as a distinct disadvantage. In 1839, there was a campaign for the shops to be pulled down so that the bridge could be widened and visitors look out over the river But the bridge survived and today vies with the Royal Crescent and the Abbey for the title of Bath's most famous building.

Our ninth excursion starts outside the gift shop at 15-16 Pulteney Bridge. In the early 1860s, a tobacconist at 16 Pulteney Bridge obtained a licence to sell beer. Later he expanded into No 15 and called his establishment the **Pulteney Stores**. It only lasted till 1903, but what a glorious place to sit, drink, and, no doubt, smoke it must have been, looking out of the window at the weir below. The bar had a four-motion beer engine, a painted, panelled, mahogany-topped counter, a glazed cigar cabinet, seven snuff jars and two spittoons. The smoking room had fixed seating round the walls, a couple of chairs, two drinking tables, a long deal form, a crib board, a card board, and three pictures on the wall. Today 15 & 16 Pulteney Bridge sells souvenirs and doll's house miniatures. Dolls are obviously fond of a tipple, because you can still buy beer here, although, at £2.50 for a bottle no bigger than your little finger, this must be, on any reckoning, the most expensive pint in Bath. And what, one wonders, would it taste like.

Although it lost its licence in 1903, Nos 15-16 Pulteney Bridge remained a tobacconist's until well into the twentieth century.

THE LOST PUBS OF BATH

The former Argyle Coffee House as it is today ...
... and in the 1950s, as the offices of the Bath Coal Company.

There was at least one other alcoholic establishment on Pulteney Bridge. In January 1795, John Gould, a "private bookseller and stationer" at 18 Pulteney Bridge, "opened vaults for the sale of British and Foreign Spirits at the following reduced prices":

Best Coniac Brandy	18/- gallon
Fine Jamaica Rum	14/- gallon
Holland Geneva	12/6 gallon
Best British Cordial	7/- gallon

At the far end of Pulteney Bridge, by the steps leading down to the river, is the old **Argyle Coffee House & Tavern**. It was opened in April 1791 by Mr Blew from the Star & Garter in Pall Mall. He was not there long; just over a year later an advertisement appeared in the *Bath Chronicle*:

> To lett – a Coffee House & Tavern called Argyle House, being the first on the south side of the Argyle Buildings, and commanding from its principal rooms unique and most beautiful prospects of land and water.

A few months later, the **Argyle House Tap** was advertised to let. This was underneath the Argyle Coffee House & Tavern and catered for sedan chairmen and servants. It was reached from the steps leading down to the river.

In September 1797, Horatio Nelson, who had lost an arm at the Battle of Santa Cruz a few weeks earlier, joined his wife in Bath. A dinner to celebrate his arrival

The Duke of Cambridge ...
... and the pub named after him.

in the city was held at the Argyle Coffee House & Tavern, which by then had been renamed the Argyle Hotel. A notice in the *Bath Chronicle* informed readers that,

> as the admiration blended with esteem which the conduct of this brave man has excited in general, the meeting is not formed on an exclusive principle. Such gentlemen, therefore, who wish to join the party already formed may be furnished with tickets. The festive pleasure of the day will no doubt receive additional zest from the consideration of the object of the meeting is to congratulate on the safety and not lament the loss (so nearly expected) of one of Britain's bravest naval sons.

In 1800, John Gould, who had started selling spirits from his bookshop on Pulteney Bridge five years earlier, took over the Argyle Hotel and changed its name to the Argyle Inn & Tavern.

In 1828, a tythingman called William Hawkins was looking out of the window of the Argyle Tap when he saw a boat with three people in it heading straight for the weir. He called to the landlord who ran outside and shouted to the young man at the oars to row as hard as he could with his left hand. It was to no avail. The boat shot over the weir, and, although it did not capsize immediately, a young woman in the boat panicked, stood up and tried to walk towards the bow. With that, they were all tipped into the water. Although the other two were saved, the woman was drowned.

Both the Argyle Inn and the Argyle Tap closed around 1830, but the sign about the Tap can still be seen in the hairdressing salon in the basement.

The lease of the Duke of Cambridge up for auction in 1928.

Grove Street, leading off Argyle Street, was one of the first of Bathwick's streets to be built. The only pub left in

---

LOT 23

"THE DUKE OF CAMBRIDGE" Beer House

With Seven days' On-Licence, and being

No. 7, Grove Street

of stone elevation, four stories in height, and containing :—ON THE THREE UPPER FLOORS : Seven Rooms. ON THE GROUND FLOOR : Bar, Smoke Room, Kitchen and Scullery, with Garden in rear. IN THE BASEMENT : Two Cellars, Outer Yard and W.C.

Let to the Bath Brewery Limited, on the terms of a Lease which will expire on the 24th June 1929, at the low Rent of £25 per annum.

THE LOST PUBS OF BATH

Grove Street in the nineteenth century.

Grove Street, the Rising Sun, opened in 1788. Three doors along, at No 7, was a beerhouse called the **Duke of Cambridge**, opened around 1870 by a shoemaker called William Field, and closed in 1928. It was a serious contender for Bath's smallest pub, consisting of a serving bar in the passage, and a tap room at the back.

The row of buildings beyond the Duke of Cambridge, leading down to the old gaol, were built in 1890 to replace those put up just over a century earlier. Despite William Pulteney's high ideals, it was perhaps inevitable that, with a gaol at the end of the street, this area should have gone rapidly downhill. A newspaper report from 1846 gives an idea of the sort of thing the residents got up to in the mid-nineteenth century:

> Hannah Pearce was summoned for assaulting Louisa Wickham, by throwing water over her in Grove Street. The assault was admitted by the defendant, but in her defence she pointed out that the water was clean. The magistrates told her this did not excuse the act and fined her 10/- and costs or in default 14 days in prison.

Almost inevitably, Grove Street had a choice of pubs for residents to while away their time – or stay out of the way of water fights. Near the prison was a pub called the **Ostrich**, built by John Eveleigh and first licensed by him in 1791. By 1793 it had been acquired by the Northgate Brewery, and, although intended as a fashionable hostelry, its proximity to the gaol and, later, to the malthouses of the Northgate Brewery, ensured that, by the mid-nineteenth century, it was far from respectable. At the back of the Ostrich, where Eveleigh may originally have intended to lay out

A pewter tankard bearing the name of Thomas Hunt, who kept the Ostrich between about 1819 and 1824, dredged from the mud near Pulteney Weir in the 1970s.

a pleasure garden, Ostrich Court, one of the least desirable bits of old Bathwick, was built. The Ostrich, along with Ostrich Court, was pulled down in 1890 in an early example of slum clearance.

One of the other buildings that went was No 14, where, in 1837, John Jones had opened an exceedingly short-lived beerhouse called the **King's Arms**.

To find our next lost pub we need to walk the length of Great Pulteney Street and head into Bathwick Street. Two of Bathwick Street's pubs – the Crown and the Barley – are still open, as is the Pulteney Arms in Daniel Street. On the southern corner of Daniel Street and Bathwick Street was another pub, a beerhouse called the **Rifleman's Arms**. Its history, though brief, is convoluted. In 1841, Edwin Organ was running a grocery store at 35 Bathwick Street. It was later taken over by William Organ, who left in 1853. The property stood empty for a while, but by 1858 No 35 was occupied by a dairyman called Sam Bonython, while, in a new extension on the corner of Daniel Street (No 35a), Henry Rudge had opened a beerhouse called the Sydney Porter Stores. Two years later, a butcher called (appropriately) Robert Ham had moved into No 35, and George Wolfe had taken over the Porter Stores. By 1864, Robert Ham had moved on, and George Wolfe had expanded the Porter

The former Rifleman's Arms – now a former Post Office.

Stores into No 35 and renamed it the Rifleman's Arms.

This marked the high point of the beerhouse's fortunes. Within four years, George Wolfe had moved out of No 35, which became O'Leary's grocer's, keeping just 35a as the Rifleman's Arms. Around 1870, a plumber and gasfitter called Henry Seymour took over the beerhouse, but closed it a couple of years later.

The shop fronts which now stretch from 27 to 35 Bathwick Street were added in 1896, long after the Rifleman's Arms had closed. Today, a launderette occupies 35a Bathwick Street; No 35, which until recently was Bathwick Post Office, is currently empty. All that is left to remind us of the Rifleman's Arms is the elaborate sign bracket hanging over No 35.

A short walk past the Holburne Museum, along Darlington Street and up Raby Place, brings us to Sydney Wharf and the **Cleveland Arms**, on the corner of Raby Mews. It was built in 1830-31 by William Robinson, a local brewer. Little is known of it beyond a tragic story from July 1845:

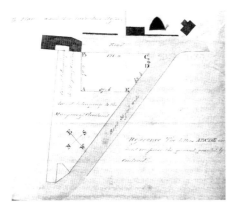

Top left A plan of the Cleveland Arms in 1830.
Top right The former Cleveland Arms, with part of its sign still legible.
Above The Cleveland Arms was built over a tunnel.
Right A letter to Mr Bowler from the Cleveland Arms.

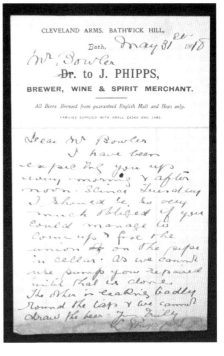

In the nineteenth century, Bathwick was synonymous with beer. The Bathwick Brewery, its name emblazoned on a horse tram outside the Kensington depot, stood across the road from the Rifleman's Arms.

On Monday morning AH English, Esq. held an inquest at the Cleveland Arms near Sydney Wharf, Bathwick, on the body of Charles M Theodore Trischler, the landlord of the house, who was found on Sunday morning by his wife, suspended by a bell cord to the tester of his bed. The widow of the deceased being examined as a witness as to his state of mind, stated that he was subject to delirium tremens from intemperance and had not been sober for the last four months. She had, however, never heard him talk of destroying himself, though he would sometimes make exclamations as if weary of life. On Sunday morning at about seven o'clock she got up and left him as if asleep. She took a walk in the garden as she was accustomed to do ... and after her return she went up to the room to call deceased to breakfast; when she found him as already described.

At the time of the 1903 report, the Cleveland Arms consisted of a bar, glass room, tap room and brewery. The brewery closed in 1926, and the pub called last orders six years later, when its licence was transferred to the Trowbridge House on Coronation Avenue.

There was another beerhouse on Sydney Wharf called the **Bargeman's Tavern**, which opened around 1850 and closed in the 1860s, although there is no indication of where it was.

To find our next pub, we need to go back along Sydney Wharf, up George Street, and along Sydney Buildings to the **Bathwick Tavern** at 10 Sydney Buildings (now No 13!). John Smith opened this as a beerhouse in the 1840s, and its licence was surrendered on 24 June 1877.

The former malthouse on the canal.

To view the malthouse behind Sydney Buildings, now converted into offices, we need to head down George Street and double back along the canal bank. To find our next lost pub, though, we need to head along the canal in the other direction, past Sydney Gardens, until we come to a row of early nineteenth-century cottages, the last five of them boarded-up and derelict. Hampton Row, built by John Pinch the Elder in 1816-17, blighted by the railway in the 1840s, given its own station for a mere ten years, and blighted once again by an abortive road scheme in the 1960s, has a rich and eccentric history of alcoholic indulgence.

Things started relatively quietly. In 1826, Thomas Pope opened a brewery at Myrtle Cottage. Then the railway came. Brunel decided that the only way to bring his line into Bath was to move the canal. He also moved the river, diverting it through Grosvenor Meadows so that an embankment could be built. The diversion of the river was temporary; that of the canal was permanent. The massive retaining wall behind which the canal now runs, with the railway running below on the canal's old course, gives some idea of the scale of what happened here between 1839 and 1841. Hundreds of men worked on the scheme. To cater for them, no less than four beerhouses opened on Hampton Row.

The former Queen Victoria.

Starting from the top, at 1 Hampton Row was the **Queen Victoria**. This was the only one of Hampton Row's beerhouses with any staying power. In 1895 it was extended into the adjoining house. The 1903 report gives a detailed description of the property. There was an exit into the garden at the back, which led down to the river. At the side of the front entrance was a way through to the garden of No 2, from which the garden of No 1 could be reached. There was a urinal in the front garden and a WC in the basement "for the use of everyone." A bar and a glass room made up the ground floor accommodation of No 1, while a doorway led through into the ground floor of No 2.

Hampton Row was a tight-knit community and the Queen Victoria was very much a locals' pub. In the 1960s, it was decided to knock down Hampton Row and build a road. The pub closed in 1965 and the residents were dispersed throughout the Bath area. The project to build the road came to nothing. The squatters moved in

Beerhouses opened at Nos 7, 9 and 11 Hampton Row to serve the navvies building Brunel's railway.

and that was that. The destruction of a community which had evolved over 150 years had been for nothing. It was, of course, like so many other instances of malicious incompetence, nobody's fault.

There were also beerhouses at No 7, No 9 (the **Lamb**), and No 11. They all closed when the railway opened and the navvies departed.

Around 1852, John Brown opened a beerhouse called the **Hampton Museum** at 14 Hampton Row. He also had a shop at 15 Pulteney Bridge where he practised his trade as a "bird and animal preserver" – in other words, a taxidermist. No prizes,

The former Hampton Museum at the end of Hampton Row.

THE LOST PUBS OF BATH

then, for guessing what sort of exhibits were on display in his miniature museum. The Victorians were crazy about stuffed birds and animals, combining, as they did, ornament with instruction. In the vaults of the Royal Literary and Scientific Institute in Queen Square, there is case after crumbling case of stuffed birds and animals, some of them preserved, perhaps, by John Brown. Through a century and a half of dust, their plumage and coats still dimly shine, imparting to us a gust of Victoriana as potent and portentous as the febrile strains of William Wordsworth's worst poem:

> While Anna's peers and early playmates tread,
> In freedom, mountain-turf and river's marge;
> Or float with music in the festal barge;
> Rein the proud steed, or through the dance are led;
> Her doom it is to press a weary bed –
> Till oft her guardian Angel, to some charge
> More urgent called, will stretch his wings at large,
> And friends too rarely prop the languid head.
> Yet, helped by Genius – untired Comforter,
> The presence even of a stuffed owl for her
> Can cheat the time; sending her fancy out
> To ivied castles and to moonlight skies,
> Though he can neither stir a plume, nor shout;
> Nor veil, with restless film, his staring eyes.

People who could sit and read things like that without laughing would, one feels, have had no problem sitting in a room full of stuffed birds and drinking beer. But they did not have long to enjoy it, for the Hampton Museum closed around 1855. Today the building is one of those boarded up, awaiting their fate.

Now we come to the grand finale of our tour of Bathwick. Beyond Hampton Row lies one of Bath's most fascinating lost pubs. This is not some ancient inn or time-worn hostelry that disappeared a century or more ago. It lies tantalisingly just out of reach, like a vision glimpsed in the moments before sleep. Yet it is lost just as surely, just as irrevocably, as any Roman taverna or medieval alehouse.

In a damp, dark tract of land, ringed by high embankments, a few shattered lumps of stone, hidden deep in the undergrowth, and a flight of steps leading nowhere, mark the remains of the **Folly**.

The Folly first appears as an unnamed building on Thorpe's 1742 map of Bath. On Harcourt Masters' 1795 map of Bath, it appears, as the Folly, linked by a free ferry with the new pleasure gardens at Grosvenor. There is no indication as to its purpose, but a glance at the map suggests a possible explanation for its name. Grosvenor Gardens was planned on a lavish scale – grander than anything seen in Bath before. In 1792, £5,000 was raised in shares. A fantastic gothic gateway, surmounted by the jawbone of a whale, was built at the entrance to the gardens. Although wonderful spectacles could be created in the gardens themselves, the view across the river was something of an anticlimax. Taking an old building and turning it into a folly by the addition of a few eye-catching features would have been an ideal way of transforming a rather uninteresting view into a picturesque landscape. This is merely a guess, however, and, as Grosvenor Gardens had already been hit by financial crisis by the time Harcourt Masters published his map, and was never fully completed, it is impossible to substantiate it.

We do know, however, that the Folly kept its name after the failure of Grosvenor Gardens and was leased by William Hulbert as a dairy farm. The Kennet & Avon Canal cut across the land behind it in 1800, bringing a steady flow of barges – including pleasure barges – and walkers to this previously remote spot. As an enterprising businessman, Mr Hulbert must have seen the potential for making a bit of extra income by offering refreshment to thirsty travellers, and it is tempting to think that he turned part of his land into a tea garden around the time the canal opened. An even more intriguing thought – although one that must forever remain unproved – is that Jane Austen stopped by for a cup of tea on her way to visit the caisson lock at Combe Hay in 1805.

On 23 July 1829 the Folly featured in a shocking report in the *Bath Chronicle*:

> On Monday morning, about a quarter before eleven o'clock, several young men were bathing in the Canal a little beyond the Folly, on the Bathampton side, and while so engaged, three young ladies happened to come up from the adjoining fields. On seeing the young ladies, one of the fellows actually rushed out of the water, and offered them the greatest indignities. The ladies not being attended by a protector, the rascal escaped unpunished.

The year after the unknown rascal hauled himself – and his great indignities – out of the canal, a bridge was thrown across the river just below the Folly. Captain Mainwaring described it in glowing terms:

> In November 1830 a neat and commodious suspension bridge across the river Avon, at the termination of Grosvenor Buildings, was completed and opened to the public. It was planned by, and constructed at the sole expense of Thomas Shew, Esq., on whose property it stands. The structure is of free-stone and wrought iron. The entire span is 160 feet. The river span is about 130 feet; the centre of which rises 30 feet above the margin. The ornamental effect of the bridge instantly strikes the eye; and its utility is demonstrable from the circumstance of its uniting the extremities of Walcot, Bathampton and Bathwick parishes, by a pedestrian access, which otherwise could not be obtained but by a long circuitous route. The delightful walks which this bridge enables the pedestrian to accomplish are, indeed, infinite and unbounded. The beautiful scenery which unfolds itself in every direction, is enchanting to the eye of a picturesque traveller, and affords a rich display of subjects for his prolific pencil.

The question Captain Mainwaring does not answer is why Mr Shew built the bridge. Was he inspired solely by altruistic motives – or did he have a more mercenary aim in mind? We know he owned the land on which the bridge stood. Bath was expanding eastward and a riverside location with easy access from both sides of the river was clearly a prime piece of real estate. Was he attempting to succeed where the original

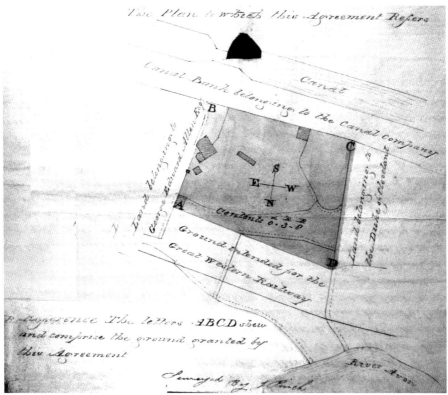

The Folly as rebuilt in 1839.

promoters of Grosvenor Pleasure Gardens had failed – and did the Folly form part of his plans? Mr Shew also owned a fleet of boats which carried goods between Bath and London on the canal. Was the bridge somehow connected with this business? Unfortunately, we do not know. What is certain, however, is the footpath past the Folly was now busier than ever.

In 1833 William Hulbert retired to a house near Cleveland Baths and his son, Matthew, took over the Folly. In 1839, Matthew Hulbert entered into an agreement with the Duke of Cleveland, who owned the land on which the Folly stood, to "take down, remove or alter the messuage or tenement and buildings standing on the said plot of ground and also erect and build and by such means cause to be erected and built ... one good and substantial messuage or dwelling house with proper offices." In other words, the Folly was redeveloped just as the railway was about to be built alongside it. Matthew Hulbert also agreed not to make a carriage road to Shew's suspension bridge, which was reserved for pedestrians. That same year, Thomas Shew hanged himself in his house at Grosvenor. Although no motive was discovered, the threat posed by the railway to his canal carrying business may have played a part in it.

It is likely that the Folly opened as a pub around this time, to cater for the navvies building the railway. Brunel drove his line through on a high embankment in front of

The old swing bridge on the canal, just above the Folly.

Grosvenor Suspension Bridge, looking towards the Folly.

THE LOST PUBS OF BATH

the Folly in 1839. Building a railway is thirsty work and the thousands of men employed to build the difficult section between Bath and Bathampton would have provided a lineside tavern with a fabulous – if somewhat boisterous – source of income.

The first reference to the Folly as a pub comes on 8 April 1847, when the *Bath Chronicle* reported that "the son of Mr Hulbert of the Folly Public House" raised the alarm when he saw a woman drowning in the river. The victim was taken to the Folly, which, like other pubs near the river, was a "receiving house" for the Bath Humane Society.* As such, it had to keep a drag net, a barrel float, a grappling iron, two reels with cords and two 17-foot poles with hooks for pulling people out of the water. It also had to keep a box of "resuscitating instruments" to deal with them once they had been rescued. The box contained

> a pair of hand bellows and flexible tubes for inflating the lungs via the mouth or nostril. Alternatively the bellows could be used to administer an enema of tobacco smoke or other herbs. In this case ivory tubes were used for the rectum and a wood-covered box of brass, containing the smouldering herbs, was interposed between the bellows and the rectal tube. A grating prevented the hot ash from being carried through the tube.

It brings tears to the eyes just to think about it.

It did not take long for the Folly to acquire a dubious reputation. In August 1852, the city's Watch Committee instructed the Chief of Police "to look after Folly House in Bathwick which the Board understands is the harbour for loose characters." Despite attempts by subsequent landlords to raise the tone, this remained the official view of the Folly until the end.

By 1854, Mary Hulbert was still running the dairy but had moved to Fir Cottage, the easternmost of the three cottages to the west of Cleveland Row. The licence was transferred to Jabez Smith, who had previously kept the Raven in Quiet Street. Jabez Smith, in spite of renaming his new pub the Folly Inn, did not last long. The following year, George Gait from the King William in Thomas Street took over. He was replaced in October 1856 by John Stowell.

In 1862, the licence passed to Thomas Osmond, from the Theatre Tavern in St John's Place, who attempted to give the Folly a new image by renaming it the Cremorne Pleasure Gardens. The original Cremorne Gardens were off the Kings Road in Chelsea. They opened in 1845 and developed a fairly bohemian reputation, counting artists such as Dante Gabriel Rossetti and James Macneil Whistler among their habitués. A stylish painting of dancers at the Cremorne Gardens by Whistler, dating from around 1870, hangs in the Metropolitan Museum of Art, New York, although

---

Cremorne Pleasure Gardens
BATHWICK.

Open Every MONDAY & WEDNESDAY EVENING
throughout the Summer Months.

For AMUSEMENT with DANCING
On the Monster Platform, to a Full Band.

ADMISSION FREE.

THOMAS OSMOND, Proprietor.

Dancing at Cremorne Gardens in the 1860s.

---

*Other pubs which acted as receiving stations were the Cleveland Arms, the Ostrich, the George at Bathampton, the White Hart at Batheaston, the Bladud's Head in Walcot Street, the White Hart and Jolly Boatman in Widcombe, the Dolphin in Lower Weston, the Hop Pole on the Upper Bristol Road, and the Green Park Tavern.

another painting by an artist called Phoebus Levin, entitled *The Dancing Platform at Cremorne Gardens*, which shows a group of prostitutes and their clients playing with a performing monkey mounted on a poodle led by a dwarf, probably gives a better idea of what they were really like. In 1872, London's Cremorne Gardens had their dancing licence withdrawn, leading to the following attack in a periodical called *Here and There*:

> It was found out that Cremorne was far from what it used to be. Canon Cromwell and his studious young men could not sleep for the bursting of

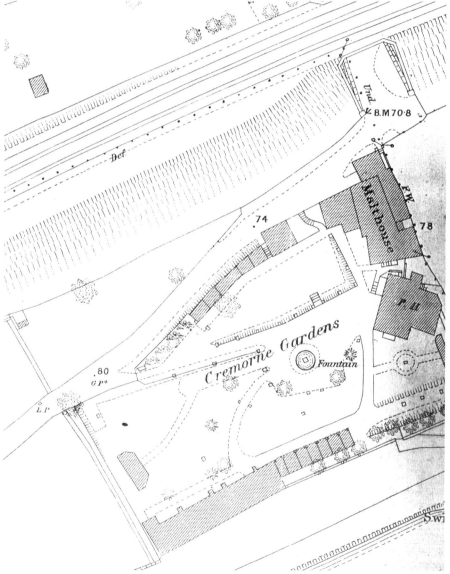

Cremorne Gardens in the 1880s.

THE LOST PUBS OF BATH

bombs and the fizzing of squibs. A spinster in the King's Road was kept awake by the rattling of cabs after midnight. A Middlesex magistrate had visited these Chelsea gardens, and had actually been asked for a glass of lemonade by a young lady he had never seen before. This shocking state of things could not go on. Such immorality must be stopped. But how? Did Mr Pownall and his Draconic colleagues order the siege of Strasbourg to be discontinued; decree that cabs should not run after twelve o'clock at night; and render it penal to ask unprotected old gentlemen for lemonade? Oh, dear, no. What they did was to take away the dancing licence. This seems to me very much like having your chimney swept to stop the cats rooting up your back garden … Granted that the Cremorne is open at all, why should not the visitors dance? There is no logic in the prohibition … It seems to me – but then I am an outrageous character, of course – that the more you can adulterate vice, the better it is for the people … Stamp out every outward sign of vice and dissipation; put down the casino and the music hall and the suburban pleasure garden … Push vice into dark corners, where she can work untold and unthought of horrors; banish profligacy into back streets, where it can do what it pleases; and cover sin with the domino of secrecy, and leave it alone. This is the gospel according to the nineteenth century moralists.

Five years later, London's Cremorne Gardens was closed as "a nursery for every kind of vice." The news must have confirmed respectable Bathonians' view of the sort of thing that went on at the back end of Bathwick under cover of darkness.

Thomas Osmond certainly pulled all the stops out at Bath's Cremorne Gardens, which was "open every Monday & Wednesday Evening throughout the Summer Months for Amusement with Dancing on the Monster Platform, to a Full Band." There were "Old English Brewings from the Hampton Springs, Foreign Wines & Spirits of the Highest Quality, and Foreign Cigars of the Highest Quality." And it did not just have any old skittle alley – it had "the Longest and most Comfortable Bowling Alley in Bath." A large-scale map of the gardens published in 1888 also shows a large fountain in the middle of the gardens. On gala nights the gardens were brilliantly lit by "Vauxhall Lamps," coloured glass globes filled with oil and a floating wick, or with dwarf candles known as "night lights."

Although Thomas Osmond was fined for opening on Sundays on at least two occasions, he was clearly held in some esteem by his peers, for in 1870 he was elected president of the Bath Licensed Victuallers' Association. Yet the name of Cremorne Gardens, like that of the Folly, continued to crop up in Watch Committee Reports. On 3 June 1865, for example,

a letter was received from Miss Aime Barlow complaining of the annoyance she sustained by people going from the Cremorne on Gala Nights; shouting and screaming so that it was impossible for her to sleep; particularly on the night of the 30th when she was awakened twice.

The Committee "ordered Chief Inspector Hughes to make special arrangements to prevent the inhabitants of the Cremorne and the approaches thereto, being annoyed on Whit Sunday, Monday and Tuesday." They also "resolved that the Sergeant and the Constable on duty on the beat on the night of the 30th should be summoned to attend the Committee on Friday next, to account for their not interfering to prevent the nuisance complained of."

A few days later, on 9 June, Thomas Osmond attended the Watch Committee himself, not to answer charges, but to complain of "persons" bathing in the canal near the Cremorne Gardens. Given his pub's reputation, there must have been something fairly serious going on for him to take this step. Perhaps the unapprehended rascal who offered great indignities to the young ladies on the canal bank 36 years earlier had made an unwelcome return. Nevertheless, the committee took his complaint seriously, resolving "that the police be instructed to prevent persons from bathing in the canal before nine o'clock in the evening until the first of August next."

In 1883, the licence passed to Emily Backhouse, with William Damon taking over in 1886. He lasted less than a year, because in March 1887 Cremorne Gardens was bought by the Great Western Railway (GWR). Why they waited almost 50 years to buy it, or what commercial advantage they saw in it, is not known. What is known is that they placed Lotta Matilda Buckley in it as licensee and changed its name back to the Folly.

A succession of other licensees soon followed. In 1890 Sidney Membury, who had once had a grocery store in Bathwick Street and still ran a tobacconist's on Pulteney Bridge, took over. He lasted about four years, before decamping to become landlord of the New Inn at Widcombe. By then the GWR had leased the Folly to Edmund Parfitt of the Albion Brewery, Newbury, who changed its name to the Grosvenor Brewery. It was an interesting choice. Grosvenor had been the name of the gardens on the other side of the river which foundered in the early nineteenth century. Did Mr Parfitt's choice of name reflect a desire on his part – and perhaps on the part of the GWR – to have one last attempt to turn the Folly from a "harbour for loose characters" into a respectable pleasure garden? Whatever the case, the Folly remained the Grosvenor Brewery – officially at least – until the end. Unofficially, people continued to refer to it as the Folly.

Meanwhile, licensees came and went with alarming regularity – Alfred Lee in 1894, George Marchant in 1895, R&E Russell in 1897 – and then the enigmatic Charles Sandbach. Sandbach came from nowhere. He did not appear in the 1898 *Bath Postal Directory*, but by 1899 he owned not only the Folly but also the Corn Street Brewery, and was living in style at The Grange, Bathampton. By 1902, however, he had moved to 3 Clarendon Villas, and had no commercial interests. His attempt to take the Bath pub trade by storm – if that is what it was – had come to nothing. The licence of the Folly was taken by Cissie Roots; Charles Cobb, of 35 Grosvenor, took over the brewery, the Albion Brewery's lease having been revoked.

In 1903, Henry Weston (who had a day job as a pork butcher) took over the Folly from Cissie Roots. In the same year, the Clerk to the Licensing Authorities visited to report on the condition of the premises. There were, he recorded, two entrances to the gardens – one from the lane leading from the suspension bridge to Hampton Row and another down some steps from the canal towpath. The premises consisted of a large serving bar, with a small glass room within, and a tap room with a bagatelle table. There was a bar in the garden used on Sundays and Bank Holidays and a skittle alley. The garden also contained "stands with a number of arbours" and a brewery, over which, he reported, the licensee had no control. He concluded his report with the terse comment, "three bedrooms available for guests, but no applicants."

Henry Weston stayed at the Folly for two years before handing over to John Langford in 1905. An inventory drawn up when Mr Langford took over gives more details of the property. At the top of the gardens was a series of arbours containing six tables. There were ten more tables outside, plus 22 benches. In the lower part of the grounds were nine more drinking tables, twelve painted forms, and an iron garden arch. The outside bar was portable and had a cast iron roof. There was a skittle alley and a bagatelle room, complete with a cottage piano in a walnut case, two piano stools, a bagatelle table with a stained deal cover, seven ivory balls, three cues and a marking board, ten Windsor chairs, six framed pictures, and five spittoons. Five more spittoons could be found in the linoleum-floored bar, along with a card board, a "push halfpenny board" and a pair of buffalo horns. All the fixtures in the bar, the inventory noted, were the property of the GWR.

It was at this point that perhaps the most intriguing development in the history of the Folly occurred. On 18 March 1907 the GWR opened a halt at the bottom of Hampton Row, next to the footbridge leading to the Folly. It did not last long, closing, along with many other GWR halts, as part of wartime emergency measures, on 29 April 1917. For a few brief years, though, you could climb down from a GWR railmotor at a wayside halt on the outskirts of Bath, wander a few yards down a narrow track and sit in a GWR-owned pub, watching the trains go past.

The question all of this begs is, why did the GWR choose to open a halt at Hampton Row, right on the edge of Bath? Perhaps they thought that, as well as attracting passengers from Bathwick, they might get people walking over the suspension bridge from the Grosvenor area rather than going all the way into town. Or perhaps – and here we enter the realm of speculation – they had ideas of turning the Folly Gardens into something more elaborate, such as a country house hotel. It was an era of massive expansion in the hotel industry – the Empire was less than seven years old – and the GWR was keen to develop into new areas.

But, if the GWR did have plans for the Folly, they came to nothing. In 1912 the licence was transferred to Eli Hatton from the Beefsteak Tavern in Newmarket Row. The following year, the pub and brewery was taken over by George Austen, a "horticultural and rustic summerhouse builder." Perhaps, given his background, he had plans to rejuvenate the gardens, but he had no time to put them into effect, for on 25 September 1914 an inventory and valuation was carried out "on behalf of the executors of Mr Austen, deceased." It was a litany of dilapidation. Six panes of glass were cracked in the drawing room, the kitchen table was broken, most of the interior walls were in urgent need of painting or papering, the roof was leaking, and the iron fencing and stone piers around the gardens were "more or less dilapidated." The cellars were singled out as being "very dilapidated," but when the attention of the GWR was drawn to them, they replied that they did "not propose to do any repairs." All they were prepared to do was give the incoming tenant a letter advising him of the state of the premises.

The new tenant was Henry Saunders. The pub-cum-brewery he took over in 1914 may not have been one of Bath's finest, but it still attracted regular crowds, especially on Sundays. Despite all the dilapidations, the gardens, on a summer's evening, with the sound of birdsong interrupted only by the passing of an occasional train, and fairy lamps winking in the trees, must have been a magical spot. You did not even have to go inside for a drink, for the outside bar had its own four-pull beer engine, with three taps linked to barrels in the cellar and one to a stout barrel in the bar. For amusement there was an automatic pistol machine on an iron stand. If you got really bored you could watch the hens in the two "fowl houses" and "hen coops" or help yourself to watercress from the beds in the kitchen garden.

When Henry Saunders went off to war, his wife took over the Folly and continued brewing beer – 400 gallons at a time. A few days after Hampton Row Halt closed, in April 1917, William Wiltshire from 2 Avon Cottages, below Hampton Row, set off for a lunchtime drink at the Folly. Passing the Halt, he saw a man he knew on the platform looking at the timetable. He told him that trains no longer stopped there, to which he replied, "oh, my blessed!" Mr Wiltshire continued over the footbridge to the Folly, and was just going through the door when he heard an engine coming from Bath whistle two or three times before braking sharply. As it came to a screeching halt next to the Folly, the driver jumped down and ran back along the line. Mr Wiltshire, realising what must have happened, scrambled up the embankment and hurried back to the Halt where he found the man's body on the line.

After the war, the wooden huts in the Folly garden were taken down and replaced by a children's bar where lemonade and biscuits were served. In 1926, Joseph Phipps, a sanitary engineer from George's Place, Bathwick Hill, took over the Folly. Four years later he was replaced by Abia Sims, a beer retailer from 17 Dorset Street, who stayed for less than a year before moving on to the New Inn in Monmouth Place. In 1931, Alfred Burgess, a boot repairer from 2a Beaufort Place, took over.

It is likely that, at some stage, beer ceased to be brewed at the Folly. All we know for certain is that, sometime after 1934, the GWR leased the entire property to the Oakhill Brewery.

Between the two world wars, the Folly remained a popular place for family outings, with swings and other games for the amusement of children. It was also noted for a culinary speciality – "Faggots & Beer." Alfred Burgess stayed at the Folly until one fateful night in 1942 when a stray German bomber brought an abrupt end to the Folly's long and somewhat chequered history. The report on the condition of the building stated that, although the damage was considerable, the building was still usable. Since the ARP Warden that night found the "considerable" damage amounted to some windows blown out, which had not greatly disturbed the regulars, it is obvious it could have been saved. But, given the Folly's less than salubrious reputation and dilapidated state, it was decided it should be allowed to slip gracefully into oblivion. The GWR was probably glad to see the back of one of the least prestigious parts of its empire.

Alfred Burgess later became the landlord of the Beehive on Belvedere. In 1958 the licence of the Folly was transferred to the Richmond Arms in Richmond Place, which until then had only had a beer licence. Today all that remains of the Folly are a few shattered stones, a short flight of steps that once led from the bar to the brewery, and a thick tangle of undergrowth. Yet it is still remembered with affection by many in Bathampton and Bathwick who went there as children.

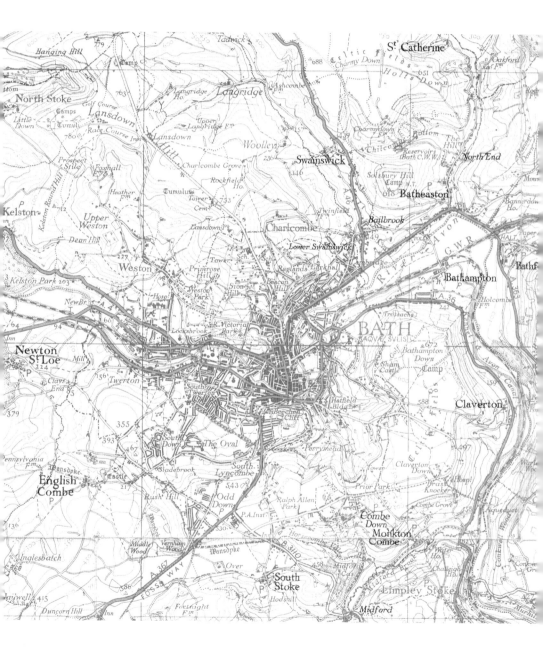

346   THE LOST PUBS OF BATH

BATH'S VILLAGES

Due to requests from residents of villages around Bath, we have included the following brief survey of the lost pubs of Bailbrook, Batheaston, Bathford, Claverton, Combe Down, Englishcombe, Monkton Combe, Newton St Loe, South Stoke, Midford and Swainswick. Although much of the information is drawn from original research, we have also drawn on the work of local historians, as acknowledged in the bibliography.

BAILBROOK

In 1855, the Vicar of Batheaston, whose parish included Bailbrook, wrote that its inhabitants,

The former King's Arms at Bailbrook.

having no chapel among them nor any of the better classes resident ... are for the most part an unsatisfactory and disorderly set. On Sunday afternoons they congregate together in the lanes or fields to gamble or create disturbances to the great annoyance of the few better disposed. I have gone among them myself to try to stop this, and at one time my churchwarden regularly went up there every Sunday afternoon. The only result was to force them to change their quarters to the adjoining parish.

The reason they were in the lanes or fields was because their local beerhouse, the **King's Arms**, was, like other licensed houses, closed on Sunday afternoons. Being

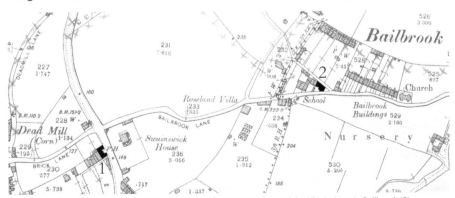

The Bladud's Arms in Lower Swainswick (1) – see entry for Swainswick – and the King's Arms in Bailbrook (2).

hounded out of the parish by the local parson must have added insult to injury.

The first landlord of the King's Arms was Thomas Beale, who also ran a small grocery store there. Around 1870, it was taken over by James Bolwell, a French polisher. It stayed in the Bolwell family until the First World War, when it was taken over by Walter Fellows.

Bailbrook eventually got a chapel – the famous tin church – but, like the beerhouse, it no longer serves its original purpose, having been converted to a dwelling-house-cum-artist's studio. The King's Arms closed around 1960 and is now a private house. A link with the past is maintained, however, by the words THOMAS BEALE: Licensed dealer in Tea, Coffee … painted above the door (the references to beer have inexplicably been removed).

There was – briefly – another beerhouse at Bailbrook in the 1880s run by George Maggs. The 1874 *Postal Directory* also lists Thomas King as a brewer at 5 Bailbrook Buildings.

BATHEASTON WITH ST CATHERINE'S

Batheaston's most famous lost pub is the **Lamb & Flag** – originally the Lamb – which stood on the corner of the Batch. The earliest record of it comes from 1684, when it was kept by a carpenter called Richard Cock. In 1751, the landlord, Richard Fuller, was fined ten shillings for allowing tippling on Sunday. It was rebuilt in the 1770s. For much of the nineteenth century, it was run by the Vezey family, who renamed it the Lamb & Flag around 1870. In a Directory of 1872, Edward Vezey is listed as brewer, maltster, farmer and innkeeper. The Lamb & Flag closed in 1962. After standing empty for several years, it was demolished in 1968.

Other inns recorded in Batheaston in the eighteenth century included the New Inn (1728), the Bell (1744), and the Crown (1755).

A tram outside the Lamb & Flag in Batheaston.

THE LOST PUBS OF BATH

Looking along Batheaston High Street with the Lamb & Flag on the corner …

… the same view today.

Above and below The former Cooper's Arms at North End.

Right The Sandybank Inn.

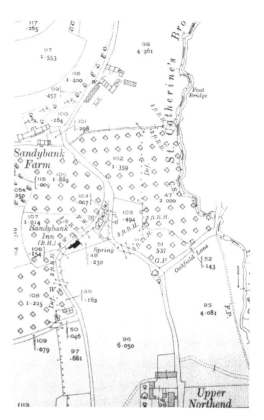

North End once had two beerhouses – the North End Inn (which is still open) and the **Cooper's Arms** on the corner of Seven Acres Lane. This was opened by a cooper called William Cook in the 1870s and closed around 1950. The painted signs on its walls have survived.

Beyond North End, as the valley dividing Somerset from Wiltshire narrows, with a maze of little lanes twisting along the contours, was the **Sandy Bank Inn**, opened as a beerhouse by a market gardener called Edward Every around 1870. It closed in 1966. The building is still there, still known as the Sandy Bank Inn, and still missed by older residents. Yet, with no parking and with only a scattering of farms and cottages round about, it seems astonishing it lasted as long as it did.

BATHFORD

The only pub left in Bathford is the ancient Crown Inn at the bottom of the hill. There were at least four others. The last to close was the **New Inn** in the High Street, first recorded in 1733. At one time it was known as the Old Inn, presumably to distinguish it from the Crown. It was renamed when it was refronted in the early nineteenth century. In 1965, Usher's, who had taken it over in 1920, renamed it The Inn at Bathford. It is now the village post office.

The former New Inn at Bathford.

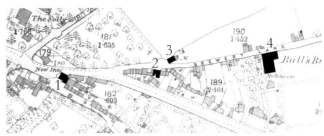

Lost pubs of Bathford: 1) the New Inn; 2) the Star; 3) the Smith's Arms; 4) the Brewery Inn.

The former Brewery Inn at Bathford.

The former Star at Bathford.

The former Smith's Arms at Bathford.

Ashley Road, which branches off the High Street a little further up the hill, was originally the London Road until a new road – the present High Street – was built around 1760. Around a century later, the Old London Road was renamed Brewery Lane. The Bathford Brewery, occupying two cottages at Northfield, opened as a brewery in the early nineteenth century. There was also a beerhouse known as the **Brewery Inn**, which closed in 1908. Brewery Lane was renamed Ashley Road in 1923.

Fading words on a blocked-up window at the former Smith's Arms.

At the bottom of Ashley Road were two beerhouses, the **Star** and the **Smith's Arms**. The Star, at 4 Ashley Road, was opened by a quarryman called John Pillinger around 1850. For a brief period in the late nineteenth century it was also known as the Rising Sun. It closed in 1957. The Smith's Arms, at 1 & 3 Ashley Road, was opened by a blacksmith called William Brooks in 1866. It closed in the mid-1930s and the building was split into two houses. To the left of the front door of No 3, the words USHER'S BEER ALE & STOUT can still be seen painted on the blocked-up window.

The Old Brew House on the corner of Prospect Place, with the prospect in the background.

The Old Brew House on the corner of the High Street and Prospect Place, was once a beerhouse called the **Quarryman's Arms**. It opened in the 1830s and closed in 1870.

CLAVERTON

The location of Claverton's lost pub is a mystery. The only reference to it comes from the *Bath Journal* for 26 July 1779:

> A Carnation Feast will be held at Michael Payne's, at the **Horse & Jockey** on Claverton Down on Wednesday the 28th of July. Whoever produces the best-blown flowers will be entitled to a silver spoon, value £1.

Its name suggests that it was near Claverton Racecourse, which closed in 1784 when the racecourse at Lansdown opened. The Horse & Jockey may well have closed at the same time.

Refreshment was, of course, available at the racecourse itself. The following advertisement appeared in the *Bath Journal* on 20 September 1773:

> Bath Races, 1773
> The best Madeira, Claret, Lisbon, Mountain, and Port Wines,
> Brandy, Rum, Shrub, Cordials, Beer, etc.,
> Also Cold Ham and Beef,
> Sold in the Under Part of the Grandstand on Claverton Down
> During the Races.
> NB Chops, Stakes, etc. dressed.

Unfortunately, the location of the racecourse, which would give us a clue to the location of the Horse & Jockey, is also unknown, although it has been suggested that the standing stones in Bushy Norwood field near the University may have been course markers.

COMBE DOWN

Originally part of Monkton Combe, Combe Down became a separate parish in 1854. It did not become part of Bath, however, until 1967. Although stone has been quarried in this area since Roman times, the village of Combe Down owes its existence to Ralph Allen, who not only developed the underground quarries but also built cottages for his workmen. Even so, as late as 1780, Edmund Rack, of the Bath & West Society, could write that the village consisted of only eleven houses.

By the late eighteenth century, cottages were being let out to invalids who found Combe Down an ideal spot to convalesce. Combe Down soon developed a reputation as a health resort, and terraces and villas were built for genteel visitors. So refined was this little enclave that, when a church was built in 1835, it was stipulated that there should be no burials in the churchyard for fear of reminding those who had come here for a rest cure what would happen if it did not work.

Not all Combe Down was gentrified, as can be seen by the rows of quarrymen's cottages, many of which survive. And, quarrying being thirsty work, it will come as no surprise to learn that Combe Down had more than its fair share of pubs. Despite numerous closures, it is still well served today. For those whose only experience of Combe Down is driving through on the main road, a walk round the old village will be a revelation. Quiet, tree-lined streets, early eighteenth century terraces, Regency

The former Crown at Combe Down.

villas and workmen's cottages linked by ancient drungways – as well as a scattering of fascinating old pubs – await discovery. Four pubs – the Foresters' Arms, the King William IV, the Horseshoe, and the Hadley Arms – are still open. Six more have gone.

Our journey round the lost pubs of Combe Down begins in Combe Road. For a short period in the mid-nineteenth century, No 26 was a beerhouse called the **Crown**. It is said that its licensing details can still be seen on the front wall behind the roof of the porch, although, on a recent visit, lush vegetation frustrated attempts to observe them.

The former Jupiter at Combe Down.

A little further along Combe Road is the old **Jupiter** beerhouse at the top of Summer Lane. This opened some time before 1889 and closed in the 1950s. A link with the past is maintained by Bath Crockhire and Party Wines, which now occupies part of the building.

A little further along Church Road, a turning to the left takes us down Rock Road. At the bottom of Rock Road is an old quarry known as Davidge's Bottom. This was one of two loading bays for Ralph Allen's tramway which took stone down to the wharf at Widcombe, and had access to the underground Firs Quarry. According to an early history of Combe Down, "in 1805, when De Montalt Mills were founded, cottages were erected in … Davidge's Bottom to take the place of wooden booths, which labourers and workmen had hitherto occupied for the day and in which they had sometimes slept during the week." In the nineteenth century, Davidge's Bottom was

a Sunday rendezvous of Combe Down quarry workers, who were attracted by a popular beerhouse. It is related that to avoid interference by the village constable, whose duty it was to see that they attended a place of worship, they would get

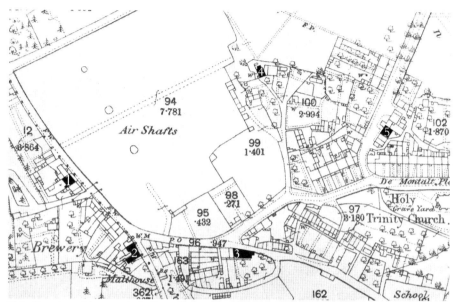

Of the five pubs on this map, only the King William IV (2) is still open. The Crown (1), the Jupiter (3), the Rock (4), and the Carriage (5) are long gone.

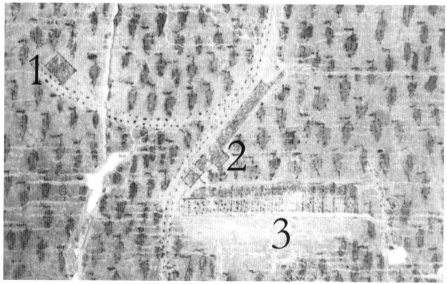

A section from a map of Ralph Allen's estates, showing 1) Davidge's Bottom; 2) the Carriage Inn; 3) the Rank cottages, built by Ralph Allen for his quarrymen. The dotted lines indicate the tramway.

THE LOST PUBS OF BATH

their mugs filled at a back window, and taking their pipes disappear into the depths of the quarry where they knew many hiding places.

The beerhouse was officially called the **Rock**, although everyone knew it as Davidge's. In the late nineteenth century, George Davidge, a descendant of the

Davidge who had given this area its name, was the quarrymaster; his wife, Sarah, ran the beerhouse. The Rock had its own brewery, but, although the old beerhouse has survived, the brewery was demolished years ago. Some lettering from when Rock House was a pub can still be seen on the false window above the entrance.

The former Rock at Combe Down.

The former Carriage Inn.

Continuing along Church Road and turning left into the Avenue, we come to the site of the **Carriage Inn**. This was the first pub in Combe Down and took its name from the carriages that carried the stone down to the wharf at Widcombe. In the late eighteenth century, William Smith the geologist, recorded that one side of the inn sign showed a carriage descending the tramway, controlled by a brakeman, while the other side showed it being towed back up by three horses. The Carriage probably opened in the late 1720s, although it was first recorded in 1786, with William Butler as landlord. He was there until at least 1805, but by 1818 Sarah Allen had taken over. The Carriage later passed to Robert Hansford, who went bankrupt in 1825. Next came John Payne, who had a rude awakening one February morning in 1828:

The Avenue a century ago, with the former Carriage Inn on the right.

THE LOST PUBS OF BATH

Thursday morning, about half past one o'clock, the Carriage Inn, kept by Mr Payne, was entered by thieves who stole two fowls, a rabbit, etc. It appears the villains were disturbed by Mr Payne, who hearing a noise, opened his bedroom window, which being heard by the thieves, they decamped, leaving a bludgeon, which was found next morning, with several articles strewn about.

The following year's *Postal Directory* listed it as the Carriage Inn & Tea Gardens, but, despite this bid for respectability, the tap room was no place for the faint-hearted. At about 8.30pm on 10 November 1841, a fight spilled out of the tap room; by the time it was over, one man was dead.

The Carriage Inn closed in the 1870s. Its last landlord, Frederick Mitchell, continued to run a coach and carting business from the inn yard, but turned the pub into a grocers. In 1878, he sold the coach house and stable to Henry Gould, a livery stable keeper from Lansdown Road, along with a wagonette and four horses, and a bus, which was kept in a separate "bus house."

Carrying on along the Avenue and turning right along North Road at the Hadley Arms, we soon come to an old pub that still looks like a pub – the **Mason's Arms**. This opened as a beerhouse around 1841 and was granted a full licence in 1961. In 1976 Fred Pearce described it as a "tiny little local so short on space there are usually more people in the skittles alley than the combined lounge/public bar." Today, even though it looks like a pub, it is not. It is, in fact, an undertaker's.

Dear reader, I see the smile trembling on thy foamy lips, thine eye a-twinkle. But hold hard, desist, refrain, wipe that budding snicker from thy visage. And ask thyself, is not this a work of scholarly import, a dipsichorean diatribe on the boozy beatifications of Aquae Sulis? It is. The temptation, therefore, to expatiate on stiff

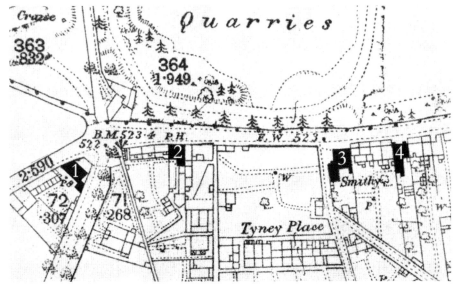

North Road showing: 1) the Hadley Arms (open); 2) the Mason's Arms (closed); 3) the Horseshoe (open); 4) the Three Crowns (closed).

North Road a century ago, with the Three Crowns on the right. Note the pole above the signboard, with a horse and jockey on top.

The Three Crowns today.

drinks, to lucubrate on last orders or to muse on the meaning of Gone for a Burton, will, with heavy heart (and to spare the reader any inappropriate felicitations), be resisted, and we will move swiftly on, past the Horseshoe, to the our last lost pub, the **Three Crowns** at 134 North Road. This opened around 1875, had a bar parlour, shop, tap room and brewery, and closed in the early 1960s.

ENGLISHCOMBE

Englishcombe had several pubs in the nineteenth century. Harold Lewis, writing in the 1870s, said that "in Tudor times there was a manor house here which is now

The former Malt & Hops at Nailwell.

converted into an alehouse." In 1840, Joseph Perrin opened a beerhouse opposite the vicarage, possibly in the house known as Yeoman's Cottage. South of the village, in the hamlet of Nailwell, was another beerhouse called the **Malt & Hops**.

Englishcombe's most celebrate lost pub, however, is the **Grove Tavern** beerhouse at Padley Bottom. It was opened by William Hucklebridge around 1870. In 1894, he went bankrupt and an inventory of the property was drawn up. The public area consisted of two rooms – a parlour and a tap room. The parlour contained an oak table, three cases of stuffed

THE LOST PUBS OF BATH

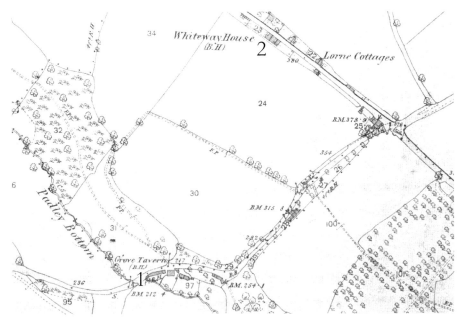

The Grove Tavern at Padley Bottom, with Whiteway House (now the Jubilee) to the north.

birds, eight spittoons, and a squirrel. The tap room contained a settle, a mahogany-topped drinking table, four forms and three wooden spittoons. There was no serving counter or beer engine in either room. The pub was taken over by the Davis family who ran it for around 50 years. The Grove closed around 1953, due mainly to lack of sanitation. The last landlord was William Noad. Today the green and gold sign which used to welcome passers-by to this idyllic spot in the heart of the country is no more than a fading memory; and the Lilliputian cottages that stood behind it have been razed to make way for a large house.

Over 50 years on, it seems hardly possible there ever was a pub in this remote spot. The Grove at Padley Bottom seems a name dreamt up by John Betjeman – or Vivian Stanshall – or even Noel Edmonds. Yet some people can still remember when the Englishcombe Harvest Supper was held there, and when, on summer Sunday afternoons before the war, tea was served on its lawns.

The former Grove Tavern at Padley Bottom.

MONKTON COMBE

On the east side of Brassknocker Hill is the old **Brassknocker Inn**. The brass knocker from which the inn – and the hill – took its name – was on its front door. Originally called the Crown, the inn dated back to coaching days, when weary horses (and weary passengers who had to get out of their coaches and walk uphill) stopped there for a reviving drink. It lost its *raison d'être* when the road along the valley was opened in the 1830s, but stayed open until about 1870. It is possible that its licence

The former Brassknocker Inn.

was transferred to the Wheelwright's Arms, first recorded as a beerhouse in 1872, but upgraded to a fully-licensed house by 1875.

The Brassknocker's last landlord was William Goff, who also held the lease of Lyncombe Farm and ran a cider merchant's on the Lower Bristol Road. After he gave up the Brassknocker, it was bought by Major Vaughan-Jenkins, who lived at the Manor House across the road. William Goff later became the landlord of the Plough on Wells Road, staying there until it closed in 1883. As Oscar Wilde might have said, "to oversee the demise of one pub may be regarded as a misfortune; to oversee the demise of two looks like carelessness."

The Brassknocker was recalled in an article in the *Bath Journal* in 1899:

The long-lost hostelry, the Brassknocker Inn, was a favourite resort, especially with the workmen of many of our old Bath firms, at which to hold their annual shop dinner – for trips and excursions had not begun, or, if they had, were neither as cheap nor as convenient as now – and the breezy walk over Claverton Down, either by Bathwick or Widcombe hills, tended to sharpen and invigorate the most fastidious or impaired appetite, as well as gratifying the most exacting taste for the beautiful and grand ... The accommodation was of the most excellent description, the viands superior, and boniface a most pleasant and agreeable individual, which always made the function looked forward to as a red-letter day in the year.

After closure, the inn was converted to three cottages. A history of Monkton Combe, written in 1924, informed readers that

the old leaping stone for women to mount the pillion from can still be observed in front, and the size of the house with the large stables at one end and the brewhouse at the other marks its ancient importance.

In 1935, a correspondent in the *Bath Chronicle* recalled that, as the Brassknocker lay just over three miles from Bath Guildhall, it could open on Sunday afternoons. The vagaries of the licensing laws in the late nineteenth century meant that pubs within a three-mile radius had to shut. As a result, the Brassknocker did very good business on Sunday afternoons.

Although the Brassknocker closed well over a century ago, its name lives on – a possibly unique instance of a road being named after a minor piece of pub decoration. It is, however, a distinction it shares with an Oxford College that was also named after a brass knocker – Brasenose.

At the bottom of Brassknocker Hill was the **Viaduct Inn**, built at the same time as the road along the valley and named after the viaduct that carried it over Midford Brook. It had its own brewery, divided from the inn by a narrow alleyway. When Fred Pearce visited in 1976, he filed the following report:

> The entertainments bar is the dominant feature here – that and the affectionate yellow-eyed cat in the public bar. Discos on Tuesdays and Thursdays, Country & Wetsern night is Wednesday and there's "organ time" on Saturdays and Sundays … This hotel on the main road overlooking the Limpley Stoke Valley also brings the pennies in with its meals in the upstairs restaurant. The main bar is an unexceptional split-level, wrought iron, carpet and leather seats bar which serves morning coffee.

The former Viaduct Inn.

Had this book been published twelve months ago, it would not have included the Viaduct. But time has finally been called at this former coaching inn. Although close to a canal marina, it stood at a very busy crossroads, with little provision for pedestrians. It was also hampered by lack of parking. If the pub is converted to flats, as now seems likely, the old three-storey brewery, which has hardly changed since it closed, will be transformed out of all recognition. Railway enthusiasts may like to note that the GWR branch from Limpley Stoke to Camerton branch, which ran next to the pub, featured in the film *The Titfield Thunderbolt*.

NEWTON ST LOE

Newton St Loe's old coaching inn, the George, open by 1725, is still in business;

The former Rising Sun at Newton St Loe.

the **Rising Sun** beerhouse closed over a century ago. Built by James Wiltshire in 1818, it became a beerhouse after the passing of the Beerhouse Act. James Wiltshire was still running the beerhouse in 1861, but shortly afterwards it passed to his widow, Mary Ann. Around 1870, it was taken over by a Mrs Smith, who closed it a couple of years later. After closure, some outbuildings, which may have been in use as a brewery, were demolished.

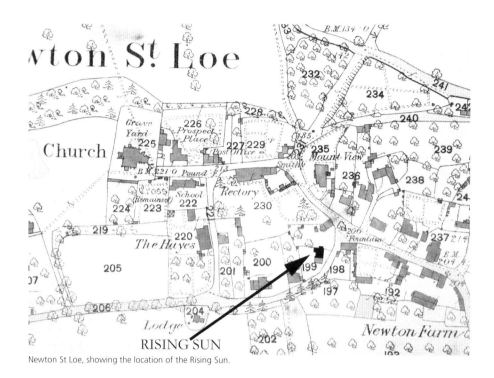

Newton St Loe, showing the location of the Rising Sun.

South Stoke, showing: 1) the former Packhorse Inn, now Packhorse Farm; 2) the present Packhorse Inn; 3) the former South Stoke Brewery.

SOUTH STOKE WITH MIDFORD

The Packhorse in South Stoke may look as though it has been an inn for centuries, with licensing records stretching back at least as far as 1674, the date on the stone above its entrance. In fact, it only opened as a beerhouse around 150 years ago. But there was a Packhorse Inn in South Stoke dating back to the 1600s, which closed when the present one opened. It was almost a mile to the east of the village centre, on Midford Hill, and closed, like many other coaching inns, when a new road was built.

The former Packhorse Inn.

The old Packhorse was a farm as well as an inn. In 1786, it was advertised to let "with stabling for 30 horses, garden, outbuildings, 15 acres of arable and pasture and an orchard." Over 20 years earlier, in March 1765, "a wagon load of grain [had been] seized at the Packhorse, Midford Hill, and hauled without the aid of horses to Bath Market and there sold at moderate price." Commandeering of basic commodities by mobs during times of food shortage and high prices was common in the eighteenth and early nineteenth centuries. Sometimes, as in this case, the initiative was successful; sometimes troops were ordered to disperse the mob.

A few months later, in January 1766, the Packhorse made the news again as the headquarters for a tea-smuggling operation:

> Tuesday last about noon, upwards of two hundredweight of smuggled tea was seized at the sign of the Packhorse on Midford Hill ... The smugglers were dividing it into small parcels when seized but immediately took their horses from the stable and made off.

Thirteen years later, in June 1779, another raid was made on the Packhorse:

> On Saturday last, Mr Hayden, Supervisor [of excise], being informed that a large quantity of tea (supposed to be about two tons) was concealed in a barn at the Packhorse on Midford Hill, he with three of his officers made a seizure of the same but an alarm being directly given, the smugglers attacked the officers with pistols, blunderbusses and bludgeons, when, after a combat of half an hour, the smugglers overpowered them (being six to one) and immediately loaded their horses and proceeded in triumph through Combe Hay and Wellow and, as supposed, by way of Old Down to Bristol. The Supervisor and one of the officers are very dangerously wounded. This is the second cargo of tea that has been lodged at the same place within these ten days.

The most surprising thing about Bath's own Jamaica Inn is that it was run by two women – Ann Grace, a widow, and her daughter, Grace Grace. They were clearly resourceful women, and shrewd enough to avoid criminal proceedings being taken against them. They also had useful family connections. Ann Grace's son-in-law, for example, was a carrier between Trowbridge and Bristol – and almost certainly an integral part of the tea-smuggling operation. When he died in 1775, rather than see his business go outside the family, she took it over and ran it herself.

The tradition of female landladies staying one step ahead of the law was maintained at the new Packhorse in South Stoke village. The first licensee was Elizabeth Lucas, who was charged in February 1853 with serving beer during Divine Service on Sundays. The summons was dismissed.

Midford forms part of the parish of South Stoke. Unlike South Stoke, which was by-passed by road, canal and railway, Midford was something of a transport hub. On the coach road from Bath to Frome, it was also an important intermediate point on the Somersetshire Coal Canal, and had two railway stations – Somerset & Dorset and Great Western. The opening shot of the *Titfield Thunderbolt* shows an express roaring across the viaduct through Midford as a local train trundles through the arches beneath. Today, only the road remains – and an inn, the Hope & Anchor, originally the White Hart, but renamed when the canal opened.

There was another eighteenth-century coaching inn in Midford, the **Fox**, first recorded in 1782, when it was taken over by George Flower. In September 1807, it was advertised to let as

> all that long-established and well-accustomed inn called the Fox … with spacious malthouse, brewhouse, cellars, gardens, stables and appurtenances thereunto belonging … The inn adjoins the great road from Bath to Frome and Warminster, and is only three miles from Bath … is situated close by the Coal Canal from Radstock and the several collieries in that neighbourhood.

It was taken by Arthur Baily from Bath, who placed a notice in the *Bath Chronicle* on 21 December 1809:

FOX INN, MIDFORD, NEAR BATH

> Arthur Baily returns sincere thanks to friends and the public for past favours and solicits their support in future; and particularly begs leave to inform carriers and

The Harbutt family outside the Fox at Midford. Traces of the sign behind the car are still visible today.

THE LOST PUBS OF BATH

owners of carts that in consequence of his not having possession of the premises opposite to his house, he has recently erected very commodious stabling for their accommodation and flatters himself that the persons travelling with wagons or carts will not in future be reduced to the necessity of seeking such accommodation from the occupier of the opposite premises, who being licensed to keep an alehouse, cannot entertain them in the manner A Baily is authorised to do.

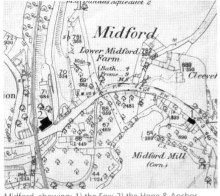

This is the only reference to an alehouse opposite the Fox. The faint outline of a door in the wall on the opposite side of the road is the only clue as to where it might have been.

The Fox had a wonderful location, next to a mill, with lawns sloping down to the river, looking across to the water meadows on the far bank. But on the other side, it opened directly onto a busy road, with little or no room for parking. It closed shortly before the Second World War.

Midford, showing: 1) the Fox; 2) the Hope & Anchor.

There was another beerhouse at Upper Midford, on the road to Combe Hay. The **Boatman's Arms** opened sometime before 1840, and, like many canalside pubs, was a sizeable establishment, with stables, accommodation, and other facilities for men working on the canal. It closed around 1889 and today, as Hyver Kennels, provides accommodation for dogs.

The canal at Upper Midford – the building on the far left is the old Boatman's Arms

SWAINSWICK
Lower Swainswick

The former Bladud's Arms at Lower Swainswick.

On the west side of the Gloucester Road, at its junction with Ferndale Road, stood the **Bladud's Arms**. It started life as a pair of cottages, one of which was opened as a beerhouse around 1840 by a butcher called John Bush. It later expanded into the adjoining cottage and was granted a full licence sometime before 1860.

In 1970, Harry Weston, the 75-year-old licensee of the Bladud's Arms, was notified that the Trustees of St John's Hospital, who owned the pub, were selling the freehold to Bath City Council, so that they could pull it down to build houses. In the event, however, the price they wanted (£10,000) was too high and the council removed the Bladud's Arms from their plans. Mr Weston, who had been at the pub since 1934, stayed on for another two years, retiring in 1973. A new licensee took over for a couple of years, but, when she left, Watney Mann decided to close it, because of problems with the lease.

Eventually, Don Meylan, a greengrocer (and CAMRA activist) from Kingsmead Square, took it over and reopened it in August 1976. For a time it was one of Bath's top real-ale pubs, but eventually – and regrettably – the Trustees of St John's Hospital got the price they were looking for and the Bladud's Arms closed, not to be demolished, but to be converted into private housing.

Upper Swainswick

The former Rising Sun at Upper Swainswick.

On the east side of the Gloucester Road, just below where it now joins the dual carriageway, was the **Rising Sun** beerhouse, opened around 1870 and closed around 1960. It is now a private house.

There were three other pubs in Swainswick, whose exact whereabouts are unknown. The **Green Tree** was recorded in the alehouse recognizances for 1798 with James Garroway as licensee. There was also two beerhouses – the **Lamb**, open for a few years in the mid-nineteenth century, and the **New Inn**, which closed in the early 1870s.

THE LOST PUBS OF BATH

THE LOST PLEASURE GARDENS OF BATH

Although a comprehensive history of Bath's lost pleasure gardens lies outside the scope of this book, they all served alcohol, and most of them had pubs – or taps – for coachmen or sedan chairmen.

SPRING GARDENS

The first of Bath's pleasure gardens opened on the opposite bank of the river to the Orange Grove around 1735. It had no serious competition, apart from three small pleasure gardens in Lyncombe Vale, until the closing years of the century.

Spring Gardens were reached by ferry from the Orange Grove. Spring Gardens Stairs led down to a wharf originally constructed by John Wood to unload stone for building Queen Square. The boats, which held up to 30 people, were covered at the top and sides as "a shelter against everything which might incommode." When the Rev John Penrose visited Spring Gardens in 1766, they were at their peak. He left this record of his visit:

Spring Gardens around 1770, showing the proposed Pulteney Bridge (1), Spring Garden Stairs (2), the Parade Coffee House (3), Gyde's Assembly Rooms (4), Simpson's Assembly Rooms (5).

> The Gardens are a most delightful spot, laid out in gravel and grass walks, some straight, others serpentine, with a fine canal in one place, and a fine pond in another, with the greatest variety of shrubs, trees, and other vegetables that the most curious could desire. In these Gardens is a large handsome building, wherein is a breakfast room capacious enough to hold many sets of company, having six windows in the side ... When we entered the room the tables were laid out with exemplary neatness. Upon a cloth as white as snow were ranged coffee cups, tea dishes of different sizes, chocolate cups, teapots, and everything belonging to the equipage of the tea table, with French rolls, pots of butter, all in decent order, and interspersed with sweet briar, which had a pretty effect both on the sight and smell.

After drinking "but one cup of chocolate, two of coffee and two of tea," the Rev

Penrose, not surprisingly, turned "from filling ... to emptying." The lavatorial facilities were so far in advance of those customary in the eighteenth century that he felt the need to record them in detail:

> Every one's eyes in search of a Fro. As need required, we found two. Over the door of one was written "For the Ladies only;" over that of the other, "For the Gentlemen only." Against the wall, within the Gentlemen's, was written with a pencil, "Whosoever comes into this place, is desired to be cleanly, to let down the lid, and shut the door." ... Whatever relates to the Ladies' Fro must be kept an inviolable secret.

Breakfasts were accompanied by music played on french horns and "clarionets." Later in the day alcoholic refreshments, of a suitably refined order, were available, and "proper music for dancing cotillons" was provided. Among the directors of music at Spring Gardens was William Herschel.

Spring Gardens could not hope to maintain its exclusivity next to a major building site, with a prison just down the road.

When Pulteney Bridge was thrown across the river just north of Spring Gardens in the early 1770s, it not only put paid to their exclusivity, but also cut off the view of Beacon Hill to the north. When the development of Bathwick New Town got under way in earnest, it marked the beginning of the end for Spring Gardens. Instead of willow-fringed water meadows and winding footpaths, they now looked over a massive building site, while the choice plants in their flower borders were covered with stone dust.

In the late eighteenth century, Meshach Pritchard took over not only Spring Gardens but also the Parade Coffee House on Terrace Walk. He gave up both leases around 1798. William Ball took over, but Spring Gardens closed a couple of years later. There was also a Spring Gardens Tap, but where it was, or when it opened, we have no idea. The only record of it comes from 1798, when the licence was held by John Townsend.

LYNCOMBE SPA

Lyncombe Spa, now the Paragon School, was more of a health resort than a pleasure garden. Nevertheless, French Horn Concerts were given there as early as 1751, and it was certainly possible to get a drink. When the Rev John Penrose visited in 1766, he was so exhausted by the climb that he "was glad of a glass of wine," and drank several more glasses after dinner.

BAGATELLE

The Bagatelle Pleasure Gardens in Lyncombe Vale opened in July 1769 when John Wicksteed announced the discovery of a spring. He built an enclosure round it and advertised it as a spa. Fulsome advertisements for the health-giving properties

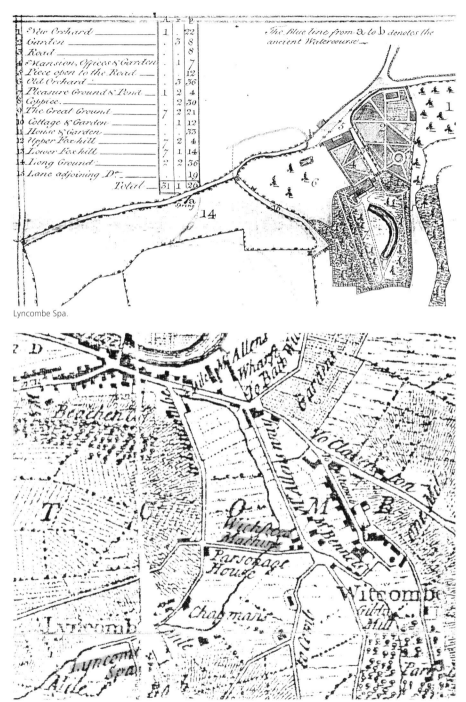

	A	r	p
1 New Orchard	1	.	22
2 Garden	.	3	8
3 Road	.	.	8
4 Mansion, Offices & Garden	.	1	7
5 Piece open to the Road	.	.	12
6 Old Orchard	.	3	36
7 Pleasure Ground & Pond	1	2	4
8 Coppice	.	2	30
9 The Great Ground	7	2	21
10 Cottage & Garden	.	1	12
11 House & Garden	.	.	33
12 Upper Fox hill	7	2	4
13 Lower Fox hill	7	1	14
14 Long Ground	2	2	36
15 Lane adjoining D⁰	.	.	19
Total	31	1	20

The Blue line from a to b denotes the
ancient Watercourse

Lyncombe Spa.

A map of 1742 showing Lyncombe Spa and Wicksteed's Machine, otherwise known as the Bagatelle.

of the water, along with complaints about people turning up to drink it without subscribing, appeared regularly in the *Bath Chronicle*. The Bagatelle was also known as Wicksteed's Machine, after an ingenious contraption for making seals, which was kept there. In 1771, it was advertised for sale, and by 1774 it had been renamed Cupid's Gardens. The new name suited its rather indecorous reputation as a place where the ardour of gentlemen could be assuaged. It was, in other words, a high-class knocking shop.

In 1778, it was once again offered for sale. The property consisted of "two dwelling houses and a summer apartment," plus a garden with "shrubbery, canal and walks." "It is," an advertisement in the *Bath Chronicle* informed its readers, "a place of great resort, and much wanted near Bath, but has never yet been conducted with a degree of propriety."

It was taken by Mr Harrison of London, who reopened it in June 1778. It closed shortly afterwards, possibly because the lack of propriety which had marked its previous history kept respectable society away.

KING JAMES'S PALACE

King James's Palace is Bath's most elusive and intriguing pleasure garden. It was first recorded in 1777, when the Royal Cumberland Masonic Lodge held a meeting there. In May 1778, a correspondent in the *Bath Chronicle* expressed "surprise and delight at St James's Palace," the proprietor of which had gone to great expense in establishing the gardens and house for company." The unknown correspondent

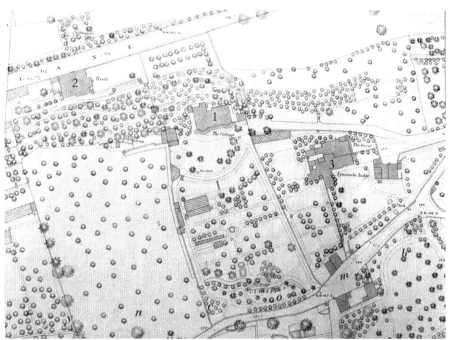

King James's Palace (1) in the late nineteenth century, when it was known as the Cottage. Tivoli (2) on Greenway Lane and Lyncombe Lodge (3), both built later, are also shown.

THE LOST PUBS OF BATH

seems to have been so taken with it that he got its name wrong, for this is the only time it is referred to as St James's Palace.

In July 1779, "public tea drinking" was advertised "at King James's Palace opposite Lyncombe Spaw. The best and pleasantest road," prospective visitors were informed, "is by the Bagatelle, to enter at the lower gate by the Spaw." The gardens also had an upper gate on Greenway Lane.

In May 1792, Robert Tanner took over King James's Palace, but he went bankrupt two years later, and it was put up for sale. Tanner soon bounced back as the landlord of the Elephant & Castle Inn in Monmouth Street, and the Palace was taken by Thomas Read, a wine merchant from Great Pulteney Street. By 1805, he too had left and the gardens were advertised for sale as "the former King James's Palace."

The reason for its name has never been satisfactorily established. There is an ingenious theory, however, which involves gin, revolution, and the procreative effects of Bath's waters. More than any other city in England, Bath was responsible for the eighteenth-century gin epidemic – indirectly and unwittingly, it is true, but responsible none the less. On 18 August 1687, James II arrived in Bath from Portsmouth, where he was joined by his second wife, the Catholic Mary of Modena. James II was not the most popular of monarchs, particularly among those who feared that his Catholic leanings – and Catholic wife – threatened the Protestant order. They were prepared to tolerate him because he was already in his fifties when he came to the throne and had no son. His heir was Mary, his daughter by his first wife. She was married to the Protestant William of Orange, so it seemed only a matter of time before Britain got a true Protestant king. The possibility of Mary giving James a son was remote, because they had already been married for 14 years without issue.

What nobody had reckoned with was the power of Bath's healing springs. James left the city after only a few days, but Mary stayed for almost two months, following a regime of daily bathing as a treatment for infertility. Incredibly, it worked, and on 2 June the following year, the bells of Bath rang out to celebrate the birth of a son to James and Mary. The prospect of a Catholic succession led to a mass uprising, known as the Glorious Revolution. James and Mary fled to France, William of Orange landed at Torbay to claim the throne, and the infant James Edward Stuart became, in due course, "the Old Pretender." William not only made the country safe for Protestantism; by encouraging the import of spirits from Holland and the distillation of spirits from grain, he precipitated the gin epidemic.

It has been suggested that the gardens in Lyncombe Vale were called King James's Palace because the house which stood in them was a country retreat for Mary of Modena during her stay in the city. It is a good story, even if the only evidence for it is the name of the gardens.

King James II.

Grosvenor Gardens offered for sale in
November 1793.

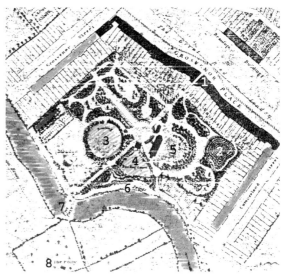

Grosvenor Gardens, showing: 1) the Hotel; 2) the Labyrinth; 3 & 4) Bowling
Greens; 5) Space for Fireworks; 6) Swings; 7) Free Ferry; 8) the Folly.

GROSVENOR GARDENS

Grosvenor Pleasure Gardens were a spectacular
flop. Too far out of town, they were conceived at
the height of a building boom. Hardly had they got
off the ground before the most spectacular slump in
Bath's history put paid to the vaulting ambitions of
their developer, John Eveleigh. Grosvenor Gardens
struggled on for a while, but the loss of momentum
transformed them from an exciting new enterprise
into a partly-built white elephant.

The first stone of the hotel which formed the
entrance to the gardens was laid on 24 June 1791.
In the following year John Eveleigh took out a licence
to serve alcohol there. At the end of May 1792, the
Bath Chronicle announced that Grosvenor Gardens
were "already in so forward a state that some idea
may be formed of their future elegance and utility."
By August 1792, pleasure boats were running to
the gardens from the Rising Sun in Grove Street,
and "tea, wines, etc." were available for visitors.
In the following year, Eveleigh went bankrupt and
Grosvenor Gardens were sold.

In 1794, John Townsend appeared in the
licensing records as the landlord of the Grosvenor
Gardens Tap. In April 1795, Mr Hewlett, a carpenter

THE LOST PUBS OF BATH

and property speculator, took over Grosvenor Gardens. He soon followed Eveleigh into bankruptcy and, in December 1795, they were once again advertised to let. A sad footnote to Mr Hewlett's brief tenure of the Gardens came two and half years later, when a Benefit Breakfast for Martha Hewlett, "whose husband [had] died under confinement," was held at Sydney Gardens.

In 1798, John Townsend left the Grosvenor Tap to take on the Spring Gardens Tap. The last record we have of the Grosvenor Tap comes in 1805 when Edward Jones was the landlord. Grosvenor Gardens, which never fulfilled their early promise, closed around the same time, and now lie under a housing estate. All that remains is the hotel – the central building in Grosvenor Place – once a college, but long since converted to residential use. Almost 200 summers have passed since the Grosvenor Hotel closed its doors, but it still stands, frozen in time, its blank panels and uncarved garlands mute testimony to John Eveleigh's never-realised dream.

SYDNEY GARDENS

Although Sydney Gardens are still with us, they have changed beyond recognition. In June 1791, plans were announced for a "New Vauxhall" in the middle of Sydney Place. The plans were approved by Miss Pulteney and, in October of the following year, a meeting to discuss "the intended Vauxhall & Ranelagh Gardens in New Town" was held at Spring Gardens. By late spring the following year, Sydney Gardens were ready to receive their first visitors. The opening was accompanied by an "Irish pipe concert."

Two years later, John Gale, "late of Wade's Passage," added two bowling greens and three swings. Advertisements stressed that there was to be no swinging between nine and five on Sundays. This may seem like a slightly overzealous edict, but swinging in the eighteenth century was not the innocent pastime it is today. Without putting too fine a point on it, young ladies went knickerless. As they swung to and fro, and their dresses billowed out, young men would position themselves strategically in the hope of catching a glimpse of their feminine charms. Once you know that, you'll never look at Fragonard's painting of the girl on the swing in quite the same way again. And you'll understood why they banned swinging on Sundays.

John Gale also laid out a labyrinth and "a capital swing on Merlin's construction," which, despite some teething problems, came into use later that summer. The labyrinth was "so puzzling" that a map of it was sold at the entrance. In October 1795, Mr Gale placed a notice in the *Bath Chronicle*, thanking patrons "for the very liberal encouragement given him," and promising to continue "to render the refreshments, of all kinds, as reasonable as possible, and of the best quality." He claimed that Sydney Gardens were already "the pleasurable resort of the most fashionable company residing in, or resorting to, Bath," and begged "leave to inform the publick that the garden is constantly receiving improvement, and from the superior and novel style in which it is designed, its visitants, and particularly admirers of picturesque plantations, will be most gratified in contemplating its rising beauties."

In November 1796, the first stone of "Sydney House," designed by Charles Harcourt Masters (now the Holburne Museum), was laid. In January 1799, Sydney Gardens were advertised to let, complete with three swings and "a new built tavern." The tavern was Sydney House, or, as it was usually known, Sydney Hotel, although it was closer to what we know as holiday apartments today, with suites of rooms hired out at a guinea a week.

In 1825, Sydney Gardens were remodelled. The ride round the Gardens was macadamised, the cascade removed, a theatre and an aviary built, and a military band engaged to entertain visitors. In 1830, the gas mains were extended to Bathwick and a gas star, seven feet in diameter and with 127 flames, was erected over the door of the hotel to illuminate the Gardens. Two years later, Mr Norrison took over the Gardens and held a Grand Gala to mark the occasion. In 1834, he held a meeting to raise money to enlarge the hotel. The following year, celebrations to mark the twentieth anniversary of Waterloo attracted about 4,000 people to the Gardens. The *Bath Chronicle* somewhat tersely commented that, "we cannot refrain from mentioning the great improvement which has been made in bringing the amusements to an early termination."

In 1835, extensions were added to the Hotel, including new stables. The following year, plans for more improvements to the Gardens were announced. Mr Norrison took to advertising them as Royal Sydney Gardens for a time, doubtless influenced by the success of Royal Victoria Park.

Two years later, a new proprietor took over. By now, the gardens had been sliced in two by the Great Western Railway, and new walks "from which the railway trains may be seen passing" were advertised. The following year, the labyrinth, which had been destroyed by the railway, was restored, and a Gothic Concert Hall was built. One of the first events held in the hall was a temperance demonstration.

Moving quickly on from that chill blast of abstinence, let us consider the alcoholic history of the Gardens. Like Spring and Grosvenor Gardens, Sydney Gardens had a tap for coachmen and servants. In 1907, Mr Sydenham described it as follows:

> At the south-east angle of Sydney House, or as it was afterwards known, Sydney Hotel, in the basement was carried on for many years a public-house, presumably for the accommodation of coach and chairmen, and other attendants of fashionable frequenters of the Gardens; as in common with all the other Bath pleasure resorts, announcements continually recur: "Servants in Livery will not be admitted" to the gardens.

The title of this public-house was frequently changed; in 1805 it was known as the Sidney Tap, in 1809 as the Royal Tap, then as the Sydney Gardens Tavern, later as the Pulteney Tap ... The quaint old-fashioned fittings of this, certainly not an open-air resort, the writer saw some years ago, slowly decaying relics of a bygone age.

This account has puzzled later researchers, and is flatly contradicted in Brenda Snadden's history of Sydney Gardens:

The Sydney Tap was not in the basement, as often stated; this would have involved mere coachmen entering by the same door as their employers. It was a separate building and let to a sub-tenant.

An advertisement from the *Bath Chronicle* in March 1822 confirms this:

To be let ... those celebrated Pleasure Gardens, with a convenient and handsome Hotel and Tavern, also an adjoining public house known by the name of the Sydney Tap ... The Sydney Tap, which is detached, has hitherto been let off to a sub-tenant.

It seems that Mr Sydenham, having seen the fittings stored in the basement of the old Sydney Hotel, assumed – or was told – that the Sydney Tap had been down there. And once it appeared in print it became received wisdom.

But, having established that it was not in the basement, where was it? In the 1822 advertisement it was described as "detached" but "adjoining" the Sydney Hotel. A further clue to its location comes from an aquatint in a book called *Bath Illustrated*, published in 1805, on display in the Holburne Museum. The words SYDNEY TAP are clearly visible on the portico to the right of the building (which now leads to the tea room). The tea room is not the old tap, for, despite its chinoiserie trimmings, it is less than a hundred years old.

There is, however, another building which fits the bill. Early maps of Sydney Gardens show a curved line of arbours running from the south-east corner of the Sydney Hotel to a small unidentified building. From the evidence of the newspaper advertisement and the aquatint, this seems the most likely candidate for the Sydney Tap. The arbours were entered from the lawn at the back of the Sydney Hotel and

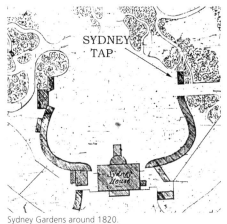

Sydney Gardens around 1820.

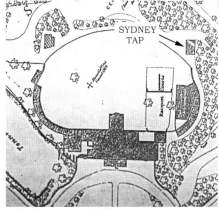

Sydney Gardens around 1880.

looked across to a similar line of arbours running from the north-east corner of the building. If the unidentified building was the Sydney Tap, however, it would have been entered from the back – through the archway beside what is now the tearoom. Ladies and gentlemen ensconced in the arbours would thus be screened from the chairmen and coachmen walking around the back for a drink.

The arbours have long since gone and it seems reasonable to assume that the Sydney Tap went with them. But did it? There are still the remains of a small building, once used as a store by the Parks' Department, hidden behind a high wall, which dates back to the early days of Sydney Gardens. Moreover, it stands in same spot as the unidentified building at the end of the arbours. Was the equipment seen by Mr Sydenham in the basement of the Sydney Hotel moved out so that the building could be used as a store? And is this unknown shed Bath's sole surviving pleasure garden tap? Although we cannot be certain, the evidence suggests that it is.

Turning from these intriguing possibilities to the licensed history of the gardens, it appears that Sydney House was first licensed in 1794, the year after the gardens opened. The licensee was George Clark and the name of the gardens was given as "Vauxhall Ranelagh." Sydney House was renamed the Sydney Hotel in 1816, became the Pulteney Hotel by 1841, and the Royal Pulteney Hotel by 1849. Its licensees included John Gale (1798), John Holloway (1799), Robert Lansdown (1815), James Hoskins (1816), Thomas Parker (1817), George Farnham (1818), William Brindle (1828), Mr Norrison (1832) and James Ivatts (1849). The hotel and gardens proved to be a poor investment for several of the tenants. William Brindle was one of those who suffered bankruptcy. He took his grievances to Sir Robert Peel, the Prime Minister, and, when denied access to him, smashed a window and got himself arrested to publicise his case.

The Sydney Tap first seems to have been licensed separately in 1805, when William Ball, who had previously held the licence for Spring Gardens, took it on. By 1809, Elizabeth Smith held the licence of what she called the Royal Tap. In 1812, William Selman took it over and renamed it the Sydney Gardens Tap. It became the Sydney Tap once more when William Gammon took it over around 1818.

By 1840, when the navvies arrived to build Brunel's railway through the Gardens, it had been renamed the Pulteney Tap. As it was the closest pub to the line, business must have boomed. But once the line was open, its days were numbered. Its end came suddenly one November morning in 1850:

> About a quarter past twelve on Monday morning, Mr Harford, landlord of the Pulteney Hotel Tap, discovered a strong smell of gas, and on entering the bar parlour to ascertain whence it proceeded, a tremendous explosion took place, by which the windows of that and another room were smashed, the door forced off its hinges and the ceiling shaken. The landlord was knocked down, his hair was singed and his hand blistered with the flames. It is supposed that some boys, who had some beer in the room on Sunday evening, turned off the gas, and attempted to steal the pipe, thus producing a leakage.

It never reopened. Three years later, the hotel and gardens were taken over by Bath Proprietary College, and the Tap was patched together as a store room, a function it continued to perform until the roof collapsed in 2004.

There have been plans to restore Sydney Gardens to something like their former glory for years. It would be wonderful to think that an unloved and uncared for part of Bath's heritage – the Sydney Tap – could be saved from demolition and become a focus for the regeneration of the Gardens. Given its recent history, that seems unlikely. Very sad to think to that a building from which Jane Austen may have heard the sounds of carousing coachmen, in a World Heritage city, should be treated with so little respect.

Bath's least-loved building? The Sydney Tap just before the roof collapsed.

The story of Bathwick Villa Pleasure Gardens is told on pages 51-52 of *Bath Pubs*, but there was one other pleasure garden which never even opened. It is one of the most tantalising might-have-beens of Bath's licensed history.

The story of Beckford's Tower has been rehearsed so often and so thoroughly, there is no need to go into it again here. There is, however, one aspect of its history that most commentators ignore or gloss quickly over: Beckford's Tower very nearly became a pub.

After William Beckford's death in 1844, his estate was auctioned off. It was one of the sales of the century, lasting eight days and netting over £25,000, an enormous sum in those days. The Tower, however, failed to find a buyer, and was offered for sale again at a public auction on 10 May 1847. It was bought, together with an acre of land, by William Knott, the landlord of the Freemasons' Tavern on Abbey Green, for £1,000. Despite its name, the Freemasons' Tavern by this time was one of Bath's less salubrious hostelries. Four years later the police tried to close it down, claiming it was the haunt of prostitutes and vagabonds. What the pleasure gardens Mr Knott intended to open on Lansdown would have been like is anyone's guess: in all probability they would have acquired the same sort of reputation as the Cremorne Gardens in Bathwick.

We will never know. Less than four months after the sale, on 4 September 1847, the Duchess of Hamilton, Beckford's daughter, having got wind of Mr Knott's plans, bought the tower and the land back off him for an undisclosed sum and presented them to the Rector of Walcot for use as a cemetery. Although the tower has had a somewhat chequered history since then – at least until its recent restoration by the Bath Preservation Trust – it is fairly safe to say that it would have been more chequered still had Mr Knott's plans gone ahead.

Even so, it would be nice to think that in a parallel universe someone could flip open the 2006 *Good Beer Guide* and find an entry such as:

Beckford's Tower

Lansdown Road BA1 9BH

12-2.30; 6-11 (12-11 Sat; 12-10.30 Sun) (closed Mon in winter)

Abbey Bellringer, Wickwar BOB, Bath Barnstormer, Butcombe Blonde; guest beers

Housed in a tower built by "England's wealthiest son," Beckford's Tower features in Roger Protz's 100 Pubs to Visit Before You Die, plus just about every pub guide published in the last 20 years. It's recommended you attempt the climb up the tower before you get stuck into a session – as the drop down the vertigo-inducing spiral staircase is a long one.

The long walk up the hill might tempt you to stay for the night, although at £80 plus for a room (£120 plus if you opt for the Vathek Suite) you might think twice. The gardens, with grottoes and arbours, are a delight, and the food is excellent, if a little on the pricey side. Beer festivals April and October. Bands on the lawn in summer. ✿ ☉ ☾ ●◆P

What might have been: the Beckford Pleasure Gardens.

THE LOST PUBS OF BATH

ENVOI

THE NAMING OF PUBS

In which the authors reveal some of the problems they have faced in their dipsychorean odyssey and take a fond farewell of the reader.

Traditionalists decry the current passion for renaming pubs, and hark back to the good old days when pubs names never changed. If that were the case, compiling this book would have been a great deal easier. The truth is that, while some pubs have kept the same name, the majority have not.

Some pubs had a bewildering variety of names. Take one on Walcot Street, open for less than 30 years, which was called, at various times, the Duke of Wellington's Arms, the Wellington Arms, the Duke of Wellington, the Wellington Arms & Newmarket Tavern, and the Newmarket Tavern. Or one in Southgate Street known as the Plume of Feathers, the Blucher, the Gladstone Arms, and the Oxford Stores.

The further back one goes, the more fragmentary the records of Bath's pubs become. Sometimes, it is only possible to establish exactly where pubs were if plans or later records are available. Often they are not. As pubs often changed their names when a new landlord took over, it can be impossible to establish continuity of use.

Some landlords had long runs, but others came and went with bewildering frequency. Take the Prince Frederick on Beaufort Square, for example, which closed in 1909. Between 1806 and 1811, it had no less than five landlords. First was William Robinson, who in April 1808 handed over to Robert Hockley. Hockley lasted only three months before moving to the Bell in Walcot Street. He was succeeded by James Norton who was there until early 1809, when he moved to the Rodney Arms in Westgate Place. Benjamin Osmond took over but only lasted 18 months, before handing over to Jonathan Shepherd. We only know about these changes because comprehensive records for this period have survived. Records for other periods have either been lost or survive in a fragmentary form, so that this sort of detailed survey is impossible. Just imagine if the records for this period had not survived and one of the Prince Frederick's landlords had decided to change its name. We would – in the absence of other information – have no way of knowing if it was the same pub.

There are numerous cases of pubs moving premises within the same street. When we go back over 200 years, it is sometimes impossible to determine whether a pub with a particular name in a particular street is the same pub as one with the same name in the same street a few years later.

Street numbers did not start to be used until the late eighteenth century – the first example we have found is that of Benjamin Fordes's Ice Cream Shop at 13 Pulteney Bridge in 1774.* Street numbering was far from universal well into the nineteenth century. But even when buildings were numbered, identifying them is not always straightforward. In the early days, numbering was a somewhat fluid process. Take the case of the Golden Lion in Southgate Street. In 1805, it was at No 12, but by 1848 it was at No 11. Four years later it was at No 10, where it remained until it closed in 1923. Surviving plans show that the inn stayed in the same place; it was the numbering that changed. That is one example from hundreds. Many streets were renumbered at least once as houses were fitted in, pulled down, knocked together, or divided up. Another problem is that many terraces were originally numbered separately and later renumbered as part of the street in which they stood. Cornwell Buildings and Ladymead, for example, were numbered separately until around 1911, but then became part of Walcot Street.

In the eighteenth and nineteenth centuries, some pubs were renamed for political reasons. The Raven is said to have indicated Jacobite sympathies, while radical politicians like Charles Fox and Bath's own JA Roebuck lent their names to pubs which, if the landlords were questioned, could be passed off as having innocuous animal connections. In the late nineteenth century, there was even a pub called the Gladstone in Bath (just imagine someone calling a pub the Old Blair & Bush or the Thatcher's Arms today). Patriotic sentiment was a major reason for pub renaming, as were major events, either national or local.

If a pub was taken over by somebody in a particular line of business or associated with a particular organisation, then its name often changed too. Plasterers, cabinet makers, saddlers, carpenters, masons, joiners, blacksmiths, volunteer riflemen – not to mention Oddfellows, Foresters, Druids, and Freemasons – all featured on eighteenth- and nineteenth-century pub signs, with the all-important word "arms" after them.

Until the eighteenth century, many of Bath's inn signs were taken from heraldic emblems. Sometimes these came from the coat of arms of the ruling monarch. Often, though, they came from the leaseholder's coat of arms or that of the profession to which he belonged. As far back as the fifteenth century, wealthy merchants or professional men leased inns, along with other property, as a form of investment, and appointed tenants to run them. Using an heraldic emblem as an inn sign was a way of proclaiming ownership, and, perhaps, had a more functional role. A professional man, arriving in a strange town, could make for the inn whose sign bore the arms of his guild, there to find not only a welcome, but also an entrée into local society. The Coat of Arms of the Worshipful Company of Apothecaries, for example, included two unicorns and the figure of Apollo holding a bow and arrow. This suggests a possible origin for the names of two of Bath's inns – the Crossbow and the Unicorn. The practice of wealthy citizens

---

*The actual address, which appears in the *Bath Journal* for 6 January 1774, is "No 13 on the New Bridge leading to Spring Gardens."

THE LOST PUBS OF BATH

acquiring inns and pubs as an investment did not so much die out as undergo a radical transformation in the latter part of the eighteenth century. Developments in brewing technology led to brewing empires being built on the back of property empires.

It was a similar story with alehouses. A mason would open an alehouse called the Mason's Arms. Itinerant masons or labourers in search of work would call in to enquire about work. Employers would drop by to look for workers. It was, in effect, an employment exchange, with the added advantage that, instead of having to watch a video about job-seeking skills, you could get a drink.

It was not just inns and alehouses that had signs, however. In an age of widespread illiteracy, signs were everywhere. There was a lodging house and shop in the Orange Grove called the Golden Fleur de Lis (1755) and a milliner's at 13 Bath Street called the Three Pigeons & Sceptre (1796). Another Bath Street milliner's was called the Pheasants (1797). John Kendall had a china shop in Pierrepoint Street called the Golden Canister (1774). Mr Palmer, a weaver and mercer, called his shop in Union Passage the Peacock (1774). Warren & Rosser's Perfumery at 8 George Street was called the Golden Fleece (1794) There was another Golden Fleece opposite the Three Tuns in Stall Street – this one was a draper's (1759). A linen warehouse at 11 Union Street was called the Beehive (1812). The Three Pigeons in Milsom Street was a Haberdashery, Hosiery, Glove and Fur Warehouse (1791), while the Plume of Feathers "on the walls and fronting the North Parade" was Mr Marriott's Hosiery, Perfume and Snuff Shop (1789). In 1783, Joseph Dibbens, Cheese Monger, Cheese & Corn Chandler from the Borough Walls moved to the Phoenix next to the Three Cups in Northgate Street, where there was a "genteel dining room to let" (1783). And, in the eighteenth century, if you asked someone directions to the Green Tree or the Star, you could have ended up being sent on a wild goose chase, if these two advertisements from the Bath Journal are anything to go by:

> Francis Bennett at the Star in the Church Yard, Bath, sells all sorts of linen drapery, woollen drapery and haberdashery goods; all sorts of blanketting, flannels, swan-skin and shags; all sorts of teas, coffee, chocolate and sugar; with all other sorts of grocery wares; all sorts of fine snuffs, and cards: all of which are sold as cheap as in London, for ready money. (4 June 1744)

> Now open for sale by hand, at Mrs Dart's, known by the name of the Green Tree House, in Stall Street, a most curious and valuable collection of fine foreign and English ornamental china. (17 November 1768)

These few examples will give some idea how wary we have had to be, and why we may sometimes appear to have erred on the side of caution. Where we have thrown caution to the winds, rushed in where angels fear to tread, or gone out on a limb, as with the story of Prior Gibb, we have, we hope, made this abundantly clear. But however cautious we have, when dealing with matter so recondite and hoary it is inevitable that errors will, like Shakespeare's whining schoolboy, creep in.

When we wrote *Bath Pubs*, we said that the old Bear on Bear Flat closed after it was bombed in 1942. Not only was there photographic evidence of extensive bomb damage; everyone we spoke to told us that it never reopened - until the book was published. Someone who had drunk there regularly throughout the 1950s got in touch because he thought we would like to set the record straight. Which we now have.

But if we can get things that happened within living memory wrong, who knows what transgressions we may have made in delving into the substrata of days beyond recall. All that we can claim is to have done our best and marked a trail for future chroniclers of times past to follow. For the rest, in the words of the Immortal Beard,

> As you from crimes would pardon'd be,
> Let your indulgence set us free.

One thing became abundantly clear during the writing of this book: the Sack of Bath, generally supposed to have been confined to the 1960s and 1970s, has been going on for centuries. Until about 50 years ago, however, it was generally agreed that replacing old buildings (apart from a few honourable exceptions) with new ones was a good thing. When a warren of seventeenth- and eighteenth-century buildings was demolished in 1900 to make way for the Empire Hotel, everybody thought it was a great improvement.

Our current craze for conservation would have been as incomprehensible to anyone living before the mid-twentieth century as it is to people from many non-European countries today. The notion that new buildings are better than old has been accepted, almost without question, throughout most of recorded history. How long our present attitude to old buildings will last is open to debate.

People in Bath may be forgiven for thinking that, in essence, nothing will change, and that the city will continue to look much as it does today for the foreseeable future. Listed building constraints are such a powerful inhibitor of change, they may lull us into the belief that things will stay the same for ever.

They won't. Look at Southgate, look at the Western Riverside, look at the Rec. Who knows what Bath will look like a hundred – or a thousand – years hence? Or how many pubs will be left. All things, as George Harrison said, must pass away. Or in the words of a wordier wordsmith:

> Our reuels now are ended: These our actors,
> (As I foretold you) were all Spirits, and
> Are melted into Ayre, into thin Ayre,
> And like the baseless fabricke of this vision,
> The Clowd-capt Towres, the gorgeous Pallaces,
> The solemne Temples, the great Globe it selfe,
> Yea, all which it inherit, shall dissolue,
> And like this insubstantiall Pageant faded
> Leaue not a racke behinde: we are such stuffe
> As dreames are made on; and our little life
> Is rounded with a sleepe.

APPENDIX ONE

BREWERIES

This is not a complete listing of the breweries that owned pubs in Bath, but a resumé of the main ones mentioned in the text. It does not include the many home-brew pubs in the city, many of which had the word Brewery in their names. For more information on Bath's breweries, see Mike Bone's article, "The Rise and Fall of Bath's Breweries: 1736-1960," in *Bath History VIII*.

Abbey Ales, Lansdown Road, founded 1997

Albion Brewery, Albion Place, Upper Bristol Road, Bath, c1808-1854. Demolished.

Anchor Brewery, Southgate Street, Bath, c1783-1843. Demolished.

Anglo-Bavarian Brewery, Shepton Mallet. c1860-1921. Brewing revived 1934-39. Building survives.

Bath Brewery (Pinch's), Kingsmead Street, Bath. Founded 1835. Date of closure unknown. Demolished.

Bath Brewery Co. Formed from six smaller breweries, including the Kensington, Bathwick, Morford, and Edgecumbe Breweries. Brewing concentrated at the Bathwick Brewery until a new brewery at Lower Weston opened in 1896. Absorbed by George's of Bristol 1923. Building demolished.

Bathwick Brewery, Bathwick Street, Bath. Opened c1791. Absorbed into Bath Brewery, 1889. Brewing continued until 1896.

Bear Brewery, Bear Flat, Bath, c1852-1902. Demolished.

The old brewery at Batheaston.

Burlington Brewery, Julian Road, Bath, c1791-1870. Demolished.

Charlton Brewery, Shepton Mallet. Founded 1844. Absorbed by Bristol United Breweries 1937. Brewing ceased 1961.

Combe Down Brewery, King William IV Inn, Combe Down, c1840-c1885. Building survives.

County Brewery. Established by three local brewers, Pearce, Reynolds, and Withers, in 1904, at the old Avondale Brewery in Batheaston, previously used by the English Lager Brewery. Absorbed by the Bath Brewery Co., 1912. Building survives.

Crown Brewery, New Orchard Street, Bath. Absorbed by George's, 1924. Demolished.

Edgecumbe Brewery, Weston, Bath. Absorbed into Bath Brewery Co., 1889. Building survives.

English Lager Brewery Ltd. Acquired Avondale Brewery, a mid-nineteenth century brewing concern near the Toll Bridge at Batheaston, in 1890. In receivership 1893. Building later taken over by the County Brewery (see above).

Frome United Breweries. Founded 1889, merged with the Lamb Brewery in 1955 to form Frome & Lamb, which was absorbed by Usher's and Stroud Breweries in 1957.

George's Brewery, Bristol. Founded c1730. Absorbed by Courage's 1961. Brewing continued till 1999.

Kensington Brewery, next to Porter Butt, London Road, Bath. Opened c1809. Absorbed into Bath Brewery Co. 1889. Building survives.

Lamb Brewery, Frome. Founded c1850.

Mole's Brewery, Melksham, founded 1982.

Morford Brewery, Lampard's Buildings. Established in the late eighteenth century. Absorbed into Bath Brewery Co. 1889. Demolished.

Norfolk Brewery, Albion Place, Upper Bristol Road, Bath, 1826-1861. Demolished.

North Parade Brewery, Gallaway's Buildings, Bath, c1870-1923. Building survives.

Northgate Brewery, Northgate Street, Bath, c1770-1868. Demolished.

Oakhill Brewery, Oakhill, 1767-1938. Building survives.

Pointing's Brewery, Weston, Bath, closed 1926. Building survives.

Portland Brewery, Portland Place, Bath, closed c1877. Demolished.

Ruddles' Brewery, Bradford on Avon, closed 1924.

Sainsbury's Brewery, Nelson Place East, London Street, Bath, c1793-1901.

Southstoke Brewery, Southstoke, 1849-c1906. Building survives.

Spencer's Brewery, Bradford on Avon, 1889-1913.

Walcot Brewery, opposite Walcot Terrace, London Road, Bath, c1792-1887. Later used as a depot by the Anglo-Bavarian Brewery. Part of building survives.

Thatcher's Brewery (later Welton Brewery), Midsomer Norton. Absorbed by George's c1918.

Williams & Sons Brewery, Broad Quay, Bath, c1779-1849. Demolished.

ROBINSON & MORGAN,
Edgecumbe Brewery,
WESTON, BATH.

Ales, and Stout Brewed especially for families.

Excellent Dinner Ales, Mild or Bitter, from 1/- per Gallon.

*Mr Stoddart reports of their F.R.A. One Shilling (Bitter Ale),
as follows :—*
Western Counties Laboratory,
Masonic Hall, 1 and 2, Park Street Bristol,
Messrs. ROBINSON & MORGAN,   November 30th, 1880.
Edgecumbe Brewery,
Gentlemen,
Having carefully analysed your Bitter Ale. I am of the opinion, that it is a very wholesome and invigorating tonic. It is flavoured with an agreeable and perfectly innocuous bitter, containing at the same time a full average of all its constituents, and is certainly a most excellent and palatable beverage.
I remain Gentlemen, yours truly,
F. WALLIS STODDART,
Public Analyst for Bristol, &c.

APPENDIX TWO

A TAVERN SONG POPULAR IN BATH, 1616

Records of the Proceedings of the Star Chamber from 1616 contain a transcript of the kind of scurrilous song common in Bath's inns and taverns in the seventeenth century. When Anne of Denmark, the wife of King James I, visited Bath, she was attended by the wife of Peter Perman, a prominent citizen. Tavern wags put it about that she was generous with her favours, and nicknamed her "Muddy Mall." The raw hides of oxen which were a common sight in the city, being carried through the streets "with their horns hanging thereon," were dubbed "Peter Perman's nightgowns" – a reference to the horns traditionally worn by cuckolds. Because of her connection with the royal family, the following song (which contains nudity and strong language) landed its author in the highest court in the land :

> Of all the whoores that I have knowne,
> From Courte that came into our Towne,
> There's none compares with Muddy Mall,
> That playes the whoore from springe to fall;
> From springe to fall was never see,
> A Poxie Jade worse than Marie,
> All honest women doe her scorne,
> Because she was a bastard borne,
> A bastard borne of noble race,
> Which makes here wear a brazen face,
> A brazen face of Opall hue,
> An arrant whoore fytt for a stewe;
> If you have golde she showes her arse,
> If you have none she burnes your tarsse [trousers].
> She keepes herselfe juste like a puncke,
> And layes her heeles against a truncke,
> Against a truncke she layes her feete,
> And wipes her c*** with a foule sheete ...

... And the residue and other parte of ye said lybell ryme and verses is so obscenous and fowle as it is not fytt herein to be written or remembered, neyther is the same fyttinge or decente for any modest eyes to reade or eares to heare.

STOP PRESS

Not many books have a stop press section. This one is an exception. Here's why:

On the morning of Monday 31 October 2005, preparations were being made to send the book to the printers when an email was received from Steve Plumridge, editor of *Pints West*, the local CAMRA newsletter. A lady called Jackie Douglass from Kent had contacted him with information about the Royal Oak on Lower Bristol Road (see pages 125-27). Eliza Beard, Bath's longest-serving landlady, was her husband's great-grandmother; she not only had a photograph of her but another showing the pub as it looked over a century ago.

Eliza Beard around 1900, with her daughter, Alethea Davis, and her son-in-law, Seth Davis. Their sons, Ernest and Harry, were born in 1894 and 1896 respectively.

She had never seen the pub and assumed it had disappeared – until she took a train journey to visit her daughter in Weston Super Mare, which, due to engineering works, had to be made partly by bus. After calling at Bath Spa station, the bus headed along the Lower Bristol Road, past the recently reopened Royal Oak. A couple of days later, she picked up a copy of *Pints West* in Weston and saw Andrew Swift's article on the reopening of the Royal Oak, which mentioned Eliza Beard. The rest, as they say, is history. We contacted Jackie who kindly agreed to the photographs appearing in the book. We received them by email later that afternoon. Worth taking the slightly unconventional step of including a stop press, we think you'll agree.

The Royal Oak, with the railway viaduct on the right and a now-demolished building on the left. Note the slats on the right-hand side of the building, indicating the location of the brewery.

BIBLIOGRAPHY

Primary sources include a vast range of material held in the Bath, Somerset and Wiltshire Record Offices, as well as the Mompesson Records in Buckinghamshire Record Office.

An invaluable source of primary material has been local newspapers held in Bath Central Library. Some information has also been gleaned from early eighteenth-century Bristol newspapers held in Bristol Reference Library.

Bath Postal Directories, a near-complete run of which is held in Bath Central Library and Bath Record Office, have been consulted extensively. As almost every entry post-1800 draws on information in Postal Directories, this has not been specifically acknowledged in most cases. We have also consulted Kelly's Directories for Somerset extensively, especially for outlying parishes which were not covered comprehensively in early Bath Postal Directories.

Other works consulted include:

A Record of the Great Floods in Bath and the Surrounding District, November 13 & 15, 1894, Reprinted from the Bath Herald, Bath 1894.

Bath and Bristol Guide, Bath, 1755.

Kegs & Ale: Bath and the Public House, Bath, 1991.

Old English Coffee Houses, London, 1954.

Aspinall, A, ed., *Mrs Jordan & her Family, Being the Unpublished Letters of Mrs Jordan and the Duke of Clarence, later William IV*, London, 1951.

Barber, Norman, *A Century of British Brewers, 1890-2004*, Longfield, Kent, 2005.

Beaton, Mark, Mike Chapman, Andrew Crutchley, Jane Root, *Bath Historical Streetscape Survey*, 2 vols, Bath, 2000.

Bickerdyke, John, *The Curiosities of Ale & Beer*, London, 1889.

Blackmantle, Bernard (pseudonym of Charles Westmacott), *The English Spy*, London, 1826.

Bold, Alan, *Drink to Me Only: The Prose and Cons of Drinking*, London, 1982.

Bone, Mike, "The Rise and Fall of Bath's Breweries, 1736-1960," in *Bath History, VIII*, Bath, 2000.

Boston, Richard, *Beer and Skittles*, London, 1976.

Brackenbury, DN, "The Folly 1742-1942, Farmhouse, Pleasure Garden & Tavern," unpublished MS, Bath Central Library, 1970.

Canvin, John, *Southstoke History*, typescript in Bath Central Library, n.d.

Chandler, John, *John Leland's Itinerary*, Stroud, 1993.

Chapman, Mike, *An Historical Guide to the Ham and Southgate Area of Bath*, Bath, 1997.

Chapman, Mike & Elizabeth Holland, *Bimbery and the South-Western Baths of Bath*, Bath, 2001.

Chudley, Ron, *Thomas Dunckerley: A Remarkable Freemason*, London, 1982.

Clark, Peter, *The English Alehouse: A Social History, 1200-1830*, London, 1983.

Cotterell, Thomas Sturge, *Historic Map of Bath*, Bath, 1939

Crawford, Anne, *Bristol and the Wine Trade*, Bristol, 1984.

Cruikshank, George, *Eccentric Excursions*, London, 1814.

Dallimore, John, *Newton St Loe, NE Somerset: A Study of the Vernacular Building Survey*, Bath, 2001.

Dallimore, Keith, *Exploring Combe Down*, Bath, 1988.

Davis, Charles, *The Mineral Baths of Bath: The Bathes of Bathe's Ayde*, Bath, 1883.

Davis, Dorothy, *A History of Shopping*, London, 1966.

Davis, Graham, *Bath Beyond the Guide Book: Scenes from Victorian Life*, Bristol, 1988.

Davis, Graham & Penny Bonsell, *Bath: A New History*, Keele, 1996.

De la Beche, Sir Henry, *Report on the City of Bath & Its Sanatory Condition*, London, 1845.

Delderfield, Eric, *British Inn Signs and Their Stories*, Exmouth, 1965.

Dillon, Patrick, *The Much Lamented Death of Madam Geneva: The Eighteenth-century Gin Craze*, London, 2002.

Disney, Francis, *Shepton Mallet Prison*, Shepton Mallet, 1992.

Dixon, Roger & Stefan Muthesius, *Victorian Architecture*, London, 1978.

Dobbie, BM Willmott, *An English Rural Community: Batheaston with St Catherine*, Bath, 1969.

Dunkling, Leslie & Gordon Wright, *Pub Names of Britain*, London, 1987.

Egan, Pierce, *Walks Through Bath*, Bath, 1819.

Eglin, John, *The Imagainary Autocrat: Beau Nash and the Invention of Bath*, London, 2005.

Fagan, Garrett G, *Bathing in Public in the Roman World*, Ann Arbor, 1999.

Fawcett, Trevor, *Bath Entertain'd*, Bath, 1998.

Fawcett, Trevor, *The Bagatelle & King James's Palace*, unpublished article, Bath Record Office, n.d.

Fawcett, Trevor, *Voices of Eighteenth-century Bath*, Bath, 1995.

Fawcett, Trevor and Marta Inskip, "The Making of Orange Grove," in *Bath History V*, Bath, 1994.

Forsyth, Michael, *Pevsner Architectural Guide to Bath*, New Haven & London, 2003.

French RV, *Nineteen Centuries of Drink in England*, London, 1884.

Fryer, Peter, *The Man of Pleasure's Companion*, London, 1968.

Girouard, Mark, *Victorian Pubs*, London, 1975.

Grafton, Frank, *Tipple & Temperance*, Unpublished article, BRO, n.d.

Gregory, W, *The Beckford Family: Reminiscences of Fonthill Abbey and Lansdown Tower*, Bath, 1898.

Hackwood, Frederick, *Inns, Ales and Drinking Customs of Old England*, London, 1985 (reprint).

Hare, Arnold, ed., *Theatre Royal, Bath: The Orchard Street Calendar, 1750-1805*, Bath, 1977.

Hargood-Ash, Joan, *Two Thousand Years in the Life of a Somerset Village; Weston, Bath*, Weston, 2001.

Harper, Duncan, *Bath at Work*, Bath, 1989.

Harrison, Brian, *Drink and the Victorians*, London, 1971.

Haydon, Peter, *The English Pub: A History*, London, 1994.

Hecht, J Jean, *The Domestic Servant in Eighteenth-Century England*, London, 1980.

Holland, Elizabeth, *The Kingston Estate*, Bath 1992.

Holland, Elizabeth & Mike Chapman, *Bath Guildhall and its Neighbourhood*, Bath 2000.

Hudson, Thomas, *Temperance Pioneers of the West*, London, 1887.

Hutt, Christopher, *The Death of the English Pub*, London, 1973.

Ison, Walter, *The Georgian Buildings of Bath*, Revised edition, Bath 1980.

Laurence, Godfrey F, *Bathford Past and Present*, Bathford, 1985.

Lewis, Harold, *The Church Rambler*, Bath, 1878.

Lowndes, William, *The Theatre Royal at Bath*, Bristol, 1982.

McGrath, Patrick & Mary E Williams, eds., *Bristol Inns and Alehouses in the Mid-Eighteenth Century*, Bristol, 1979.

Mainwaring, Captain Rowland, *Annals of Bath from the Year 1800 to the Passing of the New Municipal Act*, Bath, 1838.

Manco, Jean, *The Parish of Englishcombe: A History*, Englishcombe, 1995.

Manco, Jean, *The Spirit of Care: The 800 Year Story of St John's Hospital, Bath*, Bath, 1998

Manco, Jean, "Bath and the Great Rebuilding," in *Bath History IV*, Bath, 1992.

Manco, Jean, "Saxon Bath," in *Bath History VII*, Bath, 1998.

Marwick, Arthur, *Britain in Our Century*, London, 1984

Measom, George, *Official Illustrated Guide to the Great Western Railway*, London, 1852.

Meehan, JF, *A Few Famous Inns of Bath and District*, Bath, 1913.

Meehan, JF, *Famous Houses of Bath & District*, Bath 1901.

Minnit SC, J Durnell, AJH Gunstone, *Somerset Public House Tokens*, Bridgwater, 1985.

Morris, Dr Claver, *The Diary of a West Country Physician*, ed. Edmund Hobhouse, London, 1934.

Neale, RS, *Bath: A Social History, 1650-1850, or A Valley of Pleasure, yet a Sink of Iniquity*, London, 1981.

Parfitt, Robert, ed., *The Book of South Stoke with Midford*, Tiverton, 2001.

Paston-Williams, Sara, *The Art of Dining*, Oxford, 1993.

Peach, REM, *The Annals of the Parish of Swainswick*, London & Bath, 1890.

Peach, REM, *Street Lore of Bath*, Bath, 1893.

Pearce, Fred, *The Critical Guide to Bath Pubs*, Bristol, 1976.

Penley, Belvill, *The Bath Stage*, London & Bath, 1892.

Penrose, Rev John, *Letters from Bath, 1766-1767*, ed. Brigitte Mitchell & Hubert Penrose, Gloucester, 1983.

Pitcairn, Rev D Lee & Rev Alfred Richardson, *An Historical Guide to Monkton Combe, Combe Down and Claverton*, Bath, 1924.

Poole, Steve, *Another Utopia: A Fringe Guide to the Sites of Bath's Other Heritage*, Bath, 1996.

Pound, Christopher, *Genius of Bath: The City & its Landscape*, Bath 1986.

Putler, Richard, *Bath City Police: A Brief History*, Bath, 1985.

Robertson, Charles, *Bath: An Architectural Guide*, London, 1975.

Scott, Maurice, *Discovering Widcombe & Lyncombe*, Bath, 1993.

Shickle, Rev CW, ed., *Ancient Deeds Belonging to the Corporation of Bath*, Bath, 1921.

Simond, Louis, ed. Christopher Hibbert, *An American in Regency England*, London, 1968.

Skinner, John, *The Journal of a Somerset Rector*, ed. Howard & Peter Coombs, Oxford, 1971.

Snadden, Brenda, *The Last Promenade: Sydney Gardens, Bath*, Bath, 2000.

Southey, Robert, *Letters from England,* London, 1807.

Sporgersi, Dr EP, *Doctor Dee and the Mad Abbot of Bath,* Bath, 2003.

Stone, Barbara, *Bath Millennium*, Bath, 1973.

Sydenham S, *Bath Pleasure Gardens of the Eighteeenth Century Issuing Metal Admission Tickets*, Bath, 1907.

Sydenham, S, *Bath Tokens of the Seventeenth Century*, Bath, 1905.

Symons, Katherine E, *The Grammar School of King Edward VI, Bath, and Its Ancient Foundation*, Bath, 1934.

Ward, Ned, *A Step to the Bath*, London, 1700.

Waugh, Ken & Margaret, *A Glimpse of Bathford, the Walled Village*, Bathford, 1982.

Westmacott, Charles, *see Bernard Blackmantle*.

Wilcox, Ronald, "Bath Breweries in the Latter Half of the Eighteenth Century," in *A Second North Somerset Miscellany*, (pp. 23-31), Bath, 1971.

Wood, John, *A Description of Bath*, 2nd edition, London, 1749.

Woodforde, James, *Diary of a Country Parson*, ed. John Beresford, 5 vols.

Wroughton, John, *A Community at War: The Civil War in Bath and North Somerset, 1642-1650*, Bath, 1992.

Wroughton, John, ed., *Bath in the Age of Reform*, Bath 1972.

Wroughton, John, *Stuart Bath: Life in the Forgotten City, 1603-1714*, Bath, 2004.

PUB INDEX

Abbreviations LBR Lower Bristol Road   LBW Lower Borough Walls   UBR Upper Bristol Road   UBW Upper Borough Walls

Cooper's Arms, Claverton St, 258
Corn Market Tavern, Walcot St, 163
Corn Street Brewery, Corn St, 310
Cremorne, *see Folly*
Crescent, Milk St, 288
Crispin Tavern, LBW, *see Bell*
Cross Daggers, White Hart Lane, 51
Cross Keys, Orange Grove, 94-97
Crossbow, Stall St, 51
Crown & Anchor, Upr Hedgemead, 199-200
Crown & Cushion, Bridewell Lane, 71
Crown & Cushion, Milk St, 288
Crown & Raven, Broad St Pl, 192
Crown & Thistle, Barton St, 214
Crown & Thistle, Slippery Lane, 104
Crown Brewery, New Orchard St, 317-18
Crown, Batheaston, 348
Crown, Claremont Row, 203
Crown, Combe Down, 353
Crown, High St, 23-24
Crown, Nr Hot Bath, 61
Crown, Stall St, 83

Darby & Joan, Guinea Lane, 197-99
Devonshire House, Kingsmead St, 287-88
Distill Head, Kingsmead Sq, 283-84
Dolphin, Broad St, 154, 193
Don Cossack, Walcot St, 172-73
Dorset House, Morford St, 245
Duke Of Cambridge, Grove St, 328-29
Duke Of Cumberland, Old Orchard St, 323
Duke Of Edinburgh, Walcot St, 165-66
Duke Of York, Avon St, 298

Eagle, Bath St, 51-52
East Twerton Hotel, LBR, 124-25
Edinburgh Arms, James St W, 229
Edinburgh Castle, Newark St, 315-16
Elephant & Castle, Monmouth St, 222-27, 371
Empire Hotel, 97-98
Engineer's Arms, LBR, 121-22
Exeter Inn, Southgate St, 113

Fencer's Arms, High St, *see Noble Science*
Fleece, St Michael's Pl, 61
Folly, Bathwick, 335-45, 372
Fortt's, Milsom St, 208-9
Fountain, Avon St, 295-96
Fountain, Southgate St, 115
Fox & Hounds, Beaufort Sq, 215
Fox & Hounds, Walcot St, 160-61
Fox, Midford, 364-65
Freemason's Tavern, Abbeygate St, *see Raven*
French Horn, LBW, 81-82
Full Moon, Southgate St, 116-21
Full Moon, UBW, 12-13
Fuller's Wine Vaults, Broad St, 193-94

Gallon Pot, Avon St, 298
Gardener, Southgate St, 116
Gardener's Arms, LBR, 123
Gardener's Arms, Primrose Hill, 249
Garibaldi, Avon St, 297
Garrick's Head, St John's Pl, 11, 220
Gay's Hill Tavern, Gay's Hill, 200-2
George, Nr Hot Bath, 57-60
George, Twerton, 132-33
George, UBW, 69
George, Walcot St, 154-55
Gladstone, Southgate St, *see Oxford Stores*
Globe, Kingsmead Sq, 283
Globe, Long Acre, 182

Globe, Weston, 252-53
Gloucester House, Charles St, 228
Gloucester Inn, Somerset Blgs, 177-80
Golden Fleece, Pulteney Rd, 260-61
Golden Lion, Southgate St, 109-10
Golden Lyon, Stall St, 82
Grand Pump Room Hotel, Stall St, 47-49
Grapes, Westgate St, 62
Great Western Hotel, Dorchester St, 313-15
Green Man, Broad St, 194
Green Park Tavern, LBR, 124
Green Tree, Swainswick, 366
Greyhound (New), Claverton St, 259
Greyhound Vaults, UBW, *see Squirrel*
Greyhound, Claverton St, 121, 256-57
Greyhound, High St, 19-22, 67, 69-70
Grove Tavern, Orange Court, 99
Grove Tavern, Padley Bottom, 358-59
Guildhall Tavern, High St, 29

Half Moon, Half Moon St, *see Berkeley Arms*
Half Moon, Holloway, 273
Hampton Musuem, Hampton Row, 334-35
Hand & Flower, Lansdown Rd, 195-97
Hand & Shears, Walcot St, 152
Hare & Hounds, High St, 24
Hare & Hounds, Widcombe, 266-67
Hat & Feather, London St, 13-14, 174
Heart & Compass, Cumberland Row, 227
Heart In Hand, Ambury, 308
Heath Robinson, St James's Parade, 311
Hen & Chicken, Wlacot St, 159
Highbury Arms, Highbury Terr, 202
Hole In The Wall, Avon St, 298
Hole In The Wall, Somerset St, 313
Hope & Anchor, Somerset Blgs, 177
Hope & Anchor, Southgate St, *see Exeter Inn*
Horse & Groom, Princes St, 217
Horse & Jockey, Barton St, 212-13
Horse & Jockey, Beau St, 56
Horse & Jockey, Claverton St, 352
Horse's Head, High St, 29
Huntsman, Terrace Walk, *see Parade Coffee House*

Isabella, Wine St, 312

Joiner's Arms, Pulteney Rd, 260
Joiner's Arms, Southgate St, 116
Jolly Butchers, Boatstall Lane, 103
Jolly Footman, Stall St, 47
Jolly Sailor, Avon St, 298
Jolly Sailor, Claverton St, 257
Jolly Sailor, Walcot St, 152
Joyner's Arms, Frog Lane, 208
Jupiter, Combe Down, 353

Katherine Wheel, High St, 22-24
Kettle & Pipes, Southgate St, 107
King Bladud, Parsonage Lane, 62
King Of Wessex, James St W, 15
King William, Thomas St, 14
King's Arms, Bailbrook, 347-48
King's Arms, Broad St, 189-90
King's Arms, Grove St, 330
King's Arms, High St, 28
King's Arms, Walcot St, 151-52
King's Arms, Widcombe, 267
King's Head, Bartlett St, 238
King's Head, Cheap St, 30
King's Head, Dafford's Blgs, 186
King's Head, Lilliput Alley, 88-89
Kingsmead Wine Vaults, Kingsmead St, 228, 287

Abbreviations LBR Lower Bristol Road   LBW Lower Borough Walls   UBR Upper Bristol Road   UBW Upper Borough Walls

THE LOST PUBS OF BATH

Rifleman's Arms, Bathwick St, 330
Rifleman's Arms, Walcot St, 168
Ring Of Bells, Church St, Widcombe, 267
Ring Of Bells, Lambridge St, 186
Ring Of Bells, Orange Grove, 93-94
Ring Of Bells, Stall St, 83
Ring Of Bells, Twerton, 131
Rising Sun, Circus Pl, 239
Rising Sun, Newton St Loe, 361-62
Rising Sun, Richmond Pl, 205
Rising Sun, Swainswick, 366
Rising Sun, Union Passage, 65
Rivers' Arms, Camen Pl, 202
Roaring Cannon, Dolemeads, 264
Robin Hood, UBR, 231
Rock, Combe Down, 353-55
Rodney, Broad St, 194
Roebuck, Holloway, 275
Roebuck, Quiet St, 209
Rose & Crown, Little Corn St, 304
Rose & Crown, Milk St, 288
Rose & Crown, Northgate St, 136
Rose & Crown, Southgate St, 108-9
Rose, Avon St, 298
Rose, Morford St, 245
Rose, Westgate St, 63
Royal Oak, LBR, 15, 125-27
Royal Oak, Monmouth Pl, 229-30
Royal Oak, Northgate St, 136
Royal Oak, Stall St, 82
Royal Sailor, Wells Rd, 270
Rummer, Southgate St, 116

Sadlers Arms, Stall St, 49-50
Sam Weller's, UBW, see Full Moon
Sandy Bank Inn, Batheaston, 350
Sedan Chair, Bridewell Lane, 71-72
Seven Dials, 77
Seven Stars, Claverton St, 259
Seven Stars, Twerton, 129
Seven Stars, UBW, 65-69
Shakespeare, Old Orchard St, 321-23
Shakespeare, Westgate St, 64
Shamrock, Avon St, 297-98
Ship, Southgate St, 114
Ship, St James's St S, 317
Shoulder Of Mutton, Stall St, 83
Silver Lion, Southgate St, 108
Smith Bros, Westgate Blgs, 11
Smith's Arms, Avon St, 297
Smith's Arms, Bathford, 351
Smith's Arms, Dolemeads, 264
Smith's Arms, Holloway, 275
Somerset Arms, Dolemeads, 264
Somerset Arms, Somerset St, 312-13
Somerset Arms, Winifred's Lane, 248
Somerset Wine Vaults, Southgate St, 113
Sot's Hole, Orange Grove, see Ring Of Bells
South Pole, Dorchester St, 313
Spread Eagle, Avon St, 298
Spread Eagle, Southgate St, 113-14
Squirrel, UBW, 21, 69
St George's Brewery, UBR, 231
St James's Tavern, St James's Parade, 312
Stag's Head, Widcombe Parade, 259
Star & Garter, Lilliput Alley, 89
Star, Bathford, 351
Still House, Southgate St, 116
Summerhill Tavern, Primrose Hill, 249
Sun, High St, 28-29
Sun, Orange Court, 98
Swan, Twerton, 128

Sword, Twerton, 128

Talbot, Abbeygate St, 83
Tankard, Beaufort Sq, 215-16
Tanner's Arms, Twerton, 128
Thatched House, Walcot St, 173-74
Theatre Tavern, Monmouth St, 219-20
Three Blackbirds, Frog Lane, 208
Three Blackbirds, Holloway, 275
Three Blackbirds, Little Stanhope St, 208, 230-31
Three Blue Posts, Back St, 304
Three Crowns, Combe Down, 358
Three Crowns, London St, 174-76
Three Crowns, Quiet St, 209
Three Cups, Northgate St, 136-37
Three Cups, Walcot St, see Pelican
Three Horseshoes, Northgate St, 137-38
Three Tuns, Stall St, 41, 53, 58
Times Taven, Monmouth St, 219
Trafalgar Tavern, Calton Rd, 267
Traveller's Rest, Lower Dover St, 184
Turk's Head Coffee House, High St, 28
Turk's Head. Broad St, 192-93

Unicorn, High St, 25
Unicorn, Northgate St, 137-40, 142-43, 190
Union Tavern, York St, 52

Viaduct, Monkton Combe, 361
Victoria Arms, Eldon Pl, 186
Victoria Wine & Spirit Vaults, Monmouth St, 221

Wagon & Horses, Catsley Pl, 187
Walcot Wine Vaults, Walcot St, 168-70
Waterloo, Gallaway's Blgs, 89
Waterman's Arms, Broad Quay, 303-4
Wellington Arms, Walcot St, 162-63
West's Grill, UBW, see London Dining Rooms
Westgate House, 73-75
Westgate Tavern, New Westgate Blgs, 75-77
Weymouth Arms, Julian Rd, 242-43
Wheatsheaf, Broad St, 190-91
Wheatsheaf, Stall St, 83
Wheatsheaf, Twerton, 133
Wheelchair, Cumberland Row, 227
Wheelchair, Kingsmead Sq, 283
White Hart Tap, Westgate St, 50-51
White Hart Vaults, UBW, 70
White Hart, Avon St, 298
White Hart, James St W, see Edinburgh Arms
White Hart, Stall St, 36-47
White Hart, Twerton, 131-32
White Horse Cellar, Somerset Blgs, 176-77
White Horse, Stall St, 83
White Lion, High St, 24-28
White Lion, Hopmead Blgs, 125
White Lion, Lambridge Blgs, 186
White Lion, Milk St, 288
White Lion, Weston, 251
White Swan, LBW, 81
White Swan, Walcot St, 174
White Swan, Westgate St, 63-64
Widcombe Brewery, Pulteney Rd, 261
William IV, Claverton St, 257
Wiltshire House, Brunswick St, 185
Windsor Castle, UBR, 235
Woodman, Gallaway's Blgs, 89
Woolpack, Twerton, 131

York House Tap, Broad St see Fuller's Wine Vaults
Young Fox, Holloway, 273-74

Abbreviations LBR Lower Bristol Road   LBW Lower Borough Walls   UBR Upper Bristol Road   UBW Upper Borough Walls

THE LOST PUBS OF BATH

GENERAL INDEX

Also from AKEMAN PRESS

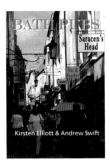

BATH PUBS
by **Kirsten Elliott & Andrew Swift**
Taking the waters – that's the reason visitors have flocked to Bath for centuries. Other books about Bath focus on this abstemious activity. This book offers a different history and a different tipple. Beer has a long and honourable tradition, and Bath's pubs are just as much part of the city's story as the Roman Baths and the Assembly Rooms. The tale the authors tell is one of high life and low life, where temperance campaigners rub shoulders with sozzled soldiers, and magistrates deal out punishment to hat-removing harlots.

Paperback £12.99 ISBN 0 9546138 0 5

AWASH WITH ALE: 2000 YEARS OF IMBIBING IN BATH
by **Andrew Swift & Kirsten Elliott**. Illustrated by **Julian Landau**
Drinking has reached crisis level – or so we are told. The truth is that drinking has been at crisis level for centuries. This is the story of how Britain's first pleasure resort coped with our ancestors' relentless desire to drink more than was good for them. From the Gin Epidemic to the Beerhouse Boom, from the Cider Rebellion to the Drunken Election – Awash with Ale tells the story of Bath in a way you've never heard it told before.

Paperback £12.99 ISBN 0 9546138 1 3

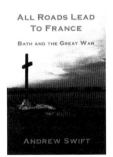

ALL ROADS LEAD TO FRANCE: BATH AND THE GREAT WAR
by **Andrew Swift**
Interweaving letters from men at the front with stories of life at home, and illustrated with over 300 photographs, this book describes the Great War's impact on the city of Bath. It is a story of grief, suffering and anger – but there is laughter too. And although Andrew Swift tells the story of one community, this could be, with minor variations, the story of hundreds of other British towns and cities as they lived through the time when all roads led to France.

Hardcover £30 ISBN 0 9546138 3 X

THE MYTH-MAKER: JOHN WOOD, 1704-1754
by **Kirsten Elliott**
John Wood was not only one of the eighteenth century's most famous architects, but also one of its most assiduous mythmakers. From a desire to restore Bath to its former position as a centre of Druidic culture, his researches led him into Rosicrucianism and alchemy. He even completed the first accurate survey of Stonehenge – or Choir Gaure as he called it. In this lavishly illustrated book, Kirsten Elliott attempts to provide the key to a re-evaluation of one of the eighteenth-century's most fascinating figures.

Paperback £10 ISBN: 0 9546138 2 1

Postage & packing on all items is FREE in the UK

To order contact Akeman Press, 58 Minster Way, Bath BA2 6RL
Phone: 01225 310364; email: info@akemanpress.com

www.akemanpress.com

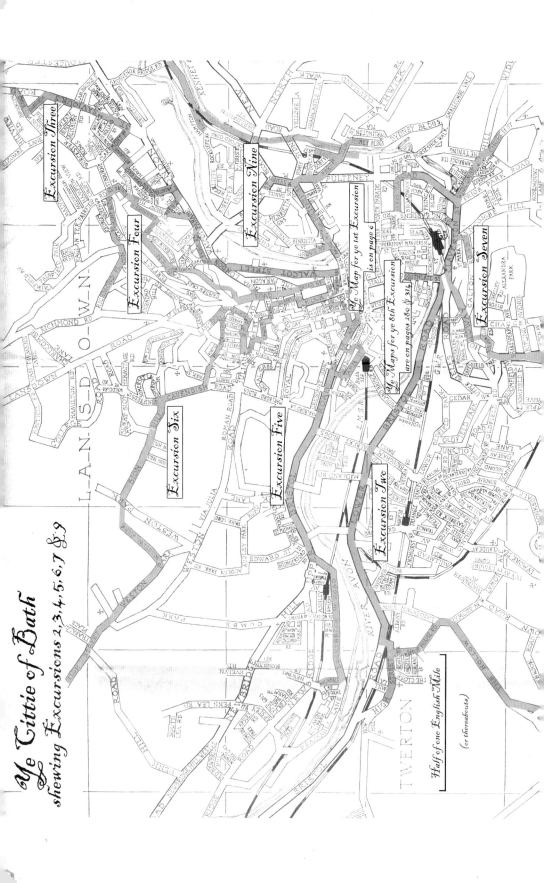

Ye Cittie of Bath
shewing Excursions 2, 3, 4, 5, 6, 7 & 9

Excursion Three
Excursion Four
Excursion Nine
Excursion Six
Excursion Five
Excursion Two
Excursion Seven

Ye Maps for ye 1st Excursion 'tis on page 6

Ye Maps for ye 8th Excursion are on pages 280 & 314

Half of one English Mile
(or thereabouts)